The ESG Framework and the Energy Industry

James Thewissen · Özgür Arslan-Ayaydin ·
Wim Westerman · André Dorsman
Editors

The ESG Framework and the Energy Industry

Demand and Supply, Market Policies and Value Creation

Springer

Editors
James Thewissen
Université Catholique de Louvain
Louvain-la-Neuve, Belgium

Wim Westerman
Faculty of Economics and Business
University of Groningen
Groningen, The Netherlands

Özgür Arslan-Ayaydin
Department of Finance
University of Illinois Chicago
Chicago, USA

André Dorsman
Amsterdam, The Netherlands

ISBN 978-3-031-48456-8 ISBN 978-3-031-48457-5 (eBook)
https://doi.org/10.1007/978-3-031-48457-5

This Springer imprint is published by the registered company Springer Nature Switzerland AG
The registered company address is: Gewerbestrasse 11, 6330 Cham, Switzerland

Paper in this product is recyclable.

Foreword

Environmental, social and governance "ESG" has rapidly evolved from being a buzzword to becoming a business concept. Many start-ups and some forward-looking companies are showing the way while the consultancy industry is reinventing classical accounting and auditing models. Yet, major economic players and consumer societies are still addicted to carbon energy while temperatures are rising faster than forecast based on current scientific knowledge. It is important to distinguish between the different obstacles that stand in the way of addressing the global climate challenge. On the one hand, there are short-term economic and political interests that often frustrate choices and sacrifices that would generate more sustainable outcomes in the long run. On the other hand, a still more fundamental problem is the reality of development inequality and unfulfilled basic needs in large parts of the world. How to reconcile economic growth aspirations, either out of luxury or out of necessity, with the sustainability paradigm that requires a new balance between planet, people and (private and public) profits to an extent not known since the industrial revolution in the early 1800s?

The contribution and future potential of the energy industry are at the heart of this pressing, if not being an existential issue that humankind is confronted with. It is therefore a more than welcome contribution to the necessary scientific underpinning and public debate promotion that the ninth collection of chapters by the Center for Energy and Value Issues focuses on the implications of the ESG framework for and by the energy industry through multiple lenses.

Reflecting on energy demand and supply trends and bottlenecks, and their implications for long-term sustainability could hardly be timelier since the start of the war between Russia and Ukraine and the unprecedented volatility of natural gas markets. Linking this new reality to the ESG performances of energy companies and their impact on energy prices and investments addresses fundamental questions concerning sector capacity reform. Analyzing what this all could or should mean for company performance and value creation offers industry insiders, academics, journalists and politicians important insights into the dimensions at play in the rapidly changing global landscape of energy production and consumption—bringing together the universally shared urgency of protecting planetary sources and the justified aspirations of billions of humans still living under or around the absolute poverty line to improve their living conditions. The independent research in this volume on the environmental, social and governance criteria and practices that could guide the way forward offers important outcomes to accelerate the change that is required to meet the universally embraced UN climate commitments. May it be of inspiration to all concerned—the global community joining minds and hands to make that change happen.

The Netherlands

Ad Melkert
Former UN Under-Secretary-General
World Bank Executive Director and
Cabinet Minister

Contents

The ESG Framework and the Energy Industry: Demand and Supply, Market Policies, and Value Creation 1
James Thewissen, Özgür Arslan-Ayaydin, Wim Westerman, and André Dorsman

Energy Resources and ESG Criteria: Demand and Supply Issues

The Causal Relationship Between ESG and Economic Growth: Evidence from the Panel of Commonwealth Independent States 9
Nermin Yasar Baskaraagac

Macroeconomic Determinants of Energy Poverty in Türkiye 17
Goktug Sahin and Savas Gayaker

Towards Economic Growth Without CO_2 Emissions: The Case of Türkiye 39
Wietze Lise

The Natural Gas War Between Europe and Russia After the Invasion of Ukraine 61
Mehmet Baha Karan, Kazim Baris Atici, Burak Pirgaip, and Göktuğ Şahin

Market-Based Policies for ESG Activities in the Energy Sector

ESG Performances of Energy Companies in OECD Countries: A Clustering Approach 87
Cem Menten, Bulent Cekic, Kazim Baris Atici, Selin Metin Camgoz, and Aydin Ulucan

The Impact of Renewable Energy Incentives on Carbon Prices in the USA 113
Esin Hilal Çoşkun, A. Sevtap Selcuk-Kestel, and Serdar Dalkir

Static and Dynamic Connectedness Between Green Bonds and Clean Energy Markets 137
Ayşe Nur Şahinler, Fatih Cemil Ozbugday, Sidika Basci, and Tolga Omay

Do Green Bonds Improve the Stock and Environmental Performance of Energy Firms? International Evidence 159
Burak Pirgaip, Mehmet Baha Karan, and Seçil Sayın Kutluca

Dealing with ESG Issues: Creating Corporate Value

Resilience in Power Generation: Two Case Studies from Turkey 187
Fatih Avcı and Volkan Ş. Ediger

The Effect of Environmental Scores on Financial Performance of Energy Companies in the European Region 209
Gizem Arı and Z. Göknur Büyükkara

The Impact of Executive Pay Gap on Environmental and Social Performance in the Energy Sector: Worldwide Evidence 241
Halit Gonenc and Deniz Kartal

Sector and Country Effects of Carbon Reduction and Firm Performance 265
Robin van Emous, R. Krušinskas, and W. Westerman

The ESG Framework and the Energy Industry: Demand and Supply, Market Policies, and Value Creation

James Thewissen, Özgür Arslan-Ayaydin, Wim Westerman, and André Dorsman

Abstract This chapter introduces the book. This ninth collection in a series published by the Center for Energy and Value Issues (CEVI) discusses environmental, social, and governance (ESG) topics in the energy industry, and it does so from the perspectives of macro-economic demand and supply, micro-economic market policies, and financial value creation by companies. The book employs an international approach, by taking examples from specific countries and country blocks. In doing so, it contributes to the global research body on an increasingly being recognized as pivotal topic for this planet. The book is meant for reading by academics and practitioners alike, and the editors trust that it will be well received.

Keywords Energy industry · ESG framework · Demand and supply · Market policies · Value creation

1 Introduction

Environmental, social, and governance (ESG) concerns are now high on the agendas of policymakers, firms, investors, and academics worldwide. Climate change, social inequality, biodiversity loss, and corporate governance scandals regularly attract

---

J. Thewissen (✉)
Louvain School of Management, Université Catholique de Louvain, Louvain-La-Neuve, Belgium
e-mail: James.thewissen@uclouvain.be

SILC Business School, Shanghai University, Shanghai, China

Ö. Arslan-Ayaydin
Department of Finance, University of Illinois at Chicago, Chicago, IL, USA
e-mail: orslan@uic.edu

W. Westerman
Faculty of Economics and Business, University of Groningen, Groningen, The Netherlands
e-mail: w.westerman@rug.nl

A. Dorsman
Dorsman Van Hees BV (Dorsman van Hees Ltd), Amsterdam, The Netherlands

J. Thewissen et al. (eds.), *The ESG Framework and the Energy Industry*,
https://doi.org/10.1007/978-3-031-48457-5_1

global attention due to the widespread and growing recognition of their impact on business and economic activities. Particularly, in the 2020–2023 period, the COVID-19 pandemic has highlighted the impact of environmental, social, and governance standards on the performance of firms and beyond.

Against this backdrop, recent empirical evidence shows that the ESG paradigm is increasingly affecting the value of companies. For instance, leading institutional investors are progressively tracking the greenhouse gas emissions of listed firms and now demand compensation for their exposure to carbon emission risk.[1] The adherence to ESG principles cannot be ignored, and it needs to be better understood how following ESG principles impacts firm value and, more importantly, what the consequences are if a company fails at adhering to such principles.

The energy sector, in particular, has raised concerns on the value-relevance of ESG principles.[2] Due to reliance on fossil fuels and the related carbon emissions, the energy industry is one of the leading actors in the climate change challenges.[3] It needs to be noted that transitioning to low-carbon economy as well as maintaining and enhancing the environmental sustainability requires a significant long-term financing for the firms in this industry.

While, until recently, ESG mainly referred to the impact of a firm's activities on the environment, the COVID-19 pandemic and other events have progressively shifted the ESG focus to the impact of the social and governance components on firm value. For instance, employment in the energy sector also exposes significant health and safety risks. Therefore, today's energy industry is not only exposed to considerations regarding its impact on the environment, but the sector now also has to reconsider its social and governance policies in order to meet ESG expectations. Yet, prior literature remains rather silent on such influences on the value of energy firms specifically.

In this vein, energy firms need to be proactive and holistic in addressing ESG issues for creating financial value. The industry has been working to tackle this challenge. For example, there are several trade organizations providing resources for their industry members to help them implement and report on ESG initiatives. Meanwhile, the Sustainability Accounting Standards Board (SASB) has developed guidelines specific to the industry. While these initiatives are showing the willingness of the energy industry for meeting investors' demands, it is likely be that much more is expected from the sector by both the society at large.

In this book, we contribute to a better understanding of the importance of ESG principles for the value of firms in the energy industry. In particular, we highlight how the sector is embracing change in the light of demand and supply of energy resources and how it addresses ESG issues, how it reacts to market policies on ESG activities, and how its firms create value through environmental, social, and

[1] Refer to: Bolton and Kacperczyk (2021).

[2] For more information, see: Flin et al. (2000) and Walsh (2010).

[3] The International Energy Agency estimates that 39% of CO_2 emissions come from electricity and heat production, (https://www.iea.org/media/statistics/Energy_and_CO2_Emissions_in_the_OECD.pdf).

governance initiatives. These issues are elaborated within the frameworks of, but not limited to: financial markets, financial risks, asset pricing, value at risk, capital structure, capital budgeting, corporate (re)structuring, corporate governance, behavioral finance, financial performance, asset pricing, cost control, financial accounting, fiscal issues and institutions, as well as political risks. Our chapters are not only concentrated on single countries, but also have a wider span with a scope of global and regional approaches.

2 Chapter Contributions

The contributions start from an economic demand and supply perspective. The chapter by Yasar Baskaraagac analyzes the causal relationship between ESG and economic growth for the Commonwealth of Independent States. The results show that the adaptation of macroeconomic policies stimulating the economic growth process in these states may also encourage the ESG indicator levels of the economy. The next chapter by Sahin and Gayaker sheds light on the determinants of energy poverty in Türkiye, emphasizing the roles of economic growth, industrial production, and oil prices. The policy implications derived from their findings are expected to inform the design and implementation of targeted policies and interventions aimed at alleviating energy poverty and fostering sustainable, inclusive economic growth. Lise analyzes the energy situation and the development of CO_2 emissions in Türkiye, which has a high potential of economic growth, and it is still possible to achieve the growth targets with reduced carbon emissions. This chapter shows that the economic growth is possible without both environmental degradations in terms of CO_2 emissions and increasing the level of energy consumption. The chapter by Karan, Atici, Pirgaip, and Sahin discusses the Euro-Russian natural gas war, which is the result of Russia's attack on Ukraine in 2022. The authors conclude that while both sides will suffer from the natural gas war, in the medium term, Europe's developing LNG market and renewable resources may emerge stronger from this war.

The preceding part of the book is followed by one on market policies. The chapter by Menten, Cekic, Atici, Camgoz, and Ulucan proposes clustering as a tool for ESG analysis of public energy companies in OECD countries, and they find that clustering enables identifying the conflicting areas of ESG performance without any predefined information on clusters or any controversies in weighting. The authors discuss the patterns with a more macro-look through the business classifications and countries of headquarters. The chapter by Coskun, Selcuk-Kestel, and Dalkir analyzes the US energy markets and shows that CO_2 prices are influenced strongly by the renewable portfolio standards as well as carbon allowances and industrial production. Furthermore, Sahinler, Ozbugday, Basci, and Omay show in their chapter that clean energy market movements have a spillover effect in the green bond market, which has become one of the most promising mechanisms to raise funds for environmentally beneficial projects, hence achieving carbon–neutral goals. Moving along with the green bonds, the chapter by Pirgaip, Karan, and Kutluca analyzes 239 green bonds issued by 80 energy firms in 2013–2021. Their results imply that green bond issuance has a lagged and temporary effect on stock prices, as environmental achievements are not that obvious particularly in the short term.

The number of studies examining the effect of environmental responsibility activities on financial performance of companies operating in the energy sector is still limited. Resilience in power systems to extreme climate events is closely linked with ESG and is especially important during the power system planning and implementation, whereby enhancement can accelerate a country's energy transition. By examining the lignite-fired Çan and hydroelectric Eğlence power plants as two cases in Türkiye, the chapter by Avci and Ediger concludes that the concept of resilience needs to be immediately taken into consideration in designing new power plant investments and in adapting already existing ones to make them more flexible to any abrupt changes in climate. The contribution of the chapter by Ari and Büyükkara is about examining the impact of environmental responsibility on financial performance within the framework of companies operating in the energy sector in the European Region. They show that activities aimed at reducing the use of environmentally harmful resources have a reducing effect on financial performance, whereas a neutral effect is dominant between the environmental responsibility activities and financial performance carried out in European energy companies in general. Gonenc and Kartal provide worldwide evidence on the impact of executive pay gap on environmental and social performance in the energy sector. The results of their chapter show that firm-level corporate governance is not as effective as country-level market institutions, supporting the notion that the development of country-level institutions drives corporate social performance in the energy sector. The final chapter of this book is by Van Emous, Krušinskas, and Westerman, who analyze the differences between sectors and various groupings of countries on carbon reduction and firm performance in terms of accounting and market performances. The findings of this chapter indicate that differences in carbon reduction are limited when various ways of grouping the countries are allowed, for instance, the services sector shows a positive result in relation to most of the corporate financial performance variables, yet a negative relationship is obtained for agricultural and mining firms.

3 Conclusion

To conclude, the key message that emerges from the relationship between the ESG framework and the energy industry is that we need a better understanding of the impact of ESG-related activities of energy firms and their impact on firm value, but also that there is an urgent need for a sounder regulatory framework to address possible failings in the energy industry.

References

Bolton, P., & Kacperczyk, M. (2021). Do investors care about carbon risk? *Journal of Financial Economics, 142*(2), 517–549. https://doi.org/10.1016/j.jfineco.2021.05.008

Flin, R., Mearns, K., O'Connor, P., & Bryden, R. (2000). Measuring safety climate: Identifying the common features. *Safety Science, 34*(1–3), 177–192.

Walsh, B. (2010). Oil Spill: *A damning indictment of BP's safety culture.* Retrieved from http://science.time.com/2010/10/26/oil-spill-a-damning-indictment-of-bps-safety-culture

Energy Resources and ESG Criteria: Demand and Supply Issues

The Causal Relationship Between ESG and Economic Growth: Evidence from the Panel of Commonwealth Independent States

Nermin Yasar Baskaraagac

Abstract This paper analyzes the causal relationship between ESG and economic growth for CIS member states over the sample period 1996–2020. Since the results of the varied panel stationarity tests suggest mixed findings on the order of integration, the ARDL model is employed to determine the co-integration relation among the series. The result of the VEC model, which is estimated to explore the long-run and short-run dynamics of this casual relation between the series in a basic way, suggests that there is a causal relationship running from income level to ESG criteria. This implies that the adaptation of macroeconomic policies which will stimulate the economic growth process in CIS countries may also encourage the ESG indicator levels of the economy.

1 Introduction

Correspondence between income and environmental, social, and governance (ESG) criteria has been one of the urgent and major subjects for a considerable number of studies in the recent economic literature. For instance, Ho et al. (2019) suggest that three main opinions are featured in applied research predicting the correspondence between ESG performance and economic growth. First, some argue for a bidirectional causality between these two variables based on a causal relationship running from ESG indicators to per capita income and vice versa. Along with the second view that predicts a partial causality between economic growth and ESG, there is also a third opinion based on the neutrality hypothesis, which predicts an absence of causality between ESG performance and GDP. Following Cracolici et al. (2010), which is one of the guiding studies in this field, development in the economic dimension of the country, such as increasing per capita GDP, may stimulate the non-economic side of this country, namely better health conditions, longer life expectancy, or higher literacy rate. At the same time, a higher level of non-economic well-being indicators

N. Y. Baskaraagac (✉)
Department of Foreign Trade, Cankaya University, Ankara, Turkey
e-mail: nerminyasar@cankaya.edu.tr

J. Thewissen et al. (eds.), *The ESG Framework and the Energy Industry*,
https://doi.org/10.1007/978-3-031-48457-5_2

may encourage a country to manage its resources more effectively leading to better economic performance such as improvements in productivity levels. According to Margaretic and Pouget (2018), ESG performance may diminish asymmetries of information in the economic system and establish trust between the investors and relevant institutions of the country stimulating investment and income growth. Another study that determines the positive impact of ESG on the countries' economic system is Crifo et al. (2017), which argues that economies with a better ESG dimension may have lower sovereign borrowing costs that may lead to a better ability for these countries to refund the public debt. Moreover, while some other studies such as by Cracolici et al. (2010), Wang et al. (2020), and Diaye et al. (2022) also archive evidence of a positive influence of ESG performance on economic growth, Schneider et al. (2010) and Murtin et al. (2011) based on "degrowth" theory and envy theory state that ESG targets and policies may have a hindering effect on the economic growth process by leading to a recession in demand and supply sides of an economy. On the other side as Castiglione et al. (2015) and Ho et al. (2019) argue that the impact of ESG determinants on economic growth may differ based on the income group a country belongs to.

As it can be understood from above-mentioned studies, although the relationship between income and ESG performance is a well-studied topic within the scope of large number of studies based on different countries or country groups, time periods, methods, and variables there is neither an ultimate result on the existence of this causal relationship nor consensus on a single appropriate economic policy inference in the economic literature. These mixed results may be related to selected variables, model specifications, time periods of the studies, as well as employed applied techniques.

This paper analyzes the casual relationship between ESG, and economic growth employing newly developed applied methods such as ARDL and VEC models and propose feasible economic policies for 12 Commonwealth Independent States (CIS) countries, which are classified as transition economies and mainly belong to the middle-income countries group.[1] With the collapse of the Soviet Union, CIS countries attempted to switch from a centralized economic structure to a capitalist free-market economy system by implementing a series of economic reforms and institutional changes. In this process, the impact of the ESG strategies adopted by these states on the economic growth process gains importance in terms of the effectiveness of the implemented policies. To the best of our knowledge, there is no other study that explores this causal relationship for CIS economies.

The remainder of the paper is structured as follows. Section 2 describes the econometric methodology used in this research. In Sect. 3, we present and discuss the test results, and Sect. 4 concludes.

---

[1] This group of countries with different economic features is established in 1991 immediately after the collapse of the Soviet Union and contain countries such as Armenia, Azerbaijan, Belarus, Georgia, Kazakhstan, Kyrgyz Republic, Russian Federation, Tajikistan, Turkmenistan, Uzbekistan, and Ukraine. As Korhonen and Wachtel (2006) states, the CIS consists of both upper middle-income and lower middle-income economies as well as countries that are energy-exporting and energy-importing.

2 Methodology

Since panel data analysis may carry time series features and problems, we first test stationarity properties of ESG indicators and income by employing the conventional panel unit root tests such as in Breitung (2000), Levin et al. (2002), Im et al. (2003), Maddala and Wu (1999), and Choi (2001). While Breitung (2000) and Levin et al. (2002) emphasize homogeneity among the series and examine the existence of a common unit root process in panel data considering that the lag order ρ_i is identical ($\rho_i = \rho$) for all cross-sectional units, Im et al (2003), Choi (2001), and Maddala and Wu (1999) consider the heterogeneity in the dynamics of autoregressive coefficients in the null hypothesizes. As Yasar (2021) indicates, the common feature of these first-generation panel unit root tests is to consider cross-sectional units of the observed panel as independent and test the null hypothesis of a non-stationarity.

To investigate the co-integration relationship between ESG criteria and economic growth in this study we apply an autoregressive distributed lag (ARDL) regression procedure asserted by Peseran et al. (2001), which handles the series at different lag orders by measuring co-integration relation at upper bound I (1) and lower bound I (0). The ARDL model estimated by OLS may be expressed as follows:

$$\Delta Y_t = \propto_{10} + \sum_{i=1}^{n} \beta_{1i} \Delta Y_{t-i} + \sum_{i=1}^{m} \gamma_{1i} \Delta X_{t-i} + \sigma_{1Y} Y_{t-1} + \sigma_{1X} X_{t-1} + \int_{1t} \quad (1)$$

$$\Delta X_t = \propto_{20} + \sum_{i=1}^{n} \beta_{2i} \Delta Y_{t-i} + \sum_{i=1}^{m} \gamma_{2i} \Delta X_{t-i} + \sigma_{2X} X_{t-1} + \sigma_{2Y} Y_{t-1} + \int_{2t} \quad (2)$$

where n and m are maximum lag orders, σ refers to the long-run relationship, β indicates the short-run dynamics of the regression model, X denotes the ESG indicators, and Y is income.

To test the null hypothesis of no co-integration between the series ($H_0 : \sigma_{iX} = \sigma_{iY} = 0$), Peseran et al. (2001) suggest upper (for I (1)) and lower (for I (0)) bounds statistics. The lower critical bound demonstrates that there is no co-integration relationship between variables, whereas the upper critical bound allows for co-integration among series. If the calculated critical value is between the lower and upper bounds, then the result obtained from this analysis may be inconclusive.

If the variables under consideration are co-integrated, then the vector error correction model (VECM) based on the Granger causality analysis can be used to examine the long-term and short-term information among observed series.

$$\Delta Y_t = \propto_{10} + \sum_{i=1}^{n} \beta_{1i} \Delta Y_{t-i} + \sum_{i=1}^{m} \gamma_{1i} \Delta X_{t-i} + \delta_Y \mathrm{EC}_{t-1} + u_{1t} \quad (3)$$

$$\Delta X_t = \propto_{20} + \sum_{i=1}^{m} \gamma_{2i} \Delta X_{t-i} + \sum_{i=1}^{n} \beta_{2i} \Delta Y_{t-i} + \delta_X \mathrm{EC}_{t-1} + u_{2t} \quad (4)$$

Following Yasar (2021), EC_{t-1} is a lagged error correction term obtained from the long-term association and shows the speed of adjustment to the long-term equilibrium after a shock in the model. If the coefficient of this error correction term, i.e., δ_X or δ_Y, is positive, then the observed series diverge from each other, whereas the negative coefficient represents a convergence between these variables. As Telatar (2015) states, the F-value of the coefficient of the lagged dependent variables of Eqs. (3) and (4) demonstrates the significance of the short-term effects, whereas the t-value of the lagged error correction term shows the significance of the long-term causal impact.

3 Data and Empirical Results

Following Ho et al. (2019), in this paper, we will use the following indicators of ESG for the observed countries; CO_2 emission, life expectancy at birth, and Corruption Control Index. The data set covers annual data for CIS economies from 1996 to 2020, which is obtained from the World Bank's World Development Indicators and Worldwide Governance Indicators.

For preliminary analysis based on the stationarity features of the observed series, Table 1 reports the result of panel unit root tests such as Maddala and Wu (1999), Choi (2001), Breitung (2000), Levin et al. (2002), and Im et al (2003) for the CO2 emission, life expectancy at birth, and Corruption Control Index and GDP series and their first difference.

The results displayed in Table 1 do not provide definite evidence of the presence or absence of unit root in the examined panel data. According to the findings of some of these panel unit tests, considered series are stationary in the level, e.g., CO_2 emission, life expectancy at birth, and Corruption Control Index, and GDP series are integrated of order 0. However, other panel stationarity analyses suggest that these variables contain a unit root and are integrated into order one.

These mixed results encourage us to apply the ARDL regression process to study the possible co-integration relation between the components of the considered panel data, which may be employed regardless of series integration order.

Table 2 reports the chi-squared test statistics used to test the null hypothesis of no co-integration relation. Based on these results, we may summarize that the co-integration relation between CO_2 emission, life expectancy at birth, and Corruption Control Index and GDP series is found for most of the cases.

Table 3 shows the estimation results from the VEC regression process that is used to determine the long-term association reflected by the error correction term (ECT). This table clearly indicates that the t-statistics of ECT in all cases for estimated VECM are statistically significant at an alpha level of 0.05, confirming the long-run relation between GDP and ESG, if GDP is considered as an independent variable in the considered panel. In addition, the Wald test statistics of the relevant coefficients that are employed to test the null hypothesis of no relation among the variables do not demonstrate statistically significant results for all cases at an alpha level of 0.05,

Table 1 Panel unit root tests

Variables	Levin et al. (2002)		Im et al. (2003)		ADF—Fisher		PP—Fisher		Breitung (2000)
	Intercept	Intercept + trend	Intercept	Intercept + trend	Intercept	Intercept + trend	Intercept	Intercept + trend	Intercept + trend
CO_2	−0.25	−0.95	1.44	0.10	15.75	24.88	18.95	20.23	−0.08
ΔCO_2	−4.75***	−4.04***	−6.01***	−4.85***	81.82***	68.08***	153.57***	154.04***	−4.16***
LE	−13.80***	−22.78***	−5.06***	−12.19***	95.88***	361.73***	34.88**	15.78	3.82
ΔLE	−10.97***	−11.57***	−8.40***	−8.12***	120.45***	132.06***	49.26**	30.34	−2.81**
CR	0.51	−1.70**	−0.90	−1.20	26.40	27.74	36.22	30.01	−0.64
ΔCR	−4.10***	−1.66*	−7.02***	−4.87***	90.32***	64.04***	201.68***	206.51***	−3.84***
GDP	−4.77***	2.36	−0.66	3.97	24.65	8.46	25.45	10.69	4.65
ΔGDP	−1.22	−3.09***	−3.10***	−3.40***	47.76**	54.72***	73.45***	59.83***	0.24

Note ***, **, and * denote rejection of the null hypothesis of unit root at 1%, 5%, and 10% significance levels, respectively

Table 2 Co-integration tests

F-statistic	
ARDL$_{CO2}$  GDP	2.0838 (0.1266)
ARDL$_{GDP}$  CO2	14,003.16* (0,000)
ARDL$_{LE}$  GDP	8.1777* (0.0004)
ARDL$_{GDP}$  LE	7.4967* (0.0007)
ARDL$_{CR}$  GDP	2.1528 (0.1186)
ARDL$_{GDP}$  CR	6.1945* (0.0024)

Note *indicates significance at the 5% level. The parenthesis implies the sum of the coefficients. The appropriate lag lengths are specified based on the Schwarz information criterion (SIC)

Table 3 Panel causality tests

	Long run	Short run
CO_2  GDP	–	–
GDP  CO_2	−2.8551* (0.0047)	0.83766 (0.4341)
LE  GDP	−4.0519* (0.0001)	0.0233 (0.9770)
GDP  LE	−3.4826* (0.0006)	0.7213 (0.5401)
CR  GDP	–	–
GDP  CR	−3.5272* (0.0005)	0.0297 (0.2138)

Note * indicates significance at the 5% level. The parenthesis implies the sum of the coefficients. The appropriate lag lengths are specified based on the Schwarz information criterion (SIC)

implying the nonexistence of the correlation between observed series in the short term.

4 Concluding Remarks

From the results of this study, several conclusions can be formulated including statistically significant evidence of the long-run unidirectional causal relationship running from income to CO_2 and Corruption Control Index for all CIS economies. The possible reason for this finding for most CIS economies is the heavy use of carbon-intensive techniques in industrial production, transportation, and domestic needs as well as the electrical energy generating process. In this context, it will be beneficial for CIS economies to support domestic and foreign investments that predict switching from consumption of traditional fuels to renewable energy systems in the production process in the leading sectors of the economy as well as taking the required steps to generate green electricity.

Secondly, our results are consistent with the Lipset theory, which asserts that expansion in income effectively promotes democracy. Moreover, development in living standards may increase the quality of political institutions and positively affect the fight against corruption in any economy. As such, we may conclude that the economic and political reforms carried out in recent years nearly in all CIS countries lead to better governance, which is associated with higher-income levels and lower corruption.

Finally, our findings show that life expectancy has a significant long-term impact on per capita income and vice versa for the observed panel of countries. This result matches with the endogenous theory of economic growth, which suggests that higher health conditions in CIS economies may stimulate productivity and economic growth by raising the level of human capital. Nelson and Phelps (1966) also state that healthier societies are much more capable of adapting and inventing new technologies, which will stimulate income growth. On the other hand, the evidence of a correlation running from human capital to economic growth coincides with Mukherjee and Chakraborty (2010) arguing that there is a positive and linear relationship running from democracy and income to the human development level. It clearly demonstrates that the implementation of macroeconomic policies that will stimulate economic growth along with better democratic conditions in CIS countries may also encourage the life expectancy index of the economy.

References

Breitung, J. (2000). The local power of some unit root tests for panel data. In B. Baltagi, et al. (Eds.), *Advances in econometrics: Nonstationary panels, panels cointegration and dynamic panels* (vol. 15, pp. 161–178+.

Castiglione, C., Infante, D., & Smirnova, J. (2015). Environment and economic growth: Is the rule of law the go-between? the case of high-income countries. *Energy, Sustainability and Society, 5*, 1–7.

Choi, I. (2001). Unit root tests for panel data. *Journal of International Money and Banking, 20*(2), 249–272.

Cracolici, M. F., Cuffaro, M., & Nijkamp, P. (2010). The measurement of economic, social and environmental performance of countries: A novel approach. *Social Indicators Research, 95*(2), 339–356.

Crifo, P., Diaye, M.-A., & Oueghlissi, R. (2017). The effect of countries' ESG ratings on their sovereign borrowing costs. *The Quarterly Review of Economics and Finance, 66*, 13–20.

Diaye, M.-A., Ho, S.-H., & Oueghlissi, R. (2022). ESG performance and economic growth: A panel co-integration analysis. *Empirica, 49*, 99–122.

Engle, R. F., & Granger, C. W. J. (1987). Co-integration and error correction: Representation, estimation, and testing. *Econometrica, 55*(2), 251–276.

Granger, C. W. J., & Newbold, P. (1977). Spurious regressions in econometrics. *Journal of Econometrics, 26*, 1045–1066.

Gründler, K., & Potrafke, N. (2019). *Corruption and economic growth: New empirical evidence.* Working Paper, No. 309, ifo Institute—Leibniz Institute for Economic Research at the University of Munich.

Im, K. S., Pesaran, H. M., & Shin, Y. (2003). Testing for unit roots in heterogeneous panels. *Journal of Econometrics, 115*(1), 53–74.

Johansen, S. (1988). Statistical analysis of co-integrating vectors. *Journal of Economic Dynamics and Control, 12*(2), 231–254.

Johansen, S., & Juselius, K. (1990). Maximum likelihood estimation and inference on co-integration—With applications to the demand for money. *Oxford Bulletin of Economics and Statistics, 52*(2), 169–210.

Ho S.-H., Oueghlissi, R., & El Ferktaji, R. (2019). *The dynamic causality between ESG and economic growth: Evidence from panel causality analysis.* MPRA Paper No. 95390. https://mpra.ub.uni-muenchen.de/95390/

Korhoneni, I., & Wachtel, P. A. (2006). Note on exchange rate pass-through in CIS countries. *Research in International Business and Finance, 20*(2), 215–226.

Levin, A. C., Lin, F., & Chu, C. S. J. (2002). Unit root tests in panel data: Asymptotic and finite—Sample properties. *Journal of Econometrics, 108*(1), 1–24.

Maddala, G. S., & Wu, S. (1999). A comparative study of unit root tests with panel data and a new simple test. *Oxford Bulletin of Economics and Statistics*, Special Issue, 631–652.

Margaretic, P., & Pouget, S. (2018). Sovereign bond spreads and extra-financial performance: An empirical analysis of emerging markets. *International Review of Economics and Finance, 58*, 340–355.

Metz, B., Davidson, O., De Coninck, H. C., Loos, M., & Meyer, L. (2005). *IPCC special report on carbon dioxide capture and storage.* Cambridge University Press.

Mukherjee, S., & Chakraborty, D. (2010). *Is there any relationship between environment, human development, political and governance regimes? Evidence from a cross-country analysis, MPRA paper 19968.* University Library of Munich.

Murtin, F., De Serres, A., & Alexander, H. (2011). *The ins and outs of unemployment: The role of labour market institutions.* OECD Economics Department, working papers. OECD Publishing, Paris.

Nelson, R., & Phelps, E. (1966). Investment in humans, technological diffusion, and economic growth. *American Economic Review, 61*(1/2), 69–75.

Nkoro, E., & Uko, A. K. (2016). Autoregressive distributed lag (ARDL) co-integration technique: Application and interpretation. *Journal of Statistical and Econometric Methods, 5*(4), 63–91.

Pesaran, M. H., Shin, Y., & Smith, R. (2001). Bounds testing approaches to the analysis of level relationships. *Journal of Applied Econometrics, 16*(3), 289–326.

Pfister, U., & Suter, C. (1987). International financial relations as part of the world-system. *International Studies Quarterly, 31*(3), 239–272.

Schneider, F., Kallis, G., & Martinez-Alier, J. (2010). Crisis or opportunity? Economic degrowth for social equity and ecological sustainability. Introduction to this special issue. *Journal of Cleaner Production, 18*(6), 511–518.

Telatar, M. E., et al. (2015). Electricity consumption, GDP and renewables. In A. Dorsman (Ed.), *Energy technology and valuation issues* (pp. 109–126). Springer Verlag.

Wang, J., Yu, J., & Zhong, R. (2020). Country sustainable development and economic growth: The international evidence (SSRN Scholarly Paper ID 3350232). *Social Science Research Network.*

Yasar, N. (2021). *The causal relationship between foreign debt and economic growth: Evidence from commonwealth independent states foreign trade review* (pp. 1–15).

Macroeconomic Determinants of Energy Poverty in Türkiye

Goktug Sahin and Savas Gayaker

Abstract Energy Poverty refers to the lack of access to modern energy services necessary for a decent standard of living, including access to electricity, clean cooking facilities, and reliable heating and cooling systems. This study examines the macroeconomic factors influencing Energy Poverty in Türkiye between December 2009 and August 2022 with the ARDL model. The research sheds light on the determinants of Energy Poverty in Türkiye, highlighting the role of economic growth, industrial production, and oil prices. The policy implications derived from these findings can support the design and implementation of targeted policies and interventions aimed at alleviating Energy Poverty and promoting sustainable, inclusive economic growth.

1 Introduction

The objective of this study is to identify the macroeconomic determinants of Energy Poverty in the scope of Türkiye spanning the time period between 2009 and 2022. For this purpose, a new approach to measuring Energy Poverty is used in the study. Even though household surveys and indices are frequently used to measure Energy Poverty in Türkiye and the World, two significant issues arise. First, survey studies are conducted on a microscale and susceptible to change based on sample selection, rendering them inadequate for revealing macroeffects. It is crucial to identify the macrovariables that influence Energy Poverty in a country for developing effective policies, evaluating existing interventions, and promoting greater public awareness and engagement on this critical issue. Second, survey and index data are cross-sectional and lack time-dependent characteristics. Investigating Energy

G. Sahin (✉)
Faculty of Economics and Administrative Sciences, Department of Economics, Ankara Haci Bayram Veli University, Ankara, Türkiye
e-mail: goktug.sahin@hbv.edu.tr

S. Gayaker
Faculty of Economics and Administrative Sciences, Department of Econometrics, Ankara Haci Bayram Veli University, Ankara, Türkiye
e-mail: savas.gayaker@hbv.edu.tr

J. Thewissen et al. (eds.), *The ESG Framework and the Energy Industry*,
https://doi.org/10.1007/978-3-031-48457-5_3

Poverty through a time-series allows for an understanding of its evolution in response to factors like seasonal shifts, economic cycles, or policy changes. It enables the forecasting of future trends and the evaluation of policy impacts over time. This perspective can reveal causal relationships between Energy Poverty and macroeconomic factors or energy prices, thereby informing more effective strategies. Thus, identifying the macrovariables that influence Energy Poverty becomes critical for effective policy development. Despite the complexities, it is vital to identify the macrovariables that influence Energy Poverty through a time-series analysis. This approach enables a deeper understanding of the temporal dynamics of Energy Poverty, which is essential for the development of effective policies.

In order to establish a time-series representation of Energy Poverty, the trend separation method was employed in the study, which mirrors the technique typically utilized in economics literature to calculate the output gap. In the context of Türkiye, Energy Poverty was estimated by examining the discrepancy between potential and actual electricity consumption. The potential electricity consumption was determined using the Kalman Filter method, a standard tool in time-series analysis. Moreover, the Autoregressive Distributed Lag (ARDL) model was used to determine the effects of macroeconomic variables on Energy Poverty. As a result of the literature review, no studies regarding our calculation technique for Energy Poverty have been found. Also, as stated, the macroeffects on Energy Poverty are scarcely mentioned in the literature, especially from an empirical point of view. Accordingly, the approach used to measure Energy Poverty in this study is an innovative contribution to the literature and shows that it is pioneering in this sense. Moreover, the scarcity of empirical studies on the macroeconomic determinants of Energy Poverty, especially about Türkiye, in the literature further increases the value of this research. By helping to understand better the relationship between Energy Poverty and key macroscale factors, this study will contribute to fill a knowledge gap for policymakers and researchers.

In a nutshell, this study consists of seven sections: Introduction, Information About Literature and Measuring Energy Poverty, Türkiye's Energy Posture in the Scope of Energy Poverty, Methodology, Data, Empirical Findings, and Conclusion. The following section provides a concise overview of Energy Poverty and relevant literature. Section 3 offers insights into Türkiye's energy landscape concerning Energy Poverty. The methodology employed in the analysis of the study's subject is detailed in Sect. 4, while Sect. 5 outlines the data and measurement of Energy Poverty. Empirical findings are discussed in Sect. 6. Finally, the study is concluded in Sect. 7.

2 Information About Literature and Measuring Energy Poverty

Actually, energy is a fact that has significant impacts on almost every aspect of human life, as well as societies, from the beginning to the end. These effects can be observed in both basic and higher-level needs. However, it is noteworthy that there are substantial differences in terms of access to energy resources between advantaged and disadvantaged countries, which, in turn, can create disparities within these countries in terms of economic growth and development levels. Notably, there is a strong correlation between energy and macroeconomic factors (Sahin, 2021).

Feldman et al. (2016) define economic development as the extension of capacities that advance society by maximizing the potential of individuals, firms, and communities, where economic development depends on economic growth. In the most general sense, economic development implies providing a better living for every human being (Hartwick & Peet, 2009). Modern economic development is a concept that should not be confused with economic growth, as Lucas (1988) stated. Besides, the United Nations Development Program (UNDP) defines poverty as the lack of opportunities for human welfare, such as lifelong physical well-being, a creative life, adequate living standards, individuality, self-confidence, and dignity (UNDP, 2020). On the other hand, energy is defined as the power generated through the use of physical or chemical resources (Oxford Learner's Dictionary, 2022) and is also described as the capacity and ability to do work (EIA, 2022). Moreover, energy plays a critical role in building a sustainable future economically, socially, and environmentally. At the same time, it is essential to industrialized society and our daily lives since individuals can convert energy into work (Sahin, 2021).

Accordingly, there is a close relationship between access to crucial modern energy sources and economic development in a macroeconomic manner. Sen (1979) suggested that energy and energy services are essential drivers for creating secondary capabilities. Low-income households allocate more of their income to necessary energy expenditures than high-income households, raising the issue of scalability. Additionally, since the energy sources preferred by low-income households have relatively lower efficiency, greater costs arise. In this respect, accessibility to modern energy resources significantly impacts poverty and is essential for prosperity and development. Furthermore, governments' inability to create effective and fair energy policies prevents qualified energy consumption.

One of the most critical factors in increasing the living standards of people with low incomes is their access to modern energy sources. In this context, the energy policies to be developed by governments and the adequate provision of modern energy services, such as improved cooking facilities, quality heating, and lighting to households, will increase the welfare level of people. It is unmanageable to end poverty, boost economic growth, create more jobs, strengthen social service initiatives, and advance human development without ensuring reliable access to energy sources. Development indicators such as augmented economic growth, decreased poverty, and improved welfare are impossible to achieve without reliable access to energy sources (Johansson et al., 2012).

In the 1990s, a new concept known as Energy Poverty emerged as a refined iteration of the earlier idea of Fuel Poverty, which had existed since the late 1970s. The poverty emphasized here is in terms of access to energy and should not be confused with the concept of economic poverty, while they are related. Although the contents of Energy Poverty and Fuel Poverty are similar, a clear consensus has not been reached. From a conceptual perspective, Energy Poverty can be defined as the inability to access sufficient energy levels necessary for basic social and material needs such as heating, cooling, lighting, and cooking, at the required level and quality for households' income level (EU, 2022). According to UNDP (2000), Energy Poverty is characterized as an inability to access adequate, affordable, healthy, high-quality, environmentally friendly, and secure energy services or, in other words, modern energy opportunities that enable development. This concept, which was developed in England and Ireland, has been examined in an increasing number of countries and from different perspectives. Especially after the 2008 crisis, Energy Poverty has been discussed in the context of being unable to meet energy expenditures in both developed and developing countries. This issue exists in both developing and developed economies, and it has a detrimental impact on welfare due to low energy usage and the consumption of fuels that have a high risk of pollution. Energy-poor households cannot adequately utilize essential energy services due to factors such as increased energy expenditure levels, low income, and specific energy necessities (Herrero, 2017). Although each issue is unique and anchored in a distinct area of policy and practice, Energy Poverty exists at the intersection of three separate topics: high energy costs, low income, and inadequate housing structure. Moreover, the reasons for the emergence of Energy Poverty differ around the world. The criteria addressed for the Energy Poverty concept vary significantly between developed-developing, rich-poor countries, and various climatic regions (Schuessler, 2014).

The International Energy Agency (2022) states that approximately 770 million individuals worldwide lack access to electricity, with a significant number concentrated in Africa and Asia. The COVID-19 Pandemic further weakened the energy purchasing power of households in developing countries. It is also reported that for the first time since 2013, sub-Saharan Africa experienced an increase in the number of individuals without access to electricity, with 77% of the population lacking access. The IEA also indicates that over 2.5 billion people in the world rely on solid biomass, kerosene, or coal as their primary cooking fuel, lacking access to clean cooking facilities. These situations create undesirable conditions and contribute to the issue of Energy Poverty, hindering economic and social development.

Despite advancements in technology and increasing global energy demand, many individuals worldwide still face difficulties in accessing clean, sufficient, and affordable energy sources. Inadequate access to modern energy resources and services constitutes a significant obstacle to achieving development targets at the global level. Sustainable Development Goal 7, established by the United Nations (UN), aims to achieve universal access to affordable, reliable, and modern energy by 2030 (IEA,

2022; UN, 2022). However, the usage of traditional energy sources creates unfavorable conditions for fundamental development indicators, perpetuating poverty and hindering access to modern energy sources for already marginalized households and individuals.

The literature highlights the relationship between energy use and economic development, with key macroeconomic indicators including GDP, industrial production, international trade, inflation, energy consumption, and CO_2 emissions. In addition to the linkage between macroeconomic development and energy usage, Energy Poverty has become an increasingly important economic and political issue, leading to more detailed studies on its measurement and conceptual dimensions (González-Eguino, 2015).

Energy Poverty is closely related to access to modern energy services, and its measurement requires careful consideration of identifying energy-poor households and reflecting their deprivation. However, measuring Energy Poverty is a complex and challenging task due to its dependence on location, time, and well-designed data. The difficulties in assessing Energy Poverty can be attributed to several factors, including the fact that energy services cannot be substituted for one another, there is no consensus on which energy services are fundamental, and defining the poverty level for each energy service is arbitrary. Energy access, measuring inputs, measuring outcomes, and the quality of energy delivered are all approaches that can be used to measure Energy Poverty (Culver, 2017). In the academic literature, Energy Poverty is calculated using a variety of methods that can be categorized as either single-indicator or multi-indicator approaches. Several studies have reviewed and critiqued these assessment methods in detail. For details, please refer to studies such as Nussbaumer et al. (2012), Bouzarovski (2014), Culver (2017), Thomson et al. (2017), Herrero (2017), Thema and Vondung (2020), Siksnelyte-Butkiene et al. (2021), and Robina et al. (2022).

Furthermore, the concept of Energy Poverty defines poverty as the lack of access to energy based on a specific threshold value in technological, physical, or economic aspects. The technological threshold approach views Energy Poverty as a problem of accessing modern energy services, typically referring to electrical energy and its various forms for activities such as cooking and home heating. In the physical threshold approach, the minimum energy consumption associated with basic needs is estimated, and households that consume less than this threshold are considered energy poor. On the other hand, the economic threshold approach seeks to determine the maximum required and reasonable income percentage for energy expenditures. This method is primarily used to measure Energy Poverty in developed countries (González-Eguino, 2015).

3 Türkiye's Energy Posture in the Scope of Energy Poverty

Türkiye, the application area of the study, is located between Asia and Europe, called Eurasia, with a total population of about 85 million people in 2021. Türkiye is a developed country with an upper-middle-income status. Türkiye has a GDP of about 815 billion dollars (current US dollar), GDP per capita of about 9587 dollars (current US dollar), and GINI index value of about 0.40 in 2021. Besides, Türkiye has an economic growth of about 11% in 2021. Moreover, Türkiye's CO_2 emissions are 4.8 metric tons per capita in 2019. Türkiye's access to electricity is reported as 100% (WB, 2022). According to the poverty line, which is determined by considering 50% of the equivalent household disposable median income, the poverty rate is 14.4% in 2021. Also, in 2021 the share of the highest income group in the total income is 46.7% (TURKSTAT, 2022).

If we refer to the information about energy in Türkiye, Table 1 presents the total consumption amounts of total and each primary energy sources in order to analyze the situation regarding Türkiye along with European, OECD, and global levels to make comparisons. Compared to 2020, total primary energy consumption increased by 6.1% in Türkiye, 4.4% in Europe, 4.4% in the OECD, and 5.5% globally in 2021. In 2021, the total primary energy consumption in Türkiye represented 1.1% of the total primary consumption worldwide, approximately the same as the previous year. It is also evident that oil, coal, and natural gas have the largest share of Türkiye's total primary energy consumption for all three years. Another important point to consider is that total primary energy consumption decreased in all four regions in the table in 2020 compared to the previous year. The reason for both the relative decrease in 2020 and the relative increase in 2021 can be attributed to the COVID-19 Pandemic.

Figure 1 illustrates that the per capita primary energy consumption has exhibited an upward trend in both Türkiye and the World, albeit at a faster pace in Türkiye. In fact, after 2016, Türkiye's per capita primary energy consumption surpassed that of the world. In the comparison of the years 2020 and 2021, the per capita primary energy consumption has increased by 5.4% in Türkiye and 4.8% in the World.

The Eleventh Development Plan, covering 2019–2023, aims to ensure a continuous, high-quality, sustainable, safe, and cost-effective energy supply in Türkiye. The plan outlines various targets and objectives for the energy and mining sectors,

Table 1 Türkiye's primary energy consumption by sources in 2019, 2020, and 2021 in comparison with Europe, OECD, and the World (Exajoule)

	Europe	OECD	World	Türkiye						
	Total	Total	Total	Coal	Oil	Natural gas	Nuclear energy	Hydroelectric	Renewables	Total
2019	83.46	234.48	591.51	1.76	2.01	1.56	–	0.79	0.39	6.51
2020	78.93	220.20	564.01	1.70	1.84	1.66	–	0.74	0.50	6.44
2021	82.38	229.89	595.15	1.74	1.89	2.06	–	0.52	0.61	6.83

Sources BP (2021), BP (2022)

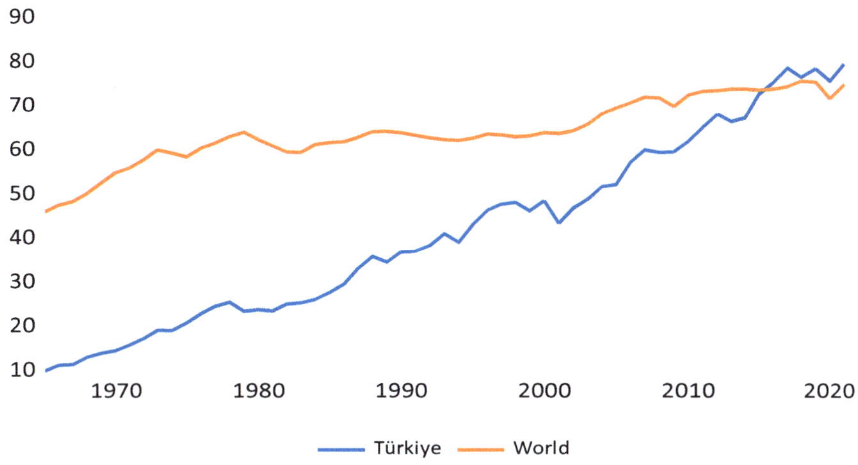

Fig. 1 Primary energy consumption per capita for Türkiye and World between 1965 and 2021 (Gigajoule). *Source* BP (2022)

including the development of a competitive investment environment, completion of rehabilitation of public power plants, increased use of lignite reserves in electricity generation, strengthening natural gas supply security, and increasing electricity generation from renewable energy sources. Other objectives include developing efficient buildings, strengthening electricity networks and systems, increasing cross-border trade opportunities, and reducing foreign dependency on energy. The plan also includes increasing exploration and production activities for domestic resources, developing domestic production in energy and mining machinery and equipment, and accelerating exploration activities for oil, natural gas, and geothermal resources. The goal is to reduce financial risks and increase exploration activities in the private sector. The data on targets for energy and related mining sectors for the year 2023 are presented in Table 2 (SBB, 2019).

On the other hand, The Medium-Term Program for the years 2022–2024 outlines several targets related to energy and mining. New R&D projects will be initiated to support groundbreaking technologies, such as quantum, artificial intelligence, biotechnology, genetics, and new-generation nuclear energy. The program also aims to support green transformation and circular economy in various industries, including transportation and energy, and to increase exports' competitiveness in line with climate change policies. Investments in environmentally friendly production and renewable energy sources will be supported to minimize the adverse effects of global climate change. The program also aims to increase transparency and competition-oriented practices in energy markets, support the energy efficiency of industrial enterprises, and strengthen physical, human, and technological infrastructure to achieve technological transformation in the industry. Additionally, the development model, which ensures sustainable growth, will be continued by observing macroeconomic balances and implementing structural reforms (OVP, 2022).

Table 2 Energy and related mining sector targets for 2023 within the scope of Türkiye's Eleventh Development Plan

	2018[a]	2023[b]
Primary energy demand (kTOE)	147.955	174.279
Electrical energy demand (TWh)	303,3	375,8
Primary energy consumption per capita (TOE/Person)	1,8	2,0
Electrical energy consumption per capita (kWh/Person)	3.698	4.324
Share of natural gas in electricity production (%)	29,9	20,7
Share of renewable resources in electricity generation (%)	32,5	38,8
Amount of electricity produced from domestic sources (TWh)	150,0	219,5
Installed power capacity (MW)	88.551	109.474
Proved lignite reserve (billion tons)	18,9	20,0

Source SBB (2019)
[a] The year in which the plan was prepared is included in the data to facilitate comparisons
[b] The targets specified in the plan serve as benchmarks for evaluation

The 2019–2023 Strategic Plan of the Ministry of Energy and Natural Resources (MENR) outlines the current needs of the energy sector and the development of necessary policies for natural resources. The main topics include ensuring sustainable energy supply security, prioritizing and increasing energy efficiency, strengthening institutional and sectoral capacity, increasing regional and global efficiency in energy and natural resources, technological development and localization in the field of energy and natural resources, increasing predictability in markets, and increasing sustainable production capacity with mining. The plan aims to achieve sustainable energy and resource management while promoting economic growth and development (MENR, 2019).

To gain insight into Türkiye's evaluation of the sustainability of national energy policies and Energy Poverty and to compare with other countries, one practical analysis is the World Energy Trilemma Index. This index is published annually by the World Energy Council and provides an indication of how well countries are achieving energy security, environmental sustainability, and access to energy, which together constitute the energy trilemma. The energy equity dimension of the index can be useful for monitoring Energy Poverty issues. The index's performance score covers three primary dimensions (energy security, energy equity, and environmental sustainability) that constitute 90% of the overall grade, with an additional dimension (Country Context) covering the remaining 10%. The score depends on which quartile the country's score corresponds to, with A representing the first 25%, B representing the first 25–50%, C representing 50–75%, and D representing 75–100%. Türkiye's ranking in the World Energy Trilemma Index 2022 is 44th among 127 countries, with a score of 64.1 and a BBBd grade. Furthermore, Türkiye's energy security, energy equity, and environmental sustainability ranks in the index are 53, 50, and 50, respectively. There has been a noticeable improvement in Türkiye's relevant scores and ranks compared to previous years. The World Energy Trilemma Index can thus provide valuable information for evaluating Türkiye's energy policies and identifying potential areas for improvement (WEC, 2022).

4 Methodology

This study uses two different models for generating and analyzing Energy Poverty. The Kalman filter was used for generating Energy Poverty, and the ARDL model was for analyzing the determinants of Energy Poverty. The Kalman filter developed by Kalman (1960, 1963) and Kalman and Bucy (1961) is an algorithm for generating predictions with the smallest mean square error in a state-space model. Specifically, it is a recursive technique for updating successively the one-step-ahead estimation of the state mean and variance based on incoming information. The Kalman filter is an extremely useful tool because the state-space model provides a fairly broad formulation for linear models in which time-varying parameters, measurement errors, and missing data can all be readily handled. After Energy Poverty was obtained, the ARDL model was used to reveal the effects of macroeconomic variables on Energy Poverty. The ARDL model is a dynamic model in which the effect of an independent variable on a dependent variable occurs over time rather than all at once. In addition, the ARDL model generates unbiased estimates in addition to accurate t-statistics, regardless of the endogeneity of the regressors that are being used in the analysis (Harris & Sollis, 2003; Jalil & Ma, 2008). The following section gives the fundamental concepts of the Kalman filter and the ARDL model, respectively.

4.1 Kalman Filter

The Kalman filter is used to estimate state-space models. Therefore, Eqs. (1) – (5) are used for this reason.

The measurement equation,

$$Y_t = X_t \beta_{t-1} + v_t \tag{1}$$

and the transition equation can be given as,

$$\beta_t = \mu + F\beta_t + e_t. \tag{2}$$

Here Y_t is the observed data, β_t is the unobservable component or state variable, and $X_t\prime$ is the constant term and the vector containing all lagged values of Y_t. Moreover,

$$\begin{bmatrix} v_t \\ e_t \end{bmatrix} \sim i \cdot i \cdot d \cdot N\left(\begin{bmatrix} 0 \\ 0 \end{bmatrix}, \begin{bmatrix} R & 0 \\ 0 & Q \end{bmatrix} \right), \tag{3}$$

where μ, F, R, and Q are previously known matrices, the aim here is to estimate the state variable β_t, which includes time-varying coefficients.

While the initial values of $\beta_{0|0}$ and $p_{0|0}$ are given, steps (4) and (5) are applied for the standard Kalman filter.

$$\beta_{t-1|t-1} = \beta_{0|0} \tag{4}$$

$$P_{t-1|t-1} = p_{0|0} \tag{5}$$

In steps (4) and (5), initial values are assigned for the Kalman filter and here can be taken as $\beta_{0|0} = 0$ and $p_{0|0} = 1$ (Mumtaz & Rummel, 2015). Equation (6) is the first equation of the Kalman filter estimation step.

$$\beta_{t|t-1} = \mu + F\beta_{t-1|t-1} \tag{6}$$

Equation (7) is used to calculate the variance of $\beta_{t|t-1}$.

$$P_{t|t-1} = FP_{t-1|t-1}F' + Q \tag{7}$$

Then, with Eqs. (8) and (9), the prediction error and the variance value of the prediction error are calculated, respectively.

$$\eta_{t|t-1} = Y_t - X_t\beta_{t|t-1} \tag{8}$$

$$f_{t|t-1} = X_t P_{t|t-1} X_t{'} + R \tag{9}$$

The Kalman gain value is calculated with the help of Eq. (10).

$$K_t = P_{t|t-1} X_t{'} f_{t|t-1}^{-1} \tag{10}$$

Backward iteration continues until $t = 0$. The updated formulas of backward repetition for time t are given in Eqs. (11) and (12) (Neusser, 2016: 325). The equation numbered (11) weights the state variable β_t with the Kalman gain value and ensures that it is updated with the help of the prediction error. Similarly, Eq. (12) is used to update the variance of the state variable.

$$\beta_{t|t} = \beta_{t|t-1} + K_t\eta_{t|t-1} \tag{11}$$

$$P_{t|t} = P_{t|t-1} - K_t X_t P_{t|t-1} \tag{12}$$

4.2 Autoregressive Distributed Lag Model

An Autoregressive Distributed Lag (ARDL) model is an Ordinary Least Square (OLS)-based model applicable for both non-stationary time series and times series with mixed order of integration. This model takes sufficient lags to capture the data-generating process in a general-to-specific modeling framework. Thus, it becomes a model approach in which the lagged values of the dependent and independent variables are included in the system. In general, the ARDL model with n-independent variables is as given in the following:

$$y_t = \alpha_0 + \sum_{i=1}^{p_1} \beta_i y_{t-i} + \sum_{i=0}^{p_2} \delta_i x_{1,t-i} + \cdots \sum_{i=0}^{p_{n+1}} \gamma_i x_{n,t-i} + u_t. \tag{13}$$

Equation (13) can be estimated with the help of OLS. The optimal lag length can be determined with the help of information criteria such as AIC, SIC, and HQ.

5 Data

Data for the empirical analysis conducted in the study are consisted of monthly observations from December 2009 to August 2022. The dataset included domestic inflation rate (π) computed as the log difference of seasonally adjusted Consumer Price Index (CPI); change in the nominal exchange rate (e) computed as the log difference of the basket rate over the previous month obtained by weighting 50% for USD/TRY and 50% for EUR/TRY rates; change in Brent oil prices (π^{oil}) and natural gas prices (π^{gas}) computed as the log difference of Brent oil and Henry Hub Natural Gas spot prices over the previous month; change in the industrial production index (ip) computed as the log difference of seasonally adjusted IPI ($2015 = 100$) over previous month; and finally Energy Poverty (ep) which is derived from the Kalman filter using seasonally adjusted electricity consumption. Key variables include inflation and exchange rates, which directly influence energy affordability, Brent oil and natural gas prices, which shape the cost of energy, and the industrial production index, a mirror of broader economic activity, including energy production. These factors provide a comprehensive understanding of the dynamics of Energy Poverty in the country's macroeconomic context. Details of the data are presented in Table 3.

5.1 Energy Poverty

In the existing body of literature, indices created by different institutions are generally used to measure Energy Poverty. Many of the indices created have annual and limited historical values. In this study, unlike the existing studies, Energy Poverty

Table 3 Description of the data

Variable	Symbol	Data source
Consumer price index (2003 = 100)	π	The Central Bank of the Republic of Türkiye—Electronic Data Delivery System
Exchange rate basket	e	The Central Bank of the Republic of Türkiye—Electronic Data Delivery System
Brent oil price	π^{oil}	US Energy Information Administration
Natural gas price	π^{gas}	Thomson Reuters Eikon
Industrial production index (2015 = 100)	ip	The Central Bank of the Republic of Türkiye—Electronic Data Delivery System
Electricity consumption	ec	Energy Exchange Istanbul

is obtained similarly to the approach used to get an output gap. In other words, Energy Poverty is formed by indicating the difference between actual and potential energy consumption. Here, the Kalman filter is used to obtain the potential energy consumption. With the help of the Kalman filter, the trend of the energy consumption is estimated. Consequently, the estimated trend is considered as the potential energy consumption, offering a fresh perspective in the assessment of Energy Poverty.

A basic model for representing a time series, y_t, is the additive model, also known as the classical decomposition. It seeks to decompose a time series, y_t, into an exhaustive set of—unobserved—underlying components:

$$y_t = \tau_t + c_t + \gamma_t + v_t + \varepsilon_t \tag{14}$$

Which—in its most general form—models the dependent time-series variable, y_t, as consisting of a slowly changing unobserved component, τ_t (trend); a periodically recurring unobserved component, c_t (cycle); a periodic unobserved component, γ_t (seasonal); an unobserved autoregressive component, v_t; and an unobserved irregular component, ε_t (disturbance). The trend component, τ_t, can be modeled either deterministically as $y_t = \tau_t + \varepsilon_t$ with $\varepsilon_t \sim iid\ N(0, \sigma_\varepsilon^2)$ or stochastically by a random walk plus noise, giving rise to the so-called local level or random walk with noise model:

$$y_t = \tau_t + \varepsilon_t \quad \varepsilon_t \sim iid\ N(0, \sigma_\varepsilon^2) \tag{15}$$

$$\tau_t = \tau_{t-1} + \eta_t \quad \eta_t \sim iid\ N(0, \sigma_\eta^2), \tag{16}$$

where $E(\varepsilon_t \eta_t) = 0$.

Models (15) and (16) can be estimated by the Kalman filter (Harvey, 1990). After the model estimation, the Energy Poverty is obtained with $ep_t = -(\tau_t - y_t)$. Here, y_t represents the logarithm of monthly electricity consumption after seasonally adjusted. In Fig. 2, actual energy consumption and potential energy consumption are given together. The Energy Poverty obtained is presented in Fig. 3.

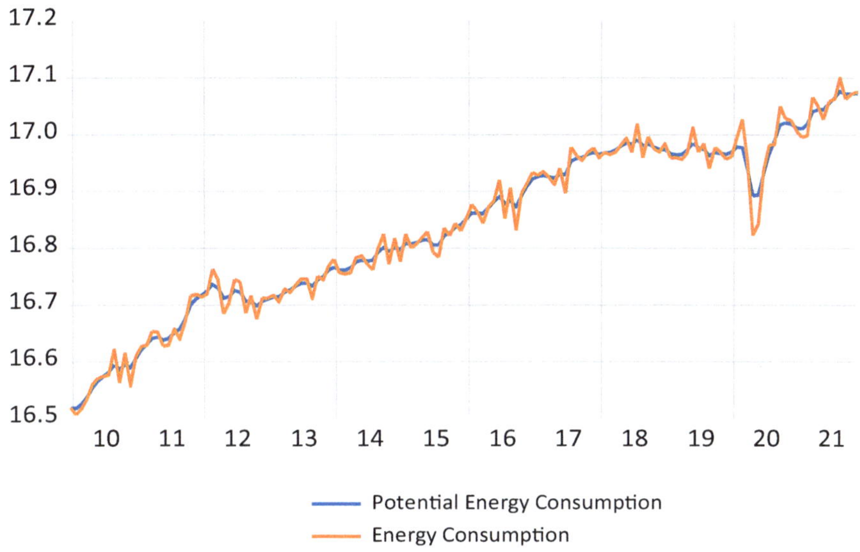

Fig. 2 Actual and potential energy consumption

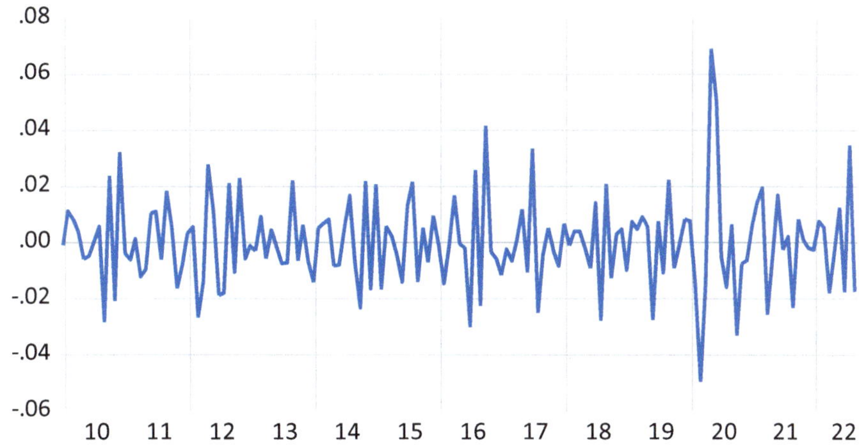

Fig. 3 Energy Poverty

Actually, when Fig. 3 is examined, the period with the highest Energy Poverty level is on the period of 2020:04. During this period, serious actions regarding the COVID-19 Pandemic began to be taken in Türkiye and the COVID-19 Pandemic has had a significant impact on Energy Poverty in Türkiye.

6 Empirical Findings

In this part of the study, the empirical findings, and the estimation results of the ARDL model (17) are reported (Table 4).

$$ep_t = \alpha + \sum_{i=1}^{y} \varphi_i ep_{t-i} + \sum_{i=0}^{p} \beta_i \pi_{t-i} + \sum_{i=0}^{q} \gamma_i e_{t-i} + \sum_{i=0}^{m} \omega_i \pi_{t-i}^{\text{oil}} + \sum_{i=0}^{n} \partial_i \pi_{t-i}^{\text{gas}} + \sum_{i=0}^{q} \delta_i i p_{t-i} + v_t \tag{17}$$

The estimation results of the ARDL model reveal several insights about the relationship between Energy Poverty and the chosen independent variables.

The findings indicate that Energy Poverty is affected by its lagged values, suggesting that past levels of Energy Poverty have an impact on current Energy Poverty. Interestingly, the relationship is negative, meaning that an increase in Energy Poverty in the past reduces Energy Poverty in the future. However, there could be several reasons for this result, such as policy response, behavioral changes, and market adjustments. An increase in Energy Poverty might prompt the government to implement targeted policies or interventions to address the issue. This could include providing financial support, increasing access to modern energy sources, or implementing energy efficiency programs to reduce energy consumption. As these policies take effect, they can lead to a reduction in Energy Poverty in subsequent periods (policy response). As households experience higher Energy Poverty, they may adopt energy-saving behaviors or invest in energy-efficient appliances to reduce their energy expenses. These changes can have a lasting impact and contribute to a reduction in Energy Poverty over time (behavioral changes). In response to higher Energy Poverty, market forces may drive innovation in the energy sector. This could include the development of more affordable and efficient energy sources, which can help alleviate Energy Poverty in the long run (market adjustments).

Both the instantaneous and lagged values of economic growth have a significant effect on Energy Poverty. The relationship is negative, which means that an increase in economic growth leads to a reduction in Energy Poverty. The negative relationship between economic growth and Energy Poverty can be explained by a combination of factors, including increased income, job creation, and infrastructure development. The fact that this effect is valid for all delays suggests that the benefits of economic growth on Energy Poverty reduction persist over time. Higher economic growth

Table 4 Estimation results of model (17)

Dependent Variable: ep_t				
Variable	Coefficient	Std. error	t-Statistic	Prob.
ep_{t-1}	– 0.403	0.090	– 4.496	0.000
ep_{t-2}	– 0.258	0.105	– 2.465	0.015
ep_{t-3}	– 0.295	0.095	– 3.088	0.002
π_t	– 0.077	0.077	– 1.001	0.319
π_t^{gas}	0.010	0.008	1.155	0.250
e_t	0.015	0.034	0.433	0.666
ip_t	– 0.088	0.033	– 2.682	0.008
ip_{t-1}	– 0.074	0.030	– 2.480	0.014
ip_{t-2}	– 0.108	0.031	– 3.503	0.001
ip_{t-3}	– 0.093	0.026	– 3.600	0.000
ip_{t-4}	– 0.099	0.026	– 3.899	0.000
π_t^{oil}	0.025	0.012	2.079	0.040
α	0.003	0.001	1.964	0.052
R-squared	0.363	Mean dependent var		0.000
Adjusted R-squared	0.306	S.D. dependent var		0.016
S.E. of regression	0.014	Akaike info criter		– 5.669
Sum squared resid	0.025	Schwarz criter		– 5.406
Log-likelihood	432.498	Hannan–Quinn criter		– 5.562
F-statistic	6.402	Durbin–Watson stat		2.145

typically leads to increased income levels for households. As household incomes rise, their ability to afford energy services also improves, reducing Energy Poverty (income effect). Economic growth often results in job creation, which can provide employment opportunities for those previously struggling with Energy Poverty. As more people secure stable employment, their financial situation improves, making it easier for them to access and afford energy services (job creation). Economic growth can lead to investments in infrastructure, such as improved electricity generation and distribution networks, and it can increase access to modern and reliable energy sources, helping to alleviate Energy Poverty (infrastructure development). A growing economy can foster innovation and technological advancements in the energy sector. This situation can lead to the development and deploying more efficient and affordable energy technologies, which can ultimately help reduce Energy Poverty (technological progress).

The analysis shows that Energy Poverty is affected by the instantaneous value of oil prices. An increase in oil prices leads to an increase in Energy Poverty. The positive relationship between oil prices and Energy Poverty can be attributed to high energy costs. Energy Poverty becomes more prevalent when oil prices increase, especially among low-income households. When oil prices rise, so does the cost of energy

Table 5 Diagnostic test of model (17)

Tests	F-stats	p-value
Ramsey RESET	2.052	0.154286
ARCH	0.675	0.415632
Breusch–Godfrey	1.324	0.269463

derived from petroleum, such as gasoline, diesel, heating oil, and other petroleum products. This can make energy cheaper, especially for low-income households, leading to increased Energy Poverty (higher cost of energy).

Finally, exchange rate, inflation, and gas prices do not statistically affect Energy Poverty. In summary, the ARDL model analysis reveals that Energy Poverty in Türkiye is influenced by its own lagged values, economic growth, and oil prices. Higher economic growth reduces Energy Poverty, while an increase in oil prices exacerbates it. Interestingly, Energy Poverty is negatively affected by its lags, which implies that higher levels of Energy Poverty in the past contribute to lower levels in the future. Meanwhile, exchange rate, inflation, and gas prices do not appear to have a statistically significant effect on Energy Poverty.

Table 5 presents the diagnostic tests for the residuals of Model (17). To ensure the efficiency of the estimated model coefficients, the residuals must not exhibit autocorrelation or heteroskedasticity. Additionally, it is crucial to assess the model's functional form for correctness.

The Breusch–Godfrey test is employed to detect autocorrelation issues in the residuals, with the null hypothesis (H_0) being that the residuals do not exhibit autocorrelation. The ARCH test is utilized to examine the presence of heteroskedasticity in the residuals, with the null hypothesis (H_0) stating that the residuals do not exhibit heteroskedasticity. Lastly, the Ramsey RESET test is applied to evaluate potential model specification errors, where the null hypothesis (H_0) posits that the model is correctly specified and free from specification errors.

Table 5 shows that the p-values of the ARCH, the Ramsey RESET, and the Breusch–Godfrey test statistics are greater than the significance level (α) 0.05. Therefore, H_0 hypotheses cannot be rejected at 0.05 significance level. The estimated model does not contain issues such as autocorrelation, heteroskedasticity, and misspecification.

Cumulative Sum (CUSUM) and CUSUM of squares tests are used in econometric analysis to assess the stability of estimated model parameters and to detect potential structural changes or instability in time-series data. These tests are particularly useful for evaluating the reliability and robustness of estimated models over time. In Figs. 4 and 5, CUSUM and CUSUM of squares tests show that all residuals fall within the interval bands (i.e., the critical bounds), which implies that the model parameters are stable over time, and no significant structural breaks or instability have been detected in the time-series data.

This result suggests that the estimated model is reliable and robust, as the stability of the parameters is essential for drawing accurate inferences and making well-informed policy recommendations.

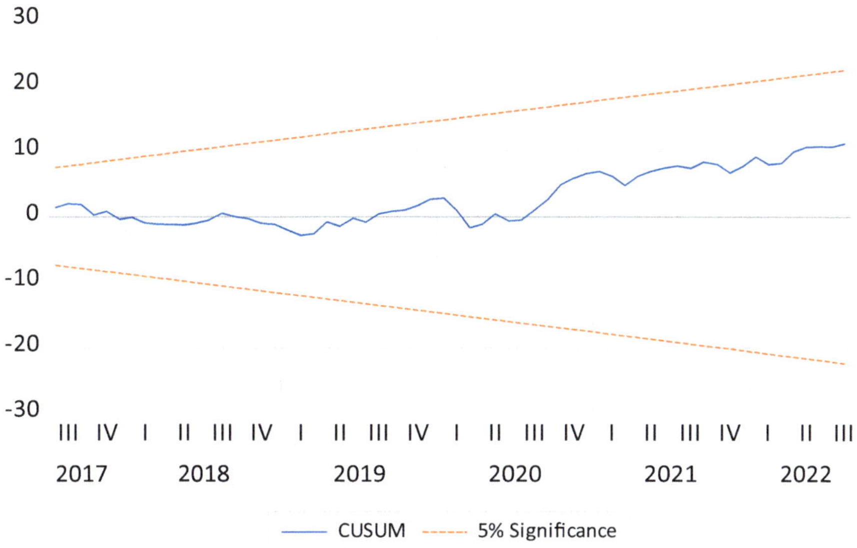

Fig. 4 CUSUM test

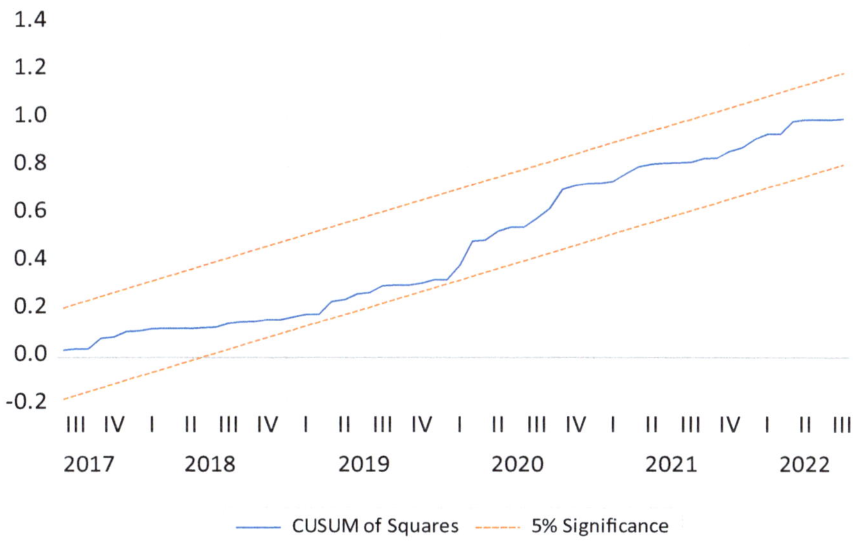

Fig. 5 CUSUM of squares test

7 Conclusion

Energy Poverty refers to the lack of access to modern energy services that are necessary for a decent standard of living, including access to electricity, clean cooking facilities, and reliable heating and cooling systems. Energy Poverty is a significant challenge for low- and middle-income countries, where access to modern energy services is limited or nonexistent, and people rely on expensive and polluting sources of energy, such as kerosene and diesel generators, to meet their energy needs besides the adverse impacts.

Moreover, it is essential to recognize the significance of the macroscale factors that impact the issue of Energy Poverty in a country. The term macrovariables refer to the broad and overarching economic, social, and environmental factors that affect energy consumption patterns and access to energy resources. Energy Poverty is a complex phenomenon that refers to the inability of a household or community to meet their basic energy needs, which can have severe consequences on their health, education, and overall well-being. So, it is essential to identify the macrovariables affecting Energy Poverty for several reasons. Firstly, it can aid in designing effective policy interventions that address the fundamental causes of Energy Poverty. Understanding the underlying factors that contribute to this problem can help policymakers devise targeted and tailored solutions that can address the specific needs of affected communities. Secondly, identifying these macrovariables can enable stakeholders to evaluate the impact of existing policies and programs. This can help determine the effectiveness of current measures and identify areas that require further attention and resources. In addition, recognizing the macrovariables that influence Energy Poverty can help to raise awareness and promote a more comprehensive understanding of the issue. This fact can foster greater public engagement and support for efforts to address the problem, leading to greater cooperation among stakeholders and more sustainable outcomes.

This study investigates the macroeconomic factors affecting Türkiye's Energy Poverty between December 2009 and August 2022 with the ARDL model. Energy Poverty is obtained by subtracting the energy consumed from the potential energy consumption. The Kalman filter is used from a different perspective in getting the potential energy consumption. Eventually, measuring Energy Poverty has two main purposes. First, energy-poor households should be identified, and second, poverty aspects should be reflected.

Relying on the abovementioned facts, the ARDL model-based empirical analysis of macroeconomic determinants of Energy Poverty in Türkiye yields several key insights. Energy Poverty can be mitigated through increased industrial production, which drives economic growth. Higher oil prices exacerbate Energy Poverty, exerting a more significant influence on Energy Poverty than natural gas prices. Notably, Energy Poverty is negatively impacted by its lagged values, indicating that past increases in Energy Poverty contribute to future reductions. These findings offer several policy implications for stakeholders and policymakers involved in addressing Energy Poverty in Türkiye. First, fostering economic growth and industrial production is essential, given their significant negative effect on Energy Poverty. Policymakers can achieve this by implementing policies that encourage job creation, infrastructure development, and technological progress, ultimately enabling households to access and afford modern, reliable energy services. Second, the strong positive relationship between oil prices and Energy Poverty highlights the necessity of devising effective strategies to mitigate the impact of rising oil prices on vulnerable households. Such strategies could encompass diversifying energy sources, promoting energy efficiency, and offering targeted financial assistance to low-income households burdened by high energy costs. Third, the negative relationship between Energy Poverty and its lagged values underscores the importance of prompt policy interventions and support measures to combat Energy Poverty. Policymakers should closely monitor Energy Poverty trends and proactively respond with targeted policies aimed at enhancing access to modern energy sources, promoting energy efficiency, and fostering innovation within the energy sector. Finally, the lack of a statistically significant effect of the exchange rate, inflation, and gas prices on Energy Poverty suggests that policymakers should prioritize addressing more impactful determinants, such as economic growth and oil prices.

To conclude, this study sheds light on the determinants of Energy Poverty in Türkiye, emphasizing the roles of economic growth, industrial production, and oil prices. The policy implications derived from these findings can inform the design and implementation of targeted policies and interventions aimed at alleviating Energy Poverty and fostering sustainable, inclusive economic growth.

References

Bouzarovski, S. (2014). Energy poverty in the European Union: Landscapes of vulnerability. *Wiley Interdisciplinary Reviews: Energy and Environment, 3*(3), 276–289.

BP (2021). *BP statistical review of world energy 2021*. Retrieved from BP: http://www.bp.com/statisticalreview

BP (2022). *BP statistical review of world energy 2022*. Retrieved from BP: http://www.bp.com/statisticalreview

Culver, L. C. (2017, May). Energy poverty: What you measure matters. In *Proceedings of the Reducing Energy Poverty with Natural Gas: Changing Political, Business and Technology Paradigms Symposium, Stanford, CA, USA* (pp. 9–10).

EIA (2022). *What is energy?* Retrieved from U.S. Energy Information Administration: https://www.eia.gov/energyexplained/what-is-energy

EU (2022). *Energy poverty in the EU*. Retrieved from European Commission: https://energy.ec.europa.eu/topics/markets-and-consumers/energy-consumer-rights/energy-poverty-eu_en

Feldman, M., Hadjimichael, T., Lanahan, L., & Kemeny, T. (2016). The logic of economic development: A definition and model for investment. *Environment and Planning C: Government and Policy, 34*(1), 5–21.

González-Eguino, M. (2015). Energy poverty: An overview. *Renewable and Sustainable Energy Reviews, 47*, 377–385.

Harris, R., & Sollis, R. (2003). *Applied time series modelling and forecasting*. Wiley.

Hartwick, E., & Peet, R. (2009). Theories of development: Contentions, arguments, alternatives. *Journal of Urban and Regional Analysis, 3*(1), 105–117.
Harvey, A. C. (1990). *Forecasting, structural time series models and the Kalman filter*. Cambridge University Press
Herrero, S. T. (2017). Energy poverty indicators: A critical review of methods. *Indoor and Built Environment, 26*(7), 1018–1031.
IEA (2022). *SDG7: Data and projections*. Retrieved from IEA: https://www.iea.org/reports/sdg7-data-and-projections
Jalil, A., & Ma, Y. (2008). Financial development and economic growth: Time series evidence from Pakistan and China. *Journal of Economic Cooperation, 29*(2), 29–68.
Johansson, T. B., Patwardhan, A. P., Nakićenović, N., & Gomez-Echeverri, L. (Eds.). (2012). *Global energy assessment: Toward a sustainable future*. Cambridge University Press
Kalman, R. E., & Bucy, R. S. (1961). New results in linear filtering and prediction theory. *Journal of Basic Engineering, Transactions ASME Series D, 83*, 95–108.
Kalman, R. E. (1960). A new approach to linear filtering and prediction problems. *Journal of Basic Engineering, Transactions ASME Series D, 82*, 35–45.
Kalman, R. E. (1963). New methods in Wiener filtering theory. In J. L. Bogdanoff & F. Kozin (Eds.), *Proceedings of the First Symposium on Engineering Applications of Random Function Theory and Probability* (Vol. 14). Wiley
Lucas, R. E. (1988). On the mechanics of economic development. *Journal of Monetary Economics, 22*(1), 3–42.
MENR (2019). *2019–2023 Dönemi Enerji ve Tabii Kaynaklar Bakanlığı Stratejik Planı*. Retrieved from Republic of Türkiye Ministry of Energy and Natural Resources: http://www.sp.gov.tr/tr/stratejik-plan/s/1971/Enerji+ve+Tabii+Kaynaklar+Bakanligi+2019-2023
Mumtaz, H., & Rummel, O. (2015). *Centre for central banking studies. Economic modelling and forecasting-recent developments in structural VAR modelling*. Bank of England.
Neusser, K. (2016). *Time series econometrics*. Springer.
Nussbaumer, P., Bazilian, M., & Modi, V. (2012). Measuring energy poverty: Focusing on what matters. *Renewable and Sustainable Energy Reviews, 16*(1), 231–243.
OVP (2022). Orta Vadeli Program (2022–2024). Retrieved from Presidency of the Republic of Türkiye Presidency of Strategy and Budget: https://www.sbb.gov.tr/orta-vadeli-programlar
Oxford Learner's Dictionaries (2022). *Energy*. Retrieved from Oxford Learner's Dictionaries: https://www.oxfordlearnersdictionaries.com/definition/academic/energy
Robina, V. K. G., Židov, B., & Robert Fabek, R. (2022). Measuring and monitoring energy poverty in the EU—Examples of good practices, 2022, April 1. Retrieved from https://www.odyssee-mure.eu/publications/policy-brief/measuring-energy-poverty.html
Sahin, G. (2021). *Natural gas economics in the scope of long-term contracts of Turkey*. Gazi Press.
SBB (2019). *On Birinci Kalkınma Planı (2019–2023)*. Retrieved from Presidency of the Republic of Türkiye Presidency of Strategy and Budget: https://www.sbb.gov.tr/kalkinma-planlari
Schuessler, R. (2014). Energy poverty indicators: Conceptual Issues-Part I: The ten-percent-rule and double median/mean indicators. *ZEW-Centre for European Economic Research Discussion Paper*, (14-037)
Sen, A. (1979). The welfare basis of real income comparisons: A survey. *Journal of Economic Literature, 17*(1), 1–45.
Siksnelyte-Butkiene, I., Streimikiene, D., Lekavicius, V., & Balezentis, T. (2021). Energy poverty indicators: A systematic literature review and comprehensive analysis of integrity. *Sustainable Cities and Society, 67*, 102756.
Thema, J., & Vondung, F. (2020). *EPOV indicator dashboard: Methodology guidebook*. Wuppertal Institut für Klima, Umwelt, Energie GmbH.
Thomson, H., Bouzarovski, S., & Snell, C. (2017). Rethinking the measurement of energy poverty in Europe: A critical analysis of indicators and data. *Indoor and Built Environment, 26*(7), 879–901.

TURKSTAT (2022). Gelir ve Yaşam Koşulları Araştırması, 2021. Retrieved from Turkish Statistical Institute: https://data.tuik.gov.tr/Bulten/Index?p=Gelir-ve-Yasam-Kosullari-Arastirmasi-2021-45581

UN (2022). *Sustainable Development Goal 7*. Retrieved from UN-Energy: https://un-energy.org

UNDP (2000). *World energy assessment: Energy and the challenge of sustainability*. Retrieved from UNDP: https://www.undp.org/publications

WB (2022). *World Bank Open Data: Türkiye*. Retrieved from The World Bank: https://data.worldbank.org/country/TR

WEC (2022). *World Energy Trilemma Index 2022*. Retrieved from World Energy Council: https://www.worldenergy.org/publications/entry/world-energy-trilemma-index-2022

Towards Economic Growth Without CO_2 Emissions: The Case of Türkiye

Wietze Lise

Abstract This chapter studies the energy situation and the development of CO_2 emissions in Türkiye. Türkiye is of interest here, as it has a high economic growth potential, and it is still possible to achieve the growth targets with reduced carbon emissions. Factors that explain the increase in CO_2 emissions are derived by undertaking a complete decomposition analysis for Türkiye over the period 1987–2018. The analysis shows, as is common to relatively fast-growing economies, that the main contributor to the rise in CO_2 emissions is the expansion of the economy (scale effect). The carbon intensity and the change in composition of the economy, also contribute to the rise in CO_2 emissions, but much less. Moreover, the carbon intensity has started to decrease in the 2010–2018 period. The energy intensity of the economy, which is decreasing at an accelerating rate after 2000, is responsible for a significant reduction in CO_2 emissions. A regression analysis with the data shows that a process of decoupling both carbon emissions and energy consumption with respect to economic growth has started in Türkiye over the period 1987–2018, indicating both an environmental and an energy Kuznets curve. Hence, economic growth is possible both without environmental degradation in terms of CO_2 emissions and without increasing the level of energy consumption.

Keywords Decomposition analysis · Türkiye · Energy · CO_2 emissions · Economic growth

1 Introduction

Understanding long-term 'energy transitions' and 'development trajectories' is a great challenge in the move towards sustainable development and a circular economy in a globalizing world. Energy transitions are defined as investments in possibly

W. Lise (✉)
Energy Markets, Management Consultancy Department, MRC Türkiye, ODTÜ Teknokent Met Alanı, Mustafa Kemal Mahallesi, Dumlupınar Bulvarı No: 280, D Blok No:3 Çankaya, Ankara, Turkey
e-mail: wietze.lise@mrc-tr.com

J. Thewissen et al. (eds.), *The ESG Framework and the Energy Industry*,
https://doi.org/10.1007/978-3-031-48457-5_4

cleaner technologies to replace and expand the depreciating capital stock. When considered over a longer time horizon, but also across countries, significant changes in energy technologies and consumption can be observed.[1] Development trajectories can be characterized by sectoral changes in the economy, which transform the society from traditional (agricultural/industrial sector) to modern (service/ITC sector).[2]

This chapter studies the energy situation and the development of CO_2 emissions for the specific situation of Türkiye. The case of Türkiye is particularly interesting for the following reasons. Official projections show that Türkiye has a yearly GDP growth potential of around 5% (SBP, 2022). Recent projections of the Climate Action Tracker (CAT, 2021) indicate that the level of CO_2 emission is going to rise in the post Covid-19 current policies scenario with 50% until 2030 with respect to the level of emissions in 2018. It is a great challenge to both meet the growth target and keep the CO_2 emissions under control. Thereupon, this chapter tries to unfold factors that drive increasing levels of CO_2 emissions by undertaking a complete decomposition analysis for Türkiye over the period 1987–2018.

There are various reasons for studying both the energy situation and the development of CO_2 emissions in Türkiye, as a country with a high economic growth potential, and Türkiye is still able to achieve the growth targets with reduced carbon emissions. First, Türkiye is a candidate for becoming an EU member and Türkiye can strengthen their strategic position as a gas and oil transit country (see also: Demirkan & Eryiğit, 2014; Van der Linde, 2004). Second, Türkiye is listed as an Annex I country[3] of the United Nations Framework Convention on Climate Change (UNFCCC) framework, but not as an Annex B country.[4] Moreover, Türkiye has ratified the Paris Agreement on 6/10/2021, and has set a target to lower greenhouse gas emission (GHG) to 21% below business-as-usual (BAU) (CAT, 2021). CAT (2021) provides an overview of Türkiye's plans for reducing GHG emissions energy situation and energy related environmental issues until 2030. They project a 50% increase in greenhouse gas emissions by 2030 in the baseline with respect to 2018 levels (ibid.), named as post COVID-19 current policies scenario. Finally, the Turkish economy has a strong growth potential, where official projections, namely the mid-term plan for 2023–2025 (SBP, 2022), show that Türkiye has a yearly GDP growth potential of around 5%.

---

[1] See for instance IRENA (2020) which reports on the energy transition in South and Eastern Europe. Even though it does not include Türkiye, the situation of Türkiye will have many similarities with the analysis for this region. Türkiye is currently still highly dependent on fossil fuel imports and local lignite, but also has an enormous potential for renewable energy. Türkiye still needs to make significant steps for an energy transition to low carbon economy. The roadmap as presented in the IRENA (2020) report also provides important lessons and directions for development for Türkiye.

[2] Türkiye has still a long way to go from the agricultural base economy to a services-based economy on their development trajectory. See for instance OECD (2021) with the latest assessment of OECD for Türkiye concerning their state of economic development from various perspectives.

[3] There are 43 parties to the Kyoto protocol, also known as Annex I countries and Türkiye is among them. A list of Annex I countries can be found in: OECD (2023).

[4] There are 36 industrialised countries listed in Annex B to the Kyoto protocol and Türkiye is not among them. These Annex B countries had specific greenhouse gas emission reduction targets. See for instance: MFA (2023).

There is a wide array of economic theories available with which to derive solid policy advice on achieving economic growth without harming the environment. However, any policy change to be translated into a change in legislation and/or doing things differently, would ideally have an appropriate theoretical foundation. Two applicable theoretical frameworks can be identified, namely cost–benefit analysis (CBA) and (regulatory) impact assessment (IA). First, an appropriate cost–benefit analysis[5] aims at quantifying all costs and revenues and translating them into a net present value (NPV); here an important parameter is the value of time as measured by the discount rate. Second, a proper (regulatory) impact assessment[6] will assess and present the impacts of a particular policy measure on economic growth (GDP), employment, investment costs, environment, among others. These impacts can be presented qualitatively but are ideally quantified as well.

The question at hand in this chapter is to find ways to achieve economic growth while slowing down CO_2 emissions. Since Türkiye has committed itself to the Paris Agreement, they will need to find ways to reduce CO_2 emissions in the most cost-effective manner, whereas possibilities to generate revenues and other positive social impacts, such as employment generation, should also be accounted for. However, before going into the nitty–gritty details of CBA or IA, it is possible to analyse past data to find the main causes of CO_2 emissions and it is possible to derive whether GDP growth can be achieved without negative environmental impacts in terms of additional CO_2 emissions. The former can be done through a decomposition analysis, whereas the latter can be done by testing the so-called Kuznets curve hypothesis.[7] Achieving this is the purpose of this chapter. Hence, the decomposition analysis aimed at in this chapter can be seen a first step prior to undertaking an CBA or IA.

Based on the literature on decomposition analysis in general and not for Türkiye in particular, an important comprehensive work surveying the literature on decomposition analysis is done by Xu and Ang (2013). Their paper reviews around eighty papers that have been published in academic peer-reviewed journals during the period ranging from 1991–2012. This is a review of studies undertaken in both developed and developing countries generally at the national level including various sectors and total emissions at the country level.

Dietzenbacher and Los (1998) give a critical assessment of the use of (structural) decomposition analysis with the main points being that the results often differ considerably from method to method. The authors argue that it is well-known that structural decompositions are not unique, both the extent of the problem and the implications have been mainly ignored. Their paper clearly points out one of the weak aspects of IDA. However, this can be overcome by structurally applying the same complete decomposition method in various contexts and to test whether the derived policy insights work in practice. Therefore, this chapter also undertakes a

[5] For more in depth assessment of the theory of CBA see, for instance, Dreze and Stern (1987).

[6] There is a practice at the EU level to subject all key regulatory policy changes to an impact assessment; see, for instance, EU (2022).

[7] For an application of the environmental Kuznets curve (EKC) hypothesis to Black Sea countries, see for instance, Saraç and Yağlıkara (2017).

regression analysis, in addition to the complete decomposition analysis, to find additional support for the derived conclusions. The quadratic regression equation is also known as "inverted-U" or the environmental Kuznets curve hypothesis. This will be explained in further detail below.

The literature also has important work on decomposition analysis on Türkiye as well. An assessment of various decomposition methods and key studies performed on Türkiye is given in the paper by Yılmaz-Ataman (2022). The author shows that all decomposition methods can be classified as Index Decomposition Analysis (IDA) of which the refined Laspeyres additive method, which will be applied to Türkiye in this chapter, is one option among them. Other options are multiplicative Laspayres methods, divisia additive and divisia multiplicative methods. This study responds to the need for a common understanding and methodological consistency in empirical studies using IDA, as stated by Ang (2004). Additionally, Su and Ang (2012) made a different classification, namely distinguishing between structural decomposition analysis (SDA) and IDA. Actually, it is the author's opinion that not so much the type of IDA, e.g. the chosen decomposition method, is important, but rather the policy conclusions that can be achieved with a careful application of a selected and applicable IDA. Another purpose of this chapter is to draw policy conclusions for Türkiye related to their commitment to the Paris Agreement in terms of reducing CO_2 and other greenhouse gas emissions.

Even though a decomposition analysis may appear simplistic at first glance, the method can lead to very useful energy policy recommendations on how to continue economic growth and reduce CO_2 emissions simultaneously. Moreover, there is a large body of literature on applications of decomposition analyses worldwide. However, work is lacking on the situation in Türkiye considering the current context of CO_2 emission reductions.

The approach in this chapter is unique in the sense that prior to presenting the results of the decomposition analysis, the underlying factors are presented and discussed as well. This consists of three variables:

1. The year-to-year changes in the sectoral shares of key economic sectors.
2. The year-to-year changes in the sectoral index of energy intensity.
3. The year-to-year changes in the sectoral index of carbon intensity.

The presentation of that information is required in order to find the intuition behind the results as derived with the complete decomposition analysis.

Thereupon, the following question is studied within this chapter, using a complete decomposition analysis:

- Which factors –i.e. scale, composition, energy and carbon intensity– explain changes in CO_2 emissions?

  In addition, the following questions are addressed:

- How has the sectoral composition of the economy changed over time?
- How have the shares of the main fossil fuels and renewables in the energy mix changed over time?

- How has the energy and carbon intensity changed over time and per sector?
- What is the link between national income and carbon emissions or energy consumption?

The outline of this chapter is as follows. Section 2 presents the methods used in this chapter. Section 3 discusses the changes in the energy situation in Türkiye by presenting graphs of three key variables, namely sectoral shares of key economic sectors, sectoral index of energy intensity, and sectoral index of carbon intensity. Furthermore, a complete decomposition analysis is undertaken and both the energy and environmental Kuznets curve hypothesis is tested for Türkiye. The final section concludes and provides responses to the raised research questions, based on the analysis undertaken in this chapter.

2 Method

2.1 Decomposition Method

A commonly used method to derive the causes of carbon emissions is to undertake a so-called decomposition analysis. As a first step, a partial decomposition analysis can be undertaken. However, this would lead to an unexplained residual term, which could also be relatively large. To give an example, CO_2 emissions (Em) can be decomposed into CO_2 emissions per GDP and GDP. This can be summarized into the following so-called Kaya identity, which reaches equivalence by striking out the GDP in the denominator and numerator:

$$\mathrm{Em} = \tfrac{\mathrm{Em}}{\mathrm{GDP}}\mathrm{GDP} \tag{1}$$

A change in CO_2 emissions can then be decomposed into a change in CO_2 emissions per GDP weighed with GDP and a change in GDP weighed with CO_2 emissions per GDP. The following formula shows this, where 'Δ' is used to denote change:

$$\Delta\mathrm{Em} = \Delta\mathrm{GDP} \cdot \left(\tfrac{\mathrm{Em}}{\mathrm{GDP}}\right) + \Delta\left(\tfrac{\mathrm{Em}}{\mathrm{GDP}}\right) \cdot \mathrm{GDP} \tag{2}$$

In Eq. (2) CO_2 emission are decomposed into two effects, namely the scale effect (growth in GDP) weighed by the emission intensity and emission intensity effect (change in emissions per GDP) weighed by the size of the economy. However, this decomposition is not complete, as there is a residual term, namely: $\Delta\mathrm{GDP} \times \Delta\left(\tfrac{\mathrm{Em}}{\mathrm{GDP}}\right)$. To eliminate this residual term, Sun (1998) proposed a complete decomposition analysis where the residual term is distributed among the considered effects. Zhang and Ang (2001) also refer to this technique as the refined Laspeyres method, which has been widely adopted due to ease of both calculation and for understanding the policy implications of the results. This chapter follows the same route as in Sun (1998), namely by equally assigning the residual term to both effects. This leads to the following extension of Eq. (2):

$$\Delta\text{Em} = \underbrace{\left(\frac{\text{Em}}{\text{GDP}}\right) \cdot \Delta\text{GDP} + \frac{1}{2} \cdot \Delta\left(\frac{\text{Em}}{\text{GDP}}\right) \cdot \Delta\text{GDP}}_{\text{scale effect}} \\ \underbrace{+ \text{GDP} \cdot \Delta\left(\frac{\text{Em}}{\text{GDP}}\right) + \frac{1}{2} \cdot \Delta\left(\frac{\text{Em}}{\text{GDP}}\right) \cdot \Delta\text{GDP}}_{\text{emission intensity effect}} \quad (3)$$

The mechanism as explained in the example of Eqs. (1)–(3) can also be used to decompose the level of CO_2 emissions into more effects. There is sufficient data to make a division into four different effects. This leads to the Kaya identity as presented in Eq. (4), as follows:

$$CO_2 \text{ emissions} = \underbrace{\text{GDP}}_{\text{scale effec}} \cdot \sum_i \underbrace{\frac{\text{Added value}_i}{\text{GDP}}}_{\text{composition effect}} \cdot \underbrace{\frac{\text{Energy use}_i}{\text{Added value}_i}}_{\text{energy intensity effect}} \cdot \underbrace{\frac{CO_2 \text{ emissions}_i}{\text{Energy use}_i}}_{\text{carbon intensity effect}} \\ = P \cdot \sum_i G_i \cdot I_i \cdot E_i \quad (4)$$

where

CO_2 emissions are the total for Türkiye, measured in million tons (Mtons)

GDP is the total for Türkiye, measured in billion Turkish Liras (TL) in constant 2015 prices.

Added value$_i$ is the share of GDP for sector i.

Energy use$_i$ is the share of energy use for sector i, measured in billion tons of oil equivalent (btoe)

CO_2 emissions$_i$ is the share of CO_2 emissions for sector i, measured in Mtons.

Sectors i are: Agriculture, Industry, Transport and Other,

P is GDP (scale effect).

G_i is Added value$_i$ divided by GDP (composition effect).

I_i is Energy use$_i$ divided by Added value$_i$ (energy intensity effect).

E_i is CO_2 emissions$_i$ divided by Energy use$_i$ (carbon intensity effect).

In words, Eq. (4) means that the total CO_2 emissions are fully equal to the product of total GDP (P), and the sum of the sectoral products of the added value per GDP (G_i), energy consumption per added value (I_i) and the CO_2 emissions per energy consumption (E_i).

To explain the changes in CO_2 emissions, the differences (ΔP, ΔG_i, ΔI_i, ΔE_i) with respect to the base-year 2000 is defined, for instance, as $\Delta P_{\text{current}} = P_{\text{current}}$

– P_{2000}, and so on. Then by using the four factors from the Kaya identity in Eq. (4), it is possible to decompose the change in the level of emissions into four effects. First, the scale or activity effect represents the amount of increase in CO_2 emissions due to the growth of the economy. If the scale effect is the dominating effect, then emissions increase linearly in the level of GDP. Second, the composition effect shows the increase of emissions due to changes in the composition of the economy. If the economy specializes in cleaner sectors, then the CO_2 emissions would grow more slowly. Third, the energy intensity effect shows the change in CO_2 emissions due to changes in energy intensity. For instance, the energy intensity can be improved by the introduction of energy saving technologies. Fourth, the carbon intensity effect shows the change in CO_2 emissions due to changes in the amount of carbon used per unit of energy. For instance, switching to a cleaner fuel mix in energy consumption can lower the carbon intensity. The last two effects, energy and carbon intensity, represent two types of technological change.

Equation (5) presents the required formulas, in compact form after rearranging the terms. A model is developed in excel by the author to perform the calculations.

$$
\begin{aligned}
\text{Peff}_t &= \Delta P_t \sum_i \Big[G_{i,1}\Big\{ I_{i,1}E_{i,1} + \frac{1}{2}(\Delta I_{i,t}E_{i,1} + I_{i,1}\Delta E_{i,t}) + \frac{1}{3}\Delta I_{i,t}\Delta E_{i,t} \Big\} \\
&\quad + \Delta G_{i,t}\Big\{ \frac{1}{2} I_{i,1}E_{i,1} + \frac{1}{3}(\Delta I_{i,t}E_{i,1} + I_{i,1}\Delta E_{i,t}) + \frac{1}{4}\Delta I_{i,t}\Delta E_{i,t} \Big\}\Big] \\
\text{Geff}_t &= P_1 \sum_i \Delta G_{i,t}\Big\{ I_{i,1}E_{i,1} + \frac{1}{2}(\Delta I_{i,t}E_{i,1} + I_{i,1}\Delta E_{i,t}) + \frac{1}{3}\Delta I_{i,t}\Delta E_{i,t} \Big\} \\
&\quad + \Delta P_t \sum_i \Delta G_{i,t}\Big\{ \frac{1}{2} I_{i,1}E_{i,1} + \frac{1}{3}(\Delta I_{i,t}E_{i,1} + I_{i,1}\Delta E_{i,t}) + \frac{1}{4}\Delta I_{i,t}\Delta E_{i,t} \Big\} \\
\text{Ieff}_t &= P_1 \sum_i \Delta I_{i,t}\Big\{ G_{i,1}E_{i,1} + \frac{1}{2}(\Delta G_{i,t}E_{i,1} + G_{i,1}\Delta E_{i,t}) + \frac{1}{3}\Delta G_{i,t}\Delta E_{i,t} \Big\} \\
&\quad + \Delta P_t \sum_i \Delta I_{i,t}\Big\{ \frac{1}{2} G_{i,1}E_{i,1} + \frac{1}{3}(\Delta G_{i,t}E_{i,1} + G_{i,1}\Delta E_{i,t}) + \frac{1}{4}\Delta G_{i,t}\Delta E_{i,t} \Big\} \\
\text{Eeff}_t &= P_1 \sum_i \Delta E_{i,t}\Big\{ G_{i,1}I_{i,1} + \frac{1}{2}(\Delta G_{i,t}I_{i,1} + G_{i,1}\Delta I_{i,t}) + \frac{1}{3}\Delta G_{i,t}\Delta I_{i,t} \Big\} \\
&\quad + \Delta P_t \sum_i \Delta E_{i,t}\Big\{ \frac{1}{2} G_{i,1}I_{i,1} + \frac{1}{3}(\Delta G_{i,t}I_{i,1} + G_{i,1}\Delta I_{i,t}) + \frac{1}{4}\Delta G_{i,t}\Delta I_{i,t} \Big\}
\end{aligned}
\tag{5}
$$

Equation (5) shows that in order to calculate, for instance, the scale effect there is a need to consider the difference in GDP (P) weighed with the other three factors of the Kaya identity. This first term leaves, however, a residual. The residual is then distributed on the 'jointly created and equally distributed' principle (Zhang & Ang, 2001). This explains the halves, thirds and quarters in the formula, which has terms with respectively two, three and four deltas. All these terms are added up to obtain the scale effect. The other effects are derived in a similar way. The change in CO_2 emissions with respect to base year 2000 is the sum of the scale, composition, energy intensity and carbon intensity effect. There is no residual. This above method is used to decompose the changes in the level of CO_2 emissions in Türkiye over the period 1987–2018 in Sect. 3.4.

2.2 Deriving a Kuznets Curve

A key question in energy transition and development trajectories is whether economic development is possible without negative environmental impacts. Originally, Nobel prize winner in economics, Mr. Simon Kuznets argued that income inequality will first increase, next peak out and finally decreases again, as economic growth continues over time (Kuznets, 1955), which is a classical hypothesis of development economics. This is also known as the inverted-U curve. Grossman and Krueger (1995) used this same concept to generalize this to environmental problems as well, namely that as the economy grows, the state of the environment first tends to deteriorate, reaches a valley and next starts to improve, again following an inverted-U relationship. Here, inequality in development is replaced by quality of the environment.

In order to test whether CO_2 emissions (or energy consumption (EC)) and GDP growth in Türkiye follow an inverted-U curve over time, the following two quadratic regression equations are tested for consistency and estimated using an ordinary least squares (OLS) double log-linear regression model:

$$\ln(\mathrm{CO_2}) = \alpha + \beta_1 \ln(\mathrm{GDP}) + \beta_2(\ln(\mathrm{GDP}))^2 \quad (6)$$

$$\ln(\mathrm{EC}) = \alpha + \beta_1 \ln(\mathrm{GDP}) + \beta_2(\ln(\mathrm{GDP}))^2 \quad (7)$$

In case the sign of β_2 is negative and statically significant, then the environmental (energy) Kuznets curve hypothesis holds, which would imply that economic growth is on the way to become decoupled from environmental impacts (in terms of CO_2 emissions) and is possible without continuous growth in energy consumption.

This method is used to test the EKC hypothesis for Türkiye with respect to the relation between economic growth and changes in the level of CO_2 emissions (and energy consumption) in Türkiye over the period 1987–2018 in Sect. 3.5.

3 Results and Discussion

A quantitative analysis of development trajectories and energy transitions in Türkiye is undertaken in this Section. Energy transitions can be studied from various perspectives. This section uses graphs to present and explain this process. For this purpose, it is useful to characterize energy use by two categories, namely technologies and sectors. Technologies can be divided into fossil (coal, lignite, oil, gas) and renewable (wind, solar, hydro and bio energy). Main energy using sectors are power (and heat) generation, transport, and industry, but the agricultural and services sectors also consume energy.

3.1 Data

For Türkiye, data have been collected from various sources. These data comprise yearly observations over the years 1987–2018, namely:

- Total population in millions,
- Gross domestic product (GDP) in billion TL in constant 2015 prices,
- Total primary energy supply per technology in btoe,
- Total primary energy consumption per sector per technology in btoe, and
- Total CO_2 emissions per sector in mega tons derived with the sectoral approach.

Population data is taken from TUIK (2021). Energy data are collected from IEA (2021) for the years 1990–2018. For the years 1987–1989, energy balances were collected from MENR (2021) and the same information as available in the IEA energy tables were extracted. The added value per sector is taken from the UN (2021).

To prepare the data for undertaking a (sectoral) complete decomposition analysis, the Turkish economy has been divided into four distinct sectors, namely:

- The primary agricultural sector,
- the secondary industrial sector,
- while the tertiary sector is subdivided into transport and services.

The value added has been derived from the national accounts as provided by the UN (2021). In these national accounts the value added for agriculture and transport are separately specified and can be used straightaway. However, the value added for industry is taken as the sum of mining, manufacturing, utilities and manufacturing. The remaining value added is assigned to the services sector in the economy.

The same sectoral division as for the value added is also possible for energy consumption. This is achieved simply by taking the numbers in billion tons of oil equivalents (btoe). It is also possible to derive the composition of fuel types in primary energy supply from these energy balances (this is shown in Sect. 3.3, namely Fig. 4).

Table 1 Emission factors (in ton carbon per TJ)

Coal	Crude oil	Oil oroducts	Natural gas
26.8	20.0	19.5	15.3

Source IPCC (2000)

To complete the data set, energy balances have been extended with emission factors using the IPCC guidelines II (chapter I.6) for emission inventorying (see Table 1). This extension is done to get an estimate of the CO_2 emissions for the relevant sectors of this study.

Table 1 shows the emission factors (in ton carbon per TJ) per used fuel type. The carbon content of coal is the highest with 26.8 ton carbon per TJ, while the carbon content is lowest for natural gas with 15.3 ton carbon per TJ. There are no emissions for energy generated with wood, animal waste, hydro, geothermal, wind power and traded electricity.

There are two ways to estimate CO_2 emissions. The first one is called the reference approach (IPCC, 2006). This method is based on making a carbon flow account (inputs and outputs of carbon fuels) and correcting for carbon in fuels that are not emitted. The other method is called the sectoral approach (IPCC, 2006). This method is based on consumption figures for different sectors. The outcomes of both methods are usually different, for various reasons (e.g. different sources of statistics). However, the difference is generally small and is on average around 1%. Here, the level of emissions is based on the generally preferred and more precise sectoral method. Following the sectoral method, also is enabling in deriving sectoral CO_2 emissions directly.

In addition to the agricultural, industrial, transport and services sector, there is a fifth sector, namely power generation. This conversion sector has a very low value added in the national accounts and a separate consideration would most likely lead to a distorted representation of a sectoral breakdown of the economy. Following the study by Paul and Bhattacharya (2004), the CO_2 emissions from power generation are assigned to four sectors in the economy proportional to their consumption of electricity, which is also reported as part of the energy balances.

In order to show the year-to-year changes in the key variables of interest, the data will be presented graphically. Next, to show how the change rates differ over time in tabular format, three time periods are distinguished, and these represent the following three stages of development:

- 1987–2000: natural gas is being introduced into the energy mix.
- 2000–2010: the first decade of the twenty-first century as a consolidation period.
- 2010–2018: modern renewables start to play a significant role in the energy mix.

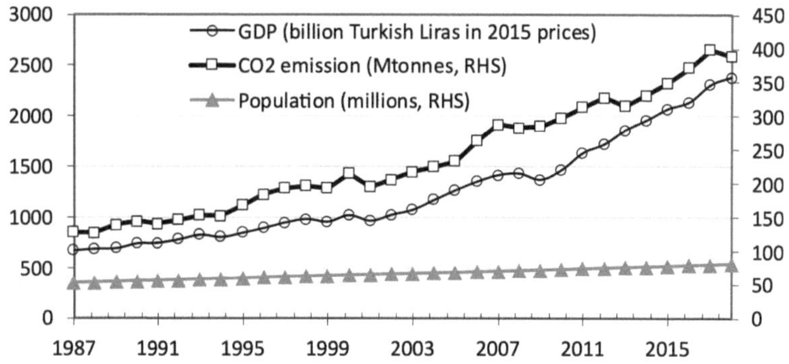

Fig. 1 Development of CO_2 emissions, GDP in real terms and population in Türkiye

3.2 GDP and Population Growth in 1987–2018

In order to obtain an insight into the Turkish economy, Fig. 1 plots the development of GDP and population over the period 1987–2018. The economy has been growing at an average yearly per capita growth rate of 2.7%. The variation in economic growth per capita is large, varying from a + 9.7% boom in 2011 to a – 6.7% bust in 2001.

To show how the Turkish economy has progressed, Table 2 compares the situation in Türkiye in 1987 and 2018 with other countries in 2018. Based on the sectoral division of the economy and the per capita exchange rates-based GDP in US$ 2010 prices, the situation of Türkiye in 1987 is somewhere near to the situation in Thailand and Iran in 2018. Thirty-one years later, the situation of Türkiye is somewhere between Chile and Croatia. This shows that the Turkish economy has made a considerable advance in the previous three decades, in spite of the so-called boom-bust economic growth characteristics.

3.3 Energy Consumption by Sector and by Fuel

Before presenting the results of the complete decomposition analysis, the nature of the data is presented graphically. Figure 2 shows the development of the share of GDP in constant prices of four sectors over time.

Figure 2 shows that the industry (from 40% in 1987 to 50% in 2018) and transport sector (from 9% in 1987 to 12% in 2018) increased in the period 1987–2018. Moreover, the share of the services sector (from 38% in 1987 to 30% in 2018) and the agricultural sector (from 13% in 1987 to 7% in 2018) decreased in the period from 1987 to 2018.

Based on traditional views on development trajectories (see for instance Kuik and Gupta (2003) for an overview), an economy tends to move from a traditional agricultural-based economy to an economy with an industrial dominance and finally

Table 2 The stage of development in Türkiye in 1987 and 2018 linked to a comparable development stage of other countries in 2018

	GDPPC in 2010 prices	Agricultural sector	Industrial sector	Services sector	Population (millions)
Thailand in 2018	6,370	8.1	34.8	57.1	69.4
Türkiye in 1987	**6,375**	**13.4**	**25.3**	**61.3**	**52.4**
Iran in 2018	6,440	9.9	35.9	54.2	81.8
Chile in 2018	15,112	3.5	29.7	66.8	18.7
Türkiye in 2018	**15,190**	**7.1**	**31.5**	**61.4**	**81.4**
Croatia in 2018	15,971	3.0	20.5	76.5	40.9

Source WDI (2021), whereas sectoral shares and population for Türkiye are derived as explained in the text

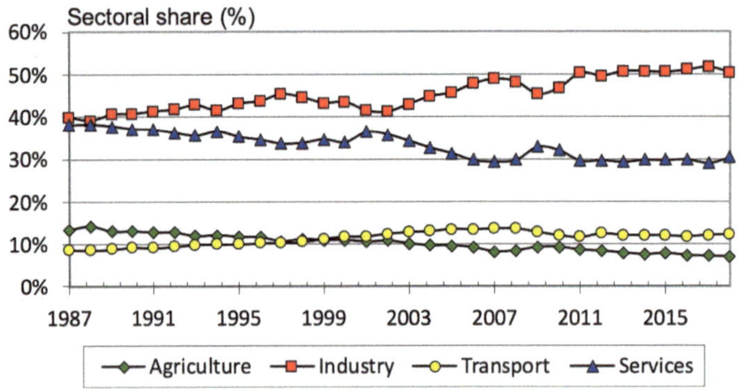

Fig. 2 Share in the Turkish economy of four considered sectors

moves towards a modern services-based economy. From that point of view, Türkiye has reached its industrialization peak, and levels of CO_2 emissions may be expected to slow down in the near future (see also CAT, 2021). This indicates that sustained economic growth with fewer CO_2 emissions may be expected in the near future and that there may be evidence for the environmental Kuznets hypothesis in Türkiye (see Sect. 3.5).

Development of Energy Intensity

The development over time of the sectoral energy consumption per value added (energy intensity) is presented in Fig. 3. The graph shows the changes of energy intensity over time, with respect to the level in the base-year 2000 to which has been assigned the value of 100. Table 3 presents the per cent changes over the periods 1987–2000, 2000–2010, 2010–2018 and 1987–2018.

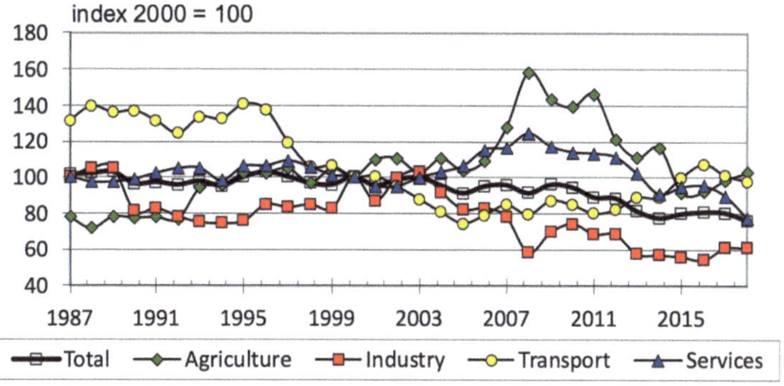

Fig. 3 Sectoral development of energy intensity (per value added) in Türkiye

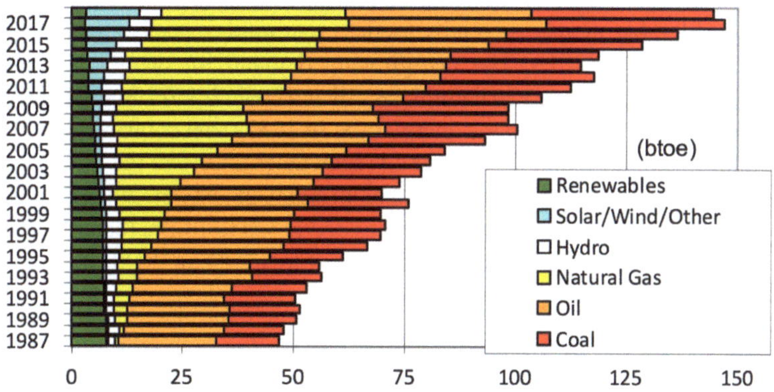

Fig. 4 Shares of fuel type in primary energy supply in Türkiye

Table 3 Per cent changes in energy intensity (per value added) in Türkiye

	Total	Agriculture	Industry	Transport	Services
1987–2000	−1.4%	28.6%	−0.4%	−23.9%	0.0%
2000–2010	−5.8%	39.2%	−26.7%	−15.6%	9.5%
2010–2018	−19.1%	−26.3%	−18.4%	15.7%	−34.9%
1987–2018	**−24.9%**	**31.9%**	**−39.3%**	**−25.7%**	**−22.5%**

Table 3 shows that the overall energy intensity decreased with 1.4% between 1987 and 2000, 5.8% between 2000 and 2010 and decreased even further between 2010 and 2018 with 19.1%. The net decrease over the period 1987–2018 is 24.9%.

For the four considered sectors in Türkiye, two extreme results are obtained for the development in energy intensity. Figure 3 shows that the agricultural sector has become more energy intensive over the period 1987–2018, with a peak in 2008; to be precise there has been an increase of + 31.9% (Table 3). At the same time there has been a change in the energy intensity in the services sector of –22.5% over the 1987–2018 period. The largest decrease in the services sector took place in the 2010–2018 period. There is also a substantial decrease in energy intensity in the transport sector, namely an overall change of –25.7% over the period 1987–2018. The energy intensity in the industrial sector decreased at the highest rate with a change rate of –39.3%.

Breakdown of Energy Mix

Next, the composition of fuel types in primary energy supply in Türkiye are considered. Figure 4 presents this, whereas Table 4 summarizes the shares in 1987, 2000, 2010 and 2018.

Figure 4 shows that the share of renewable carbon-free energy types (including hydro) has been fairly constant in tons of oil equivalents between 1987 until 2010 around 10.3 btoe (standard deviation of 0.65). From 2010 onwards this share started to grow considerably mainly driven by modern renewables, such as wind and solar, reaching 20.5 btoe in 2018. The fast-growing demand for energy in Türkiye is primarily met with an increase in natural gas, oil and coal imports. Since 1987 natural gas started to acquire a share in the energy mix. In 1987, coal contributed 30.0%, oil 47.6%, natural gas 1.4% and the sum of all renewables 21.0% to the primary energy supply in Türkiye (Table 4). In 2018, coal contributes 28.3%, oil 29.1%, natural gas 28.4% and the share of the sum of renewables decreased to 14.2% (actually the share of the total sum of renewables already decreased to 13.3% in 2000) in the primary energy supply in Türkiye.

Development of Carbon Intensity

The development over time of the sectoral CO_2 emissions per unit of energy consumed (carbon intensity) is presented in Fig. 5. Following the presentation in Fig. 3 (on energy intensity), the carbon intensity is shown with respect to the level in 2000 to which has been assigned the value of 100. Table 5 shows the per cent changes over the period 1987–2000, 2000–2010, 2010–2018 and 1987–2018.

Table 5 shows that there has been a gradual increase in the carbon intensity over time. Over the period 1987–2018, the carbon intensity increased with + 14.3%. The increase in carbon intensity has been significantly high in the services sector, which shows an increase of + 63.6% over the period 1987–2018. The services sector is

Table 4 Shares of fuel type in primary energy supply in Türkiye in 1987 and 2018

	Coal (%)	Oil (%)	Natural Gas (%)	Hydro (%)	Solar/ wind/ other (%)	Renewables (%)	Total
1987	30.0	47.6	1.4	3.4	0.8	16.8	46.9
2000	30.0	40.0	16.6	3.5	1.3	8.6	76.3
2010	29.5	29.8	29.7	4.2	2.5	4.3	105.7
2018	28.3	29.1	28.4	3.6	8.4	2.2	144.2

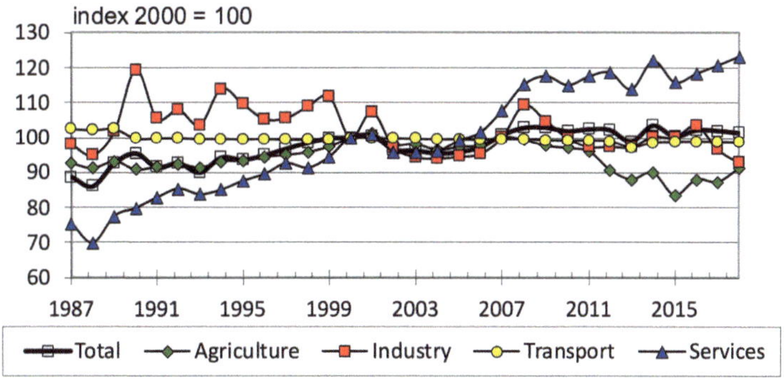

Fig. 5 Sectoral development of carbon intensity (per energy consumption) in Türkiye

Table 5 Per cent change in carbon intensity (per energy consumption) in Türkiye

	Total (%)	Agriculture (%)	Industry (%)	Transport (%)	Services (%)
1987–2000	12.7	8.0	2.0	−2.5	32.8
2000–2010	1.8	−3.0	0.0	−0.8	15.0
2010–2018	−0.4	−6.0	−7.0	−0.5	7.1
1987–2018	**14.3**	**−1.5**	**−5.2**	**−3.7**	**63.6**

the sum of residential, commercial, and other activities. Even though the rate of increase of carbon intensity is falling over time, the carbon intensity per unit of energy consumed is still found to be increasing in the services sector. The carbon intensity in the agricultural sector slightly decreased with a ratio of – 1.5% over the period 1987 to 2018. Figure 5 shows that the carbon intensity in the industrial sector is quite variable over time but only decreased slightly over the period 1987–2018 with a ratio of – 5.2%. The development of carbon intensity in the transport sector is very gradual over time (– 3.7%).

Interpretation of the result in Fig. 5 indicates that the services sector, which had a substantial decrease in energy intensity, has increased considerably in carbon intensity. The 'profit' of a reduction in energy intensity is more than offset by the 'loss' in an increased carbon intensity in the services sector. The aggregate effect of energy efficiency gain (– 23%) and the increase in carbon intensity (+ 64%) is a considerable increase of CO_2 emissions with 41%.

There is also an increase of carbon emissions in the agricultural sector, namely the energy intensity increased by 32% is partly offset by a minor carbon intensity decrease with a ratio of – 1.5%. However, the industry sector shows both a decrease in energy intensity (– 39%) and a minor decrease in carbon intensity (– 5%). This is the sector where the most significant reduction in CO_2 emissions (– 44%) can be observed in the Turkish economy.

3.4 Decomposition Analysis

A complete decomposition analysis, as originally proposed by Sun (1998), has been undertaken. Given the data availability, changes in CO_2 emissions over time with respect to the base-year 2000 can be decomposed into four distinct factors.

Figure 6 presents the results of the decomposition analysis for Türkiye. Figure 6 decomposes the total level of CO_2 emissions at the national level, where the difference in CO_2 emissions with respect to the amount of CO_2 emissions in 2000 is given. For example, the increase of 82 million tons CO_2 emissions in 2010 with respect to 2000 is the sum of 93 + 2 – 24 + 12 million tons of CO_2 emissions, respectively, due to the scale, composition, energy intensity and carbon intensity effects. Table 6 shows the percent changes over the periods 1987–2000, 2000–2010, 2010–2018 and 1987–2018.

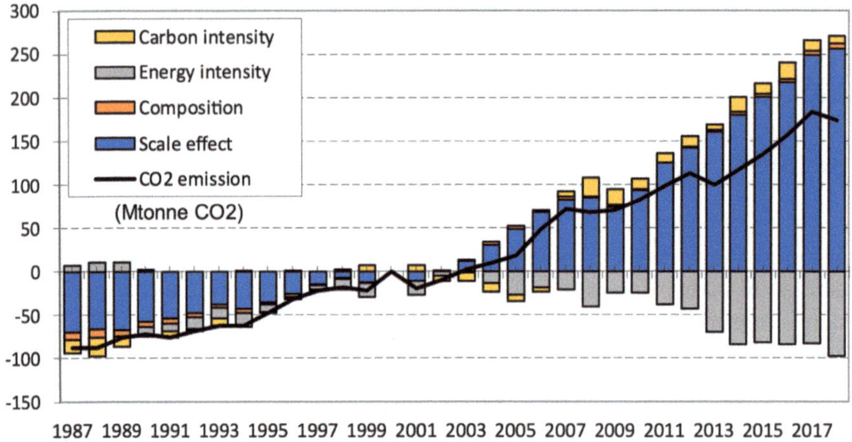

Fig. 6 Decomposition of the difference in CO_2 emissions (in Mtons CO_2) with respect to the level of emissions in 2000

Table 6 Decomposition of the change in CO_2 emissions

	1987–2000		2000–2010		2010–2018		1987–2018	
Scale effect	69.94	(80.0%)	92.95	(113.2%)	163.60	(179.4%)	326.51	(125.2%)
Composition effect	8.20	(9.4%)	1.64	(2.0%)	4.17	(4.6%)	**14.01**	**(5.4%)**
Energy intensity effect	−6.61	−(7.6%)	−24.43	−(29.8%)	−73.67	−(80.8%)	**−104.71**	**−(40.2%)**
Carbon intensity effect	15.90	(18.2%)	11.93	(14.5%)	−2.91	−(3.2%)	**24.92**	**(9.6%)**
CO_2 emissions increase	87.46	(100.0%)	82.09	(100.0%)	91.19	(100.0%)	**260.74**	**(100.0%)**

Figure 6 shows that the scale effect (growth in the economy in real terms) is the main explaining factor for the increase in CO_2 emissions in the Turkish economy. More specifically, Table 6 shows that the scale effect accounts for + 125% of change in CO_2 emissions over the period 1987–2018. The composition effect (+ 5%) and carbon intensity effect (+ 10%) nearly move in tandem. However, the carbon intensity effect gradually decreases over time and became even negative in the 2010–2018 period, whereas the composition of the Turkish economy has caused a minor increase in CO_2 emissions over time. The opposite is true for the energy intensity effect, where the CO_2 emissions have decreased over the whole period with a ratio of –40% and this effect is accelerating over time. In summary, CO_2 emission increases have been caused by the scale effect, which is partially offset by improvements in energy intensity, while the composition and the carbon intensity effects were rather small.

3.5 *Link CO_2 Emissions and EC with GDP*

To verify the link between CO_2 emissions (CO2) or energy consumption (EC) with GDP, it is also possible to test whether Türkiye has a so-called environmental Kuznets curve with respect to the greenhouse effect as measured by CO_2 emissions or an energy Kuznets curve with respect to energy consumption. Figure 7 presents a graphical plot of the data and a fitted quadratic curve following Eqs. (6) and (7).

$$\ln(CO_2) = \underset{(2.59)}{-17.76} + \underset{(0.73)}{5.63}\ln(GDP) - \underset{(0.05)}{0.33}(\ln(GDP))^2;\ R^2_{adj} = 0.989 \quad (8)$$

$$\ln(EC) = \underset{(2.09)}{-12.31} + \underset{(0.59)}{3.83}\ln(GDP) - \underset{(0.04)}{0.21}(\ln(GDP))^2;\ R^2_{adj} = 0.991 \quad (9)$$

Both estimations lead to environmental/energy Kuznets curves for Türkiye, as the estimate of the quadratic term is significant (error term in the brackets is much

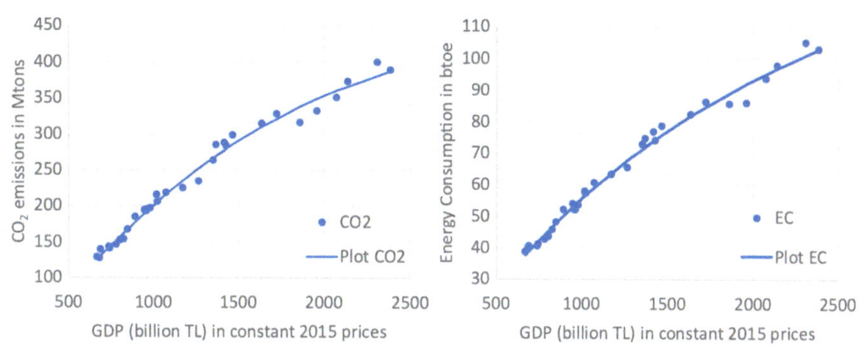

Fig. 7 The link between GDP and CO_2 emissions or EC in Türkiye

smaller than the estimated coefficient, which is then statistically different from zero; actually, with statistical significance with P-values below 1%) and it has the correct sign (negative value).

This means that based on the yearly data over the period 1987–2018, the CO_2 emissions and Energy Consumption are decoupling from the level of GDP and there is an Environmental Kuznets curve in CO_2 emissions and an energy Kuznets curve in EC for Türkiye. In a previous paper by Lise (2006), a similar approach was followed, but no evidence of Kuznets curve could be found.[8] This decoupling is also apparent graphically from Fig. 7. Hence, there is decoupling of carbon emissions or energy consumption from economic growth in Türkiye. This result is in line with the conclusion from the decomposition analysis that the decreasing energy intensity has slowed down the increase in CO_2 emissions in Türkiye over the period 1987–2018. Moreover, the carbon intensity per GDP has decreased with a ratio of – 2.9% over the period 2010–2018, which is equivalent to a yearly decarbonisation at a rate of 0.29%. Therefore, in order to reach an annual rate of decarbonisation of 2%, key to meeting long term climate change targets, an annual improvement of at least 1.71% will be required in the future.

4 Conclusions

This chapter undertook a quantitative analysis of development trajectories and energy transitions for the energy situation in Türkiye. A decomposition analysis was undertaken to answer the following question: Which factors—i.e. scale, composition, energy and carbon intensity—explain changes in CO_2 emissions? In addition, the following questions were addressed: How has the sectoral composition of the economy changed over time? How have the shares of the main fossil fuels and renewables in the energy mix changed over time? How has the energy and carbon intensity changed over time and per sector? What is the link between national income and carbon emissions or energy consumption?

Which factors—i.e. scale, composition, energy and carbon intensity—explain changes in CO_2 emissions? The decomposition analysis indicates that the largest increase in CO_2 emissions is caused by the expansion of the economy (scale effect). The scale effect is most dominant in the 2010–2018 period, where also the reduction in energy intensity is most pronounced. The carbon intensity also decreased in that period, whereas the composition effect somewhat increased. As a net total, the link between GDP with carbon emissions and energy consumption is increasing, albeit at a decelerating pace. Hence, due to energy efficiency measures, which may also be

[8] Aydın and Esen (2017), for instance, also tested the environmental Kuznets curve hypothesis for Türkiye looking at data for the period 1971–2014, but could not find evidence to support this hypothesis.

driven by cost advantages by investments in modern renewable generation technologies such as wind and solar, a significant and measurable slowdown in the increase in CO_2 emissions can already be observed in the Turkish economy.

How has the sectoral composition of the economy changed over time? The share of the industrial sector (from 40 to 50%) and transport sector (from 9 to 12%) increased in the period 1987–2018, whereas the share of the services sector (from 38 to 30%) and the agricultural sector (from 13 to 7%) decreased in the period from 1987 to 2018. It may be observed that Türkiye has reached its industrialization peak, and levels of CO_2 emissions may be expected to slow down in the near future.

How have the shares of the main fossil fuels and renewables in the energy mix changed over time? The amount of renewable carbon-free energy types (including hydro) has been fairly constant between 1987 and 2010, namely around 10 btoe, whereas this amount started to increase from 2010 onwards, mainly driven by modern renewables, such as wind and solar, reaching 20.5 btoe in 2018. The fast-growing demand for energy in Türkiye is primarily met with an increase in natural gas, oil and coal imports. In 1987, coal contributed 30%, oil 48%, natural gas 1% and the sum of all renewables 21% to the primary energy supply in Türkiye. In 2018, coal contributed 28%, oil 29%, natural gas 28% and the share of the sum of renewables decreased to 14% in the primary energy supply in Türkiye.

How has the energy and carbon intensity changed over time and per sector? The energy intensity decreased considerably over the period 1987–2018 in Türkiye. On the one hand, there has been an increase of energy use in the agricultural sector. On the other hand, the industry, transport, and services sectors had a considerable reduction in energy intensity. In contrary to the energy intensity, the amount of CO_2 emissions per unit of energy consumed (carbon intensity) has increased over the period 1987–2018. This increase took place in the services sector (total GDP minus added value of agricultural, industrial and transport sector) more than offsetting the gain achieved by the reduction in energy intensity. The industry, transport and agricultural sectors showed a minor reduction in carbon emissions.

What is the link between national income and carbon emissions or energy consumption? To provide further support for the results with the decomposition analysis, this chapter has also demonstrated shows that there is an Environmental Kuznets curve in CO_2 emissions and an energy Kuznets curve in energy consumption for Türkiye. This is an important result, because this implies a decoupling of carbon emissions (and also energy consumption) from economic growth in Türkiye. Moreover, the Turkish economy decarbonized by a rate of 0.29% annually over the period 2010–2018. The data indicated that the services sector still sees an increase in carbon intensity over time, albeit on a falling rate. This will require additional measures to reach a sustainable path of decarbonation. Hence, Türkiye must make additional steps to reach a sustainable level of 2% decarbonisation. Future policy research is needed to find ways for Türkiye to 'leapfrog' these emissions.

This study has shed light on how continued high level of economic growth may be possible, while slowing down the amount of CO_2 emissions more and more. In the sectoral composition of the economy, the share of the agricultural sector halved but is still considerable in 2018, while the share of the industrial sector has grown over the period 1987–2018. This shows that Türkiye is still in the middle of their transition towards a services-based economy. To complete this transition, a path is foreseen with initially increased in carbon emissions. However, it is expected that carbon emissions will start to slow down soon after that, even though the GDP is expected to continue on grow.

Acknowledgements The author is grateful for the discussing and feedback received during the Center for Energy and Value Issues (CEVI) (See, for instance, https://www.centerforenergyandvalue.org/) conference presentations at:

- the online 8th MULTINATIONAL ENERGY AND VALUE CONFERENCE, CEVI and ISINI, May 6–7, 2021, LIDAM group of the Université Catholique de Louvain (UCL), Belgium.
- the online MULTINATIONAL ENERGY AND VALUE CONFERENCE, CEVI session at ISINI 2022, September 1–2, 2022, Wrocław, Poland.
- the 9th MULTINATIONAL ENERGY AND VALUE CONFERENCE, CEVI and ISINI, ESG in the energy sector, May 11–12, 2023, Université Catholique de Louvain (UCL), Belgium.

Remaining errors are the author's.

References

Ang, B. W. (2004). Decomposition analysis for policymaking in energy: Which is the preferred method? *Energy Policy, 32*(9), 1131–1139.

Aydın, C., & Esen, Ö. (2017). The validity of the environmental Kuznets curve hypothesis for CO_2 emissions in Turkey: New evidence from smooth transition regression approach. Mustafa *Kemal University Journal of Social Sciences Institute, 14*(39), 101–116. https://dergipark.org.tr/tr/download/article-file/355072. Accessed January 27, 2023

CAT. (2021). Turkey country summary. *Climate Action Tracker*. https://climateactiontracker.org/countries/turkey/. Accessed 26 April 2021.

Demirkan, O., & Eryiğit, B. (2014). Turkey: Country of international pipelines. Oil Gas Law Newsl. https://www.kolcuoglu.av.tr/Uploads/Publication/iba---oil-and-gas-law-newsletter.pdf. Accessed December 22, 2022.

Dietzenbacher, E., & Los, B. (1998). Structural decomposition techniques: sense and sensitivity. *Economic Systems Research, 10*(4), 307–324. https://doi.org/10.1080/09535319800000023. https://www.scinapse.io/papers/2158678217. Accessed November 25, 2022.

Dreze, J., & Stern, N. (1987). *The theory of cost benefit analysis. Handbook of public economics* (Vol. 2, pp. 909–989). Elsevier. https://personal.lse.ac.uk/sternn/040NHS.pdf. Accessed November 25, 2022.

EU. (2022). *Impact assessments*. https://ec.europa.eu/info/law/law-making-process/planning-and-proposing-law/impact-assessments_en. Accessed November 25, 2022.

Grossman, G., & Krueger, A. (1995). Economic growth and the environment. *Quarterly Journal of Economics, 110*, 353–377.

IEA, 2021. Data and Statistics. Energy Tables for Turkey. *International Energy Agency*. https://www.iea.org/data-and-statistics/data-tables?country=TURKEY&energy=Balances&year=1990. Accessed April 26, 2021.

IPCC. (2000). *Special report on emissions scenarios* (p. 599). Cambridge University Press.

IPCC. (2006). *Reference approach*. https://www.ipcc-nggip.iges.or.jp/public/2006gl/pdf/2_Volume2/V2_6_Ch6_Reference_Approach.pdf. Accessed November 25, 2022.

IRENA. (2020). *Renewable energy prospects for Central and South-Eastern Europe Energy Connectivity (CESEC)*. https://www.irena.org/Publications/2020/Oct/Renewable-Energy-Prospects-for-Central-and-South-Eastern-Europe-Energy-Connectivity-CESEC. Accessed November 25, 2022.

Kuznets, S. (1955). Economic growth and income inequality. *American Economic Review, 45*, 1–28.

Lise, W. (2006). Decomposition of CO_2 emissions over 1980–2003 in Turkey. *Energy Policy, 34*, 1841–1852.

MENR. (2021). Energy tables for Turkey. *Ministry of Energy and Natural Resources*. https://enerji.gov.tr/enerji-isleri-genel-mudurlugu-denge-tablolari. Accessed 26 April 2021.

MFA. (2023). United Nations Framework Convention on Climate Change (UNFCCC) and the Kyoto Protocol, Ministry of Foredign Affairs, Republic of Türkiye. https://www.mfa.gov.tr/united-nations-framework-convention-on-climate-change-_unfccc_-and-the-kyoto-protocol.en.mfa. Accessed March 06, 2023.

OECD. (2021*). OECD economic surveys, Turkey*. https://www.oecd.org/economy/surveys/TURKEY-2021-OECD-economic-survey-overview.pdf. Accessed November 25, 2022.

OECD. (2023*). List of Annex I Countries*. https://www.oecd.org/env/cc/listofannexicountries.htm. Accessed March 06, 2023.

Saraç, Ş., & Yağlıkara, A. (2017). Environmental Kuznets curve: the evidence from BSEC countries. *EGE Academic Review, 17*(2), 255–264. https://doi.org/10.21121/eab.2017225203 https://dergipark.org.tr/tr/download/article-file/561703. Accessed November 25, 2022.

SBP. (2022). Orta Vadeli Programı (2023–2025). Strateji ve Butçe Başkanlığı. (Mid-term Plan 2023–2025. *Strategy and Budget Presidency*. https://www.sbb.gov.tr/wp-content/uploads/2022/09/Orta-Vadeli-Program-2023-2025.pdf. Accessed December 22, 2022.

Su, B., & Ang, B. W. (2012). Structural decomposition analysis applied to energy and emissions: Some methodological developments. *Energy Economics, 34*(1), 177–188.

Sun, J. W. (1998). Changes in energy consumption and energy intensity: A complete decomposition model. *Energy Economics, 20*, 85–100.

TUIK. (2021). Mid-year population estimations and projections, 1986- 2025. *Turkish Statistical Institute*. https://data.tuik.gov.tr/Bulten/DownloadIstatistikselTablo?p=QPWxsRHJDQcaHhpPFrUvXJ16d1OV2Zi53iFoxtk1IYeHYlODkN6RwLWf1cAXh1/e. Accessed April 26, 2021.

UN. (2021). Value added by economic activity, at constant 2015 prices. National currency. *United Nations*. https://unstats.un.org/unsd/nationalaccount/, https://unstats.un.org/unsd/snaama/basic. Accessed April 26, 2021.

Yılmaz-Ataman, A. (2022). Index decomposition analysis and energy consumption of Turkey: 2000–2014. *Journal of Research in Economics, 6*(2), 107–134, https://doi.org/10.29228/JORE.17 https://dergipark.org.tr/en/download/article-file/2676397. Accessed November 25, 2022.

WDI. (2021). *World Development Indicators*. https://databank.worldbank.org/source/world-development-indicators. Accessed April 26, 2021.

Xu, X. Y., & Ang, B. W. (2013). Index decomposition analysis applied to CO_2 emission studies. *Ecological Economics, 93*, 313–329.

Zhang, F. Q., & Ang, B. W. (2001). Methodological issues in cross-country/region decomposition of energy and environmental indicators. *Energy Economics, 23*, 179–190.

The Natural Gas War Between Europe and Russia After the Invasion of Ukraine

Mehmet Baha Karan, Kazim Baris Atici, Burak Pirgaip, and Göktuğ Şahin

Abstract This study aims to explain and evaluate the Euro-Russian natural gas war, which started after the Russian attack on Ukraine in 2022, within the scope of the energy policies of both sides before and after the war. This study evaluates short-term and medium-term measures of Europe and Russia. In addition, a SWOT analysis is made, both sides' strengths and weaknesses are discussed, and their opportunities and threats are explained. As a result, it is revealed that both sides will suffer from the gas war. However, in the medium term, Europe's developing LNG market and renewable resources may emerge stronger from this war. Still, Russia, which has lost its political and economic power over Europe, will suffer more.

Keywords Natural gas · Trade · Ukrainian war · Europe · Russia

1 Introduction

The Ottoman Empire, one of the most dominant powers in fourteenth- and fifteenth-centuries' Europe, when it started to lose its economic superiority against the rapidly developing European countries in 1683, besieged Vienna to regain this power. The defeat after this siege would cause Ottomans to lose their power forever. Similarly, the post-World War II decolonization and the Suez Crisis in 1956 publicly exposed Britain's limitations to the world. They confirmed Britain's decline on the world

M. B. Karan (✉) · K. B. Atici · B. Pirgaip
Department of Business Administration, Hacettepe University, Ankara, Turkey
e-mail: mbkaran@hacettepe.edu.tr; mbkaran@hbv.edu.tr

K. B. Atici
e-mail: kba@hacettepe.edu.tr

B. Pirgaip
e-mail: burakpirgaip@hacettepe.edu.tr

G. Şahin
Department of Economics, Hacı Bayram Veli University, Ankara, Turkey
e-mail: goktug.sahin@hbv.edu.tr

J. Thewissen et al. (eds.), *The ESG Framework and the Energy Industry*,
https://doi.org/10.1007/978-3-031-48457-5_5

stage and its end as a first-rate power. Today, history repeats itself, and Vladimir Putin, who wants to restore Russia to its former power, is viewed to invade Ukraine at the beginning of 2022. This occupation attempt inevitably turned into an energy war between Russia and Europe. When the Russians dared to wage a war that could spiral out of control at any moment, they relied not only on their military strength, but also on their decades-long monopoly position in the ex-Soviet countries of eastern Europe and their position as the most important gas supplier in the Western European market, especially in Germany.

The brutal winters of Eastern Europe, which decimated the armies of Napoleon and Hitler earlier on, could have helped the Russians against the energy-deprived Europeans. However, the Winter of 2022/23 was relatively mild in Western and Eastern Europe, contrary to many expectations, and Putin's hope might have remained for the following winter. Many questions are still on the agenda. Will Russia win the energy war and regain its former power? Can the European Union, which has taken a low-profile position for decades, overcome its difficulties with the solidarity among its members? Will this struggle benefit the USA and/or China?

The European Union (EU), whose energy policies are based on supply security, competition, and sustainability (European Commission, 2006), was forced to follow a contradictory procedure in the energy field, as being dependent on low-price natural gas resources supplied from Russia. On the one hand, the Union tried to develop alternative energy sources and obtain natural gas from different countries. In contrast, on the other hand, it increased its commitment to Russia by completing Nord Stream pipeline projects with it. Moreover, although Russia endangered world peace by annexing Crimea, it continued implementing these policies. In addition, the energy policies planned by the European states within the framework of the increased sensitivity to the climate and the policies related to sustainability had also been designed in a structure that would increase the dependence on Russia. For example, plans to phase out nuclear energy in some European countries, especially Germany, the EU's goal of reducing greenhouse gas emissions by reducing coal consumption, and the policies of depletion of local gas resources inevitably would have increased the dependence on Russia and imported approximately 150–200 bcm of natural gas annually. Note that the Union met more than 40% of its needs from this country.

Although the pre-war EU was highly dependent on Russia in the field of natural gas and energy, it did expect that the continent's problem would be solved in the long run with the development of alternative energy sources and the LNG market. However, due to physical constraints, high dependence on Russia, especially on a regional basis, delayed the problem's solution. Renewable energy sources and storage systems had not been given as much priority as necessary. With the annexation of Crimea by Russia in 2014, the EU brought energy security to the fore in its agenda, but the measures in this regard were insufficient. In a step in this direction, in February 2016, the European Commission announced a new package of energy security measures to strengthen the EU's resilience against gas supply disruptions (European Commission, 2016b). These measures were within the scope of the principle of solidarity developed by EU member states. These principles obligated EU countries to assist neighboring countries experiencing a gas supply crisis. The measures would also strengthen intergovernmental energy agreements between EU and non-EU countries, emphasizing liquefied natural gas and gas storage. It would increase energy security by facilitating new access to these resources (European Commission, 2016a). Another critical step was the plan to create an energy Union, including energy security, with the contribution of 28 European countries in March 2015 (European Parliament, 2015). The Union aims to provide secure, affordable, and clean energy for EU citizens and businesses. Developments after the Ukraine war have revealed that the energy Union's legal framework regarding energy security has significantly contributed to managing the effects of the crisis in the energy sector. Although the legislation came along with some issues like member state veto rights, the Union was crucial in facilitating cross-border coordination alongside extensive cooperation and information sharing between the member states, system operators, and relevant agents in the energy sector (Prisecaru, 2022).

However, things started to change after the second half of 2021, with a sharp increase in energy prices worldwide due to increasing demand after the pandemic and difficulties in logistics. Following this, the Russian invasion of Ukraine in February 2022, has been a turning point for the energy policies of the EU. The EU, the UK, and many other European countries, backed by the support of the USA, began rapidly changing their energy policies by embargoing the Russians. As a result of these developments, fuel prices increased even more, putting the EU, which is excessively dependent on Russia, in a problematic situation and faced with the problem of energy supply security. Russia's decision to suspend gas distribution to several EU member states has exacerbated the situation. The year 2022 has passed with mutual moves, and this tense environment has begun to harm the parties. While the growth rate of Europe decreased with increasing inflation, economic problems started in Russia, which financed the war with the hydrocarbon resources it sold to Europe (Polak, 2017).

Both Europe and Russia want to be the winners of this emerging energy war by starting to look for new options. At first glance, it is clear that there will be no real winner in this war. The IMF, IEA, and EU have conducted various research and evaluations about how this period will progress and discussed the issue of which side will be more profitable from this struggle with less damage in the short and long term. Most of these reports have described this struggle from the EU's or Russia's perspective.

In this chapter, we aim to contribute to the literature by evaluating the situation of both sides before and after the war. This study has three original contributions to the literature. The first contribution is to present the position of the two sides before and after the war. The second one discusses the parties' short- and medium-term measures. The third contribution is to employ a SWOT analysis. This method will reveal both sides' weaknesses, strengths, opportunities, and threats in more detail. The final contribution is that we develop a possible future scenario.

This chapter consists of five sections. In Sect. 2, the European natural gas market is explained around the scope of the developments and measures taken before and after the Ukraine war. In Sect. 3, Russia's options will be discussed after the Russian gas market is explained within the scope of the Ukraine war. In Sect. 4, a SWOT analysis is presented. Finally, Sect. 5 concludes the chapter.

2 European Natural Gas Market

2.1 Situation Before the Ukraine War

Until 2022, Europe received natural gas from various countries, mainly through pipelines. Pipeline gas flows reach Europe via Russia, Norway, the UK, North Africa, and the Caspian region. Russian channels enter Europe via Germany (North Stream I), Poland (Yamal), Ukraine, and Turkey (TurkStream). Apart from these, Norwegian gas entered via Germany, Netherlands, Belgium, UK, and Denmark with the completion of the Baltic Pipe (to Poland) toward the end of 2022. While North African gas comes through Spain and Italy, Azerbaijan gas enters through Turkey and Greece. In total, non-Russian pipelines accounted for 30% of the total gas import capacity, while Russian channels accounted for 42% and LNG import terminals for 28%. As of the beginning of 2022, in addition to the 28 LNG import terminals in Europe (including non-EU Turkey), there are eight small-scale LNG facilities in Finland, Sweden, Germany, Norway, and Gibraltar. Of the LNG import terminals, 24 are located in EU countries and 4 in Turkey, consisting of 23 land-based import terminals and four floating storage and regasification units (FSRU). The only import facility in Malta is a Floating Storage Unit (FSU) and an onshore regasification unit (Rogers et al., 2018).

Before 2022, Europe's natural gas markets are divided into three. Firstly, the North-West market, which is its most developed market, includes the Netherlands, Belgium, Denmark, France, Germany, Ireland, Sweden, and the UK. The second covers the Southern Market with Spain, Portugal, and France. The third market, less dependent on Russia, is the South-Southeast region of Europe with a minor infrastructure. Austria, Italy, Bulgaria, Czech Republic, Greece, Hungary, Poland, Romania, Slovakia, and Slovenia are included in this market.

Especially after the 2014 Ukraine crisis, the energy security policy became increasingly important. In this context, EU, (1) supported renewable energy sources (European Commission, 2009a). In 2021, renewable energy reached 22.1% of the energy consumed in the EU (EEA, 2022), (2) supported new natural gas pipelines with gas projects going southeast Europe, such as the TANAP project that brought Azerbaijani gas were supported and implemented (Temizer, 2018), with also bas projects in the Eastern Mediterranean being encouraged. Gas projects in Africa and Norway redeveloped (European Commission, 2018a), (3) carried out projects for the LNG market and installed LNG terminals in various European destinations (Sönnichsen, 2022a, 2022b), (4) improved gas storage capacity (European Commission, 2009b), (5) implemented a policy on energy consumption, with a target of 20% energy savings being set with the regulation known as the "Energy Efficiency Directive" (European

Commission, 2012) followed by a new agreement in 2016 and 2018 with a new level of energy savings of 32.5% by 2030 (European Commission, 2018b).

2.2 *Ukraine War and Gas Trade*

2.2.1 Post-War European Union Policies

The high price and tight supply environment in the second half of 2021 intensified after the Russian invasion of Ukraine, leading to fuel switching and a demand decline. The USA took the first step by banning all oil and gas imports from Russia in March 2022. In May, Russia imposed a series of sanctions on European companies after the EU refused to comply with a new payment system set by Russia. Then Gazprom announced that it would stop using the Yamal-Europe pipeline. In September, the Nord Stream 1 pipeline cut off gas flow, and Russian gas flows only through the TurkStream gas pipeline in 2022 and, surprisingly, also through Ukraine at much lower levels than in 2021 (Deb & Rajendran, 2022).

Gazprom accelerated its gas supply cuts to OECD Europe in the third quarter of 2022, further increasing tensions in European and global LNG markets. In contrast, Europe's LNG imports rose to seasonal highs, trying to offset the low flows in Russia partially. While the gas supply to the EU in 2022 decreased by 66% compared to the previous year, Gazprom gradually reduced the gas flow through Nord Stream with its low compressor power. Gas flow through Nord Stream had dropped to only 20% of the pipeline's capacity at the end of July and had stopped entirely at the beginning of September. Higher pipeline deliveries and record volumes of LNG inflows from alternative sources offset their lower flows from Russia. Pipeline supply from Norway increased by 8% (6 bcm) in the first eight months of 2022, and flow from Azerbaijan via the Trans Adriatic Pipeline increased by 50% (2.5 bcm) year-on-year. LNG imports were proliferating. LNG supply from the USA to the EU was 12 billion cubic meters in the third quarter, surpassing Russia's pipe exports for the first time in history (IEA, 2022c).

Prices in European stock markets also started their worst period since 2008, as there is long-term evidence of a significant balance relationship between political risk, stock prices, and global oil and gas prices (Simpson et al., 2016). While prices increased 2–3 times in the TTF spot gas market in the Spring, research reports published one after another suggested that a new market structure could create significant uncertainty in the short term. Still, the process could be managed (Trading Economics, 2023). The International Energy Agency stated in the report that planning should be done according to a situation where Russia's pipeline gas exports to the EU would fall by more than 75% compared to 2021 (IEA, 2022b). In addition, the possibility of further unilateral restriction of export flows, as Russia did before, has always remained on the agenda.

The EU and its member states have taken measures to increase supply security and market flexibility with the outbreak of the Ukrainian war. At the end of March 2022, the International Energy Agency (IEA) proposed the "10-Point Plan for Reducing EU's Reliance to Russian Natural Gas" (Iancu, 2022). In May 2022, the EU Commission presented the REPowerEU plan in line with this recommendation. This package quickly responded to the war in Ukraine and the energy crisis that exposed the EU's strong dependence on Russian energy. REPowerEU, as a plan to save energy, produce clean energy, and diversify European energy sources, is supported by financial and legislative measures to build the new energy infrastructure and system that Europe needs (European Commission, 2022a).

2.2.2 Interregional Gas Supply Imbalance

Accordingly, Russia's closure of the natural gas supply will affect European countries differently. Undoubtedly, cooperation between countries will improve this picture. In this context, according to a study conducted by the IMF, the situation on a country basis is given below (Di Bella et al., 2022).

- UK, Ireland, Spain, Portugal, Sweden, and Denmark are the countries that need Russian gas the least. The capacity of these countries to adapt to such a supply disruption is quite strong. However, opportunities to support the rest of Europe are also limited.
- France, the Netherlands, and Belgium are somewhat dependent on Russian gas but have direct access to LNG import capacity and alternative pipeline supply routes and can adapt.
- Finland, Latvia, Lithuania, and Estonia, although historically dependent on Russian gas, will be able to adapt to gas cuts and avoid physical shortages with their current facilities and alternative import capacities coming into play soon.
- Poland, with about half of the natural gas imported from Russia in 2020, is not particularly gas-intensive as it has historically been more dependent on coal. Even if the Russians cut off the gas completely, Poland can manage its gas needs.
- Bulgaria, Romania, Croatia, and Slovenia can overcome the natural gas bottleneck, whereby the share of Russian gas in total gas consumption in Bulgaria plays a less critical role in the overall energy mix since it also has alternative supply routes via Greece and Turkey.
- Germany and Austria, conversely, are highly dependent on Russian gas. Despite having relatively strong pipeline networks with neighboring countries, gas shortages, and economic problems may arise. Considering the bottlenecks with neighboring countries, the analysis by ENTSOG (2022) indicates that there will be a deficit of around 15 bcm per year, while Bachmann et al. (2022) state that stopping Russia's energy imports without energy cuts could lead to a GDP decline.
- Italy will be able to supply less than half, and there will be a remarkable gas shortage.
- The Czech Republic, Slovakia, and Hungary highly depend on Russian gas so these countries will have significant distress and high gas prices.

As a result, the inadequacy of the natural gas network in the south and east of Europe may affect Hungary, Slovakia, Czechia, and Italy the most in these regions (Flanagan et al., 2022). Oxford Analytica (2022) states that the Czech Republic, Hungary, Poland, and Slovakia are among Europe's weakest in the chain. Some Central European countries could be at the forefront of the energy war, raising the risk of domestic political instability as prices and fears of winter scarcity rise. As a matter of fact, despite the embargo decision of European countries, Hungary signed an energy agreement with Russia (Preussen, 2022) and even announced that it could use its veto right if necessary. Capolongo et al. (2022), on the other hand, stated that Energy-intensive sectors would have to cut production, thus reducing the Eurozone GDP and leading to higher unemployment.

2.3 Europe's Short-Term Measures

The EU immediately took a series of measures to alleviate this distressing picture. The first is to use existing pipelines more efficiently, the second is to improve LNG capacity, and the third is to develop storage capacity. However, as of 2023, many problems continue.

2.3.1 Using Existing Pipelines and LNG Capacity Effectively

Under normal conditions, the pipeline capacity utilization capacity was 81% from Norway and 50–60% from other non-Russian countries (Di Bella et al., 2022). Efforts are still being made to increase the capacity of these lines (European Commission, 2022b). The EU also aimed to use LNG entry terminals more effectively, including those whose capacity it had not previously used. Only 39% of the stated capacity was used in 2021. However, it should be underlined that the total stated capacity technically cannot be used in practice. Factors such as seasonal demand-pull, maintenance, and system redundancies prevent reaching total capacity, as well as the fact that pipelines are not strongly connected to Central Europe (Di Bella et al., 2022). For example, LNG import terminals in Spain and Portugal have no ties to Central European countries, and Europe's largest LNG terminals are in Spain. Due to insufficient pipeline connections between the two countries, this country can only export 10% of its import capacity to France. The capacity of the Irun pipeline, which still carries natural gas with a capacity of 1.5 bcm between Spain and France, was increased by 66% in November 2022. However, Spain still needs more connectivity to the European gas grid, limiting the transport of Spain's large gas capacity to the rest of the EU. France and Spain have decided to establish a submarine pipeline connecting Barcelona and Marseille. However, the new channel will be operational after four years at the earliest. Spain is also working to strengthen the infrastructure at the port of Barcelona to export more LNG to Italy by sea (McMurtry, 2022). The French scent the gas with some chemicals to help people identify leaks. French gas cannot be added to German gas, as this practice is incompatible with specific industrial processes. North–South bottlenecks in Germany and Italy limit sharing between these countries and restrict shipments to Central and Eastern Europe. Finally, for technical reasons, gas transport from Greece and Italy to Southeast Europe is minimal. The EU has also started work to build approximately 25 new LNG terminals and FRSUs to increase LNG capacity and hopes to expand its LNG import capacity to 40 bcm by the end of 2023 (Elliott, 2022).

In the first eight months of 2022, EU LNG imports increased yearly by about 70% (or 35 bcm). Expanding existing regasification terminals and the lease of FSRUs has allowed the EU to expand its regasification capacity by 15% (or 25 bcm/year) over the 2022/23 heating season. It is planned that most of the LNG supply, which has increased in the winter of 2022–23, will be procured from the spot market. Diversifying pipeline imports and increasing interconnections in addition to record LNG flows, EU member states have turned to diversify their imports from non-Russian pipeline suppliers.

2.3.2 Increasing Storage Capacity

Within the framework of its policy of meeting the shortage of Russian gas supply with LNG imports in 2023, the EU aimed at filling levels of at least 90% of working storage capacity to provide an adequate buffer for the European gas market during the winter seasons, and additional LNG regasification aimed at building the capacity. Although the storage capacity of the countries is close to a certain level, it is unevenly distributed over the continent. Apart from Russia and Belarus, which have the most extensive storage facilities on the continent, Ukraine and Germany have the largest gas storage capacity, accounting for around 40% of European capacity. Italy, the Netherlands, and France follow the two, and storage capacity in other countries is limited. The variation between countries and regions is quite considerable. This situation changes according to the ratio of storage to usable capacity and the share of annual capacity consumption. Storage capacities in five countries (Germany, Italy, France, the Netherlands, and Austria) account for two-thirds of the EU's total capacity. Interestingly, Gazprom also had extensive storage facilities in Germany and Austria that make up 7% of EU storage capacity (and 4% of existing stocks) and are assumed to be usable in a crisis as they fall under European legal jurisdiction.

Although the gas storage level in Europe was at historically low levels during the Winter of 2021, the storage accumulation has increased rapidly from April 2022 onwards, reaching an average gas storage fill level of 88% (European Council, 2023) and a gas storage capacity of 990.16 TWh among member countries in December 2022 (Sönnichsen, 2022a, 2022b). According to new EU regulations, countries without storage facilities must store 15% of their annual domestic gas consumption in stocks in other member countries to access the gas reserves stored in other member countries (European Council, 2023).

2.3.3 Evaluation of Europe's Short-Term Measures

With the help of European infrastructure and global supply, the decline in Russian gas deliveries was managed in 2022. The total gas consumption was reduced compared to the previous year, and alternative sources, especially LNG, have been used. The mild 2022/23 winter conditions also facilitated the management of the problem. Initially, it was thought that it would be tough to replace more than 150 bcm of gas imported from Russia under current conditions (Flanagan et al., 2022).

By the end of 2023, the European and global natural gas markets have yet to recover from the danger of Russia's interruption of gas delivery through pipelines. Underlining that the energy crisis in Europe was not a temporary shock, the IMF stated that the geopolitical reorganization of energy resources after the war was permanent and suggested that Winter 2022 would be harsh. In contrast, Winter 2023 will probably worsen (Gourinchas, 2022).

Besides, Europe's increasing demand for LNG to replace Russian pipeline gas supplies has created a highly tight global market. Record-high gas prices in Europe have made the continent an important market for LNG, resulting in supply shortages in many markets. Additional energy transition policies will need to be implemented in developed European gas markets to sustain the decline in gas consumption. Such measures can also ease pressure on prices globally and help price-sensitive emerging markets access resources that can accelerate their shift away from coal, contributing to short-term carbon intensity and air quality improvements.

2.4 Europe's Medium-Term Supply and Demand Policies

Europe will significantly reduce its gas supply dependency by 2022, and its conditions will likely improve further (Di Bella et al., 2022). In a study conducted by the IMF, it was recommended that policies aimed at increasing energy costs should protect the mechanism of formation of prices while providing targeted support in society. It was underlined that the increase in energy prices presented both opportunities and risks for climate policy and that energy policy in Europe should be carried out rapidly by transferring to targeted areas rather than broad-based price suppression measures (Ari et al., 2022). For this reason, evaluating the EU's options in terms of supply and demand is essential.

2.4.1 The Supply Side

From the supply perspective, it is seen that increasing the capacity of existing pipelines and importing LNG are the most practical solutions. Indeed, the European Gas Infrastructure Europe (GIE) industry group estimates that in the long term, LNG terminals in the EU could provide 285 bcm of excess import capacity by 2030. Europe's current import capacity is about 220 bcm annually (IEA, 2022d). However,

Europe may experience significant difficulties both in supplying gas and in transmitting gas to certain countries. Europe had the opportunity to raise its storage levels in 2022. However, with the Chinese economy accelerating again, it may help to fill the gas storage facilities that are threatened to be emptied under the conditions of 2023. The Union considers that even assuming gas prices remain current, replacing 60 bcm of Russian gas consumed in 2022 in 2023 with short-term measures will be difficult.

IMF (2022a) underlined that gas supply via LNG would slow down the effects of the Russian gas cut, but it will affect the economic situation in these countries. In the report, which states that the EU's production will also be affected, it is explained that monetary policies resulting from high gas negatively impact the economy. The report says that the EU is well-connected to the global LNG market. Still, the integration in the domestic market is flawed as it is partly geared toward Russia (Di Bella et al., 2022).

A tight market and sensitive prices boost short-term LNG trading. The share of spot and short-term contracts in total LNG trade had increased from 25% in 2017 to nearly 40% in 2021. The USA has considerably strengthened its position as a provider of LNG contracts, and US gas producers' revenues nearly tripled in 2022. Still, long-term LNG contracts are concluded with the USA, they are based on Henry Hub prices, below European (TTF) and Asian spot prices, due to bottlenecks in US export capacity. Due to competition for LNG, European and Asian spot gas prices are higher and more correlated than European and US Henry Hub prices (Di Bella et al., 2022).

European countries can provide some additional gas by increasing the capacity of non-Russian pipeline flows. The EU will be able to increase LNG imports next year modestly, under a recently announced agreement between Israel and Egypt. The situation on a country basis is as follows (EIA, 2022):

- USA: committed to providing Europe with additional LNG in 2022. Export terminals will be operating at 95% capacity in 2022. Other engineering measures could increase the capacity of existing terminals by 10% in the short term.
- Qatar: Qatar may increase its European exports by 10–15%.
- Australia: Australia's export capacity utilization is over 90% and is not expected to increase significantly.

It is also possible to increase local EU production within the community. For example, the Netherlands may delay the closure of the Groningen gas field, aimed at reducing production for environmental reasons. In addition, alternative energy sources can help minimize gas import needs further, and nuclear power can be used as an alternative. A new nuclear power plant started operating in Finland in 2022. This plant can provide a seven bcm gas equivalent (IEA, 2022a). German authorities are considering extending the use of nuclear power plants. The EU's power generation from wind and solar was expected to increase. The IEA argues that there are strong indications that production bottlenecks can strengthen this and that installing new solar and wind power plants could quickly replace 6 billion cubic meters of natural gas (IEA, 2022d). In addition, a transition from gas to coal may continue in Europe, especially in Germany and the Netherlands (Di Bella et al., 2022).

2.4.2 The Demand Side

Europe needs additional measures on the demand side. In the short term, there is expected to be only a limited demand squeeze in the household sector. Many European countries regulate consumer gas and electricity prices to protect low-income households. EU energy ministers agreed in Brussels to reduce the use of natural gas by 15%. If member states declared a warning level at the EU level, reducing demand for this gas would become mandatory (European & International Energy Policy, 2022). Since prices began to rise in 2021, additional measures have been implemented to protect consumers partially. Suppliers typically arrange such measures either through a direct subsidy or by promising higher prices in the future. However, while such actions do not provide the necessary incentives to reduce demand, higher prices will reduce household consumption, given the price elasticity of gas prices. An average European household paid 54% more monthly gas and electricity bills in the UK (Glide, 2022) in 2022 than in 2021, while a German family paid 116.86 euros for electricity in 2022, a 24% increase (Statista, 2022).

In current and projected gas prices, adjustments to the potential supply and demand balance are estimated to be sized, with savings increasing further (Di Bella et al., 2022). According to the IEA's report, the EU will be able to close the 27 bcm gap in the worst scenario by reducing gas demand by spending around 100 billion Euros.

3 The Russian Gas Market

3.1 Russian Natural Gas Market Before the Ukraine War

As one of the world's largest natural gas suppliers, Russia's economy, one of Europe's most important natural gas suppliers for decades, is based on hydrocarbon-based energy resources and industry. Income from oil and gas occupied an important place in the Russian economy and constituted 35–45% of budget revenues. Russia, the world's second-largest natural gas producer, has been exporting large-scale gas pipelines and LNG for a long time. In 2020, Russia produced 638 bcm of natural gas. The country's main export markets are the EU and Turkey, with pipeline connections, and it exports 30% of its production. In addition, Russia imports natural gas from Kazakhstan and Uzbekistan for re-export (IMF, 2022a).

For a long time, Russia has directed its export policy to the European market, exporting approximately 150–200 bcm of natural gas annually to this region (EURACTIV, 2020). However, for several reasons, the appeal of the European market had begun to wane even before the war with Ukraine broke out. The most important driver is the shale gas market developed after the 2010s. The process, which started with the USA being one of the world's most essential exporters, enlarged the LNG market. The competitive environment, especially in Europe, began to reduce natural gas prices in the European continent. In addition, the EU's policies supporting renewable resources reduced the continent's natural gas demand. In addition, natural gas coming to Europe from Africa and the Caucasus was reducing the profitability of the Russians. It maintained its European link, as all forecasts were for natural gas consumption to continue. Russia's two main export pipelines in the European market, "Urengoy–Pomary–Uzhgorod" and "Soyuz," were coming through Ukraine, which conflicted with Russia, creating a risky situation (Pirani & Yafimava, 2016). Therefore, Russia launched two gas pipeline projects at the beginning of 2020, Nord Stream-2 (Schmidt-Felzmann, 2020) and TurkStream (Mikulska, 2020), with a total volume of 70 bcm (Henderson & Mitrova, 2015).

On the other hand, Russia had begun to change its export policy for a while. In the second decade of the twenty-first century, the increasing demand for natural gas in the Far East directed the attention of the Russians to this region. Still, substantial infrastructure investments were needed for this region (Kutcherov et al., 2020). China, India, Taiwan, Japan, and South Korea were the largest energy consumers in the Asia Pacific. These countries were beginning to be considered an important market potential for Russia. Japan, India, and South Korea fully meet their natural gas consumption through LNG imports under long-term contracts, while China purchases LNG on long-term contracts and gas pipelines. In 2020, while Russia's gas exports to Japan, South Korea, and other Asian countries decreased, its exports to China increased by 30%. In 2019, Russia started to send gas 2019 with the "Power of Siberia," a 3000 km pipeline from Siberia. The capacity of this line was expected to increase to 28 bmc in 2023 (Mamakhatov et al., 2020).

Russia has started to give importance to LNG investments to turn to the Far East market. For this purpose, it has started to build new terminals in the North Sea, although climatic conditions are pretty tricky. Another problem is the difficulty of obtaining ready-to-operate LNG tankers with the growth of this LNG market in recent years. Due to Western sanctions, it cannot find tankers suitable for North Sea conditions to transport gas to the Far East (Humpert, 2022). Currently, there are LNG plants with a capacity of 18.3 and 11.1 bcm, respectively, on the Yamal Peninsula and Sakhalin Island in Russia. The country has planned LNG terminal investments in the Arctic Gydan peninsula, De-Kastri, Khabarovsk region, and Ust-Luga Leningrad region with capacities of 20.3, 6.8, and 16.6 bcm, respectively (Kutcherov et al., 2020). According to the Russian Ministry of Energy, the estimate of potential LNG production in the Russian Federation as of 2020 was over 80 million tons annually. Given the potential announced projects, production could be around 163 bcm per year. Ongoing large, medium, and low-tonnage projects had the potential to substantially impact establishing a resource base for gas production and export. Russia is one of the leading countries in LNG production and carrying capacities. According to analysts' estimates, if there were no war, Russia's share in the world liquefied natural gas market would have reached 20% by 2035 (Kharitonova et al., 2020).

3.2 *The Ukrainian War and Russia's Short-Term Plans*

In the short term, the only option for the Russians was to increase LNG production and take advantage of the rising energy prices due to the war and the embargo. For their energy-based economy to survive, their incomes had to increase. Russia's Federal State Statistics Service (Rosstat) stated that Russia's natural gas production decreased, and liquefied natural gas (LNG) production increased in 2022 (TASS, 2022). On the other hand, the increased natural gas prices in early 2022 helped Russia meet its expectations in 2022. In March–April 2022, Russia's oil and gas revenues skyrocketed to historic highs (Lee, 2022). While the maximum price in the first quarter of 2022 was 350 Euros per MWh, a sharp decline began in May. By the end of 2022, natural gas prices had fallen to pre-war levels. Prices at Europe's largest TTF center in the Netherlands decreased to a record low below 77 euros per MWh. Although it showed a very volatile character in 2022, the energy income of the Russians was close to the revenues of 2021 (Sassi, 2022).

The Ukraine war not only made it difficult for Russia to sell natural gas to European countries but also made it difficult to operate the natural gas fields around the Arctic. Russia, the largest power in the Arctic region, owns almost 60% of Arctica's coast. In 2020, 80% of Russian natural gas and 17% of its oil were produced here. However, there are significant difficulties in implementing the project due to the production areas in the Arctic region. These problems are reflected in increased capital costs throughout the entire production chain and increase the risks of not implementing the project within the planned timeframe within the budget provided (Kutcherov et al., 2020).

In the pre-war period, the Russian government had planned to invest $29 billion in LNG projects that had to start working as soon as possible. However, even before 2022, achieving these goals would not be easy. This was due to two main factors. First, there was a shortage of investment in the oil and gas sector in the 2010s. It was due to the long-term deterioration of the investment environment following the Western sanctions imposed on Russia after the annexation of Crimea in 2014. Second, the emerging green transition of advanced economies would further reduce the demand for hydrocarbon energy sources. The sanctions imposed on Russia after it invaded Ukraine further complicated Russia's prospects for development in the Arctic. In addition to the embargo on oil and gas purchases from Russia, potential trading partners' refusal to use the Northern Sea Route for the international transit of goods emerged as a separate issue. This possibility would significantly limit the demand for goods and services that the Russian Arctic can produce (Eiterjord, 2022).

Some studies suggest that there will be no new major economic projects in the Russian Arctic or the rest of the country in the near future. Undoubtedly, investments in these regions will slow down without investment funds based on Western capital. Apart from these, since the Western countries have not provided technical support since 2014, Russia has had difficulties extracting gas from the Arctic region, which has vast potential. Still, with its limited opportunities, the LNG project in the Yamal

Peninsula started on time despite difficult conditions, technological difficulties, and sanctions (Chatham House, 2018).

3.3 *Russia's Medium-Term Plans*

Russia's long-term strategy has two pillars. The most important of these is the Chinese market. For decades, China has discussed that the Arctic energy and the Northern Sea Route will offer opportunities to diversify resources and supply lines (Lo, 2009; Xing & Bertelsen, 2013). As a result of the cooperation that started with the "Power of Siberia" project, it exports 10 bcm of natural gas annually to China as of 2022. With the cancelation of the certificate of Nord Stream, which was expected to export gas to Europe, and the cessation of the activity of Nord Stream 1, Russia took action to fill this gap by building a second pipeline to China and launched the "Power of Siberia 2" Project. Power of Siberia 2 is planned to supply gas from Western Russia via Mongolia to China, and construction work will begin in 2024. The capacity of this gas, which is the continuation of the Gazprom-operated Power of Siberia 1 pipeline stretching from eastern Siberia to northern China, will be 50 bcm (Russia Briefing, 2022). Undoubtedly, this cooperation will benefit both parties. Zhang et al. (2022) claimed that strengthening cooperation between China and Russia in oil and gas resources in the Arctic ensures that China's energy security index will rise from 0.4419 in 2020 to 0.5412 in 2025. For this reason, China's technology, funding, scientific research, and other support and multilateral cooperation with Russia, paved the way for cooperation in the Arctic waterway, oil, and gas exploration and development, as well as Arctic scientific research.

Russia has received technical and financial support from China since the early 2010s and has started to develop natural gas projects with its help. In 2017, China and Russia agreed on constructing the northern waterway and the "Ice Silk Road," forming two joint research teams to complete the scientific survey of the critical waters of the "northeast channel." Thus, as China-Russia became a "strategic collaborative partner" in 2019, China increased Russia's investment in the Arctic region. The Russia-China cooperation, which started with the Yamal project, has become the world's largest oil and gas project, covering an integrated natural gas development, processing, liquefaction, and maritime transport with the Project above. The second important project is Artic 2, which is expected to build three natural gas production lines and produce a total annual production of 19.8 million tons (Zhang et al., 2022). This project depends on foreign partners as equity partners and financiers and as crucial providers of technology and project management expertise. The project will be completed in three phases. The first is almost complete, the second is not yet half completed, and the third is not yet built (Tsafos, 2022).

The research of Carnegie (2021) underlines that the interest in Russia's Arctic projects in partnership with China predates the conflict between Moscow and the West and is purely pragmatic. Despite the adverse global conditions, Russia is trying to protect itself from the risk of overdependence on China. Therefore, it has tried to diversify its partnerships as much as possible and has been successful in the Arctic LNG 2 project thanks to active commercial diplomacy and financing from Russian sources. However, China attaches great importance to holding all the cards in negotiations. At this point, China is likely to make very serious concessions due to Russia's desperation (Tsafos, 2022).

Although Russia's "Power of Siberia" and LNG projects developed in cooperation with China do not solve Russia's problems in the short term, Asia will probably be able to compete with Europe as a primary market for Russian gas in the medium term. However, according to experts, the Asian market will not be a complete alternative to Europe as a source of income and geopolitical weight. When the Power of Siberia 1 pipeline reaches capacity, Russia can ship approximately 60 billion cubic meters to China with LNG sales. At the most optimistic forecast, Russia can sell no more than 80 bcm of gas annually without new projects. While it is possible to build scenarios that Russia could sell 100–120 bcm of gas to Asia by 2030, this amount is unlikely to replace 150–200 bcm of gas sold to Europe. In addition, Europe is a more accessible market for Russia in terms of transportation in the North. Apart from pipelines, Europe is a natural Russian market for projects in the west, near Saint Petersburg. Apart from pipelines, Russia could sell approximately 20 billion cubic meters of LNG to Europe via its north (Yamal) and west (Vysotsk and Portovaya) facilities. While Europe is a year-round destination within the framework of LNG shipments from the Yamal Peninsula, it is possible to sell goods to Asia only when the northern sea route is convenient for transportation (Tsafos, 2022).

On the other hand, knowing that Russia is in trouble, China has forced Russia to make a series of price cuts to develop its LNG business while paying a much lower price for Russian gas than Europe (Sor, 2022). For this reason, Russia's income decreased considerably. Also, while China has established several joint ventures with Gazprom over time, unlike Europe, it does not seem too keen for Gazprom to set up any business within Chinese territory (Tsafos, 2022).

Russia was relatively late to enter the eastern market. Several countries share the market for this region. China bought gas from Australia ($9.55 B), Turkmenistan ($5.25 B), Qatar ($4.24 B), the USA ($2.47 B), and Indonesia ($1.62 B) in 2020 (OEC, 2020). The situation will be no different in Japan, South Korea, and Taiwan, and Russia's market share in Asia will remain small (Tsafos, 2022). Even if Russia opens to Asian markets, the inability to fill the place of the European market may lead it to new searches. In this context, it may be possible for the Russians to turn to the markets in South East Europe. It is also possible that a significant portion of the countries in this region use traditional fuels such as coal, potentially creating greater natural gas demand. There are also countries in the region that are not members of the EU and have strong historical ties with the Russians.

Developments in 2022 show that it will not be easy for Europe to continue to impose a full embargo on Russian gas. However, how much more gas Europe will be interested in buying from Russia depends on the determination of the EU concerning its policies.

- The first reason for this is that some countries that are not members of the EU will not comply with the embargo decision on Russia. Some countries heavily dependent on Russian gas and have closer political ties to Moscow will likely push for a later deadline to end gas imports from Russia and pressure that imports continue indefinitely. Non-EU countries such as Serbia will continue to buy gas from Russia. Serbia announced in May 2022 that it had signed a new agreement to supply natural gas to Russia for three years (RFERL, 2022). While this agreement showed that Russia still strongly influenced the Balkans, Bosnia, and Herzegovina also stated that it would not impose any sanctions against Russia. Albania, which will consume almost no gas by 2022 but is willing to expand its role to reduce its dependence on hydroelectric power plants (HEPPs), could also be a new market for Russian gas.
- The second reason is that countries such as Hungary continue to buy natural gas from Russia even though it is a member of the EU. Hungary continues to buy gas from Russia and calls on Europe to lift the embargo against Russia. On the other hand, Spain and France received more LNG from Russia in 2022 than the previous year. Greece continues to buy gas via Turkish Stream and buys LNG from Russia when it finds an opportunity.
- The third reason is that Russia implements secret strategies to hide its energy exports (Ioanes, 2022). It is the most common method for Russian businesses to hide behind non-sanctioned shell companies and/or transact through third-party countries that do not present enforcement issues. In addition, methods such as multiple ship-to-ship transfers, temporarily disabling ship tracking transponders, and using uncertain navigational patterns are implemented. Another tactic sanctioned countries use to disguise the origin of petroleum products is to blend them with oil from other countries. Because these processes are often difficult to monitor, it will be challenging to know how effective and widespread they are (IISS, 2022).
- Finally, the capacity of LNG facilities established or to be established in Greece or other Balkan countries is not more than 20–25 bcm. It is far from meeting the growing natural gas demand of the region (Athens News, 2022). An alternative to Russian gas has still not been established.

4 SWOT Analysis

A SWOT analysis of Europe and Russia was employed using the results of all the market information and scientific research evaluated. The outcome of the analysis is given in Table 1. While Europe's strong economy and other international relations with the USA, its access to financial markets, and its natural gas infrastructure are of a benefit, Europe still needs Russian gas. Rising gas prices are causing economic problems. As discussed in previous sections, the EU's cooperation and the physical infrastructure within the energy Union are strong. Also, the energy Union is a better tool for decision-making than the EU; while each member of the EU has a blocking vote, it provides a quick reaction in the gas war between the EU and Russia. A large storage capacity was created immediately. Although some of its members are somewhat incompatible, there is a strong solidarity in unity. Besides, It has a solid international political power and a robust economic base, with a GDP of $16.6 trillion by 2022 (IMF, 2022b). As observed during the crises, the dominant feature of the Union is more robust intergovernmental cooperation (Coman et al., 2020). However, as explained in the paper, the need for Russian gas, albeit partially, is a concern in Europe, which does not have gas resources and has a weak interregional imbalance. Some areas do not have adequate gas lines and storage facilities. It has to tolerate high gas prices, which cause inflation in the Union countries for a while. Inflation triggered by gas prices is a severe threat (Cambridge Econometrics, 2022). Although LNG entry points are being developed, they are still weak. However, having no problem with accessing international gas markets creates an opportunity for the EU. The emerging LNG market and renewable energy will diversify and develop the energy security of the EU in the future. According to surveys, there is strong public support for the energy policies of the Union (Janik et al., 2021). In 2023/24, both a cold winter and an increase in the gas demand of the Chinese economy and the increase in prices may pose a significant threat. Fortunately, China's economic recovery appears to be on track, in the first half of 2023 but is unevenly spread across sectors, likely to result in a moderate increase in natural gas imports. The prolongation and expansion of the Ukraine war is the most feared scenario.

On the other hand, although Russia is still an essential player and has strong political influence in the European market, it is in danger of losing its power in this and international markets. The third section explains that Russia gained great power from Europe's leading natural gas pipes and storage feeding. Russia is indispensable because of its relatively clean and cheap gas sales, especially for central and south-eastern European countries. The country is developing its infrastructure for supplying Far East markets. Nevertheless, Russia does not have sufficient financial and technical competence for its projects. As Russia opens to the Far East market, it will have to sell its gas cheaper and lose its political power over Europe. Undoubtedly, this situation will diversify Russia's gas export market and provide additional motivation with China's support to develop their technologies. Global warming, decreasing budget revenues, and the developing LNG market are significant threats to Russia.

The results reveal that, while both parties face high economic and social costs in the short term, the international cooperation of both parties would decline. While Europe can increase its security of supply in the medium term, Russia can diversify its exports through market diversification. Still, on the other hand, Russia inevitability loses its international political power sourced by energy resources. However, Russia can gain technological and political leverage by improving its cooperation with China.

Table 1 SWOT analysis

Europe	
Strengths	**Weakness**
Energy network	Insufficient gas production
Solidarity among member states	Interregional difference
Strong economy	High energy prices
Support of USA	Overdependence on Russia
Decision-making structure	Insufficient gas entry points
Storage capacity	Inadequate pipelines on a regional basis
International political power	Imbalance of storage locations
Opportunities	**Threats**
Access to the financial markets	Cold winter
Public support	Social unrest in some countries
The development of renewable energy sources	Different policies of member states
Supply diversification	The spread of the Ukrainian war
Emerging LNG market	China's economy grows much
Increase in supply security	Cost of high and volatile past prices
	High inflation
Russia	
Strengths	**Weakness**
Natural gas resources	Lack of export market diversity
Strong supplier of the European market	Access to financial resources
Political power	New investment need
Gas pipelines and networks in Europe	Access to high technology
Access to the Far East market	Extreme competition and low prices in the Asian market
Cheap and clean features of natural gas	Overdependence of the country's budget on energy
	Transportation problems
Opportunities	**Threads**
Market diversification	Global warming
Entering South East European market	Emerging LNG market
Developing national gas technology	Growing shale gas market
	The decline of Russia's political power
	Budget deficit and economic problems

5 Conclusion

Like many great powers whose power has waned, Russia has attempted to test its strength by invading Ukraine. However, according to the first findings, Russia is in a far position to get what it wants. A harsh winter, which helped in the past, has not appeared in 2022. Russia still hopes for the following winters, but it is clear that it has yet to succeed in the first round of the natural gas war with Europe. The energy war may continue for many years and, according to the first estimates, may leave permanent traces in Europe and Russia. The energy war not only changes the structures of the markets but also has essential reflections from the foreign policy of Europe and Russia to their economic structures.

As of May 2023, Europe did not encounter a severe gas shortage in the past year, contrary to expectations. It managed to keep its economy alive without complicating the people's daily life. European economies managed problems such as high inflation and low growth rates with their strong economies and the support of the USA. On the other hand, although Russia is at war with Ukraine, it has solved its problems in the short term by obtaining energy income close to the previous years due to the excessively rising oil and gas prices at the beginning of 2022. Still, 2023 and 2024 will be very tough for both sides. However, it is expected that Europe will have some advantages with its low-profile policy in the long term. As pointed out by previous studies and reports of international institutions, the developing LNG market, and renewable energy resources may help the continent to manage its problems. In addition to the solidarity among the members of the Union, strong US support is among the crucial assets of Europe. On the other hand, Russia is trying to replace the gas import deficit by exporting to the Chinese and Far East Asian markets. However, by investing more, Russia will have to accept gas prices falling below the price it used to sell to the European market. It may not retain its old political power as a prominent player in new markets. Russia will also have difficulty accessing financial markets and high technology.

Our research and SWOT analysis indicate that Europe is in a more advantageous position against the Russians as of mid-2023. However, the decreasing trade between Russia and Europe will cause global economic problems. While Europe's access to cheap and clean energy becomes more complex, the Russians will incur high investment costs and sell gas at lower prices in new markets. The struggle naturally negatively affects the parties and decreases growth by increasing global inflation.

As a result of this study, both sides should draw some lessons. To improve energy security, the EU should accelerate the development of renewable energy sources, reevaluate the debate on nuclear energy, increase subsidies where necessary, focus on hydrogen produced from renewable sources in the long term, and diversify gas and oil suppliers in Europe and the world.

Besides strengthening the energy cooperation between the member states, in the case of a crisis, no member state should be left alone and be empowered to act with third countries under the umbrella of the EU (Polak & Polakova, 2022). European countries outside the EU should also take a lesson from these developments. They need to improve their relations with the European Union in the energy field and reduce their dependence on Russia by diversifying their energy supply, considering that Russia can use energy as a weapon in the future. Conversely, Russia should stop using energy as a weapon and become a stronger player in the Far East by developing natural gas technology and LNG infrastructure. Undoubtedly, once the war in Ukraine is over and political risk factors are reduced, global oil prices will reach a moderate equilibrium, as research indicates (Simpson et al., 2016).

In conclusion, this research does not lead us to conclude that either side wins but indicates that Europe will be the less loser of this struggle. On the other hand, this last effort of Russia, like the great powers in history that started to lose power, may harm it. The answer to the question of who will win this war is quite clear: the USA and China. The USA will find new markets for its shale gas, increase revenues, and grow trade. China will buy natural gas at a lower price and gain technological superiority over Russia.

References

Ari, M. A., Arregui, M. N., Black, M. S., Celasun, O., Iakova, M. D., Mineshima, M. A., & Zhunussova, K. (2022). *Surging energy prices in Europe in the aftermath of the war: How to support the vulnerable and speed up the transition away from fossil fuels*. International Monetary Fund.

Athens News. (2022, December 2). Greece becomes European hub for liquefied natural gas. Retrieved from https://en.rua.gr/2022/12/02/greece-becomes-european-hub-for-liquefied-natural-gas/. Accessed January 2023

Bachmann, R., Baqaee, D., Bayer, C., Kuhn, M., Löschel, A., Moll, B., & Schularick, M. (2022). What if? The economic effects for Germany of a stop of energy imports from Russia. *Wirtschaftsdienst, 102*, 251–255.

Capolongo, A., Kühl, M., & Skovorodov, V. (2022, August 9). Cold winter ahead? Implications from a Russian gas cut-off for the euro area. *European Stability Mechanism*. Retrieved from https://www.esm.europa.eu/blog/cold-winter-ahead-implications-russian-gas-cut-euro-area%23_ftnref2

Chatham House. (2018, January 29). Russia's untapped arctic potential. Retrieved from https://www.chathamhouse.org/2018/01/russias-untapped-arctic-potential

Coman, R., Crespy, A., & Schmidt, V. A. (Eds.). (2020). *Governance and politics in the post-crisis European Union*. Cambridge University Press.

Deb, K., & Rajendran, A. (2022, October 19). Q&A|Assessing the impact of the largest OPEC+ production cut since 2020. *Center of Global Energy Policy*. Retrieved from https://www.energypolicy.columbia.edu/publications/qa-assessing-impact-largest-opec-production-cut

Di Bella, G., Flanagan, M. J., Foda, K., Maslova, S., Pienkowski, A., Stuermer, M., & Toscani, F. G. (2022). *Natural gas in Europe: The potential impact of disruptions to supply*. IMF Working Papers.

Cambridge Econometrics. (2022). Fossil fuel prices and inflation in Spain. Retrieved from https://www.camecon.com/wp-content/uploads/2022/10/Spain-report_FINALv2_PDF.pdf

EEA. (2022, October 26). Share of energy consumption from renewable sources in Europe. *European Environment Agency*. Retrieved from https://www.eea.europa.eu/ims/share-of-energy-consumption-from

EIA. (2022). https://www.eia.gov/naturalgas/U.S.liquefactioncapacity.xlsx for data on US export terminals.

Eiterjord, T. (2022, December 13). Amid Ukraine war, Russia's Northern sea route turns east. *The Diplomat*. Retrieved from https://thediplomat.com/2022/12/amid-ukraine-war-russias-northern-sea-route-turns-east/
Elliott, S. (2022, August 10). Feature: Europe's dash for new LNG import infrastructure picks up pace. *S&P Global*. Retrieved from https://www.spglobal.com/commodityinsights/en/market-insights/latest-news/natural-gas/081022-feature-europes-dash-for-new-lng-import-infrastructure-picks-up-pace
ENTSOG. (2022). *Summer supply outlook*. European Central Bank.
EURACTIV. (2020, November 14). What if Nord stream 2 is never completed? Retrieved from https://efile.fara.gov/docs/6491-Informational-Materials-20201114-165.pdf
European and International Energy Policy. (2022, July 26). EU energy ministers agree on gas demand reduction plan. Retrieved from https://www.bmwk.de/Redaktion/EN/Pressemitteilungen/2022/07/20220726-eu-energy-ministers-agree-on-gas-demand-reduction-plan.html
European Commission. (2006). *Green paper: A European strategy for sustainable, competitive and secure energy, adopted by the European Commission on 8 March 2006*. Office for Official Publications of the European Communities.
European Commission. (2009a). Directive 2009/28/EC of the European parliament and of the council of 23 April 2009. Retrieved from https://eur-lex.europa.eu/legal-content/EN/ALL/?uri=celex%3A32009L0028
European Commission. (2009b). Council directive 2009/119/EC of 14 september 2009 imposing an obligation on member states to maintain minimum stocks of crude oil and/or petroleum products. Retrieved from https://eur-lex.europa.eu/legal-content/EN/ALL/?uri=CELEX%3A32009L0119
European Commission. (2012). Directive 2012/27/EU of the European parliament and of the council of 25 October 2012. Retrieved from https://eur-lex.europa.eu/legal-content/EN/TXT/?qid=1399375464230&uri=CELEX:32012L0027
European Commission. (2016a, February 16). Regulation of the European Parliament and of the council: concerning measures to safeguard the security of gas supply and repealing Regulation (EU) No 994/2010. Retrieved from https://eur-lex.europa.eu/legal-content/EN/TXT/?uri=uriserv:OJ.L_.2017.280.01.0001.01.ENG
European Commission. (2016b, February 16). Towards energy union: The commission presents sustainable energy security package. Accessed June 5, 2017 Retrieved from http://europa.eu/rapid/press-release_IP-16-307_en.htm
European Commission. (2018a, November 19). The European Union and Algeria strengthen their energy partnership. Retrieved from https://commission.europa.eu/news/european-union-and-algeria-strengthen-their-energy-partnership-2018-11-19_en
European Commission. (2018b, June 19). Energy efficiency first: Commission welcomes agreement on energy efficiency. Retrieved from http://europa.eu/rapid/press-release_STATEMENT-18-3997_en.htm
European Commission. (2022a, May 18). REPowerEU: A plan to rapidly reduce dependence on Russian fossil fuels and fast forward the green transition. Retrieved from https://ec.europa.eu/commission/presscorner/detail/en/IP_22_3131
European Commission. (2022b, September 27). Launch of the baltic pipe. Retrieved from https://commission.europa.eu/news/launch-baltic-pipe-2022-09-27_en#:~:text=The%20Baltic%20Pipe%20will%20make,planned%20for%201%20October%202022
European Council. (2023, January 26). Infographic—How much gas have the EU countries stored? Retrieved from https://www.consilium.europa.eu/en/infographics/gas-storage-capacity/#:~:text=In%20December%202022%2C%20the%20average,among%20member%20states%20was%2088%25
European Parliament. (2015). European energy security strategy. Retrieved from https://www.europarl.europa.eu/EPRS/EPRS-AaG-559474-European-Energy-Security-Strategy-FINAL.pdf
Flanagan, M., Kammer, A., Pescatori, A., & Stuermer, M. (2022, July 19). How a Russian natural gas cutoff could weigh on Europe's economies. *IMF Blog*.

Retrieved from https://www.imf.org/en/Blogs/Articles/2022/07/19/blog-how-a-russias-natural-gas-cutoff-could-weigh-on-european-economies

Glide. (2022). Average gas and electric bill per household 2022. Retrieved from https://glide.co.uk/guides/average-gas-and-electric-bill-per-household-2022/

Gourinchas, P. (2022, October 11). Policymakers need steady hand as storm clouds gather over global economy. *IMF Blog*. Retrieved from https://www.imf.org/en/Blogs/Articles/2022/10/11/policymakers-need-steady-hand-as-storm-clouds-gather-over-global-economy

Henderson, J., & Mitrova, T. (2015). *The political and commercial dynamics of Russia's gas export strategy*. University of Oxford.

Humpert, M. (2022, September 9). Western sanctions delay opening of arctic LNG 2 project by one year. *High North News*. Retrieved from https://www.highnorthnews.com/en/western-sanctions-delay-opening-arctic-lng-2-project-one-year

Iancu, L. (2022, March 3). IEA's new 10-point plan: Reducing the European Union's Reliance on Russian natural gas. *Energy Industry Review*. Retrieved from https://energyindustryreview.com/oil-gas/ieas-new-10-point-plan/

IEA. (2022a). Gas market report, Q1-2022. Retrieved from https://www.iea.org/reports/gas-market-report-q1-2022

IEA. (2022b). Gas market report, Q3-2022. Retrieved from https://www.iea.org/reports/gas-market-report-q3-2022

IEA. (2022c). Gas market report, Q4-2022. Retrieved from https://www.iea.org/reports/gas-market-report-q4-2022

IEA. (2022d). Electricity Market Report. Retrieved from https://www.iea.org/reports/electricity-market-report-july-2022

IISS. (2022). Russia and sanctions evasion. *Strategic Comments, 28*(4), 7–9.

IMF. (2022a). IMF reports and publication by country: Russian federation. Retrieved from https://www.imf.org/en/Countries/RUS

IMF. (2022b). World economic outlook database: October 2022. Retrieved from https://www.imf.org/en/Publications/WEO/weo-database/2022/October

Ioanes, E. (2022, October 16). Despite sanctions, Russian fuel is still selling-here's who's buying. Vox. Retrieved from https://www.vox.com/platform/amp/2022/10/16/23407003/sanctions-russian-fuel-china-india-natural-gas-ukraine

Janik, A., Ryszko, A., & Szafraniec, M. (2021). Determinants of the EU Citizens' attitudes towards the European energy union priorities. *Energies, 14*(17), 5237.

Kharitonova, N. A., Pulyaeva, V. N., Kharitonova, E. N. (2020, December). *Prospects for projects of the liquefied natural gas production (Vol. 976, No. 1, p. 012032)*. IOP Conference Series: Materials Science and Engineering. 976 No. 1, s. 012032. IOP Publishing.

Kutcherov, V., Morgunova, M., Bessel, V., & Lopatin A. (2020). Russian natural gas exports: An analysis of challenges and opportunities. *Energy Strategy Reviews, 30*(100511).

Lee, J. (2022, September 20). Russian oil flows dive, hurting Putin's war chest. *Bloomberg*. Retrieved from https://www.bloomberg.com/news/articles/2022-09-20/russian-oil-flows-dive-hurting-putin-s-war-chest?leadSource=uverify%20wall

Lo, B. (2009). *Axis of convenience: Moscow, Beijing, and the new geopolitics*. Brookings Institution Press.

Mamakhatov, T., Mohammad, M. J., & Chaykovskiy, A. (2020). Analysis of the economic impact of the Power of Siberia project on the development of the eastern regions of Russia. *Geology and Mineral Resources of Siberia, 2*(42), 110–122.

McMurtry, A. (2022, November 01). Spain and France boost capacity of Irun gas pipeline by 66%. *Anadolu Agency*. Retrieved from https://www.aa.com.tr/en/europe/spain-and-france-boost-capacity-of-irun-gas-pipeline-by-66-/2726624

Mikulska, A. (2020). Gazprom and Russian natural gas policy in the first two decades of the 21st century. *Orbis, 64*(3), 403–420.

OEC. (2020). Petroleum gas in China. *The Observatory of Economic Complexity*. Retrieved from https://oec.world/en/profile/bilateral-product/petroleum-gas/reporter/chn?redirect=true#:~:text=In%202020%2C%20China%20imported%20%2436.6B%20in%20Petroleum%20Gas%2C%20mainly,and%20Indonesia%20(%241.62B)

Oxford Analytica. (2022). Russian gas cut would hurt EU's eastern members most. *Emerald Expert Briefings*, (oxan-db).

Pirani, S., & Yafimava, K. (2016). *Russian gas transit across Ukraine post-2019–pipeline scenarios, gas flow consequences, and regulatory constraints*. NG, 27: Oxford Institute for Energy Studies.

Polak, P. (2017). The trouble with nord stream 2. https://www.foreignaffairs.com/articles/europe/2017-08-23/trouble-nord-stream-2

Polak, P., & Polakova, B. (2022). Changes in the EU's geopolitical position and energy doctrine in light of the Ukraine invasion. *Society, 59*(3), 254–258.

Preussen, W. (2022, August 31). Hungary signs new gas deal with Gazprom. *Politico*. Retrieved from https://www.politico.eu/article/hungary-signs-deal-with-gazprom-over-additional-gas/

Prisecaru, P. (2022). The war in Ukraine and the overhaul of EU energy security. *Global Economic Observer, 10*(1), 16–25.

RFERL. (2022, May 29). Vucic says Serbia secures gas deal with Russia following phone talks with Putin. *Radio Free Europe Radio Liberty*. Retrieved from https://www.rferl.org/a/serbia-vucic-gas-deal-russia/31873908.html

Rogers, D., Nelson, R., & Howell, N. (2018). *LNG in Europe 2018: An overview of LNG import terminals in Europe*. King & Spalding LLP.

Russia Briefing. (2022, July 18). Mongolian transit of power of Siberia 2 pipeline construction to Begin In 2024. Retrieved from https://www.russia-briefing.com/news/mongolian-transit-of-power-of-siberia-2-pipeline-construction-to-begin-in-2024.html/

Simpson, J. L., Alsameen, A., & Evans, J. (2016). The economic drivers of the political will for social responsibility in energy policy for Fossil fuel exporting countries. In A. B. Dorsman, O. Arslan-Ayaydin, & M. B. Karan (Eds.), *Energy and finance: Sustainability in the energy industry* (pp. 145–163).

Sönnichsen, N. (2022, May 18), Number of LNG import terminals in Europe by country 2022. *Statista*. Retrieved from https://www.statista.com/statistics/326008/lng-import-terminals-by-country-europe/#:~:text=Number%20of%20LNG%20import%20terminals%20in%20Europe%20by%20country%202022&text=In%20total%20there%20are%2029,the%20planning%20stage%20in%20Europe

Sönnichsen, N. (2022, November 9). Quarterly gas storage volume in the EU 2011–2022. *Statista*. Retrieved from https://www.statista.com/statistics/1294025/quarterly-gas-in-storage-in-the-european-union/

Sassi, F. (2022, September 27). Russia's energy game in Asia. *The Diplomat*. Retrieved from https://thediplomat.com/2022/09/russias-energy-game-in-asia/

Schmidt-Felzmann, A. (2020). Gazprom's Nord stream 2 and diffuse authority in the EU: Managing authority challenges regarding Russian gas supplies through the Baltic Sea. *Journal of European Integration, 42*(1), 129–145.

Sor, J. (2022, September 8). China has secured Russian gas at a 50% discount until the end of this year. *Markets Insider*. Retrieved from https://markets.businessinsider.com/news/commodities/russia-natural-gas-china-lng-europe-energy-crisis-discount-asia-2022-9

Spivak, V., & Gabuev, A. (2021, December 31). The ice age: Russia and China's energy cooperation in the Arctic. *Carnegie Endowment for International Peace*. Retrieved from https://carnegiemoscow.org/commentary/86100

Statista. (2022, December 13). Average electricity bill for a 3-person household in Germany from 1998 to 2022. Retrieved from https://www.statista.com/statistics/1346248/electricity-bill-average-household-germany/

TASS. (2022). Gas production in Russia in January–October down by 13% yoy to 474 bcm, statistics says. Retrieved from https://tass.com/economy/1541095

Temizer, M. (2018, July 31). TANAP receives €5 million in support from EC. *Anadolu Agency*. Retrieved from https://www.aa.com.tr/en/economy/tanap-receives-5-million-in-support-from-ec/1218582

Trading Economics. (2023). EU natural gas. Retrieved from https://tradingeconomics.com/commodity/eu-natural-gas

Tsafos, N. (2022, May 4). Can Russia execute a gas Pivot to Asia? CSIS: Center for strategic and international studies. Retrieved from https://www.csis.org/analysis/can-russia-execute-gas-pivot-asia

Xing, L., & Bertelsen, R. G. (2013). The drivers of Chinese Arctic interests: Political stability and energy and transportation security. Arctic yearbook 2013: In *The arctic of regions versus the globalized arctic* (pp. 53–68). 600 Akureyri, Iceland.

Zhang, K., Hu, M., Dang, C. N. (2022). The potential of Sino–Russian energy cooperation in the arctic region and its impact on China's energy security. *Scientific Programming*, 1–10.

Market-Based Policies for ESG Activities in the Energy Sector

ESG Performances of Energy Companies in OECD Countries: A Clustering Approach

Cem Menten, Bulent Cekic, Kazim Baris Atici, Selin Metin Camgoz, and Aydin Ulucan

Abstract Examining the *Environmental*, *Social*, and *Governance* (ESG) aspects of the organizations is one of the current concerns related to sustainable investment decisions. Energy markets are one of the key areas where ESG concepts are applied due to their dynamism, scale, and effect. Noting that the ESG framework is very appropriate for use of multi-criteria decision methodologies to rank the alternatives, the current research is motivated by the idea that clustering can also serve as a tool to evaluate ESG performance. Accordingly, we propose clustering as a tool for ESG analysis for OECD energy companies that enables us to identify the conflicting areas on ESG performance while avoiding potential controversies, the requirement for predefined information, or subjectivity in aggregation. The *k-means* clustering algorithm is used to analyze a data set of 231 energy organizations under the three ESG pillars of *Environmental*, *Social*, and *Governance*. We identify the patterns across the clusters that may signify high and low performance in each pillar and discuss the properties of prominent clusters in terms of business classifications and country of headquarters.

Keywords Energy planning · Sustainability · ESG · Clustering · OECD

JEL Classification Q40 · Q56 · C38

C. Menten · B. Cekic · K. B. Atici (✉) · S. M. Camgoz · A. Ulucan
Department of Business Administration, Hacettepe University, Ankara, Turkey
e-mail: kba@hacettepe.edu.tr

C. Menten
e-mail: cemmenten@hacettepe.edu.tr

B. Cekic
e-mail: bulentc@hacettepe.edu.tr

S. M. Camgoz
e-mail: selinm@hacettepe.edu.tr

A. Ulucan
e-mail: aulucan@hacettepe.edu.tr

J. Thewissen et al. (eds.), *The ESG Framework and the Energy Industry*,
https://doi.org/10.1007/978-3-031-48457-5_6

1 Introduction

ESG stands for Environmental, Social, and Governance. The United Nations Global Compact Initiative's report "*Who Cares Wins*," published in 2004, is considered to be the earliest resource in that the term "*ESG*" was used (United Nations Global Compact Initiative, 2004). One of the most significant changes to the financial markets in recent years has been the use of ESG measures in investing decisions (Christensen et al., 2022). ESG framework covers rating the organizations under three main pillars consisting of different subcategories. Evaluations based on ESG scores are becoming common practices that have increasing importance for sustainable investment decisions in many markets (Christensen et al., 2022). A company's performance on all ESG indicators reflects its capacity to create value and implement effective business strategies (Apergis et al., 2022). Energy markets are undoubtedly one of the areas where the ESG framework has a significant potential to be utilized, given the scale, number, and consequently environmental and social impact of energy companies.

Multiple Criteria Decision Analysis (MCDA) is a research stream of a widely applied set of methods that offers a path to the decision-maker to integrate both subjective values and mathematical calculations to *select*, *rank*, *cluster*, or *classify* a group of alternatives. MCDA methods are handy to use in decision-making processes with a set of alternatives to be evaluated with respect to multiple and potentially conflicting criteria. Analogously, ESG scores for companies in any sector that present the performance in three main pillars with their subcategories establish a multiple criteria decision problem in nature. As in all multi-criteria decision problems, aggregating the scores into one representative score is an issue in ESG evaluations that may serve to select and/or rank. On the other hand, clustering or classifying the alternatives, which are among the main objectives of multiple criteria decision approaches, can serve as an alternative way to approach this multiple criteria problem. Clustering is preferable to classifying since it is unsupervised and does not require any predefined information regarding the groups of alternatives (Ishizaka et al., 2021). Considering that, the current research is motivated by this observation and asks the question "*How clustering can act as a tool for evaluating the ESG performance of the organizations?*" In answering this question, the domain is the ESG performances of energy companies listed in the stock exchanges of OECD countries. We aim to propose that alternatives that are *not strongly preferred to each other* (i.e., similar) in terms of ESG performance can be grouped with the aim of bypassing the potential controversies, the requirement for predefined information, or subjectivity in aggregation.

For our analysis, we undertake the *Refinitiv ESG Scores* framework consisting of 10 criteria in three pillars as Environmental (*Resource Use, Emissions Reduction, Innovation*), Social (*Workforce, Human Rights, Community, Product Responsibility*), and Governance (*Management, Shareholders, Corporate Social Responsibility Strategy*). The data set is obtained from *Refinitiv Eikon* for 231 public energy companies operating in OECD countries considering the data reliability. Ordinarily, the scores in each subcategory of the *Refinitiv ESG Scores* methodology are derived from more than 180 key performance metrics. The scores are combined into pillars using a weighted average method. The number of indicators that characterize each subcategory determines the weights for each one. The combined pillar ratings are then used to create an overall ESG score for each business. As an alternative to evaluating overall ESG performance through weighting averages, we utilize *the k-means* algorithm to obtain non-hierarchical clusters for the companies in each pillar and interpret findings.

Within the scope of the research, we identify the noticeable patterns across these non-hierarchical clusters and discuss the properties of prominent clusters. The findings reveal clear-cut clusters that can be representative of high and low performance in all *E*, *S*, and *G* pillars. Companies are primarily concentrated in the high-performance cluster in *G* as opposed to the low-performance clusters in *E* and *S*. Within the scope of the research, prescriptive discussions are provided with respect to two main characteristics of the companies as business classification and country of headquarters. Overall, we contribute to the literature by demonstrating that clustering enables us to pinpoint the ESG performance metrics that are in conflict without the need for predetermined information or weighting.

The chapter is organized as follows. Section 2 reviews the MCDA methodologies applied in the ESG context. In Sect. 3, we provide the basics of the *Refinitiv ESG Scores* framework so that each ESG subcategory is defined and the data set is described. Section 4 is devoted to presenting the basics of the clustering methodology utilized. In Sect. 5, we present and discuss the findings of the clustering analysis. Finally, Sect. 6 concludes the chapter.

2 ESG and Multiple Criteria Decision Analysis

Environmental, Social, and Governance (ESG) measurement and data analysis based on ESG is in the process of evolving as a contemporary research stream. In this domain, Multiple Criteria Decision Analysis (MCDA) is one of the widely applied methodologies with its fitting nature. There exists vast and relatively recent literature on implementing MCDA methods in ESG measurement. In this section, we review related research in this area. Table 1 summarizes the domain, data, and methodology of the reviewed research. As can be seen in the last column of Table 1, the MCDA methods employed vary and usually hybrid methodologies are preferred. The reader may refer to Greco et al. (2016) for miscellaneous methods cited in the table.

In various research, ESG factors are integrated into different types of decision processes through decision-maker preferences. As an example, Escrig-Olmedo et al. (2017) present a methodological approach based on fuzzy MCDM to integrate ESG investors' preferences into the evaluation process of the assets. The proposed methodology is illustrated in a clothing sector application with three decision-makers. Guedhami et al., (2022a, 2022b) also deal with investment decisions based on ESG performance. Two well-known MCDA methods are illustrated to rank the ESG performance of publicly traded companies. In a more macro-level research, a two-stage procedure

Table 1 Research on ESG using MCDA methods

Research	Domain	Data	Methodology
Escrig-Olmedo et al. (2017)	ESG performances of clothing sector companies	Thomson Reuters ASSET4 database	Fuzzy TOPSIS
Liern and Pérez-Gladish (2018)	ESG performance of energy firms worldwide	Thomson Reuters EIKON database	N-AHP-TOPSIS
Iamandi et al. (2019)	ESG performances of 1165 European companies	Thomson Reuters EIKON database	Kohonen neural network for clustering
Ziolo et al. (2019)	23 OECD countries	Expert opinions	Cognitive mapping and PROMETHEE
Ishizaka et al. (2021)	US banks' financial and non-financial (ESG) criteria	S&P's market intelligence platform and Refinitiv and ASSET4	PROMETHEE and SMAA and multi-criteria clustering
Guedhami et al., (2022a, 2022b)	ESG performance data of publicly traded companies	MSCI ESG STATS (KLD STATS)	AHP-TOPSIS and TOPSIS with entropy-based weights
Lin et al. (2022)	Shipping companies headquartered in Europe, Asia, and the USA	Survey to investment experts	DANP-mV model (hybrid DEMATEL, ANP, and modified VIKOR techniques)
Reig-Mullor et al. (2022)	ESG corporate performance in the gas and oil energy sector	EIKON database	AHP-TOPSIS
Sariyer and Taskin (2022)	ESG scores of the companies listed in the BIST sustainability index	Refinitiv and Turkey's public disclosure platform	*K-means* clustering algorithm
Vilas et al. (2022)	Five FTSE4 good sustainability indices and 11 conventional indices	Refinitiv	*K-means* clustering and agglomerative clustering and spectral clustering and mean shift and affinity propagation

is introduced and applied by Ziolo et al. (2019), in which the experts evaluate the ESG factors in the first stage and OECD countries are ranked in terms of identified criteria as the second stage. In a more recent research, Lin et al. (2022) investigate the main factors that affect the financial performance of global shipping companies. ESG is one of the four key dimensions incorporated into a hybrid multiple criteria assessment methodology with the data collected from investment experts. Liern and Pérez-Gladish (2018) introduce linguistic labels provided by the rating agencies to the decision process for defining the fuzzy ESG performance of the firms.

Clustering methodologies are also applied to ESG data. For instance, Vilas et al. (2022) evaluate sustainability stock indices and test the relationship between those and the conventional indices for stocks utilizing *Refinitiv ESG* data. Ishizaka et al. (2021) also deal with clustering organizations based on multiple criteria. They propose a hybrid methodology to evaluate US banks regarding financial and non-financial criteria, in which the non-financial criteria are represented by ESG. In another recent research that employs clustering algorithms, Sarıyer and Taşkın (2022) analyze the companies in the Borsa Istanbul (BIST) Sustainability Index using *k-means* clustering their ESG scores. Furthermore, neural network-based clustering algorithms are also applied in the ESG context in the case of big data, for instance, Iamandi et al. (2019) Kohonen Neural Network for Clustering to map the sustainability patterns of European companies at different levels.

ESG framework and MCDA methods are jointly employed also in energy markets. In a recent research, Reig-Mullor et al (2022) illustrate their proposed hybrid multiple criteria method to rank the Oil and Gas sector companies.

3 Data

The Environmental, Social, and Governance (ESG) score evaluates a company's ESG performance using publicly available and verified reported data. The ESG scores are calculated using a variety of approaches in the literature. One of the most reliable and well-known sources of ESG data is provided by *Refinitiv*. The data is available for different companies from different markets in the *Refinitiv Eikon* database. The *Refinitiv* ESG framework consists of ten subcategories that formulate the three pillar scores as well as the overall ESG score Fig. 1 depicts the components of each pillar that constitutes the ESG score for a company.

In *Refinitiv ESG Score* methodology,[1] the scores in each subcategory come from more than 180 key performance indicators. The scores are aggregated into pillars in the first stage using a weighted average method. The weights for each subcategory are obtained relying on the number of indicators that define them. The pillar scores are then aggregated into a single ESG score for each company. The percentile rank scores for the overall ESG scores and the subcategories are all scaled at a range from 0 to 100 (Berg et al., 2020; Refinitiv, 2022a, 2022b). The types of scores at each pillar and their definitions are listed in Table 2.

Within the scope of this research, ESG data for the energy companies in OECD countries are collected from *the Refinitiv EIKON* database for 231 companies. The level of data is associated with the subcategories of three main pillars of ESG. The scores are obtained for the ten subcategories listed in Table 2, separately. Therefore, the data set consists of 231 alternatives with ten criteria.

[1] The reader may refer to Refinitiv (2022a) for more information on the ESG score methodology. Note that recently, the scoring is extended to ESGC scores, where "C" stands for *ESG controversies* score. In this research, we focus on the ESG component.

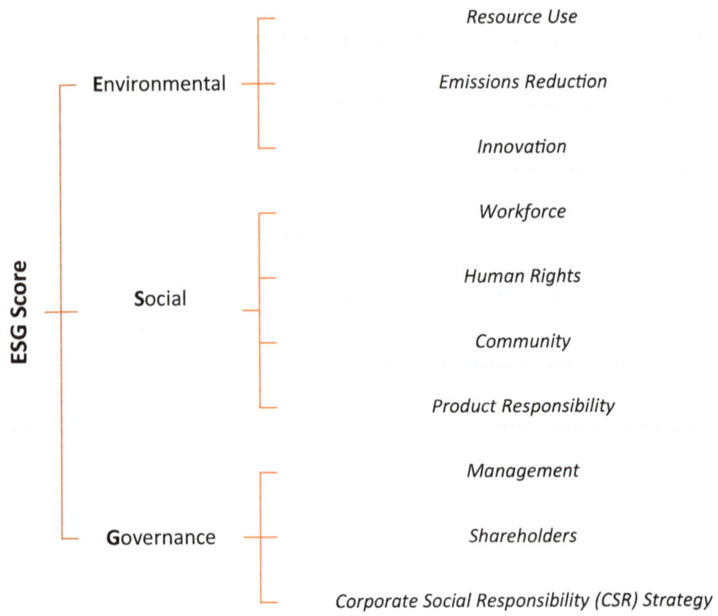

Fig. 1 Pillars and subcategories of refinitiv ESG scores

When the data set is examined, it is observed that the companies in the sample belong to ten different categories in terms of *Thomson Reuters Business Classifications (TRBC)* (see Refinitiv, 2022b). The frequencies of the companies in the data set with respect to these business classifications are given in Table 3. The majority of the companies operate in *the Oil and Gas Exploration and Production* category followed by *Oil Related Services and Equipment* and *Oil and Gas Refining and Marketing*. It is observed that Oil and Gas-related companies dominate the data set.

The companies in the data set are all headquartered in the OECD countries. The country of headquarters information for the companies in the data set is presented in Table 4. The majority of the firms are from the United States of America (USA) followed by Canada, Australia, and the United Kingdom.

The descriptive statistics in each ESG subcategory are provided in Table 5. Note that the abbreviations given in Table 2 are used to identify the subcategories. The data is quite homogeneous with mean values distributed between 40 and 60 except for the *Innovation* subcategory in *the Environmental* pillar with a mean of 19.44 and too many zeros in the data.

Considering the homogeneity of the ESG data which is scaled between 0 and 100, the companies are comparable despite the economic size difference. In the following section, we explain the basics of the clustering algorithm utilized.

Table 2 Definitions for ESG scores

Pillar	Score category	Definition
Environmental	Resource use (RES)	The resource use score represents a company's performance and ability to reduce its use of resources, such as water, energy, and materials, as well as to discover more environmentally friendly solutions by streamlining its supply chain management
	Emissions reduction (EMISSION)	The emission reduction score evaluates a company's dedication and success in decreasing environmental emissions throughout its operating and production processes
	Innovation (INNOV)	The innovation score measures a company's ability to lower customers' environmental costs and burdens, opening up new market potential through innovative environmental technology, processes, or environmentally conscious product design
Social	Workforce (WORK)	The workforce score evaluates how effectively a business treats its employees in terms of job satisfaction, a safe and healthy work environment, preserving diversity and equal opportunity, and giving possibilities for growth
	Human rights (HUMAN)	The human rights score evaluates how well a business upholds fundamental human rights principles
	Community (COMM)	The community score evaluates a company's dedication to upholding business ethics, safeguarding the public's health, and being a responsible corporate citizen
	Product responsibility (PRODRES)	The product responsibility score represents a company's ability to provide high-quality goods and services while incorporating the health and safety of the customer, integrity, and data privacy
Governance	Management (MAN)	The management score represents a company's effectiveness and dedication to adhering to the best practices in corporate governance

(continued)

Table 2 (continued)

Pillar	Score category	Definition
	Shareholders (SHAREHOLD)	The shareholder score is defined as a company's success in implementing anti-takeover safeguards and treating shareholders fairly
	CSR strategy (CSR)	The CSR strategy score is based on how well a company communicates and how it incorporates economic (financial), social, and environmental considerations into daily decision-making

Source Refinitiv (2022a)

Table 3 Thomson Reuters Business Classifications (TRBC)

	Industry name	# of companies
1	Coal	11
2	Integrated Oil and Gas	6
3	Oil and Gas drilling	6
4	Oil and Gas exploration and production	68
5	Oil and Gas refining and marketing	36
6	Oil and Gas transportation services	22
7	Oil related services and equipment	51
8	Renewable energy equipment and services	22
9	Renewable fuels	8
10	Uranium	1
Total		231

4 Methodology

Of the two main approaches of grouping a set of alternatives (classification and clustering), the current research focuses on clustering. Clustering is preferred to classification because of its unsupervised nature with no requirement for predefined information for the groups of the alternatives. With the data set of 231 companies' ESG performances in ten dimensions, we apply *the k-means* clustering approach to group alternatives that are similar without any hierarchical relationship between the clusters. *The k-means* algorithm is one of the most influential and well-recognized clustering techniques (see MacQueen, 1967; Lloyd, 1982 for seminal research). This algorithm is an unsupervised clustering method to identify patterns in multi-dimensional data. The applications of the method are widespread in the Operations Research literature and range from facility location to risk prediction (Borgwardt et al., 2017). Below, we explain the basics of the *k-means* algorithm.

Table 4 Country of headquarters

	Country	#		Country	#
1	Australia	20	14	Japan	7
2	Austria	3	15	South Korea	1
3	Belgium	2	16	Luxembourg	1
4	Canada	25	17	Mexico	1
5	Chile	1	18	Netherlands	6
6	Denmark	1	19	New Zealand	2
7	Finland	2	20	Norway	9
8	France	8	21	Spain	3
9	Germany	4	22	Sweden	6
10	Hungary	1	23	Switzerland	2
11	Iceland	1	24	Turkey	2
12	Israel	1	25	United Kingdom	19
13	Italy	2	26	United States of America	101

K-means is an iterative algorithm that divides a set X of N objects in $\mathbb{R}^{\mathrm{d}}$ into $k \geq 2$ clusters so that the objects in each cluster are distinct from one another and similar to one another (Pérez-Ortega et al., 2019; Vattani, 2009). By minimizing the sum of squared distances between each data point and its nearest cluster center (centroid), the *k-means* algorithm groups all of the data points (N) into clusters (k). We begin with defining a *d-dimensional* set of n data points as $X = \{x_1, \ldots, x_n\}$. The refined clustering as the result of an iterative method as a *d-dimensional* set of k centers is defined as $C = \{c_1, \ldots, c_k\}$.

The *k-means* algorithm minimizes the objective function given in (1) (Hammerly & Elkan, 2002).

$$\mathrm{KM}(X, C) = \sum_{i=1}^{N} \min_{j \in \{1 \ldots k\}} \|x_i - c_j^2\|. \tag{1}$$

An iterative algorithm that minimizes variance (the square of the distance between each center and the allocated data points) within the clusters is generated by this objective function. The members of clusters are obtained by *k-means'* membership and weight functions that are given in (2) and (3).

$$\mathrm{membership}(c_j|x_i) = \begin{cases} 1; \text{ if } \; I = \arg\min_j \|x_i - c_j^2\| \\ 0; \text{ otherwise} \end{cases}, \tag{2}$$

$$\mathrm{weight}(x_i) = 1. \tag{3}$$

Table 5 Descriptive statistics of the data

	RES	EMISSION	INNOV	WORK	HUMAN	COMM	PRODRES	MAN	SHAREHOLD	CSR
Mean	41.29	45.85	19.44	50.43	39.90	52.67	46.07	55.76	56.71	45.06
Median	41.35	46.36	0.00	49.34	38.37	54.74	29.37	56.76	58.41	49.71
Std. dev.	33.80	32.82	28.93	29.26	35.75	27.29	28.39	29.48	26.88	33.23
Range	99.68	99.82	83.67	99.06	94.57	98.52	99.72	96.97	93.50	99.68
Minimum	0.00	0.00	0.00	0.77	0.00	1.32	0.00	2.45	6.04	0.00
Maximum	99.68	99.82	83.67	99.83	94.57	99.83	99.72	99.42	99.55	99.68
Count	231	231	231	231	231	231	231	231	231	231

Since the method is unsupervised, the number of clusters is usually identified with an exploratory approach that relies on tests with different *k* values. Within the scope of research, the k value for the given data set is identified as 5, which produces a relatively good pattern structure after tests with a different number of clusters.

5 Findings and Implications

We design the clustering scheme around the three pillars of ESG. The energy companies in the data set are clustered in each pillar as *Environmental, Social,* and *Governance* with the data of given subcategories. *The Environmental* pillar considers three dimensions as Resource Use, Emissions Reduction, and Innovation. The *Social* pillar consists of four subcategories as Human Rights, Product Responsibility, Workforce, and Community. *Governance* takes Management, Shareholders, and CSR Strategy subcategories into account. The findings of the *k-means* analysis in three levels are presented in this section.

The number of companies in each cluster with respect to the *Environmental, Social,* and *Governance* subcategories is presented in Table 6. The majority of the companies are in Cluster 2 in *Environmental* and *Social* performance, whereas Cluster 3 is the most crowded in the *Governance* pillar. Since the clustering is non-hierarchical, these frequencies do not tell much about the performance. To better understand, we seek commonalities in each dimension in the following subsections.

5.1 Clusters in Environmental Pillar

The *Environmental* pillar consists of three subcategories as Resource Use, Emissions Reduction, and Innovation. The number of companies in each cluster is presented with respect to *Thomson Reuters Business Classifications (TRBC)* in Table 7 and with respect to the country of headquarters in Table 8 of the Appendix. To observe the patterns between clusters, Fig. 2 presents the mean values of subcategory scores in each cluster. It can be observed that in all subcategories, Cluster 3 attains the highest

Table 6 Number of companies in each cluster

Clusters	Environmental	Social	Governance
1	33	38	44
2	84	76	46
3	32	39	66
4	57	54	43
5	25	24	32
Total	231	231	231

mean value and there is a clear pattern of low mean values in Cluster 2. Therefore, it can be said that Cluster 2 and 3 can represent the low- and high-performance clusters, respectively. Note that in terms of environmental performance, the majority of the companies are in Cluster 2 (see Table 6).

After identifying that Clusters 2 and 3 are prominent in the sense of environmental performance, we can have a deeper look at these two noteworthy clusters. Figure 3 depicts the business classifications of Clusters 3 and 2, in upper and lower panels, respectively. It presents the portion of the total number of companies in each classification that are grouped into Cluster 3 and Cluster 2 by *the k-means* algorithm. For instance, 38% of all companies in the Renewable Fuels classification are in Cluster 2, whereas 25% of them are in Cluster 2. It can be seen that companies from 7 out of 10 classifications are reported to be in Cluster 3 (high performance) and companies from 9 out of 10 classifications are in Cluster 2.

Recall that the majority of the companies in the whole data set (68 out of 231) operate in *Oil and Gas Exploration and Production* (see Table 3). Interestingly, almost half of the companies in this category are members of Cluster 2 in environmental performance. Only 3% of companies in *Oil and Gas Exploration and Production* are in Cluster 3. The same pattern is observed for other populous classifications such as *Oil Related Services and Equipment* and *Oil and Gas Refining and Marketing*. In these subsectors, environmental performance tends to be lower. On the other hand, in renewable-associated subsectors, the portion of companies in Cluster 3 is higher. *Coal*, *Uranium*, and *Oil and Gas Drilling* subsectors have no companies in Cluster 3.

We perform a similar examination in terms of the country of headquarters. Figure 4 presents the distribution of countries in Clusters 3 and 2 in upper and lower panels, respectively. Some countries have no company that is clustered into Clusters 2 and/or 3. Observe that only 8% of the US companies are in Cluster 3 (high performance). On the other hand, half of the US energy companies in the data set are in Cluster 2 regarding environmental performance. Similarly, companies in Australia are mainly in Cluster 2. Only 5% of Australian companies are in the high-performance cluster (Cluster 3). 60% of Australian companies are in Cluster 2. Note that only half of the countries listed in Table 4 have companies in Cluster 3. Some countries such as New Zealand, Luxembourg, Israel, and Chile with a smaller number of companies in the data set have all their companies in Cluster 2. On the contrary, Spain and Denmark

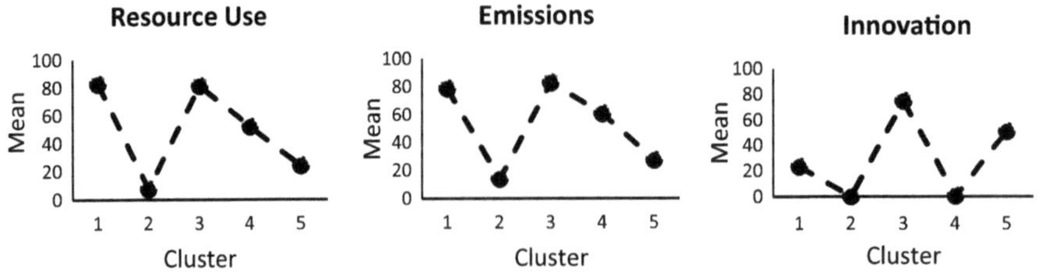

Fig. 2 Mean values of the *environmental* subcategories

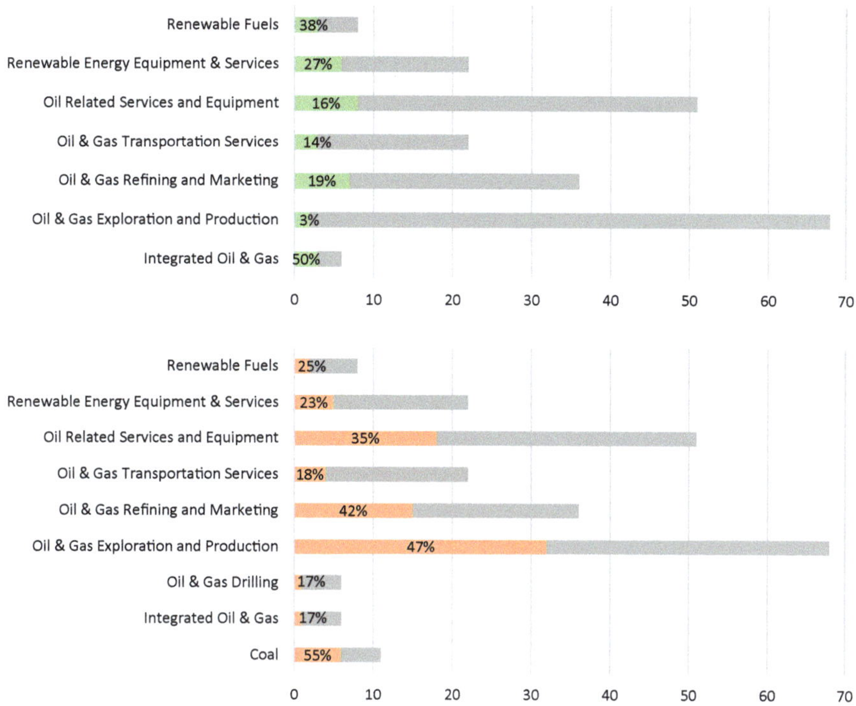

Fig. 3 Business classifications of Cluster 3 (upper panel) and Cluster 2 (lower panel) *(environmental)*

have all their companies in a high-performance cluster in terms of the *Environmental* pillar.

5.2 *Clusters in Social Pillar*

The *Social* pillar consists of four subcategories as Workforce, Human Rights, Community, and Product Responsibility. The number of companies in each cluster is presented with respect to *Thomson Reuters Business Classifications (TRBC)* in Table 9 and with respect to the country of headquarters in Table 10 of the Appendix. As in the Environmental pillar, to observe the patterns between clusters, we produce Fig. 5 which depicts the mean values of subcategory scores in each cluster. In terms of *Social* performance, Cluster 4 attains the highest mean value in all subcategories, representing a high-performance cluster. Low mean values are observed in Cluster 2. Cluster 2 is also the most populated (see Table 6).

Relying on the observations from Fig. 5, Clusters 2 and 4 are examined as representatives of low and high performance in the *Social* pillar, respectively. Different

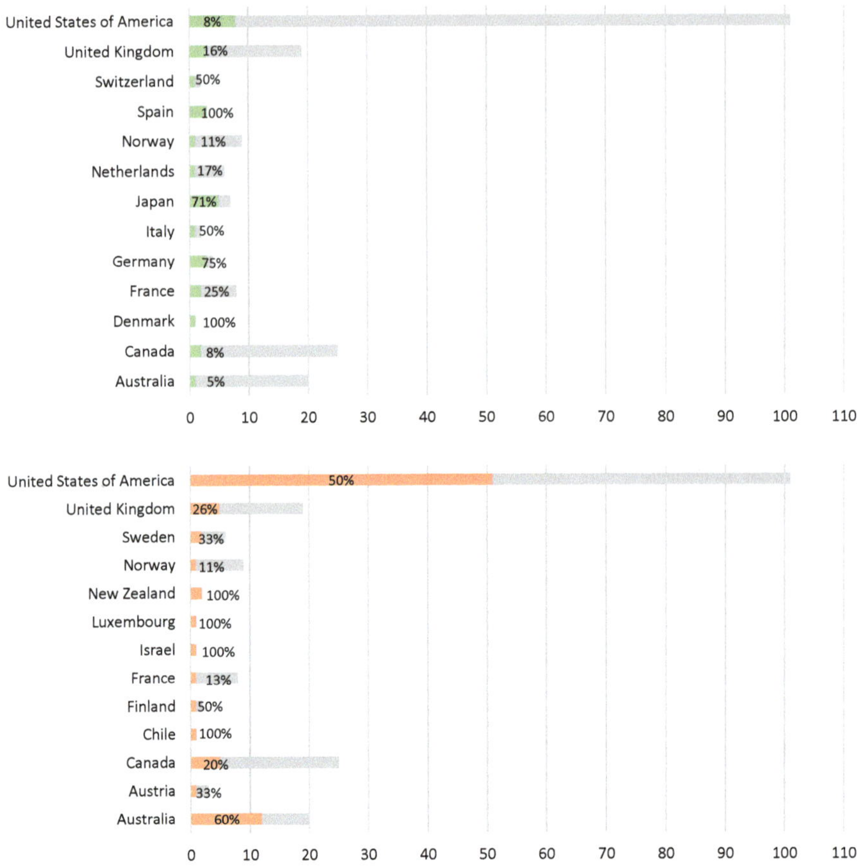

Fig. 4 Countries of headquarters in Cluster 3 (upper panel) and Cluster 2 (lower panel) *(environmental)*

classifications are observed between the two clusters. In Cluster 4, companies from *Oil Related Services and Equipment* and *Oil and Gas Refining and Marketing* classifications dominate in number, whereas in the low-performance cluster (Cluster 2) *Oil and Gas Exploration and Production* companies are dominant (see Table 9 in Appendix).

Figure 6 depicts the business classifications of Clusters 4 and 2, in upper and lower panels, respectively. It presents the portion of the total number of companies in each classification that are grouped into Cluster 4 and Cluster 2 by *the k-means* algorithm. As in the environmental performance, *Oil and Gas Exploration and Production* classification has the lowest portion in the high-performance cluster (Cluster 4) and the majority in the low-performance cluster (Cluster 2). Interestingly, the Oil and Gas Refining and Marketing subsector have the majority of the companies in either Cluster 4 (36%) or Cluster 2 (44%). As for environmental performance, there are no

Fig. 5 Mean values of the *social* subcategories

companies belonging to *Coal* and *Oil and Gas Drilling* classifications in Cluster 4. The single company from the *Uranium* classification is grouped under Cluster 4 in *Social* performance.

A similar exploration can be made in terms of the country of headquarters. Figure 7 presents the distribution of countries in Clusters 4 and 2. Similar to environmental performance, not all countries have companies in high and low-performance clusters. The major set in the whole data set (US companies) produces a similar result to environmental performance. Regarding the *Social* scores, only 15% of US companies are in Cluster 4, whereas 42% of the companies headquartered in the US are in Cluster 2 indicating low performance in *the Social* pillar. The portion of low-performance companies in Australia is slightly lower in *the Social* pillar than *in the Environmental* pillar. Turkey, Spain, Italy, Hungary, and Denmark have all their companies in high-performance clusters. On the other hand, Israel, Iceland, and Chile (that have only one company) get their companies clustered in the low-performance cluster in *the Social* pillar.

5.3 *Clusters in Governance Pillar*

The final ESG pillar to be analyzed is *Governance* consisting of three subcategories as Management, Shareholders, and CSR Strategy. The companies are also clustered using *Governance* scores. The number of companies in each cluster is presented with respect to *Thomson Reuters Business Classifications (TRBC)* in Table 11 and

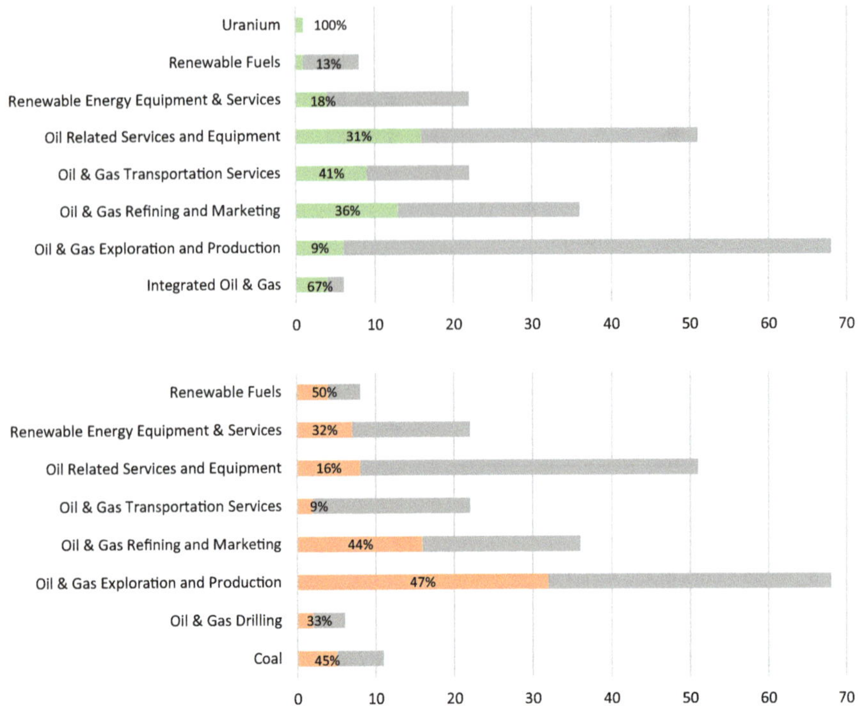

Fig. 6 Business classifications of Cluster 4 (upper panel) and Cluster 2 (lower panel) *(social)*

with respect to the country of headquarters in Table 12 of the Appendix. In Fig. 8, we seek a pattern between clusters using mean values of subcategory scores in each cluster. Regarding the *Governance* pillar, Cluster 3 seems to be representing the highest-performing cluster in all subcategories. When Table 6 is examined, it can be seen that this cluster is also the highest-populated cluster. Unlike *Environmental* and *Social* performance, in *Governance*, the majority of the companies are clustered in the high-performance group. In *Governance* performance, Cluster 4 is the low-performance cluster with the lowest mean scores in all subcategories. Let us further explore Clusters 3 and 4.

Figure 9 reveals the business classifications of Clusters 3 and 4, in upper and lower panels, respectively. It presents the portion of the total number of companies in each classification that are grouped into Cluster 3 and Cluster 4 by *the k-means* algorithm.

The domination of companies in *Oil and Gas Exploration and Production* classification in low-performance clusters is reversed in *Governance* performance. The majority of high-performance companies (Cluster 3) are from this classification (see Table 11 in the Appendix). Besides, 35% of the companies in this subsector are in the high-performance cluster (Cluster 3), whereas only 13% are in Cluster 4 indicating low performance. This case was the opposite in the *Environmental* and *Social* pillars.

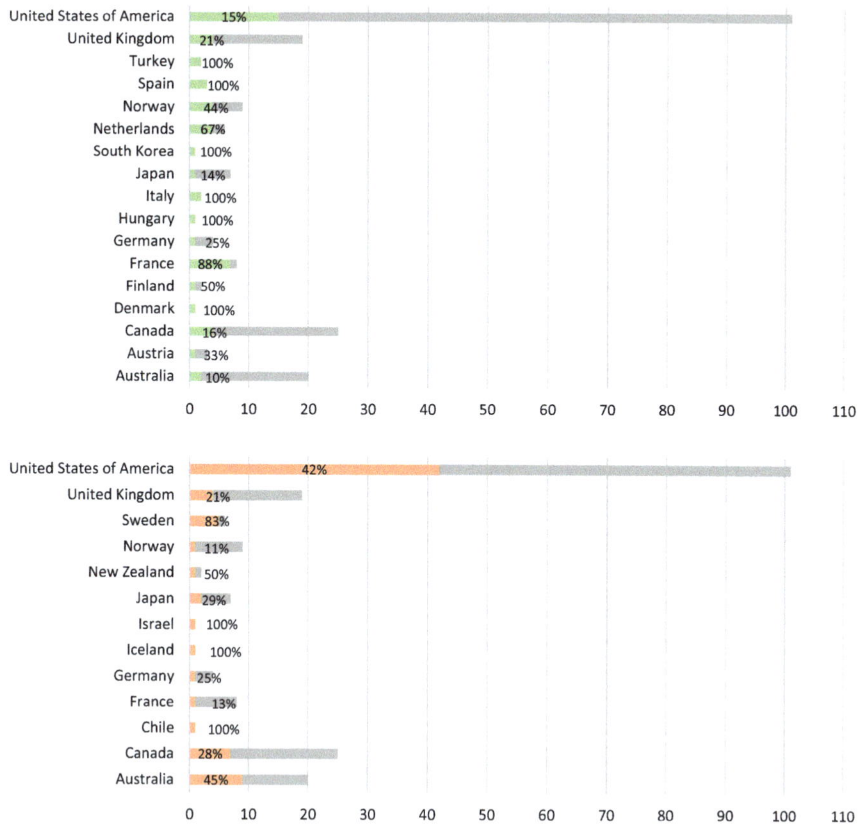

Fig. 7 Countries of headquarters in Cluster 3 (upper panel) and Cluster 2 (lower panel) (*social*)

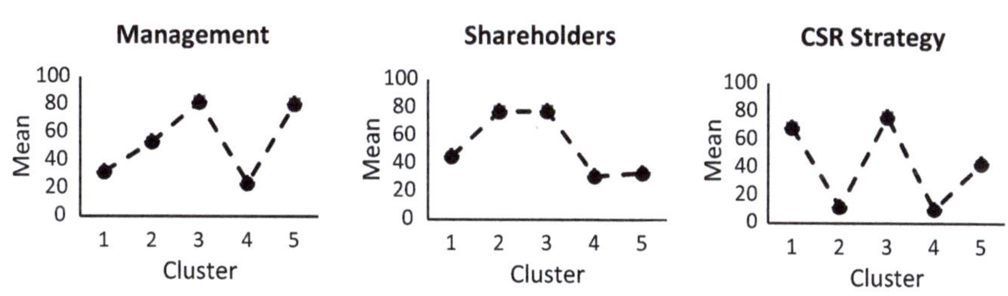

Fig. 8 Mean values of the *governance* subcategories

In Fig. 9, especially for Cluster 4, a more even distribution of the companies between the business classifications is observed compared to *Environmental* and *Social* performances. Having the majority of the companies in the high-performance cluster, we can say that the Governance performance of the companies in the data set is more balanced. Let us look at the distribution of the companies' headquarters. It

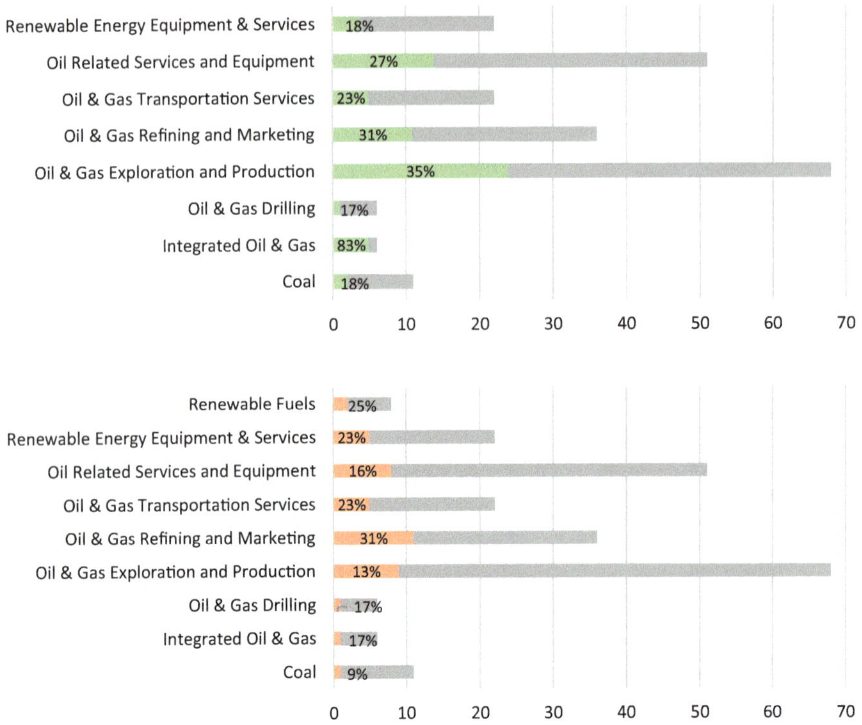

Fig. 9 Business classifications of Cluster 4 (upper panel) and Cluster 3 (lower panel) *(governance)*

is observed that US, UK, and Australian companies dominate the high-performance cluster (see Table 12 in Appendix). This pattern is also adverse to what is observed in *Environmental* and *Social* performance. Looking at Fig. 10 which presents the distribution of countries in Clusters 3 and 4, we observe that the companies from the UK, Canada, and Australia have more companies in the high-performance cluster (Cluster 3) than the low-performance cluster (Cluster 4). US companies show a more balanced distribution. The companies from Israel and Chile are also in the low-performance cluster (Cluster 4) as is the case in the other two pillars.

Above, with the help of non-hierarchical clustering, the patterns in the ESG performance of the companies are identified. Similarities regarding the distribution of the companies exist between *Environmental* (*E*) and *Social* (*S*) performance. On the other hand, the distribution has slight differences in terms of *Governance* (*G*) performance. In general, there exist clear-cut clusters that can be representative of high and low performance in all *E*, *S*, and *G* pillars. The majority of the companies are in low-performance clusters in *E* and *S*, while the majority are in the high-performance cluster in *G*. Regarding the sectors, *Oil and Gas Exploration and Production* companies, which are the majority in the data set, are mostly in low-performance clusters in *E* and *S*. These companies relatively score better in *G*. Companies of *Oil Related Services and Equipment* and *Oil and Gas Refining and Marketing* show a

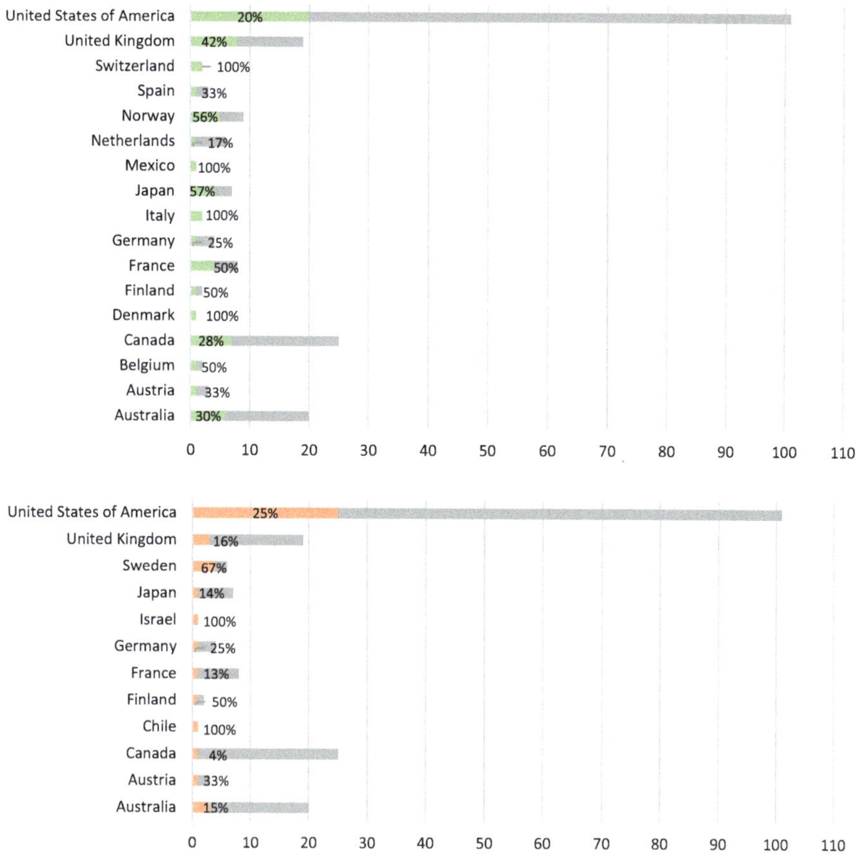

Fig. 10 Countries of headquarters in Cluster 3 (upper panel) and Cluster 4 (lower panel) (*governance)*

more balanced distribution between high and low-performance clusters. On the other hand, as would be expected, the companies from renewable-related subsectors are mainly in the high-performance cluster in *E*. Regarding countries of operation, the majority of the US energy companies in the data set are in low-performance clusters in *E* and *S*. The distribution between clusters is more balanced in *G*. Australia, Canada, and the UK have more energy companies in the low-performance cluster than in the high-performance cluster in *E*. The same is true for Canada and Australia in *S*. Nevertheless, for *G*, the relationship is reversed.

6 Conclusion

Defining and evaluating Environmental, Social, and Governance (ESG) characteristics of companies as well as integrating data consistency are contemporary issues regarding sustainable investment decisions. Energy markets with their dynamism, size, and impact are one of the main areas in that ESG concepts should be incorporated. Considering that the ESG framework is multiple criteria in nature, it is highly suitable for the utilization of Multiple Criteria Decision Analysis (MCDA) methodologies. These methods are widely used in decision-making processes with a set of alternatives to be *selected*, *ranked*, *clustered*, or *classified* with respect to multiple and potentially conflicting criteria, which is very relevant for the analysis of ESG data.

In this research, we propose clustering as a tool for ESG analysis for companies. Our domain is public energy companies in OECD countries. A data set of 231 companies are analyzed using a *k-means* clustering algorithm under three pillars of ESG as *Environmental, Social,* and *Governance* corresponding to ten different subcategories. The classification problem is undertaken in three pillars separately and the companies are clustered in a non-hierarchical order. In the identified clusters, patterns are investigated mainly in the clusters that may represent high and low performance. Prescriptive discussions are provided with respect to two main characteristics of the companies as business classification and country of headquarters.

The findings reveal that clustering enables us to identify the conflicting areas of ESG performance without any predefined information on clusters or any controversies in weighting. Within the domain of ESG performance of energy companies, we demonstrate that as a way of grouping the alternatives in an unsupervised manner, clustering can be an effective alternative tool for evaluating ESG at different levels of aggregation. We mainly discuss the patterns with a more macro look through the business classifications and countries of headquarters; however, it is also possible to present company-level evaluations by examining the clusters that the companies are assigned by the algorithm.

Appendix

See Tables 7, 8, 9, 10, 11, and 12.

Table 7 Number of TRBC industries in each cluster (environmental)

TRBC Industry Name	Cluster 1	Cluster 2	Cluster 3	Cluster 4	Cluster 5	Total
Coal		6		4	1	**11**
Integrated Oil & Gas	1	1	3	1		**6**
Oil & Gas Drilling		1		4	1	**6**
Oil & Gas Exploration and Production	7	32	2	27		**68**
Oil & Gas Refining and Marketing	12	15	7	1	1	**36**
Oil & Gas Transportation Services	3	4	3	11	1	**22**
Oil Related Services and Equipment	9	18	8	8	8	**51**
Renewable Energy Equipment & Services		5	6	1	10	**22**
Renewable Fuels		2	3		3	**8**
Uranium	1					**1**
Total	**33**	**84**	**32**	**57**	**25**	**231**

Note TRBC stands for Thomson Reuters Business Classification, which is an industry classification of global companies.

Table 8 Number of countries of headquarters in each cluster (environmental)

Countries	Cluster 1	Cluster 2	Cluster 3	Cluster 4	Cluster 5	Total
Australia	2	12	1	4	1	**20**
Austria	1	1		1		**3**
Belgium				2		**2**
Canada	4	5	2	9	5	**25**
Chile		1				**1**
Denmark			1			**1**
Finland	1	1				**2**
France	3	1	2	2		**8**
Germany			3		1	**4**
Hungary	1					**1**
Iceland	1					**1**
Israel		1				**1**
Italy	1		1			**2**
Japan			5	1	1	**7**
South Korea	1					**1**
Luxembourg		1				**1**
Mexico				1		**1**
Netherlands	2		1	1	2	**6**
New Zealand		2				**2**
Norway	3	1	1	4		**9**
Spain			3			**3**
Sweden		2		1	3	**6**
Switzerland			1	1		**2**
Turkey	2					**2**
United Kingdom	4	5	3	6	1	**19**
United States of America	7	51	8	24	11	**101**
Total	**33**	**84**	**32**	**57**	**25**	**231**

Table 9 Number of TRBC Industries in each cluster (social)

TRBC Industry Name	Cluster 1	Cluster 2	Cluster 3	Cluster 4	Cluster 5	Total
Coal		5	3		3	**11**
Integrated Oil & Gas			1	4	1	**6**
Oil & Gas Drilling	2	2			2	**6**
Oil & Gas Exploration and Production	3	32	15	6	12	**68**
Oil & Gas Refining and Marketing	7	16		13		**36**
Oil & Gas Transportation Services	6	2	3	9	2	**22**
Oil Related Services and Equipment	14	8	10	16	3	**51**
Renewable Energy Equipment & Services	4	7	6	4	1	**22**
Renewable Fuels	2	4	1	1		**8**
Uranium				1		**1**
Total	**38**	**76**	**39**	**54**	**24**	**231**

Note TRBC stands for Thomson Reuters Business Classification, which is an industry classification of global companies.

Table 10 Number of countries of headquarters in each cluster (social)

Countries	Cluster 1	Cluster 2	Cluster 3	Cluster 4	Cluster 5	Total
Australia	2	9	3	2	4	**20**
Austria	2			1		**3**
Belgium	2					**2**
Canada	5	7	4	4	5	**25**
Chile		1				**1**
Denmark				1		**1**
Finland	1			1		**2**
France		1		7		**8**
Germany	1	1	1	1		**4**
Hungary				1		**1**
Iceland		1				**1**
Israel		1				**1**
Italy				2		**2**
Japan	3	2	1	1		**7**
South Korea				1		**1**
Luxembourg	1					**1**
Mexico			1			**1**
Netherlands	1			4	1	**6**
New Zealand	1	1				**2**
Norway		1	4	4		**9**
Spain				3		**3**
Sweden		5	1			**6**
Switzerland	1				1	**2**
Turkey				2		**2**
United Kingdom	2	4	7	4	2	**19**
United States of America	16	42	17	15	11	**101**
Total	**38**	**76**	**39**	**54**	**24**	**231**

Table 11 Number of TRBC Industries in each cluster (governance)

TRBC Industry Name	Cluster 1	Cluster 2	Cluster 3	Cluster 4	Cluster 5	Total
Coal	5	3	2	1		**11**
Integrated Oil & Gas			5	1		**6**
Oil & Gas Drilling	1		1	1	3	**6**
Oil & Gas Exploration and Production	12	13	24	9	10	**68**
Oil & Gas Refining and Marketing	5	5	11	11	4	**36**
Oil & Gas Transportation Services	6	4	5	5	2	**22**
Oil Related Services and Equipment	3	16	14	8	10	**51**
Renewable Energy Equipment & Services	10	3	4	5		**22**
Renewable Fuels	2	2		2	2	**8**
Uranium					1	**1**
Total	**44**	**46**	**66**	**43**	**32**	**231**

Note TRBC stands for Thomson Reuters Business Classification, which is an industry classification of global companies.

Table 12 Number of countries of headquarters in each cluster (governance)

Countries	Cluster 1	Cluster 2	Cluster 3	Cluster 4	Cluster 5	Total
Australia	4	3	6	3	4	**20**
Austria		1	1	1		**3**
Belgium		1	1			**2**
Canada	8	3	7	1	6	**25**
Chile				1		**1**
Denmark			1			**1**
Finland			1	1		**2**
France		2	4	1	1	**8**
Germany	1		1	1	1	**4**
Hungary	1					**1**
Iceland		1				**1**
Israel				1		**1**
Italy			2			**2**
Japan	1	1	4	1		**7**
South Korea					1	**1**
Luxembourg					1	**1**
Mexico			1			**1**
Netherlands	3	2	1			**6**
New Zealand	2					**2**
Norway		4	5			**9**
Spain	1		1		1	**3**
Sweden	1	1		4		**6**
Switzerland			2			**2**
Turkey	1				1	**2**
United Kingdom	3		8	3	5	**19**
United States of America	18	27	20	25	11	**101**
Total	**44**	**46**	**66**	**43**	**32**	**231**

References

Apergis, N., Poufinas, T., & Antonopoulos, A. (2022). ESG scores and cost of debt. *Energy Economics, 112*, 106186.

Berg, F., Fabisik, K., & Sautner, Z. (2020). Rewriting history II: The (un) predictable past of ESG ratings. *European Corporate Governance Institute–Finance Working Paper, 708*, 10–2139.

Borgwardt, S., Brieden, A., & Gritzmann, P. (2017). An LP-based *k-means* algorithm for balancing weighted point sets. *European Journal of Operational Research, 263*(2), 349–355.

Christensen, D. M., Serafeim, G., & Sikochi, A. (2022). Why is corporate virtue in the eye of the beholder? The case of ESG ratings. *The Accounting Review, 97*(1), 147–175.

Escrig-Olmedo, E., Rivera-Lirio, J. M., Muñoz-Torres, M. J., & Fernández-Izquierdo, M. Á. (2017). Integrating multiple ESG investors' preferences into sustainable investment: A fuzzy multicriteria methodological approach. *Journal of Cleaner Production, 162*, 1334–1345.

Greco, S., Figueira, J., & Ehrgott, M. (2016). *Multiple criteria decision analysis* (Vol. 37). Springer.

Guedhami, O., Louton, D. A., Saraoglu, H. & Zheng, Y. (2022). ESG investing: A decision-making paradox?. *Finance Journal Articles, 91*. https://digitalcommons.bryant.edu/finjou/91

Guedhami, O., Louton, D., Saraoglu, H., & Zheng, Y. (2022). ESG investing: A decision-making paradox? *The Journal of Impact and ESG Investing.*

Hamerly, G., & Elkan, C. (2002, November). Alternatives to the *k-means* algorithm that find better clusterings. In *Proceedings of the eleventh international conference on Information and knowledge management* (pp. 600–607).

Iamandi, I. E., Constantin, L. G., Munteanu, S. M., & Cernat-Gruici, B. (2019). Mapping the ESG behavior of European companies: A holistic Kohonen approach. *Sustainability, 11*(12), 3276.

Ishizaka, A., Lokman, B., & Tasiou, M. (2021). A stochastic multi-criteria divisive hierarchical clustering algorithm. *Omega, 103*, 102370.

Liern, V., & Pérez-Gladish, B. (2018). Ranking corporate sustainability: A flexible multidimensional approach based on linguistic variables. *International Transactions in Operational Research, 25*(3), 1081–1100.

Lin, A. J., Chang, H. Y., & Hung, B. (2022). Identifying key financial, environmental, social, governance (ESG), bond, and COVID-19 factors affecting global shipping companies—A hybrid multiple-criteria decision-making method. *Sustainability, 14*(9), 5148.

Lloyd, S. P. (1982). Least squares quantization in PCM. *IEEE Transactions Information Theory, 28*(2), 129–137.

MacQueen, J. (1967). Some methods for classification and analysis of multivariate observations. *Berkeley symposium on mathematical statistics and probability, Volume 1: Statistics* (pp. 281–297). University of California Press.

Pérez-Ortega, J., Almanza-Ortega, N. N., Vega-Villalobos, A., Pazos-Rangel, R., Zavala-Díaz, C., & Martínez-Rebollar, A. (2019). The *K-means* algorithm evolution. *Introduction to Data Science and Machine Learning.*

Refinitiv. (2022a). Environmental, social and governance (ESG) scores. Available at: https://www.refinitiv.com/content/dam/marketing/en_us/documents/methodology/refinitiv-esg-scores-methodology.pdf

Refinitiv. (2022b). TRBC sector classification. Available at: https://www.refinitiv.com/en/financial-data/indices/trbc-business-classification

Reig-Mullor, J., Garcia-Bernabeu, A., Pla-Santamaria, D., & Vercher-Ferrandiz, M. (2022). Evaluating ESG corporate performance using a new neutrosophic AHP-TOPSIS based approach. *Technological and Economic Development of Economy, 28*(5), 1242–1266.

Sariyer, G., & Taşkın, D. (2022). *Clustering of firms based on environmental, social, and governance ratings: Evidence from BIST sustainability index.* In press.

UN Global Compact. (2004). Who cares wins: Connecting financial markets to a changing world. *Global Compact.* Available at: www.globalcompact.org

Vattani, A. (2009). *K-means* requires exponentially many iterations even in the plane. In *Proceedings of the twenty-fifth annual symposium on computational geometry* (pp. 324–332).

Vilas, P., Andreu, L., & Sarto, J. L. (2022). Cluster analysis to validate the sustainability label of stock indices: An analysis of the inclusion and exclusion processes in terms of size and ESG ratings. *Journal of Cleaner Production, 330*, 129862.

Ziolo, M., Filipiak, B. Z., Bąk, I., & Cheba, K. (2019). How to design more sustainable financial systems: The roles of environmental, social, and governance factors in the decision-making process. *Sustainability, 11*(20), 5604.

The Impact of Renewable Energy Incentives on Carbon Prices in the USA

Esin Hilal Çoşkun, A. Sevtap Selcuk-Kestel, and Serdar Dalkir

Abstract Many studies examining the price of CO_2 have analyzed mostly the EU ETC market and attempted to explain the relationship between energy prices and CO_2 emissions. This chapter investigates the dynamics and price determinants of the US CO_2 market and aims to capture the decrease in carbon prices (CO_2) with increasing incentives to renewable energy sources, in conjunction with economic growth, energy prices, and carbon permits. For this purpose, we analyze the carbon market prices, specific to the US energy markets, since there the carbon prices are low compared to other countries. We assume that the reason is the apparent increase in the incentives toward renewable energy sources. To explore the reasons and justifications, we employ econometric methods on data from the US market. In this context, linear regression, VEC model, and panel data analysis are performed according to their applicability and use. The findings show that CO_2 prices are influenced strongly by the renewable portfolio standards as well as carbon allowances and industrial production.

Keywords CO_2 prices · Renewable portfolio standards · Regional greenhouse gas initiative · Carbon permits

1 Introduction

Significant climate changes are associated with an increase in the atmospheric density of certain gases, particularly CO_2. Along with the utilization of the fossil sources, the energy production requires the development of new sources, especially the ones whose sustainability and efficiency against climate change remain consistent. Assessments by the Intergovernmental Panel on Climate Change show that the Earth's

E. H. Çoşkun · A. S. Selcuk-Kestel (✉) · S. Dalkir
Institute of Applied Mathematics, Middle East Technical University, Ankara 06800, Turkey
e-mail: skestel@metu.edu.tr

S. Dalkir
CRETC, Competition & Regulation Economics Testimony and Consulting LLC, Washington, DC, USA

J. Thewissen et al. (eds.), *The ESG Framework and the Energy Industry*,
https://doi.org/10.1007/978-3-031-48457-5_7

climate heated up to 0.85 °C (1.53 degrees Fahrenheit) between 1880 and 2012; and that human activities affecting the atmosphere are probably an important factor (EIA, 2019). The countries having the highest influence on the carbon emission in 2017 are ranked as China (12,454 $MtCO_2e$) and the USA (6673 $MtCO_2e$), followed by the European Union (4424 $MtCO_2e$), India (2379 $MtCO_2e$), and Russia (2199 $MtCO_2e$) (EIA, 2019).

In 1994, the United Nations Framework Convention on Climate Change (UNFCCC) and then in 1997 the Kyoto Protocol (KP) were established with the goal to stop the atmospheric greenhouse gas accumulation and prevent climate change (UN, 2015). Elasticity mechanisms (Joint Implementation, Clean Development Mechanism, and Emission Trading) and the protocol to achieve greenhouse gas decrease targets between 2013 and 2020 have resulted in 42 emission trading systems to operate in the scope of Emissions Trading as of 2015. Markets are concentrated in these regions in parallel with the USA, Canada, EU, Australia, New Zealand, China, and Japan, which are the main players in climate change negotiations. Reducing human-activity-generated greenhouse gas emissions varies by country because of costs and regulations. The flexibility mechanisms recognized in the KP are expected to lower the costs and thus to benefit the implementing countries.

The Paris Agreement, adopted in 2015 under the United Nations Framework Convention on Climate Change (UNFCCC), represents a seminal international treaty in the realm of climate change mitigation. Its overarching objective is to limit the global average temperature increase to well below 2° above pre-industrial levels, while pursuing efforts to further restrict the increase to 1.5° (Evensen, 2017). The agreement recognizes the urgent need to reduce greenhouse gas emissions and underscores the imperative of transitioning toward a sustainable, low-carbon economy.

In the USA, renewable portfolio standards (RPS) have emerged as a policy mechanism designed to advance the goals articulated within the Paris Agreement. Implemented at the state level, RPS policies mandate specific renewable energy procurement targets for utilities operating within each jurisdiction (Kelly, 2019).

A carbon market is seen as an important tool in reducing emissions if it operates following the market rules in which carbon credits (carbon certificates) are obtained within defined exchange rates and standards. These certificates are purchased and sold to prevent or reduce greenhouse gases, especially CO_2. Such a market penalizes those who emit more than the prescribed limit, while those that emit less are rewarded to ensure that the available resources are used at the lowest cost. Besides, the carbon market makes it possible to trade carbon all over the world by converting the charged pollution units into ownership rights. Thus, it encourages enterprises to use clean technology by reducing the greenhouse gas emissions. The emission trading system (ETS) sets an upper limit (cap) for greenhouse gas emissions arising from the facilities covered by the system, which provides policymakers with certainty as to the amount of emissions that will take place over a period. The Regional Greenhouse Gas Initiative (RGGI) in the USA is the first mandatory market-based cap and trade program to reduce CO_2 emissions from electricity generation in the Northeastern US states.

On the other hand, increasing the use of renewable energy is known to reduce carbon emissions as they do not contain CO_2 like fossil sources. Solar, wind, biomass, geothermal, and hydropower energies are the main types of renewable energy sources which are available depending on a country's geographical and geopolitical situation. Therefore, a tax policy that encourages the reduction of fossil fuel and the use of renewable energy sources contributes to the reduction of environmental externalities (Herber & Raga, 1995). For these reasons, it is vital to investigate the relationship between the main drivers of the carbon price in the RGGI and to explain the relationship between the CO_2 price and the renewable energy policy components. The literature offers extensive research to investigate the carbon pricing mechanism, mostly on the EU. Many studies show that energy prices are the main drivers of the carbon price in the allowance market. Also, weather conditions, policy options like the emission target, and renewable energy subsidies are found to be the main determinants of the EU-ETS carbon price (Chevallier, 2011; Mansanet-Bataller et al., 2007; Reboredo, 2013). In addition to energy prices, it is found that there exists a significant additional effect of weather conditions, such as unexpected temperature changes, on the EU-ETS carbon price (Alberola et al., 2008; Rickels et al., 2007, 2010). The economic situation of the country, the carbon price in the EU-ETS and its drivers (policy instruments such as energy prices, weather conditions, and renewable energy incentives) (Koch et al., 2014), renewable energy use (Hintermann, 2010; Van den Bergh et al., 2013; Abrell & Weigt, 2008) are the main factors affecting carbon prices. Kim and Koo (2010) emphasize that besides changes in crude oil and natural gas prices, the price of coal is also a key factor affecting the volume of carbon allowance trading and has a significant impact on the carbon allowance market. Besides, there is evidence that the temperature and economic crises in the USA have had significant impact on the carbon allowance trade volume. Research investigating the relation among the RGGI carbon price and energy prices in the northeastern USA (Kim & Lee, 2015) has found that the natural gas price has a positive effect on the carbon price of RGGI, but it is not affected by RGGI, whereas the CO_2 and coal prices are negatively related.

The literature points out that economic activity, energy prices, and renewable energy are the main drivers for carbon prices (Chun et al., 2022; Chevallier, 2011; Van den Bergh et al., 2013; Hammoudeh et al., 2014). To our best knowledge, a majority of the publications in the literature entirely pay attention to the carbon allowance market in the EU, since EU-ETS is the biggest and most important carbon trade market. Having its own dynamics, the USA being as an unique market can be taken as a guide in establishing incentives.

The aim of this chapter is to investigate the relationship between the main drivers of the carbon price in the USA-RGGI and to explain the relationship between the CO_2 price and renewable energy policy. As a non-Kyoto member, the USA constitutes a unique CO_2 market in the following aspects: (i) relative to the consumption, CO_2 price is lower compared with other ETS markets, (ii) the regulations on CO_2 market price are clearly defined, and (iii) the USA is a pioneer in renewable energy source improvements. To achieve these goals, we employ statistical models such as linear regression, multivariate time series, and panel data analysis applied on the most readily available data collected from the US market. Regarding a negative and statistically significant relationship between CO_2 prices and renewable energy portfolio targets for RGGI states, we aim to (i) find an econometric relation between energy prices (coal, oil, and natural gas), economic activity, RGGI allowance quantity, and CO_2 prices, (ii) search a time-dependent relation of the contributing factors on CO_2 prices and their causal effect, (iii) determine the influence of RGGI strategies, time, and contributing factors on the CO_2 prices.

The organization of the chapter is as follows. Section 2 gives the background on RGGI framework in the USA. In Sect. 3, the contributing factors on CO_2 in the US market are explained. The empirical analysis, the results, and findings are presented in Sect. 4. This part presents the findings as a result of three models implemented on the US monthly observations between January 2009 and June 2018. The conclusion and comments are given in Sect. 5.

2 The US Emission Trading Scheme

The Regional Greenhouse Gas Initiative (RGGI) for the ten northeastern US states beginning in, 2009 include nine states: Connecticut (CT), Delaware (DE), Maine (ME), Maryland (ML), Massachusetts (MA), New Hampshire (NH), New York (NY), Rhode Island (RI), Vermont (VT), and New Jersey (withdrew in 2012) as shown in Fig. 1a. The carbon allowance prices for the year 2018 are USD 17.80 and USD 4.94 in the EU-ETS and the RGGI states, respectively, show a remarkably huge difference (Fig. 1b) (Kossoy, 2015). The most expensive price is realized in Alberta CCIR, followed by Korea ETS, whereas the minimum is in Guangdong pilot ETS. Reasons for this can be stated as follows: The RGGI (i) is not an economy-wide system, (ii) applies only to CO_2 emissions from electric power plants (generating > 25 MW) which are fewer in number than in ETS markets, (iii) has limited regional scope and (iv) is a voluntary market. RGGI and its market are one of the voluntary carbon markets in which organizations willing to be carbon neutral buy carbon certificates that are generated as a result of emission reductions provided by a voluntary standard to reduce and offset their emissions by calculating their carbon footprints.

The historical development of yearly carbon prices between 2009 and 2012 (Fig. 1b) is low (around USD 2) even though it jumps off to its highest value in 2016. Due to several auctions during the same years, some allowances were left unsold. After 2012, a 45% cap reduction was made resulting in the demand for CO_2 allowances to rise and carbon prices to increase up to USD 8 per short ton toward 2016. Following the publication of Clean Energy Plan in 2015, bids were offered more than three times the total number of RGGI allowances which also caused an increase in the prices followed by a decrease after 2016. As the aim of the RGGI is to cap and reduce CO_2 emissions from the energy sector, the program is projected to support the states to decrease annual CO_2 emissions of the power sector under the 2005 levels by 2020. Figure 1b shows a sharp fall (around 30%) in the emission in

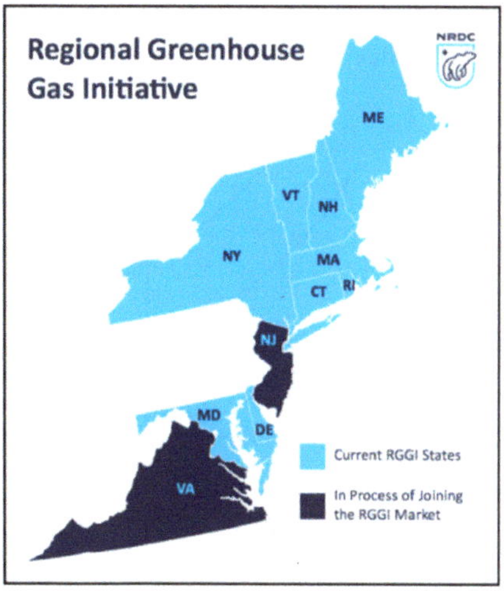

(a) Northeastern RGGI States (Ho,2018)

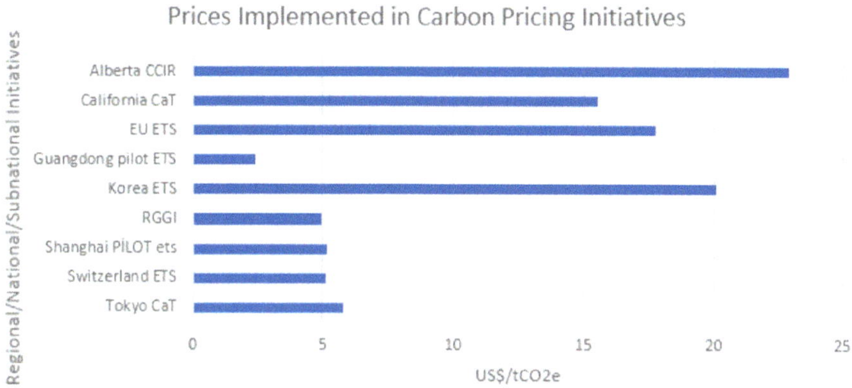

(b) CO2 market prices

Fig. 1 RGGI states and the different carbon trading systems (Kossoy, 2015)

nine states after the start of RGGI due to the transition from coal and oil to natural gas, nuclear power, and renewable sources.

The effect of the cap and trade system on CO_2 price can also be seen in Fig. 2 indicating that such policy instruments can achieve significant emission reductions (Heindl & Löschel, 2012). However, they may cause a surplus on the number of allowances in the ETS market, which leads to downward pressure on the carbon allowance prices. To achieve a reduction in emissions, setting a cap and trade system is most effective. Nevertheless, when a government combines the cap and trade system with other policy measures, the efficiency can change severely (Fig. 2) (Görlach, 2014). For instance, in such an intervention, the direct effect of these subsidies is

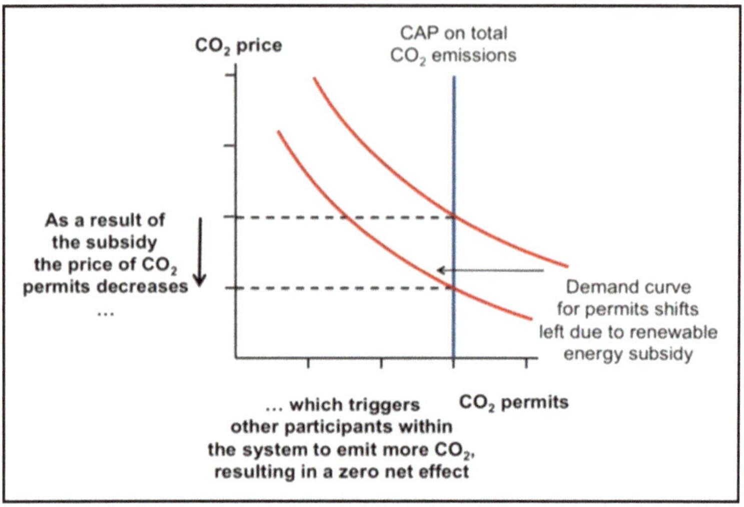

Fig. 2 Relation between carbon emission prices and renewable energy subsidy (Mulder, 2018)

the replacement of electricity produced by fossil fuel power plants with the ones by renewable techniques reducing CO_2. For this reason, electricity producers save their CO_2 permits to sell in the permit market resulting in a decline in the price of CO_2 permits.

External changes from policies complement the RGGI cap and trade programs. Some examples that can cause such exogenous shifts in emission are: (i) Renewable portfolio standards (RPS) entails a certain part of the state energy to come from non-renewable sources and thus creates reduction in emission and shifts in marginal abatement cost (MAC) which measures the cost of reducing one more unit of pollution. This mechanism imposes an obligation on electricity supply companies to generate a certain amount from a renewable energy source. (ii) The RGGI program includes emission limits, such as the use of RGGI auction revenues for energy efficiency, as well as additional measures to reduce emissions. RGGI states (collectively) allocate the auction revenues as 64% for energy efficiency, 10% for electricity bill assistance, 4% for GHG abatement, 16% for clean and renewable energy, 6% for administration, and 1% for RGGI, Inc. in 2015. (iii) All the regulations of the Federal Clean Air Act on air pollutants (i.e., sulfur dioxide, nitrogen oxide, and mercury) introduce legal requirements for coal-fueled production, which opts to replace appropriate alternatives such as natural gas and nuclear energy with renewable energy sources in RGGI states.

The decrease in CO_2 price can be due to policies that are complementary to the RGGI cap and trade system. In the framework of this study, we consider renewable portfolio (RP) of seven states as the representation of renewable energy incentives. Two states, NY and VT are excluded due to the availability of RPS parameters in the data sources. Figure 3 shows the renewable portfolio targets across seven states. The targets of the states except NH appear to increase continuously as the

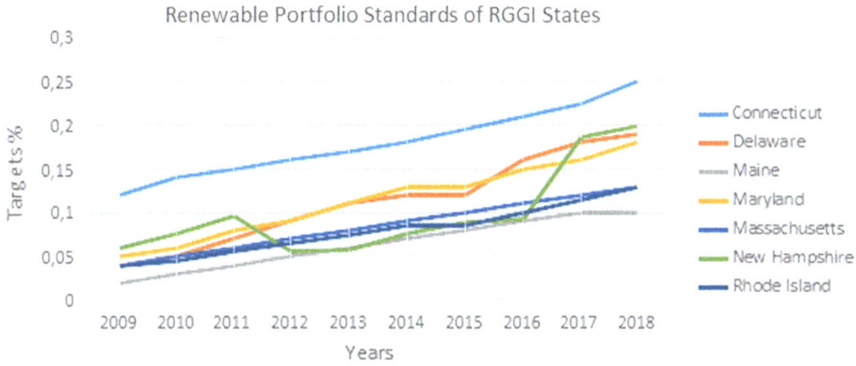

Fig. 3 RPS targets (%) of RPS across seven RGGI states (DSIRE, 2018)

renewable energy requirement of each energy source is modified. We expect that RPS requirements are strongly correlated across states so that, one state should serve as a good instrument for the RPS requirement for other ones which is justified by the high value of the Pearson correlation coefficient (ρ), specifically, between NH and all other states (around 60–71%).

3 Contributing Factors on Renewable Energy

The factors underlying the influence of renewable energy incentives on CO_2 prices (CO_2) are chosen as CO_2 allowance quantity (ALQ), industrial production index (IP), energy prices (crude oil (CROP), natural gas (NGP), coal (COP)), and renewable portfolio standards (WA) whose dynamics in the country and variable specific characteristics are summarized briefly.

3.1 CO_2 Price

RGGI for each state recorded by the Allowance Tracking Program (RGGI COATS) (RGGIb, 2019) is a platform on which each state archives and tracks occurrences of the CO_2 Budget Trading Program. It also includes the transfer of CO_2 allowances purchased by winning bidders in quarterly auctions started first in 2008 (RGGIb, 2019). These allocations are distributed free of charge or through an auction process. Allocations can also be obtained by trade between other third parties, which determines the market price of all allocations. Since there is a cost associated with greenhouse gas emissions under the ETS, there is an incentive to reduce the emissions of plants. The emissions trade offers the option to trade, thus assuring the lowest cost options for emission reduction by the market. Cap and trade system consists of two parts. In the first part, the government determines the maximum amount of emissions. The government sells or exports permits for greenhouse gas to emitters each of which needs a permit for each allowed ton of greenhouse gas. In the second part, emitters can trade carbon permits among themselves and create an equilibrium price. The market enforces stakeholders to reduce their CO_2 emissions.

Accordingly, Fig. 4a illustrates the price (right vertical axis) which changes by year. It reaches nearly to the minimum allowable bid (price floor) in 2010 after a sharp drop in 2007 and remains for more than two years because of the decline in natural gas prices leading to a fall in CO_2 emissions and a halt in the sales of some of the allowances (left vertical axis). Although the RGGI reduces its emissions cap, actual emissions stay under the cap resulting in an excess of allowances (Fig. 4a). By the declaration of RGGI in Jan 2013 to reduce its CO_2 emissions limit by 45% (Fig. 4b) starting from 2014, we observe an increase in CO_2 prices exceeding its base price (around USD 4). In February 2013, the Cost Environmental Protection Reserve (CCR) is announced to keep the number of allowances conditioned to the price reaching to a prescribed level. The CCR trigger price aims to increase the price annually by USD 2 (up to USD 10) starting in 2017, and by an increment of 2.5% per year after then. However, in 2014, a limit on allowance of 5 million and on withdrawal of 10 million are observed for all subsequent years. By the announcement of Clean Energy Plan in 2015, the total amount of RGGI allowance becomes threefold resulting in an increase in allowance prices. The downward trend in the clearing price since the beginning of 2016 indicates a low demand for RGGI allowances. Subsequently, for effectively determining the minimum allowance price adjustments, a reserve price for 2017 (USD 2.15) which is 2.3% higher than a year before, triggers more than 14 million grants to be sold with a clearing price of USD 3 at which the auction sums up to USD 43.1 million. This amount was utilized for many purposes, including supporting the energy efficiency of RGGI states, renewable energy, direct energy bill assistance, and greenhouse gas reduction programs. During the year 2018, CO_2 allowance prices remain constant with a slight rise toward the mid-year (RGGIa, 2019).

3.2 CO_2 Allowance

CO_2 allocations are provided by each RGGI state in the amount specified in the respective laws and/or regulations of each state. All CO_2 allocations distributed by all RGGI states constitute the total limit of RGGI (the total cap). Most of the allowances distributed by a regional CO_2 auction can only be retained by a certain amount in a given account and distributed quarterly based on the government-specific programs (RGGIb, 2019). Figure 4b shows the allowance offered and sold quarterly (right vertical axis) by auction in respect to the CO_2 prices (left vertical axis). It is noticed that at the beginning of the RGGI cap and trade program, all allowances are sold until the 3rd quarter of 2010 and then remained under the offered allowances, leading to a decrease in the CO_2 price, which causes more than 169 million tons of

(a) CO2 prices, allowances offered and sold in auctions

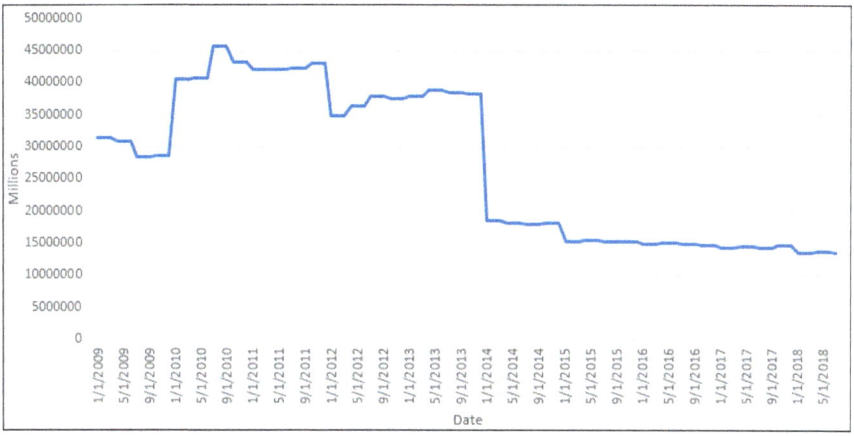

(b) RGGI allowance quantity

Fig. 4 Quarterly prices (USD) and RGGI allowances (2009–2018) (RGGIa, 2019)

allowances (26% of the total allowance) to remain unsold. In January 2012, some states (CT, MA, NY, DE, RI, VT) declare to withdraw the unsold allowances for the next compliance period and as a result of RGGI program review, the emission cap is reduced to 45% (91 million tons) by nine states, divided into 2.5% drops for each year between 2015 and 2020. The changes in the emission cap causing an allowance shortage and the trading of allowances through an auction mechanism in that case lead to an increase in CO_2 prices (Fig. 4b). The allowance quantities through the years can be roughly classified into four periods: the first period (2009–2011) with a cap of 188 million, the second period (2012–2014) with a 165 million cap, the third period (2015–2017), with a new cap of 91 million, and the fourth period (2018–2020) with a cap amount of 78 million CO_2 tons/year.

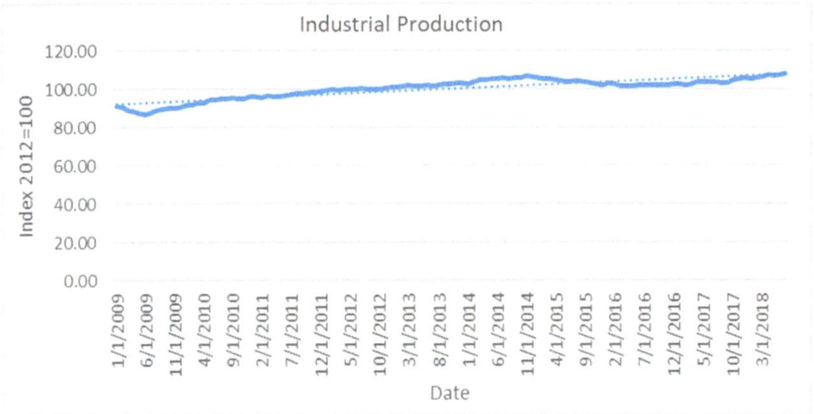

Fig. 5 Monthly industrial production index (2009–2018) (2012 = 100, seasonally adjusted) (FED, 2019)

3.3 *Industrial Production Index*

As an economic indicator, the industrial production index (IP) measures the actual output for all facilities in the country, including those in manufacturing, mining, and electricity and gas facilities (except those in the US territories). The monthly index shows the short-term changes in production and emphasizes the structural developments in the economy and is an indicator of growth in the sector (FED, 2019). The IP index is not available for each state separately. The index for the country as a whole reached to its lowest value (87.49%) across all the years due to the subprime crisis between January and June 2009 (Fig. 5). This leads to a fall in energy usage and a decrease in electricity production, less consumption of CO_2 and therefore, lower demand for carbon allowances in the market. Manufacturing industrial production falls slightly in 2015 due to a severe winter and increases after then.

3.4 *Energy Prices*

Many studies in the literature reveal the relationship between the economics of energy markets and the price of CO_2 (see Mansanet-Bataller et al., 2007; Alberola et al., 2008). Based on spot and futures prices, the literature shows that carbon prices in the EU-ETS are dependent on the use of fossil fuels (oil, natural gas, coal). In contrast to the large number of studies done for the EU-ETS market, limited research is found on the US-ETS market. Hammoudeh et al. (2014) reveal that the impact of energy prices on CO_2 emission allowance prices estimated by using a quantile regression technique shows a negative relationship between CO_2 prices and fossil energy sources. Additionally, it is experienced that, the crude oil and the natural gas prices have an inter-commodity spread; that is, when one gets increasingly costly, consumers switch to the other. As relevant energy products, oil and natural gas prices have a definite historical price relationship. Nevertheless, this connection changes in the recent years due to the detection of new natural gas reserves in the USA which alters the price relation between these two energy products. With the decline in crude oil prices at the end of 2014, the price relation between these two commodities reverts to the more normal historical levels as in the last twenty-five years. In Fig. 6a and b, it can be seen that there is mostly a negative relationship until 2014. Natural gas is the fossil fuel that emits the lowest amount of greenhouse gases, which corresponds to about 47% of the carbon dioxide that coal produces for the same level of energy output (Mitigation, 2011). In 2008, the US natural gas reserves were stated to have had a 40% increase compared to earlier estimates, due to the development of shale gas fields. The sudden development of this natural gas supply and related technical innovations caused a 46% drop in natural gas prices between 2005 and 2011, whereas coal prices increased during the same time interval (Fig. 6c). Natural gas prices, because of a relatively large supply and an economic recession, became low. In 1990, natural gas supplied 12% of electricity generation in the RGGI states. However, its market share rose to 40% until 2011. For the same duration, the share of coal decreased by 11% from its 25% share of total production in 1990.

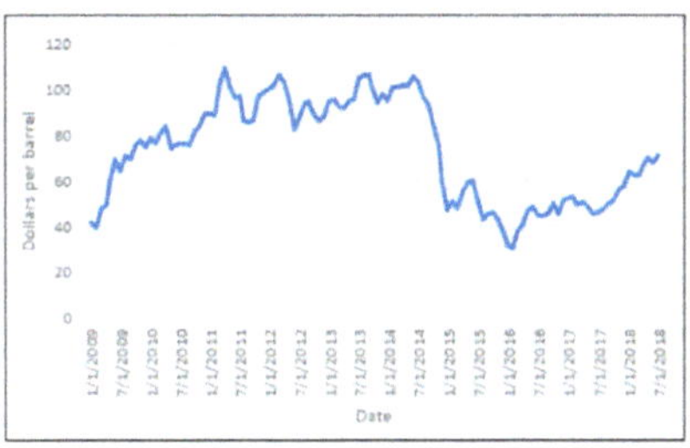

(a) Crude oil spot prices (USD/barrel) (EIAc, 2019)

(b) Natural gas spot prices (USD/mil.Btu) (EIAa, 2019)

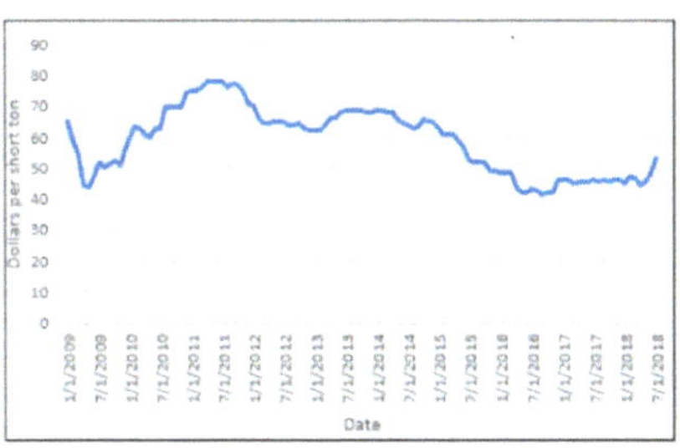

(c) Coal spot price in Northern Appalachia (EIAb, 2019)

(d) Mont hly weighted average of targets (%) of RPS over nine states (DSIRE, 2018)

Fig. 6 Monthly fuel energy prices and renewable portfolio standards (2009–2018)

There are five coal commodity regions in the USA: *Central Appalachia, Northern Appalachia, Illinois Basin, Powder River Basin*, and *Uinta Basin*. This study uses the coal prices in *Northern Appalachia* because of its regional closeness to the selected RGGI states (Fig. 6c). Between 2009 and 2010, we see a sharp decrease in the coal prices in the Appalachian Region. The price of northern coal increases by 39% in 2018 due to a strong international demand for both metallurgy and steam coal. Electricity generation by each RGGI state in 2017 is dominated by natural gas. In order to measure the effect of energy resources in RGGI states on the CO_2 price, the natural gas price is expected to capture more of the CO_2 allowance behavior.

3.5 Renewable Portfolio Standard

The RPS requires electricity services and other retail electricity providers to contribute a percentage (or absolute quantity) of the minimum customer demand from appropriate renewable electricity sources. By March 2015, twenty-nine states and Washington, D.C., had mandatory RPS requirements. The percentage increase in the renewables target in each state is represented in Fig. 6d. State RPSs are the drivers of renewable energy development in RGGI states (RGGIb, 2019).

In addition to the aforementioned factors, weather (temperature) can also be taken into account as a determinant of the CO_2 price. Price changes due to extreme weather conditions are indirectly related to the impact of energy demand, such as the cooling and the heating of homes and to the supply of carbon-free energy through such factors as rainfall, hours of sunlight, and wind speed. Using the renewable energy incentives provided to electricity producers, we include the supply/demand effects of the weather variable indirectly to avoid multicollinearity issues in econometric modeling (Alberola et al., 2008; Bunn & Fezzi, 2007).

4 Empirical Findings

To depict the impact of renewable energy incentives on CO_2 emissions, the analyses are performed in three aspects to answer the following questions: (i) How do some important exogenous factors contribute to CO_2 price movements? (ii) How does overall economic activity affect the renewable energy strategies and CO_2 prices through time? (iii) How do renewable energy portfolio standards in each RGGI influence CO_2 prices? Within this framework, CO_2 price (CO_2), CO_2 allowance quantity (ALQ), industrial production (IP), crude oil price (CROP), natural gas price (NGP), coal prices (COP), and renewable portfolio standards (RPS-WA) are considered as the main variables. The historical monthly observations on these variables are retrieved from the open-source Web sites Global Greenhouse Gas Emissions Data (EPA, 2017), Regional Greenhouse Gas Initiative Database, (RGGIa, 2019), Federal Reserve Economic Data (FEDa, 2019), Industrial Production and Capacity

Utilization (FED, 2019), US Coal Prices by Region (EIAb, 2019), US Natural gas spot prices by Region (EIAa, 2019), and Database of State Incentives for Renewables & Efficiency (EIAd, 2019) for the time period of January 2009 through June 2018 based on the availability of each variable in this time frame.

We express RPS targets as the weighted average (WA) of the nine states. The weights are given according to the monthly electricity generation capacity in each province. In the first instance, energy prices are taken as the main drivers on the CO_2 market. We exclude the electricity price to avoid multicollinearity due to its strong correlation with fossil energy prices. Each variable contains 115 monthly observations between January 2009 and July 2018. We employ the linear regression technique to estimate CO_2 prices in terms of the explanatory variables. We also make use of vector autoregression (VAR) and vector error correction (VEC) models to capture relations among variables with respect to time as well as panel data analysis to depict the influence of renewable energy initiatives on CO_2 prices. The software package STATA (V11) is used in our programming.

The descriptive statistics summarized in Table 1 show that the coefficient of variation (CV) of each variable is well below 1, yielding mostly a homogenous set of observations. The test on normality using Jarque–Bera (JB) test is rejected in the favor of non-normality (p-value < 0.001), except for crude oil prices. Coal, crude oil prices, and industrial production show negative skewness, whereas the rest are positive. A leptokurtic distribution is not observed for any of the variables. Significant Pearson correlation coefficients (p-values < 0.001) show that CO_2 prices have negative relations with ALQ (81%), CROP (63%), NGP (42%), COP (54%), and positive associations with IP (52%) and RPS-WA (58%). Associations between pairs of exogenous variables are mostly significant as well. ALQ is strongly associated with RPS-WA (-80%) and COP (75%), IP weakly is associated with other variables, CROP has a strong association with COP (79%), and NGP shows a negative association with RPS-WA (58%).

4.1 *Estimation of CO_2 Prices in Terms of Its Contributing Factors*

All the variables that may play a role in determining the change in CO_2 prices are considered in a multivariate relation using linear regression models. Our aim is to capture the information between price and other variables in order to obtain a reliable prediction for CO_2 prices. This relation is shown as follows:

$$\mathrm{CO_2} = \beta_0 + \beta_1\mathrm{ALQ} + \beta_2\mathrm{IP} + \beta_3\mathrm{CROP} + \beta_4\mathrm{NGP} + \beta_5\mathrm{COP} + \beta_6\mathrm{WA} + u. \quad (1)$$

Here, β_i, $i = 0, \ldots, 6$ are the parameters and u denotes the random error having the properties of zero mean, constant variance, and independent and identically normally distributed residuals. Throughout the modeling steps, it is depicted that the estimated

Table 1 Descriptive statistics of model variables

Variable	Abbr	Unit and/ or desc	Mean	St. dev.	CV	Min.	Max.	Skew	Kurt	JB
Carbon emission	CO_2	USD cost of CO_2 per ton	3.52	1.42	0.403	1.88	8.22	0.69	2.92	0
Allowance quantity	ALQ	Millions per short ton CO_2	27.2	11.84	0.435	13.6	45.6	0.12	1.26	0
Industrial production index	IP	Index (2012 = 100)	100.2	5.23	0.052	87.1	107.8	−0.87	2.82	0
Crude oil price	CROP	USD per barrel	73.31	22.31	0.304	30.3	109.5	−0.12	1.63	0
Natural gas price	NGP	USD per million Btu	3.45	0.87	0.252	1.73	6	0.44	3	0.1
Coal price	COP	USD per short ton	58.87	10.82	0.184	41.5	78.1	−0.04	1.76	0
Renewable portfolio standards	WA	Weighted average of targets (%) of RPS for each RGGI state	0.11	0.04	0.364	0.06	0.19	0.29	2.11	0

model incorporating the original values comes up with insignificant coefficients for NGP and COP in the equation. However, normality tests of the residuals are not justified. For this reason, after many trials on reaching a plausible model, we conclude that log-transformed (ln) variables yield the best performance measures (Table 2) with respect to overall model significance. Additionally, the normality test on the residuals (skewness/kurtosis test) justifies the required assumption on residuals (p-value = 0.83149).

The estimation results in Table 2 show that there is a negative and statistically significant (p-value < 0.05) relationship between CO_2 price and allowance quantity in the USA which is consistent with the literature (Benz & Trück, 2009). The CO_2 price in the cap and trade system is mainly affected by the supply of RGGI allowances; that is, the CO_2 allowance issued by all the RGGI states comprising the cap. If RGGI states decrease the total cap in the system due to renewable energy incentives, a reduction in CO_2 emission occurs, leading to electricity producers or permit buyers selling extra permits in the market. Because of this, the CO_2 price decreases when the allowance quantity increases. On the other hand, when IP increases, CO_2 emissions rise, and therefore electricity producers in RGGI states need more CO_2 allowances to cover their emissions as expected (Chevallier, 2013). We also mark that IP has the

Table 2 Parameter estimates and diagnostics of CO_2 prices

	Variable	Parameter	St. error	*t*-stat	*p*-value
Dependent	ln_CO2				
Independent	ln_ALQ	−0.7299	0.0864	−8.45	< 0.01*
	ln_IP	5.4585	0.9535	5.72	< 0.05*
	ln_CROP	−0.407	0.0904	−4.5	< 0.05*
	ln_WA	−0.9919	0.1739	−5.7	< 0.05*
	Constant	−22.1298	4.5432	−4.87	< 0.05*

* Statistically significant

most important influence in magnitude on CO_2 prices. In terms of energy sources, consistent with the literature (Hammoudeh et al., 2014), a negative association is found, also as an indirect influence of natural gas prices. It is well known that crude oil is the second biggest source of greenhouse gas emissions following coal. A considerable drop in CO_2 prices is observed following a rise in crude oil prices which may be due to the strong effects of high oil prices at the higher end of the carbon spectrum, but not substituting coal for oil (Hammoudeh et al., 2014). Finally, we find that the weighted average of RPS has a decreasing influence on the CO_2 price. An increasing share in the renewable energy incentives in these seven RGGI states, empowering them to utilize renewable energy sources, causes a decrease in CO_2 emissions, reducing the energy companies' need for permits to produce electricity. Thus, the demand for CO_2 permits decreases and the CO_2 price falls. Even though statistical significance of our linear model is justified through the t-tests and the F-test, and the model fit is verified by a relatively high R^2 (78%), correlation among exogenous variables may lead to biasedness. To check whether heteroscedasticity and autocorrelation may be present in the model, we run White's and Breusch–Godfrey tests. The White test applied to residuals supports that the random errors have constant variance (p-value > 0.75), and no serial correlation at lag 1 is detected by the Breusch–Godfrey test (p-value < 0.001).

4.2 *Impact of RGGI Strategies on CO_2 Prices*

Relations between multiple variables and their historical observations (lags) can best be captured using vector autoregressive (VAR) analysis. We employ VAR to investigate the interdependence between multiple time series. The VAR models are used when the series are stationary, and there is no cointegration among the variables. This condition is not attained frequently, as the series shows certain behavior due to some components such as seasonality and/or trend. If the variables are cointegrated, an error correction model (VEC model) is estimated instead. A brief summary of these methods is given in order to facilitate a proper understanding of the parameters estimated.

VAR of order p is a system of linear equations of the historical values of all variables and is often used to estimate systems of interrelated time series. A k-dimensional VAR (p) is expressed as follows:

$$Y_t = \sum_i A_i Y_{t-i} + CX_t + u_t, i = 1, \ldots, p, \tag{2}$$

where Y_t is a $k \times 1$ vector of K endogenous variables and X_t is a $d \times 1$ vector of K exogenous variables. The A_i; $i = 1, ..., p$ are a $k \times k$ matrices of lag coefficients to be estimated, and C denotes the exogenous variable coefficient. u_t is a $k \times 1$ white noise process, with the properties $E(u_t) = 0$, and $E(u_t u_s') = 0$.

On the other hand, vector error correction (VEC) model is a limited VAR that is modeled for non-stationary variables being cointegrated. The cointegration is acknowledged as the error correction term since the deviation from the long-term equilibrium is gradually adjusted by a series of partial short-term adjustments. If VEC specification assumes that there are linear trends in the series and a constant in the cointegrating equations, the change in dependent variable can be expressed as:

$$\Delta Y_{i,t} = \delta_1 + \gamma_1 \left(Y_{j,t-1} - \mu - \beta Y_{i,t-1} \right) + \varepsilon_{i,t}, \quad i = 1, \ldots, j. \tag{3}$$

Here, ε denotes the random error corrections. Equation 3 exposes that all variables vary with respect to time whose influence on the realizations should be filtered based on stationarity tests. Augmented Dickey–Fuller (ADF) test results indicate that except IP and WA, all variables have integration of order one. Time-dependent variables may have a long-term or short-term impact (cointegration) on CO_2 prices, along with their historical observations in the system of VAR equations.

To determine dependence on historical observations, Johansen cointegration test is applied to define the lag-order selection based on various selection criteria. The log-likelihood (LL), likelihood ratio (LR), final prediction error (FPE), Akaike information criterion (AIC), Hannan–Quinn Information (HQIC), and Bayesian Schwartz Information (BIC) are implemented and a majority of their results indicate agreement on a lag of one (Table 3).

Cointegration analyses using "maximum eigenvalue" and "trace test" conclude on one cointegration relation among the variables in VAR. The statistic is not strong enough to reject the existence of cointegration for higher ranks (Table 4). To capture

Table 3 Lag-order selection statistics using several tests

Lag	LL	LR	df	p-value	FPE	AIC	HQIC	BIC
0	−973.774				36.8370	17.795	17.845	17.918
1	−260.009	1427.5	25	0.000	**0.00013***	**5.272***	5.571	**6.009***
2	−238.153	**43.712***	25	0.012	0.00014	5.330	5.877	6.680
3	−226.617	23.072	25	0.573	0.00018	5.575	6.371	7.538
4	−214.540	24.154	25	0.511	0.00024	5.809	6.855	8.387

the dynamics of long- and short-term causality in VECM, the differenced variables (D) and cointegration equations (CE) with lag (L) are estimated. In consideration of the long-term relation between the CO_2 price and other variables, all CE estimates are expected to have negative signs together with significant p-values. Regarding the short-term causality between variables, individual lag coefficients and p-values for each independent variable are taken into account. Because of space limitations, only the estimates of the cointegration equations (CE) regarding CO_2 prices are listed in Table 5. The details for other parameters in VAR analyses can be found in (Çoşkun, 2019).

The findings reveal that mostly short-term influences of the variables are significant on CO_2. The second lags of coal prices and WA have short-term impacts, whereas neither long- nor short-term relations to other variables are detected in ALQ. In the short term, IP is sensitive to its own, CROP's and WA's first lags. Energy prices, CROP, NGP, and COP vary in short-term dependence. CROP and NGP have dependence to the first lag of ALQ, whereas the second lag of IP and the third lag of NGP have an influence on COP. Finally, the first lags of IP and NGP are influential on WA as well as WA's own third lag. All of these models are verified based on the parameter tests at the 5% significance level. Additionally, the normality of the residuals of each model is justified by the skewness/kurtosis test for normality (p-value < 0.05). For details see (Çoşkun, 2019).

The short-run causality of CO_2 price with coal price and weighted average of RPS is consistent with the linear regression model discussed above. Since coal price is an important source of electricity generation in RGGI regions, it is one of the important variables affecting the CO_2 price. Also, WA has a short-term relationship with IP and NGP. Increased industrial production will also increase the demand for electricity, which we expect to increase renewable energy production (Table 6). That is because the increased industrial production leads to a higher demand for electricity, which, in turn, can create a greater demand for renewable energy sources. RPS policies provide a framework and incentive for utilities to procure a specific percentage of their electricity from renewable sources. As industrial production expands, the overall electricity demand rises, increasing the need for renewable energy and incentivizing utilities to invest in renewable projects to meet the RPS requirements.

RPS policies support the integration of industrial growth and renewable energy development by aligning industrial objectives with environmental sustainability

Table 4 Johansen cointegration test results

Rank	Par.	LL	Eigenvalue	Trace Stat	Crit. Val	Max. Stat	Crit. Val
0	5	−314.65		86.9145	68.52	39.1614	33.46
1	14	−295.07	0.2907	47.7531	47.21	25.24	27.07
2	21	−282.45	0.1986	**22.5131***	29.68	16.8798	20.97
3	26	−274.02	0.1376	5.6333	15.41	5.6244	14.07
4	29	−271.21	0.0481	0.0089	3.76	0.0089	3.76
5	30	−271.20	0.0001				

Table 5 VECM estimates for CO_2 price with respect to other variables

Variable	CE L1	Par.	Std. err.	z	p-value	CE L1	Par.	Std. Err.	z	p-value
D_CO_2	1	−0.2777	0.1289	−2.15	**0.031**	4	−0.0186	0.0114	−1.62	0.104
	2	−0.0073	0.2437	−0.30	0.764	5	0.3363	0.2333	1.44	0.149
	3	0.1315	0.0688	1.91	**0.056**	6	0.0056	0.0241	0.24	0.814
D_ALQ	1	−1.0042	0.7250	−1.39	0.166	4	0.0184	0.0645	0.29	0.776
	2	−0.3435	0.1370	−2.51	**0.012**	5	−2.0355	1.3120	−1.55	0.120
	3	−0.3670	0.3869	−0.95	0.343	6	0.0957	0.1358	0.70	0.481
D_IP	1	0.0031	0.1118	0.03	0.978	4	0.0348	0.0099	3.49	**0.000**
	2	0.0090	0.0211	0.43	0.667	5	0.4878	0.2024	2.41	**0.016**
	3	−0.2344	0.0597	−3.93	**0.000**	6	−0.0428	0.0209	−2.04	**0.041**
D_ CROP	1	0.0242	1.3375	0.02	0.986	4	−0.1722	0.1191	−1.45	0.148
	2	0.6390	0.2528	2.53	**0.011**	5	1.1155	2.4204	0.46	0.645
	3	−0.1459	0.7139	−0.2	0.838	6	−0.3453	0.2506	−1.38	0.168
D_NGP	1	0.0041	0.1011	0.04	0.968	4	0.0164	0.0090	1.82	0.060
	2	−0.0021	0.0191	−0.11	0.912	5	−0.2977	0.1829	−1.63	0.104
	3	0.0089	0.0539	0.16	0.869	6	−0.0487	0.0189	−2.57	**0.010**
D_COP	1	−0.3260	0.4306	−0.76	0.449	4	0.0241	0.0383	0.63	0.529
	2	0.1360	0.0814	1.67	0.095	5	1.8055	0.7792	2.32	**0.021**
	3	0.1145	0.2298	0.50	0.618	6	−0.3174	0.0807	−3.93	**0.000**
D_WA	1	−0.0001	0.0011	−0.11	0.910	4	−0.0002	0.0001	−2.09	**0.036**
	2	−0.0002	0.0002	−1.14	0.256	5	−0.0041	0.0021	−1.94	0.053
	3	0.0011	0.0006	1.88	0.06	6	0.0004	0.0002	1.84	0.066

goals. by mandating a certain percentage of renewable energy in the electricity mix, RPS policies drive the industrial sector to adopt cleaner energy sources to meet their electricity needs. This alignment between industrial growth, electricity demand, and renewable energy production helps advance the transition toward a low-carbon economy.

In sum, Regional Portfolio Standards (RPS) stimulates renewable energy demand, drives renewable energy investment, promotes renewable energy growth, and aligns industrial objectives with environmental sustainability goals. RPS policies play a crucial role in encouraging the adoption of renewable energy sources as industrial production and electricity demand increase. Increasing demand for renewable energy is likely to negatively affect the demand (and price) of natural gas, which is the most widely used fuel for electricity generation.

Table 6 Granger causality tests

X	*Y*	Test-stat**	*p*-value	*Y*	Test-stat	*p*-value
CO_2	**ALQ**	6.4071	**0.041***	NGP	0.8384	0.658
	IP	15.812	**0.000***	COP	2.8325	0.235
	CROP	2.988	0.224	**WA**	14.467	**0.001***
ALQ	CO_2	2.045	0.300	NGP	1.5163	0.469
	IP	2.478	0.290	COP	4.3426	0.114
	CROP	2.357	0.308	WA	0.0394	0.980
IP	CO_2	0.1383	0.933	NGP	0.5545	0.758
	ALQ	2.0373	0.361	COP	6.8478	**0.033***
	CROP	23.543	**0.000***	**WA**	12.935	**0.002***
CROP	CO_2	5.3815	0.068	NGP	2.9864	0.225
	ALQ	8.0894	0.018	COP	0.8430	0.656
	IP	0.4366	0.804	WA	0.5100	0.775
NGP	CO_2	1.5676	0.457	CROP	5.0816	0.079
	ALQ	11.510	**0.003***	COP	4.3007	0.116
	IP	0.0212	0.989	WA	5.7239	0.057
COP	CO_2	0.3457	0.614	CROP	7.9779	0.019
	ALQ	8.2722	0.503	NGP	3.5023	0.174
	IP	0.4216	0.010	WA	1.5962	0.450
WA	CO_2	0.9750	0.614	**CROP**	6.7544	0.034
	ALQ	1.3746	0.503	NGP	5.2722	0.072
	IP	9.304	**0.010***	COP	3.4531	0.178

* Significant at 1% level; ** Test-Stat: Chi-square with 2 degrees of freedom

4.3 Impact of Renewable Energy Policies on CO_2

To understand if the renewable energy policies make a difference in the CO_2 prices, we investigated the variation with respect to seven selected states using panel data analysis. Because of the strong correlation between the RPS requirements of the states, we expect the policy on RPS will serve as an instrument within the RPS requirements for the rest of the states as far as CO_2 prices are concerned. We construct the panel data model as

$$Y_{i,t} = \alpha_i + \sum_{k=1}^{K} X_{i,t}\beta_{k,i,t} + u_{i,t}, i = 1, \ldots, N; t = 1, \ldots, T; k = 1, \ldots, K. \quad (4)$$

Here, the α_i's are the individual intercepts (fixed for given N), $X_{i,t}$ is the vector of variables with coefficient vector of β_k and N, T and K refer to the number of cross-sections, periods and independent variables, respectively. In this model, variation may be observed with respect to α_i and $u_{i,t}$. To decide between random effects (RE) and fixed effects (FE), we applied a Hausman test to the proposed data set. The test statistic favored the alternative hypothesis that the FE is appropriate choice (Çoşkun, 2019). The FE version of Eq. 4 is:

$$Y_{i,t} = \alpha_i + X^{'}_{i,t}\beta + u_{i,t}. \tag{5}$$

Under FE, consistency does not require that the α_i's and the random erros, $u_{i,t}$, to be uncorrelated, only that the condition $E(X_{i,t}u_{i,t}) = 0$ to hold. There are $N - 1$ additional parameters for capturing individual heteroscedasticity.

Rearranging all observations increases the number of observations to 805, with 115 time periods clustered for seven states. We apply panel data analysis to the original data to estimate CO_2 prices stratified with respect to seven states. We come up with significant parameter estimates, reasonable goodness of fit ($R^2 = 66\%$), and individual cross-sectional effects ($\rho = 31\%$) as well as homoscedastic errors. However, the model fails on serial correlation based on the Wooldridge test which verifies the existence of the first-order autocorrelation. To circumvent this, we re-estimate the model with log-transformed variables which successfully handles the autocorrelation problem compared to the model incorporating the original variables. Table 7 exposes the results of the model with the log-transformed variables. It depicts that the effect of RPS strategies on the CO_2 emission prices with respect to time is noticeable. It is seen that ALQ (−0.71), WA (−0.26), and CROP (−0.36) are negatively related to CO_2 price, whereas, in contrast to expectations, COP is positively (0.38) related to CO_2. As found in our earlier analyses, IP has a positive (1.69) impact on the CO_2 price.

It is noteworthy that all parameter estimates are significant and analysis of the residuals for Normality is supported at the 5% significance level. We conclude that the model plausibly determines the impact of the targets of the different states on CO_2. The model goodness of fit statistic (R^2) is 76% with a corresponding p-value < 0.0001 for model significance (F-test).

On the other hand, the information extracted from OLS, VAR, and panel data analyses supports one another in terms of detecting the influential variables on CO_2 prices,

Table 7 Panel data analysis with fixed effects and robust standard errors

Variable	Coefficient	Std. err.	*p*-value
ln_CO_2			
ln_ALQ	−0.71	0.014	< 0.0001
ln_CROP	−0.36	0.005	< 0.0001
ln_COP	0.38	0.026	< 0.0001
ln_IP	1.69	0.218	< 0.0001
ln_WA	−0.26	0.042	< 0.0001
Constant	−4.98	0.970	< 0.0001

even as each model focuses on a different aspect of the time-dependent multivariate relationship.

4.4 Discussion

The three-step analysis of the observations within our research agenda reveals that with respect to the relation between carbon price and other variables we show a positive impact from the industrial production index, whereas a negative relation from the crude oil price and renewable energy targets. Additionally, CO_2 price has a rather short-term association with historical occurrences of coal price and the weighted-average RPS as well as its own historical values. Although RPS programs help reduce carbon emissions, the increase in renewable energy displaces mostly natural gas which is less polluting than coal. While the price of electricity and renewable credits are expected to increase under an RPS, energy generation using either coal or natural gas should decrease. It is noticed also that the RPS programs are generally superior to alternative policies. When overall economic activity increases monthly or yearly within states, we expect renewable energy production and/or renewable portfolio standards targets to increase. Moreover, contrary to the theory and literature, coal price is found to have a positive impact on emission prices.

5 Concluding Comments

The Paris Agreement assumes profound significance as a comprehensive and internationally recognized framework for addressing the complexities of climate change. Its importance lies in the establishment of an ambitious and collective global response to the climate crisis, emphasizing the imperative of decarbonization and sustainable development. Within the USA, renewable portfolio standards (RPS) serve as a key instrument to operationalize the commitments outlined in the Paris Agreement. These state-level policies impose binding obligations on utilities to secure a predetermined percentage of their electricity from renewable energy sources, thereby fostering the growth of clean and sustainable energy generation (Kelly, 2019). Increasing the incentives to renewable energy sources, a policy complementary to RPS's, is shown to have a significant effect on CO_2 prices. Renewable energy investments also significantly impact CO_2 prices which reduces the quantity of carbon traded in the market, at least in the USA. We recommend that the use of complementary environmental policies as an auxiliary factor in reducing carbon emissions across countries should continue. This study also illustrates the necessity of understanding the dynamics of energy sources to improve renewable energy investments even in a country with relatively low allowance prices compared to EU-ETS. Even though RGGI is a relatively new and nascent market, and despite the limited and irregular nature of the financial data generated by RGGI and the energy markets, this study contributes an insight for further studies to determine the price drivers for exchange-traded emission allowances and to understand how greenhouse gas emissions change with the prices of natural resources and the incentives toward production of energy from renewable sources (Richards, 1931).

References

Aatola, P., Ollikainen, M., & Toppinen, A. (2013). Price determination in the EU ETS market: Theory and econometric analysis with market fundamentals. *Energy Economics, 36*, 380–395.

Abrell, J., & Weigt, H. (2008). *The interaction of emissions trading and renewable energy promotion.* Dresden University of Technology Working Paper no. WP-EGW-05.

Alberola, E., Chevallier, J., & Chèze 1, B. (2008). The EU emissions trading scheme: The effects of industrial production and CO_2 emissions on carbon prices. *Economie Internationale, 4*, 93-125.

ASME (American Society of Mechanical Engineers), General Position Statement on Reducing Carbon Dioxide Emissions Technology and Policy Recommendations and Goals for in the Energy Sector I. (2009). https://fc-es.net/wp-content/uploads/2012/08/National-Climate-Plan-USA-Phase-1.pdf

Benz, E., & Trück, S. (2009). Modeling the price dynamics of CO_2 emission allowances. *Energy Economics, 31*(1), 4–15.

Bunn, D. W., & Fezzi, C. (2007). *Interaction of European carbon trading and energy prices.*

Chevallier, J. (2011). *Econometric analysis of carbon markets: the European Union emissions trading scheme and the clean development mechanism. Springer Science and Business Media.*

Chevallier, J. (2013). Carbon price drivers: An updated literature review. *International Journal of Applied Logistics (IJAL), 4*(4), 1–7.

Chun, D., Cho, H., & Kim, J. (2022). The relationship between carbon-intensive fuel and renewable energy stock prices under the emissions trading system. *Energy Economics, 114*, 106257.

Çoşkun, H. E. (2019). *Influence of renewable energy on carbon prices in the USA.* Master's thesis, Middle East Technical University.

DSIRE (Database of State Incentives for Renewables & Efficiency). (2018). https://www.dsireusa.org/

EIAa (U.S. Energy Information Administration). (2019). US natural gas prices by region. https://www.eia.gov/dnav/ng/ng_pri_sum_dcu_nus_m.htm

EIAb (U.S. Energy Information Administration). (2019). US coal prices by region, Quandl. https://www.quandl.com/data/EIA/COAL-US-Coal-Prices-by-Region

EIAc (U.S. Energy Information Administration). (2019). Crude oil spor prices by region. https://www.eia.gov/todayinenergy/detail.php?id=42415

EIAd (U.S. Energy Information Administration). (2019). Database of state incentives for renewables & efficiency. https://www.eia.gov/electricity/data.php

EPA (US Environmental Protection Agency). (2017). Global greenhouse gas emissions data, https://www.epa.gov/ghgemissions/global-greenhouse-gas-emissions-data

Evensen, D. (2017). Renewable energy policy: Enumerating costs reduces support. *Nature Energy, 2*, 17106.

FED (Federal Reserve Bank). (2019). Industrial production and capacity utilization, F. R. B. of St. Louis B. of Governors of The Federal Reserve System. https://www.federalreserve.gov/releases/g17/current/

Görlach, B. (2014). Emissions trading in the climate policy mix—Understanding and managing interactions with other policy instruments. *Energy and Environment, 25*(3–4), 733–749.

Hammoudeh, S., Nguyen, D. K., & Sousa, R. M. (2014). Energy prices and CO_2 emission allowance prices: A quantile regression approach. *Energy Policy, 70*, 201–206.

Heindl, P., & Löschel, A. (2012). Designing emissions trading in practice general considerations and experiences from the EU emissions trading scheme (EU ETS). *ZEW Discussion Papers, 12*.
Herber, B. P., & Raga, J. T. (1995). An international carbon tax to combat global warming: An economic and political analysis of the European union proposal. *American Journal of Economics and Sociology, 54*, 257–267. https://doi.org/10.1111/j.1536-7150.1995.tb03422.x
Hintermann, B. (2010). Allowance price drivers in the first phase of the EU ETS. *Journal of Environmental Economics and Management, 59*(1), 43–56.
Ho, B. (2018). RGGI shows tackling climate change pays major dividends, NRDC (Natural Resources Defense Council). https://www.nrdc.org/experts/bruce-ho/rggi-shows-tackling-climate-change-pays-major-dividends.
Kelly, L. (2019). The power of renewable energy: A comprehensive analysis of renewable portfolio standards and their strengths. *CU Scholar*. https://scholar.colorado.edu/concern/undergraduate_honors_theses/h128nf13x
Kim, H. S., & Koo, W. W. (2010). Factors affecting the carbon allowance market in the US. *Energy Policy, 38*(4), 1879–1884.
Kim, M.-K., & Lee, K. (2015). Dynamic interactions between carbon and energy prices in the US regional greenhouse gas initiative region. *International Journal of Energy Economics and Policy, 5*, 2.
Koch, N., Fuss, S., Grosjean, G., & Edenhofer, O. (2014). Causes of the EU ETS price drop: Recession, CDM, renewable policies or a bit of everything?—New evidence. *Energy Policy, 73*, 676–685.
Kossoy, A. (2015). *State and trends of carbon pricing 2015*. World Bank Publications.
Mansanet-Bataller, M., Pardo, A., & Valor, E. (2007). CO_2 prices, energy and weather. *The Energy Journal, 28*(3).
Mitigation, C. C. (2011). IPCC special report on renewable energy sources and climate change mitigation. *Renewable Energy, 20*(11).
Mulder M. (2018).*The waterbed effect*. University of Groningen. https://www.futurelearn.com/courses/energy-transition/0/steps/10227
Oh, T. H. (2010). Carbon capture and storage potential in coal-fired plant in Malaysia—A review. *Renewable and Sustainable Energy Reviews, 14*(9), 2697–2709.
RGGIa (The Regional Greenhouse Gas Initiative). (2019). Regional greenhouse gas initiative database. https://www.rggi.org/
RGGIb (The Regional Greenhouse Gas Initiative). (2019). Regional greenhouse gas initiative information. https://www.rggi.org/
Reboredo, J. C. (2013). Modeling EU allowances and oil market interdependence, implications for portfolio management. *Energy Economics, 36*, 471–480.
Richards, L. A. (1931). Capillary conduction of liquids through porous mediums. *Physics, 1*(5), 318–333.
Rickels, W., Duscha, V., Keller, A., & Peterson, S. (2007). *The determinants of allowance prices in the European emissions trading scheme: Can we expect an efficient allowance market 2008?* (No. 1387). Kiel Working Paper.
Rickels, W., Görlich, D., & Oberst, G. (2010). Explaining European emission allowance price dynamics: Evidence from Phase II, No 1650, Kiel Working Papers, Kiel Institute for the World Economy (IfW Kiel).
UN (United Nations). (2015), Framework convention on climate change. https://unfccc.int/resource/docs/2015/cop21/eng/l09r01.pdf
U.S. Energy Information Administration. (2016). Greenhouse gases' effect on climate—U.S. Energy Information Administration (EIA). Eia.gov. https://www.eia.gov/energyexplained/energy-and-the-environment/greenhouse-gases-and-the-climate.php
Van den Bergh, K., Delarue, E., & D'haeseleer, W. (2013). Impact of renewables deployment on the CO_2 price and the CO2 emissions in the European electricity sector. *Energy Policy, 63*, 1021–1031.

Xu, C., Li, X., Liu, X., & Li, J. (2020). An integrated de-carbonization supercritical coal-fired power plant incorporating a supplementary steam turbine, process heat recovery and a modified boiler structure. *Applied Thermal Engineering, 178*, 115532. https://doi.org/10.1016/j.applthermaleng.2020.115532

Static and Dynamic Connectedness Between Green Bonds and Clean Energy Markets

Ayşe Nur Şahinler, Fatih Cemil Ozbugday, Sidika Basci, and Tolga Omay

Abstract The green bond market has become one of the most promising mechanisms to raise financial sources for projects with environmental benefits that not only achieve carbon–neutral goals but also allow to diversify the risk and hedging. In this study, we examine the possible interdependence between the green bond market and seven energy markets, including Wilder Hill Clean Energy Index, S&P Global Clean Energy Index, Nasdaq Clean Edge Green Energy, Ardour Global Solar Energy Index, S&P Global Water Index, and MSCI Global Green Building Index using Diebold and Yilmaz's (2012) spillover framework. Our findings show that movements in the clean energy market have a spillover effect in the green bond market. Additionally, the spread of risk is asymmetrical.

Keywords Green bond · Green equity · Time connectedness

JEL Classification Q5 · N20

A. N. Şahinler · F. C. Ozbugday · S. Basci (✉)
Ankara Yıldırım Beyazıt University (AYBU), Ankara, Turkey
e-mail: sidika.basci@aybu.edu.tr

A. N. Şahinler
e-mail: aysenursahinler@aybu.edu.tr

F. C. Ozbugday
e-mail: fcozbugday@aybu.edu.tr

T. Omay
Atilim University, Ankara, Turkey
e-mail: tolga.omay@atilim.edu.tr

J. Thewissen et al. (eds.), *The ESG Framework and the Energy Industry*,
https://doi.org/10.1007/978-3-031-48457-5_8

1 Introduction

The World Bank Group President Jim Yong Kim said, "*Climate change is not just an environmental challenge. It is a fundamental threat to economic development and the fight against poverty.*" Sustainable growth can only be achieved with environmentally friendly development, as the environment provides natural resources and sets limits on economic growth (Guo & Zhou, 2021). For this reason, the acceleration of climate change over the past few years has shown that it is necessary to take actions immediately to decrease greenhouse gas emissions and avoid destructive effects on ecosystems and human life. Developing clean energy sources is a key strategy for decarbonizing the energy system and ensuring environmental protection (Van Hoang et al., 2019). Due to the investors' interest in environmental risk and the 2015 Paris Agreement, in which a wide range of countries pledged to transition to a climate-resilient economy, the green bond market has become one of the fastest-growing segments of international capital markets for a decade (Reboredo, 2018). Although the green bond market initially grew slowly, it has shown an impressive growth of over 50% in the last five years. The Climate Bond Initiative reports that the green bond market cumulatively reached 104 billion US dollars at the end of 2015. For the first time in 2017, it broke the yearly threshold of 100 billion US dollars; and in December 2020, it reached 1 trillion US dollars. As a result, the highest growth and diversification in this market occured in 2020. From 2020 to 2021, the green bond market expanded by 75% to 522.7 billion US dollars. Hence, the total was 1.6 trillion US dollars. It reached 2 trillion US dollars at the end of September 2022. Sean Kidney, CEO of Climate Bonds, states that, in order to achieve climate-related targets, green bond issuance must reach 5 trillion US dollars annually by 2025, issued by governments, policymakers, and investors.

Green bonds are considered in the fixed-income asset class, just like government or corporate bonds, in terms of pricing and rating. However, green bonds are issued to finance investment projects that aim to provide environmental and climatic benefits such as low-carbon emissions. Nevertheless, in addition to their risk-return curves, the economic effects of green bonds also depend on the impact of other market fluctuations on them (Liu et al., 2021). Furthermore, understanding the interdependence between the green bond market and other financial markets is also important for the development of green bond markets and their role as a means of diversifying risk for investors. The risk spillovers from or to green bond markets can alter investors' incentives to allocate funds to cleaner or greener projects, which are critical for the transition to a low-carbon economy. Thus, the spillovers between green bonds and other clean energy markets have practical implications for policymakers and investors, and a comprehension of these spillovers is essential.

The phenomenon of spillover between two financial markets has different economic bases and internal transmission mechanisms. In the theoretical literature, several hypotheses have been proposed to explain the risk spillover effects between the stock and bond markets. The first hypothesis is financial contagion. According to this hypothesis, financial contagion occurs when financial distress in one market spreads to other markets without any information being released or due to an overreaction to news disclosure or noise. This hypothesis is consistent with the evidence suggesting that news announcements are not a main determinant of the observed market return connectedness (i.e., Connolly & Wang, 2000; Connolly et al., 2005; Kodres & Pritsker, 2002; Lin & Ito, 1994). The second hypothesis is the hedging demand shift hypothesis. When the price of an asset deviates too much from its true value, investors will want to shift to another safe asset for hedging (Barksy, 1986; Campbell & Ammer, 1993; Hong et al., 2014). This hypothesis predicts that good news in the stock market will push bond prices down. The final hypothesis is the asset substitution hypothesis: bonds and stocks are viewed as competing assets. Any disclosure or information affects the attractiveness of these two different assets. If one piece of information contributes to an increase in the stock price, this causes investors to convert the bonds in their portfolios into stocks or vice versa. Thus, a positive earnings shock in one market propagates as a negative shock in another (Liu et al., 2021).

Despite the relevance of practical implications, there are the few papers on the spillover effects between green bond markets and other clean energy markets, and these are rather new. The findings of these papers point to spillovers between green bond markets and other clean energy markets. To advance our limited knowledge of the spillovers between green bond markets and other clean energy markets, we investigate the interconnectedness between the green bond market, represented by the S&P Dow Jones GB Index, and six sectoral and global clean energy market indexes: WilderHill Clean Energy, S&P Global Clean Energy, Nasdaq Clean Edge Green Energy, Ardour Solar Energy, S&P Global Water, and Nasdaq OMX Green Building. Thus, our main research question is, "***what is the extent of spillover effects between green bond markets and other clean energy markets?***" To answer that question, we examine return and volatility spillover between the indexes mentioned above in a Diebold and Yılmaz (2012) framework.

The results of the empirical analyses indicate that the green bond market is substantially influenced by price spillovers from the clean energy market during extreme market conditions. From a portfolio standpoint, these findings indicate that green bonds do not provide managers/investors with an opportunity for diversification in their portfolios that include clean energy market instruments. Contrarily, the risk interconnectivity of the green bond index and clean energy exchange-traded funds (ETFs) allows for opening of short positions to protect against risks.

The paper proceeds as follows. Section 2 presents the literature review. In Sect. 3, data and methodology are explained. Results obtained from the analysis are presented in Sect. 4. Finally, Sect. 5 concludes.

2 Literature Review

Numerous scholars have discussed the effects of green bond premiums. No clear conclusions have yet been made regarding this subject. Karpf and Mandel (2017) show that there is a statistically significant positive spread between conventional and green bonds on average. Green bond premiums are also found to be positive by Bachelet et al. (2019) and Wu (2022). Nevertheless, Immel et al. (2021), Zerbib (2019), and Hachenberg and Schiereck (2018) indicate a negative premium.

Recently, some studies have started to examine the green bond market and other conventional markets. Pham (2016) finds a spillover between the aggregate and green bonds. Reboredo (2018) finds a strong correlation between green bonds and treasury and between green bonds and corporate bonds but a weak correlation between green bonds and the stock market. Reboredo and Ugolini (2020) and Hammoudeh (2020) find a one-direction Granger causality running from CO_2 and treasury to the green bond market.

A number of studies have focused on assessing the linkage between clean energy stocks and energy commodities (such as natural gas and crude oil). Findings show that oil prices and sectoral clean energy indices are weakly interrelated (Sadorsky, 2012; Managi & Okimoto, 2013; Reberedo et al., 2017; Ferrer et al., 2018; Paiva et al., 2018; Maghyereh et al., 2019; Umar et al., 2022; Farid et al., 2023). However, Kumar et al. (2012) document that oil prices affect the stock prices of clean energy firms. Similarly, Reboredo (2015) finds that oil prices symmetrically contribute to systemic risk in renewable energy stocks. In addition, some other studies have demonstrated that clean energy stocks react differently to new information on oil prices under different market conditions (Dawar et al., 2021; Geng et al., 2021; Kocaarslan & Soytas, 2019; Lee & Baek, 2018).

Furthermore, other empirical studies in the literature have begun to look at the relationship between commodity markets and green bonds after finding that green bonds and clean energy equities seem to be aiming for the same objective of reducing environmental degradation. First studies deal with the linkage overall energy market and green bonds, and they find little effect of energy commodities on green bonds (Reberedo, 2018; Reboredo & Ugolini, 2020; Nguyen et al., 2021; Ferrer et al., 2021; Arif et al., 2022). However, Park et al. (2020) reveal an asymmetric relationship between green bonds and the energy market. Their results show that the green bond market is more sensitive to positive shocks. Some researchers have attempted to address this gap with various econometric methodologies due to the absence of empirical research on determining the relationship between sub-commodity markets and green bonds. Kanamura (2020) has focused on correlations between energy commodities and green bonds (the S&P green bond and the Bloomberg Barclays MSCI); however, the findings vary depending on the green bond used. The author shows a significant negative correlation between crude oil and Solactive green bonds but a positive correlation between S&P green bond index and crude oil. Naeem et al. (2021) also extend the literature by considering the diversifying benefit of the green bond market against the price movement in commodities, including silver, gold, natural gas, heating oil, crude oil, gasoline, aluminum, copper, zinc, nickel, wheat, soybean, cocoa, coffee, corn, cotton, and sugar. They find that green bonds provide the best protection from market volatility for commodities like natural gas, aluminum, wheat, coffee, cocoa, and soybean using the cross-quantilogram methodology. Similarly, Xiang et al. (2023) investigate the green bond market and its connectedness with only natural resources commodities such as oil, coal, and natural gas by applying the quantile ARDL method. Their findings indicate that coal price has a significant positive effect on green bonds at all quantiles. Oil price also has a positive effect on green bonds, but it negatively affects green bonds at low quantiles.

The growing popularity of clean energy markets and green bonds has influenced many scholars. The study conducted by Liu et al. (2021) is the first empirical investigation into clean energy markets and green bonds. They indicate that the tail risk of green bonds will be triggered by changes in the return of clean energy assets. Pham (2021) finds strong spillovers between green stocks and bonds following sharp price fluctuations. Similarly, Tiwari et al. (2022) show that clean energy dominates the green bond market. Chatziantoniou et al. (2022) also indicate that the green bond market is the primary net recipient of shocks. Finally, Chai et al. (2022) reveal a positive link between the clean energy and green bond, but this link has some differences at different times.

The objective of the current study is to investigate the relationship between stock prices of alternative clean energy indices and the green bond market by deploying constant and time-varying connectedness methods. We also consider asymmetric and long memory properties for their unconditional volatility. Our sample period differs from earlier studies.

3 Data and Methodology

S&P Dow Jones Green Bond Index represents the global green bond market. The six green equities used are NASDAQ (Nasdaq), S&P Global Clean Energy Index (Clean), Wilder Hill Clean Energy Index (WilderHill), Ardour Global Solar Energy Index (Solar), S&P Global Water Index (Water), and MSCI Global Green Building Index (Building). Daily data in US dollars is downloaded from Datastream. The sample period is August 2010–July 2022.

Returns are calculated by taking the difference between the logarithms of two consecutive prices, first log differences of closing prices, that is,

$$r_t = (\ln p_t - \ln p_{t-1}) * 100, \tag{1}$$

where r_t is return and p_t is price at time t, $t = 1, \ldots, 3099$. Following Öztek and Öcal (2017), the extreme returns outside the confidence interval of three standard deviations around the mean are substituted with their boundary values.

Table 1 presents the descriptive statistics for the dataset, including mean returns, standard deviations, skewness, kurtosis, and results from tests Jarque-Bera (JB) and the augmented Dickey-Fuller (ADF). All mean returns are positive, except for those of S&P Dow Jones Green Bond and Ardour Global Solar Energy. The high standard deviations realized for NASDAQ (1.83), Ardour Global Solar Energy (2.40), and Wilder Hill Clean Energy (1.94) indicate a high degree of variabilities for these returns. The lowest standard deviation is for the S&P Dow Jones Green Bond (0.36), indicating the stability of this return. The skewness values are negative and significant for all returns except for green bond and other financial markets returns except Ardour Global Solar Energy. Moreover, all the kurtosis values are greater than three, showing that all return series exhibit fat-tail distributions. These are indicators of non-normality of the sample data, and Jarque–Bera (JB) test supports these indications by rejecting the null hypothesis of the normality at a 1% significance level. The augmented Dickey-Fuller (ADF) test for unit roots clearly rejects the null hypothesis that the series have a unit root.

The correlation matrix of returns is presented in Table 2. Except for the S&P Global Water Index, all of the correlations with the S&P Dow Jones Green Bond are positive. The return correlations range from −0.059, between green bonds and clean energy returns, to 0.284. For instance, green bonds have a positive correlation with Clean, with an estimated value of 0.284, and have a positive correlation with Building, with an estimated value of 0.241. However, green bonds are negatively correlated with Water (−0.059). As may be seen from Table 2, Clean energy returns

Table 1 Descriptive statistics

	Green	Nasdaq	Clean	WilderHill	Solar	Water	Building
Mean	−0.01	0.05	0.02	0.01	−0.004	0.05	0.03
Median	0	0.09	0.05	0	0.008	0.07	0.04
Maximum	1.17	5.86	4.49	6.216	12.96	2.84	3.05
Minimum	−1.18	−5.77	−4.48	−6.209	−12.99	−2.772	−3.01
Standard Deviation	0.36	1.83	1.37	1.942	2.404	0.836	0.87
Skewness	−0.16	−0.14	−0.06	−0.11	0.09	−0.21	−0.20
Kurtosis	4.55	4.41	4.56	4.44	8.40	4.59	5.17
Jarque–Bera	324.73 (0.00)	266.48 (0.000)	320.52 (0.00)	277.57 (0.00)	3776.0 (0.00)	349.38 (0.00)	631.9 (0.00)
Sum	−19.67	159.25	47.74	33.95	−15.18	141.01	95.30
Sum of squared deviation	416.62	10,330.9	5884.6	11,695.2	17,907	2165.8	2363.1
Observations	3099	3099	3099	3099	3099	3099	3099
ADF	−37.54	−13.96	−11.58	−13.72	−12.74	−14.93	−26.54

ADF stands for the augmented Dickey-Fuller unit root tests

are highly correlated between themselves but not perfectly. The correlation ranges from about 39 to 93%.

Addressing the issue of volatility spillover is based on conditional variance, which is obtained from Generalized Autoregressive Conditional Heteroskedasticity (GARCH) specifications.

We use Diebold and Yılmaz (2012) spillover framework. This approach provides both gross and net directional spillover measures that are independent of the ordering used for the volatility forecast error variance decompositions. Diebold and Yılmaz's framework is not the first to consider issues related to volatility spillovers.

The dynamic connectedness method was initially proposed by Diebold and Yilmaz (2009). However, this method has several limitations, both methodological and substantive. Firstly, as the method is based on the Cholesky factor identification of VARs, variance decompositions will be sensitive to variable ordering. The second limitation of the method is that it only addresses the **total** spillovers. Someone would also like to examine **directional** spillovers. Diebold and Yilmaz (2012) suggest a generalized vector autoregressive framework in which forecast error variance decompositions are invariant to the variable ordering. Under this approach, we can quantify spillover dynamics, examining rolling-sample total spillovers, rolling-sample directional spillovers, rolling-sample net directional spillovers, and rolling-sample net pairwise spillovers. Following Diebold and Yilmaz (2012), a covariance stationary N-variable VAR(p) model is written as

$$y_t = \sum_{j=1}^{p} \theta y_{t-j} + \varepsilon_t, \tag{2}$$

where $\varepsilon \sim (0, \sum)$ a vector of independently and identically distributed disturbances. y_t is the $n \times 1$ vector of observed variables at time t. θ_t is $N \times N$ coefficient matrices.

The H-step ahead forecast error variance decompositions are

$$\phi_{ij}^{g}(H) = \frac{\sigma_{jj}^{-1} \sum_{h=0}^{H-1} \left((\vartheta_h \Sigma)_{ij} \right)^2}{\sum_{h=0}^{H-1} \left(\vartheta_h \Sigma_h^T \right)_{ii}}, \tag{3}$$

Table 2 Correlation matrix

	Green	Nasdaq	Clean	WilderHill	Solar	Water	Building
Green	1						
Nasdaq	0.139	1					
Clean	0.284	0.774	1				
WilderHill	0.152	0.937	0.788	1			
Solar	0.157	0.720	0.734	0.741	1		
Water	−0.059	0.572	0.533	0.543	0.395	1	
Building	0.241	0.511	0.537	0.501	0.399	0.671	1

where σ_{jj} is the standard deviation of the error term for variable j, $\sum$ is the variance matrix for the error vector ε, and $\phi_{ij}^{g}(H)$ shows variables' contribution to their own forecast error variance for $i, j = 1, 2, \ldots, N$, such that $i \neq j$. Since the sum of the elements in each row of the variance decomposition is not equal to 1, $\phi_{ij}^{g}(H)$ is normalized as

$$\tilde{\phi}_{ij}^{g}(H) = \frac{\phi_{ij}^{g}}{\sum_{j=1}^{N} \phi_{ij}^{g}(H)}. \tag{4}$$

The total spillover index represents the contribution of spillovers of volatility shocks:

$$S^{g}(H) = \frac{\sum_{\substack{i, j = 1 \\ i \neq j}}^{N} \tilde{\phi}_{ij}^{g}(H)}{\sum_{i,j}^{N} \tilde{\phi}_{ij}^{g}(H)} * 100 = \frac{\sum_{\substack{i, j = 1 \\ i \neq j}}^{N} \tilde{\phi}_{ij}^{g}(H)}{N} * 100. \tag{5}$$

The net volatility spillover from one market to other markets is defined as

$$S_{ij}^{g}(H) = S_{i \to j}^{g}(H) - S_{i \leftarrow j}^{g}(H). \tag{6}$$

If the net spillover effect has a negative value, this market is a net receiver of shocks from all other markets.

Finally, net total directional connectedness captures information about how much asset i contributes to the volatility of asset j. It is formulated as follows:

$$S_{ij}^{g}(H) = \frac{\tilde{\phi}_{ji}^{g}(H) - \tilde{\phi}_{ij}^{g}(H)}{N} * 100. \tag{7}$$

4 Results

In order to examine the connectedness between green bonds and the clean energy markets, we first estimate the univariate GARCH (1,1) processes. Table 3 lists the variance equations for the GARCH model estimations. We choose the best model using the Akaike information criteria (AIC). The IGARCH specification is the best model for green bonds and solar return series, while the FIAPARCH model, which captures long memory behavior and asymmetric effects in conditional variance, is the best model for the other series. It can be seen that all parameters for the green bond and solar return series are found to be significant at the 5% significant level. The "α" and "β" parameters represent the persistence of shocks and the persistence of volatility clustering, respectively. The persistence of shocks appears to be greater in building volatility than in other market indices. The "d" parameter is the long memory feature in volatility. When d is less than 0.5, autocorrelations quickly disappear. Results show that all "d" parameters are greater than 0 but less than 0.5. We conclude that Nasdaq, Clean, WilderHill, Water, and Building return series have a long memory feature but are in a weak form. "γ" parameter indicates an asymmetric effect. Negative shocks increase volatility more than positive shocks if this parameter is greater than zero. The "γ" parameter is positive and significant at the 5% significant level for Nasdaq, Clean, WilderHill, Water, and Building. A negative shock at time $t-1$ is said to have a bigger effect on variance at time t than a positive shock. Student's t distribution for the standardized residuals and standardized square residuals are presented in Table 3. According to the Box-Pierce Q statistics, no excessive autocorrelation remains in the residuals, which is insignificant up to lag 50.

Table 4 shows spillover analysis for the full sample period. According to the spillover matrix, "From others" on the top shows that one market receives spillover from other markets, while "to others" on the bottom indicates the magnitude of spillovers transmitted from one market to the other markets. The last two columns represent the net transmitters/receivers when the net spillover computed by the difference between "to others" and "from others" has a positive value/negative value. When one looks at panels A and B, it can be seen that the green bond market is a net receiver of shocks from all other markets. Some other green equities are also receivers like solar, water, and building considering return spillover index, while global equities, namely Nasdaq and S&P Clean, and WilderHill energy, are considered contributors to the spillover effect over the entire sample period. Panel B differs from panel A in terms of the water return series. Water is a net receiver from other markets in terms of returns, while it is a net contributor of shocks from all other markets in terms of volatility.

According to Table 4, S&P Clean Energy spills more into the green bond market to 6.42%, taking into account the return spillover index, while S&P Clean Energy also spills more into the green bond market to 12.16, considering the volatility spillover index. It can be said that green bonds are influenced by global equities strongly while moderately by sectoral equities. Global energy equities also play a significant role in terms of return and volatility transmission to global markets. For example, Wilder Hill Clean Energy Index appears to be the primary transmitter of shocks considering both the return and volatility spillover index. On the other hand, in sectoral equities excluding solar, the resources of the primary shocks come from the sectoral markets. From the view of return and volatility transmission, spillover from MSCI Global Green Building Index is the largest one.

Because dynamic spillover analysis includes a great amount of information, we limit ourselves to "total" and "net" connectedness, which may be understood as total systemic risk and the net influence of clean energy markets on green bonds during the last decade.[1] Figures 1 and 2 show the time-varying total return and volatility spillover of the green bond market and green equities. Both figures indicate that

[1] The "from", "to", and "net pairwise" directional connectedness tables are presented in Figs. 7a, b, 8a, b, and 9a, b in the Appendix. "From" Diebold–Yilmaz spillover index in Fig. 7a, b shows the total spillover received by all other markets, while "to" in Fig. 8a, b indicates the total spillover effect for all equities. Directional spillovers for "to" are relatively less volatile than directional

Table 3 GARCH models

	ω	α	β	d	γ	δ	Log (L)	Q (50)	Q_s (50)
Green	0.0003 (0.020)	0.045 (0.000)	0.954				−893.70	(0.102)	(0.538)
Nasdaq	0.012 (0.866)	0.178 (0.036)	0.445 (0.000)	0.326 (0.000)	0.283 (0.001)	2.078 (0.000)	−5824.5	(0.371)	(0.184)
Clean	1.385 (0.026)	0.136 (0.125)	0.449 (0.000)	0.391 (0.000)	0.170 (0.000)	2.006 (0.000)	−4936.0	(0.037)	(0.251)
WilderHill	1.309 (0.077)	0.168 (0.099)	0.432 (0.001)	0.317 (0.000)	0.242 (0.006)	2.092 (0.000)	−6020.8	(0.215)	(0.142)
Solar	0.051 (0.016)	0.080 (0.000)	0.919				−6667.7	(0.271)	(0.116)
Water	0.044 (0.109)	0.223 (0.004)	0.389 (0.000)	0.253 (0.000)	0.389 (0.000)	1.575 (0.000)	−3479.3	(0.096)	(0.400)
Building	1.180 (0.000)	0.302 (0.000)	0.670 (0.000)	0.362 (0.000)	0.670 (0.000)	1.382 (0.000)	−3459.0	(0.447)	(0.448)

Q (50) and Q_s (50) show the Box-Pierce test for standardized residuals and squared standardized residuals. Numbers in parentheses are p-values

Table 4 Spillover index

	Green	Nasdaq	Clean	WilderHill	Solar	Water	Building	From	Net	Conclusion
Green	79.58	2.83	6.42	2.85	2.45	1.39	4.49	20.4	−14.3	Net recipient
Nasdaq	0.52	27.43	16.86	24.16	14.53	9.06	7.43	72.6	16.2	Net contributor
Clean	2.05	18.29	28.98	18.62	15.73	8.31	8.03	71	10	Net contributor
WilderHill	0.59	24.25	17.29	27.48	15.31	8.11	6.97	72.5	15	Net contributor
Solar	0.74	18.21	18.16	19.1	33.44	5.28	5.07	66.6	−6.2	Net recipient
Water	0.3	13.35	11.09	11.88	6.03	39.68	17.66	60.3	−9.9	Net recipient
Building	1.92	11.84	11.21	10.91	6.31	18.28	39.53	60.5	−10.8	Net recipient
To	6.1	88.8	81	87.5	60.4	50.4	49.7	423.9		Total spillover effect
All	85.7	116.2	110	115	93.8	90.1	89.2			60.6
Panel B: Volatility spillover index and components										
Green	62.63	5.41	12.16	4.94	2.09	5.35	7.42	37.4	−29.6	Net recipient
Nasdaq	0.91	32.02	17.55	27.79	4.22	10.26	7.25	68	18.8	Net contributor
Clean	2.18	17.92	32.37	18.4	7.41	11.33	10.38	67.6	12.6	Net contributor
WilderHill	0.7	27.9	18.06	32.44	4.74	8.76	7.41	67.6	14.4	Net contributor
Solar	0.17	9.94	9.37	8.65	64.04	4.28	3.54	36	−14	Net recipient
Water	1.69	13.67	10.81	11.58	1.62	42.34	18.28	57.7	4.9	Net contributor
Building	2.16	12	12.25	10.65	1.88	22.65	38.41	61.6	−7.3	Net recipient
To others	7.8	86.8	80.2	82	22	62.6	54.3	395.7		Total spillover effect
All	70.4	118.9	112.6	114.4	86	105	92.7			56.5

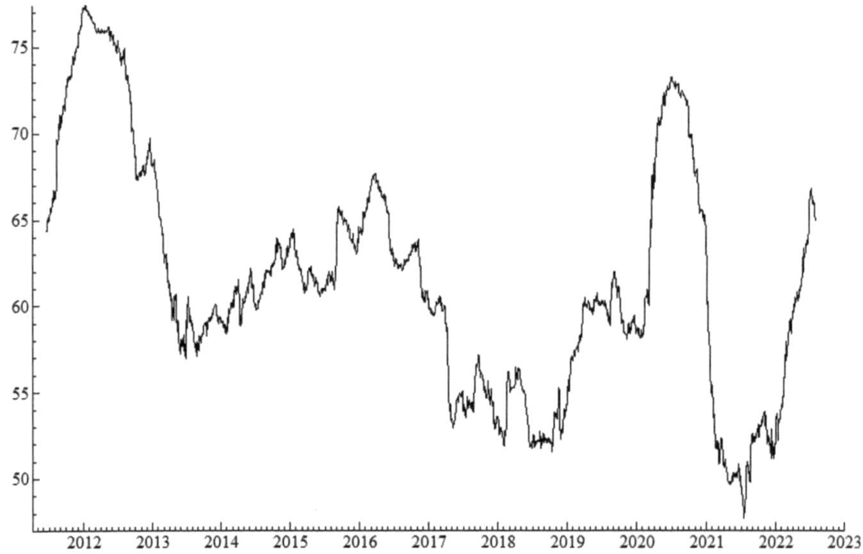

Fig. 1 Total return spillover index

spillover increases dramatically during the period of crisis and varies over time. Furthermore, we observe that dynamic return and volatility spillover are at their maximum during some different events in the market Sovereign Debt Crises in the Eurozone, 2010–2012 as well as in the recent COVID-19 pandemic crisis. Thus, our results tend to confirm that green bonds and green equities relationships are affected by shocks. When the connectedness rises substantially, opportunities for portfolio diversification will decrease.

Figures 3 and 4 reveal the time-varying evolution of the net spillover effect on returns and volatility for green bonds and different clean energy markets under this study. Net spillover analysis obtained from the 200-day rolling window estimation following Diebold and Yılmaz (2012) indicates which shocks have led to the most volatility in our variables at a particular point in time. When the spillover index has a negative (positive) value, this shows that series is a net receiver (contributor). As shown in Fig. 3, the return spillover index for the green bond is a net receiver of spillover during all periods, while the volatility spillover index for green bonds in Fig. 4 shows that it is a net contributor in sub-samples such as 2015, 2019, and 2022 years. When the sectoral markets are evaluated, the solar return spillover index is a net contributor for other markets during 2016–2019 and the beginning of the COVID-19 period. Water energy, on the other hand, has been more of a net contributor compared to the sectoral indexes, although mostly a net volatility recipient. Nasdaq,

spillovers for "from." Directional spillover effect for both increases during the crises. Dynamic pairwise spillover in Fig. 9a, b shows the difference between volatility that is transmitted from one clean energy market to another clean energy market and volatility that a particular market receives from another.

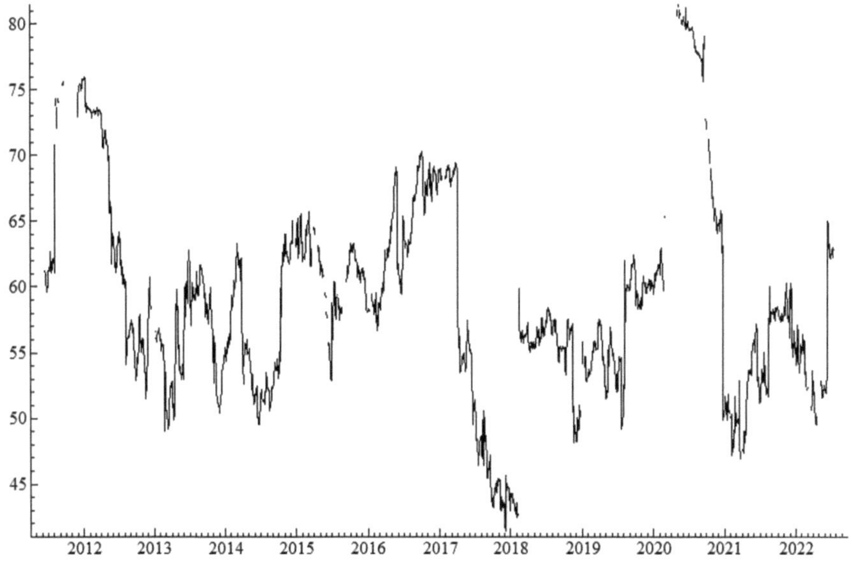

Fig. 2 Total volatility spillover index

one of the global clean energy markets, is the most net return transmitter throughout almost all periods.

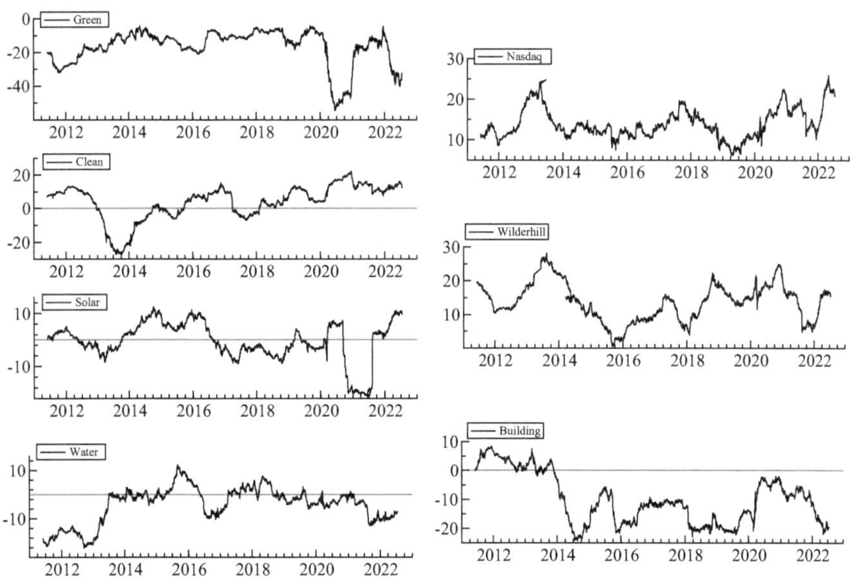

Fig. 3 Net return spillover

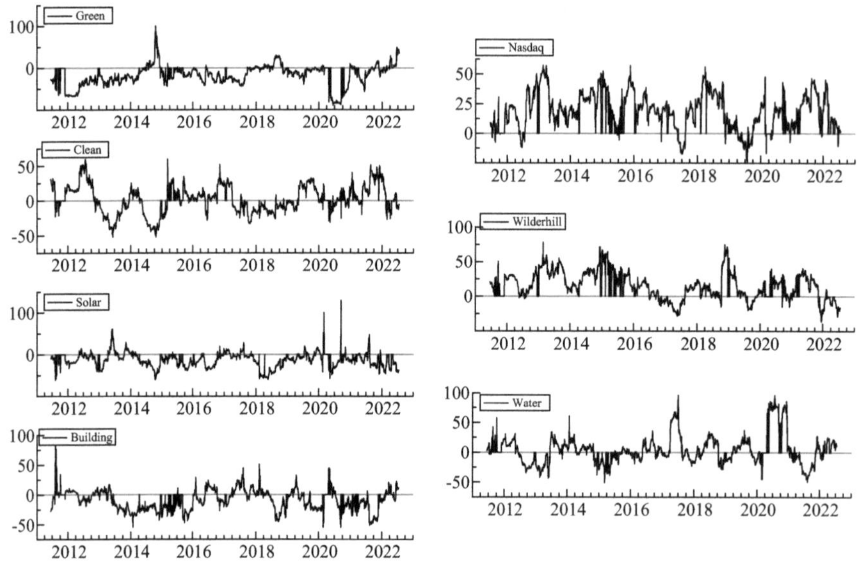

Fig. 4 Net volatility spillover

Net pairwise connectedness analysis can be used to examine the dependency relationship between certain market pairs over time. Thanks to this analysis, a practitioner or researcher can examine the relationship between two markets over time and easily decide at which periods the markets are contributing to a shock or receiving volatility from the other market. Figures 5 and 6 present net pairwise volatility spillovers between the green bond and other markets, respectively: Nasdaq, S&P Clean, WilderHill, solar energy, water, and building (see pairwise time-varying index for other series). According to Fig. 5, green bonds can be identified as net receiving from other markets for the return spillover index. However, Fig. 6 shows that the green bond is a net contributor to volatility spillover in the sub-sample. The biggest contributor to the shock for the green bond is Nasdaq energy, while the second contributor is the WilderHill energy market.

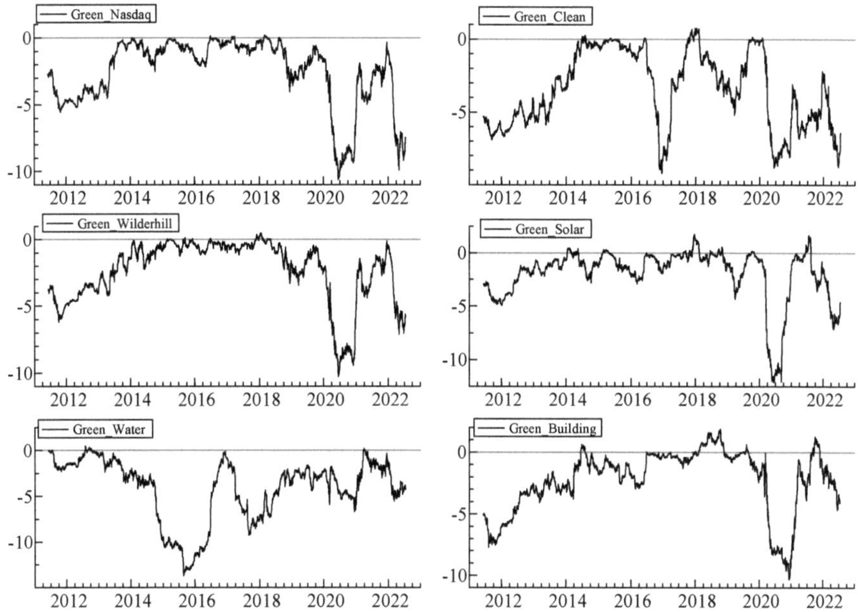

Fig. 5 Net pairwise return spillover

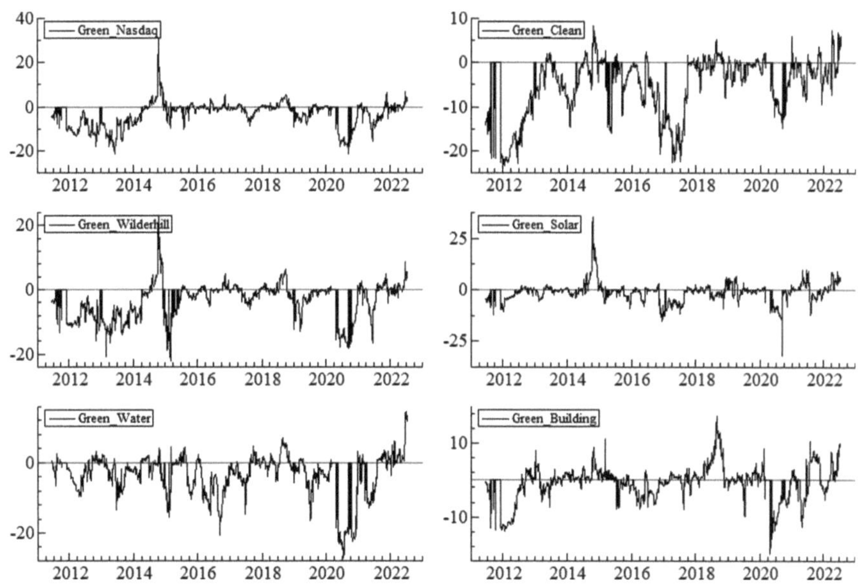

Fig. 6 Net pairwise volatility spillover

5 Conclusion

The transition to a greener economy requires raising substantial amounts of funds. As one element of sustainable finance, green bonds are becoming increasingly popular as a recent and new green finance opportunity. As of September 2022, the green bond market reached a cumulative milestone of 2 trillion US dollars, proving its essentiality for sustainable development. Thus, although green bonds have emerged as a new asset class for market participants, they have received considerable attention from policy makers and environmentally concerned investors.

Earlier empirical research has examined yields between green and ordinary bonds (Karpf & Mandel, 2017; Zerbib, 2019). In addition, several studies have focused on the relationship between green bonds and different financial markets (Pham, 2016; Reberedo, 2018; Reberedo & Ugolini, 2020; Hammoudeh et al., 2020; Ferrer et al., 2021). In this paper, we investigate interconnectedness between the green bond market, represented by the S&P Dow Jones GB Index, and six sectoral and global clean energy market indexes of WilderHill Clean Energy, S&P Global Clean Energy, Nasdaq Clean Edge Green Energy, Ardour Solar Energy, S&P Global Water, and NASDAQ OMX Green Building. Furthermore, we apply Diebold and Yılmaz (2012) framework to examine return and volatility spillover between the indexes.

Our results confirm earlier studies examining the relationship between green bonds and clean energy (Liu et al., 2021; Pham, 2021). The green bond market is substantially affected by price spillovers from the clean energy market during extreme market conditions. From a portfolio standpoint, the general findings of this study do not provide managers with an opportunity for diversification. Conversely, the risk interconnectivity of the green bond index and clean energy exchange-traded funds (ETFs) allows for opening short positions to protect against risks. This result aligns with what Liu et al. (2021) found.

Our study contributes to the newly established and limited literature on the spillovers between green bond markets and clean energy ETFs markets. The findings also have practical implications for designing sustainable finance policies to fund clean energy investments.

However, the study still has some limitations. The study does not explain economic bases and internal transmission mechanisms for the spillover effects between green bond markets and clean energy ETFs markets. To distinguish between various hypotheses, such as the asset substitution hypothesis, hedging demand shift hypothesis, or financial contagion hypothesis, for the spillovers between green bond markets and clean energy ETFs markets, we need a more micro-level research design with disaggregated variables. We leave this as future research.

Appendix

See Figs. 7, 8, and 9.

Fig. 7 **a** Directional return spillovers, FROM. **b** Directional return spillovers, TO

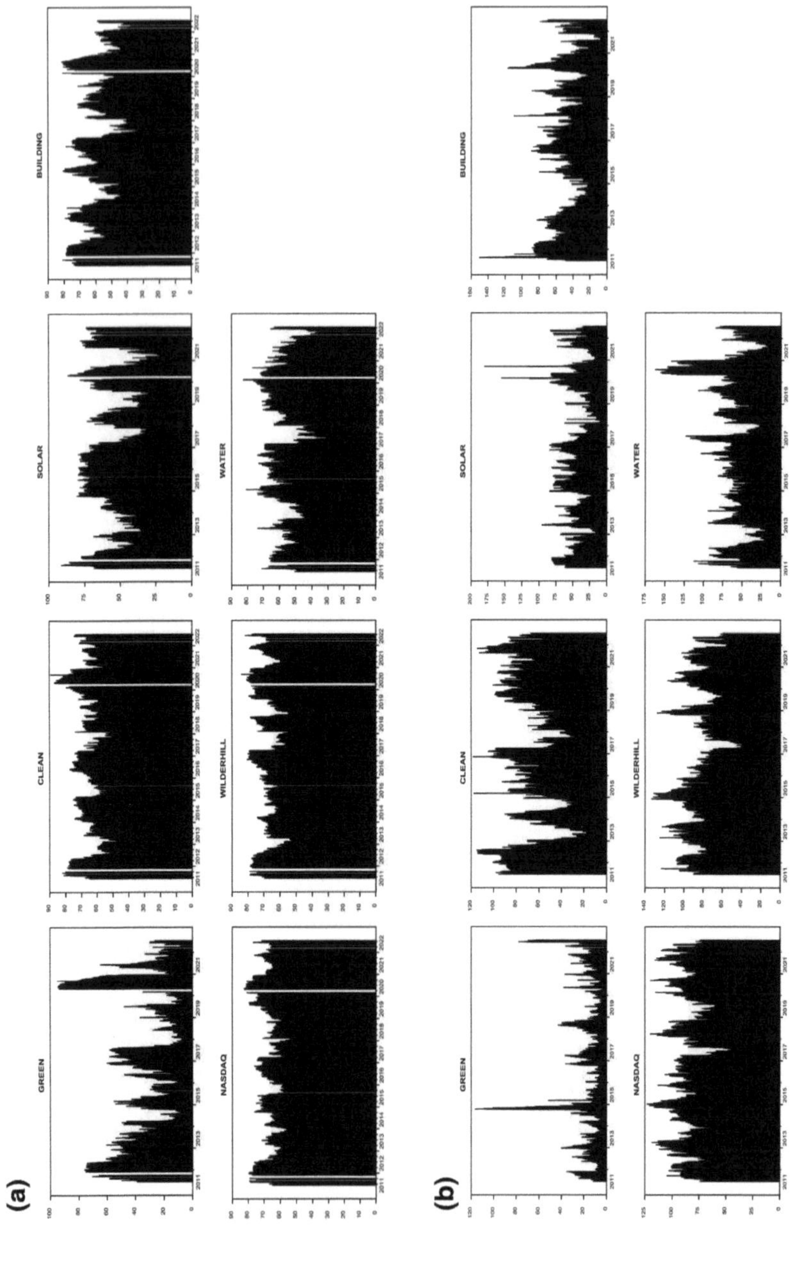

Fig. 8 **a** Directional volatility spillovers, FROM. **b** Directional volatility spillovers, TO

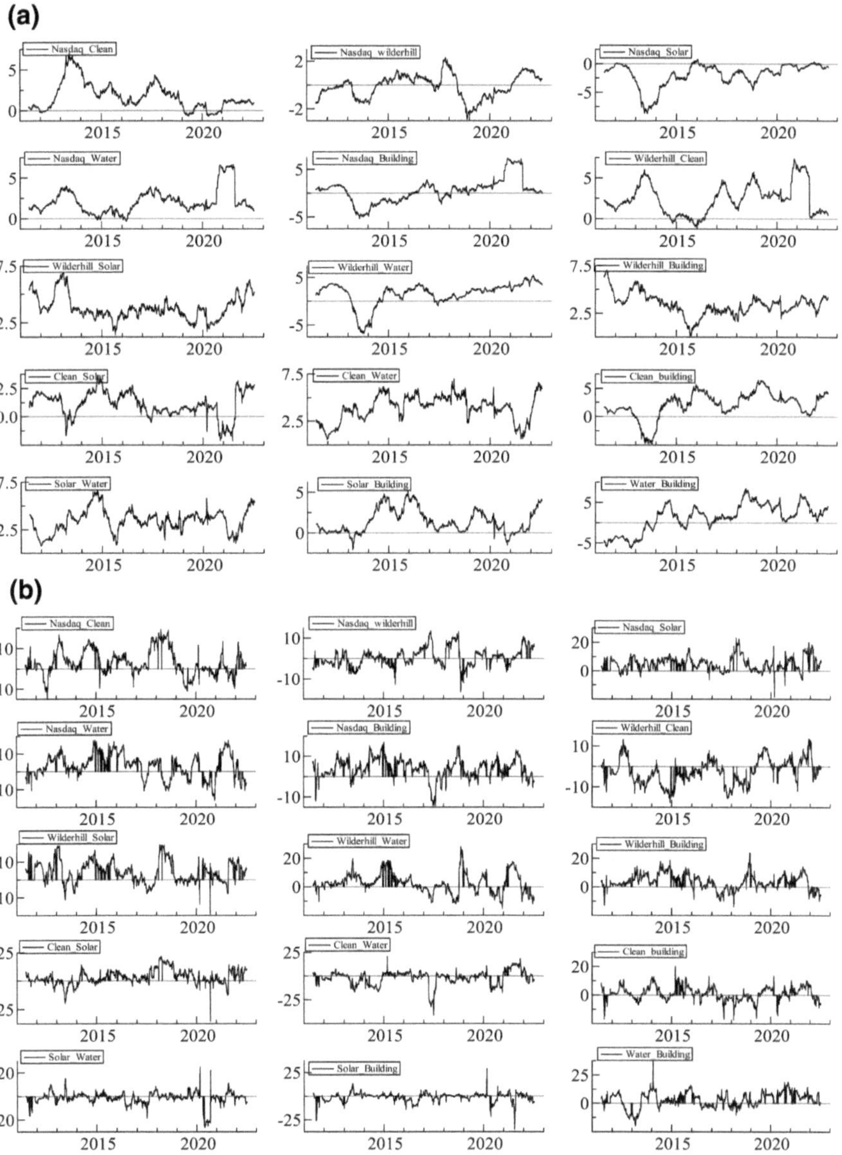

Fig. 9 **a** Net pairwise return spillovers. **b** Net pairwise volatility spillovers

References

Arif, M., Naeem, M. A., Farid, S., Nepal, R., & Jamasb, T. (2022). Diversifier or more? Hedge and safe haven properties of green bonds during COVID-19. *Energy Policy, 168*, 113102.

Bachelet, M. J., Becchetti, L., & Manfredonia, S. (2019). The green bonds premium puzzle: The role of issuer characteristics and third-party verification. *Sustainability, 11*(4), 1098.

Baker, M., Bergstresser, D., Serafeim, G., & Wurgler, J. (2018). *Financing the response to climate change: The pricing and ownership of US green bonds* (No. w25194). National Bureau of Economic Research.

Barsky, R. B. (1986). *Why don't the prices of stocks and bonds move together?* (No. w2047). National Bureau of Economic Research.

Broadstock, D. C., & Cheng, L. T. (2019). Time-varying relation between black and green bond price benchmarks: Macroeconomic determinants for the first decade. *Finance Research Letters, 29*, 17–22.

Campbell, J. Y., & Ammer, J. (1993). What moves the stock and bond markets? A variance decomposition for long-term asset returns. *The Journal of Finance, 48*(1), 3–37.

Chai, S., Chu, W., Zhang, Z., Li, Z., & Abedin, M. Z. (2022). Dynamic nonlinear connectedness between the green bonds, clean energy, and stock price: the impact of the COVID-19 pandemic. *Annals of Operations Research*, 1–28.

Chatziantoniou, I., Abakah, E. J. A., Gabauer, D., & Tiwari, A. K. (2022). Quantile time-frequency price connectedness between green bond, green equity, sustainable investments and clean energy markets. *Journal of Cleaner Production*, 132088.

Connolly, R., Stivers, C., & Sun, L. (2005). Stock market uncertainty and the stock-bond return relation. *Journal of Financial and Quantitative Analysis, 40*(1), 161–194.

Connolly, R. A., & Wang, F. A. (2000). On stock market return co-movements: Macroeconomic news, dispersion of beliefs, and contagion. *Dispersion of Beliefs, and Contagion (June 2000).*

Corbet, S., Goodell, J. W., & Günay, S. (2020). Co-movements and spillovers of oil and renewable firms under extreme conditions: New evidence from negative WTI prices during COVID-19. *Energy Economics, 92*, 104978.

Cotter, J. (2004). Minimum capital requirement calculations for UK futures. *Journal of Futures Markets: Futures, Options, and Other Derivative Products, 24*(2), 193–220.

Dawar, I., Dutta, A., Bouri, E., & Saeed, T. (2021). Crude oil prices and clean energy stock indices: Lagged and asymmetric effects with quantile regression. *Renewable Energy, 163*, 288–299.

Diebold, F. X., & Yilmaz, K. (2009). Measuring financial asset return and volatility spillovers, with application to global equity markets. *The Economic Journal, 119*(534), 158–171.

Diebold, F. X., & Yilmaz, K. (2012). Better to give than to receive: Predictive directional measurement of volatility spillovers. *International Journal of Forecasting, 28*(1), 57–66.

Edwards, S., & Susmel, R. (2001). Volatility dependence and contagion in emerging equity markets. *Journal of Development Economics, 66*(2), 505–532.

Engle, R. F., Ng, V. K., & Rothschild, M. (1990). Asset pricing with a factor-ARCH covariance structure: Empirical estimates for treasury bills. *Journal of Econometrics, 45*(1–2), 213–237.

Ferrer, R., Shahzad, S. J. H., López, R., & Jareño, F. (2018). Time and frequency dynamics of connectedness between renewable energy stocks and crude oil prices. *Energy Economics, 76*, 1–20.

Ferrer, R., Shahzad, S. J. H., & Soriano, P. (2021). Are green bonds a different asset class? Evidence from time-frequency connectedness analysis. *Journal of Cleaner Production, 292*, 125988.

Forsberg, L., & Ghysels, E. (2007). Why do absolute returns predict volatility so well? *Journal of Financial Econometrics, 5*(1), 31–67.

Geng, J. B., Liu, C., Ji, Q., & Zhang, D. (2021). Do oil price changes really matter for clean energy returns? *Renewable and Sustainable Energy Reviews, 150*, 111429.

Ghysels, E., Santa-Clara, P., & Valkanov, R. (2006). Predicting volatility: Getting the most out of return data sampled at different frequencies. *Journal of Econometrics, 131*(1–2), 59–95.

Gianfrate, G., & Peri, M. (2019). The green advantage: Exploring the convenience of issuing green bonds. *Journal of Cleaner Production, 219*, 127–135.

Guo, D., & Zhou, P. (2021). Green bonds as hedging assets before and after COVID: A comparative study between the US and China. *Energy Economics, 104*, 105696.

Hachenberg, B., & Schiereck, D. (2018). Are green bonds priced differently from conventional bonds? *Journal of Asset Management, 19*(6), 371–383.

Hammoudeh, S., Ajmi, A. N., & Mokni, K. (2020). Relationship between green bonds and financial and environmental variables: A novel time-varying causality. *Energy Economics, 92*, 104941.

Hong, G., Kim, Y., & Lee, B. S. (2014). Correlations between stock returns and bond returns: Income and substitution effects. *Quantitative Finance, 14*(11), 1999–2018.

Immel, M., Hachenberg, B., Kiesel, F., & Schiereck, D. (2021). Green bonds: Shades of green and brown. *Journal of Asset Management, 22*(2), 96–109.

Karpf, A., & Mandel, A. (2017). Does it pay to be green? Available at SSRN 2923484.

Kanamura, T. (2020). Are green bonds environmentally friendly and good performing assets? *Energy Economics, 88*, 104767.

Kocaarslan, B., & Soytas, U. (2019). Asymmetric pass-through between oil prices and the stock prices of clean energy firms: New evidence from a nonlinear analysis. *Energy Reports, 5*, 117–125.

Kodres, L. E., & Pritsker, M. (2002). A rational expectations model of financial contagion. *The Journal of Finance, 57*(2), 769–799.

Kumar, S., Managi, S., & Matsuda, A. (2012). Stock prices of clean energy firms, oil and carbon markets: A vector autoregressive analysis. *Energy Economics, 34*(1), 215–226.

Lee, D., & Baek, J. (2018). Stock prices of renewable energy firms: Are there asymmetric responses to oil price changes? *Economies, 6*(4), 59.

Lin, W. L., & Ito, T. (1994). Price volatility and volume spillovers between the Tokyo and New York stock markets. In *The internationalization of equity markets* (pp. 309–343). University of Chicago Press.

Liu, N., Liu, C., Da, B., Zhang, T., & Guan, F. (2021). Dependence and risk spillovers between green bonds and clean energy markets. *Journal of Cleaner Production, 279*, 123595.

Managi, S., & Okimoto, T. (2013). Does the price of oil interact with clean energy prices in the stock market? *Japan and the World Economy, 27*, 1–9.

Maghyereh, A. I., Awartani, B., & Abdoh, H. (2019). The co-movement between oil and clean energy stocks: A wavelet-based analysis of horizon associations. *Energy, 169*, 895–913.

Naeem, M. A., Nguyen, T. T. H., Nepal, R., Ngo, Q. T., & Taghizadeh-Hesary, F. (2021). Asymmetric relationship between green bonds and commodities: Evidence from extreme quantile approach. *Finance Research Letters, 43*, 101983.

Nguyen, T. T. H., Naeem, M. A., Balli, F., Balli, H. O., & Vo, X. V. (2021). Time-frequency comovement among green bonds, stocks, commodities, clean energy, and conventional bonds. *Finance Research Letters, 40*, 101739.

Paiva, A. S. S., Rivera-Castro, M. A., & Andrade, R. F. S. (2018). DCCA analysis of renewable and conventional energy prices. *Physica a: Statistical Mechanics and Its Applications, 490*, 1408–1414.

Park, D., Park, J., & Ryu, D. (2020). Volatility spillovers between equity and green bond markets. *Sustainability, 12*(9), 3722.

Pham, L. (2016). Is it risky to go green? A volatility analysis of the green bond market. *Journal of Sustainable Finance & Investment, 6*(4), 263–291.

Pham, L. (2021). Frequency connectedness and cross-quantile dependence between green bond and green equity markets. *Energy Economics, 98*, 105257.

Öztek, M. F., & Öcal, N. (2017). Financial crises and the nature of correlation between commodity and stock markets. *International Review of Economics and Finance, 48*, 56–68.

Reboredo, J. C. (2015). Is there dependence and systemic risk between oil and renewable energy stock prices? *Energy Economics, 48*, 32–45.

Reboredo, J. C., Rivera-Castro, M. A., & Ugolini, A. (2017). Wavelet-based test of co-movement and causality between oil and renewable energy stock prices. *Energy Economics, 61*, 241–252.

Reboredo, J. C. (2018). Green bond and financial markets: Co-movement, diversification and price spillover effects. *Energy Economics, 74*, 38–50.

Reboredo, J. C., & Ugolini, A. (2020). Price connectedness between green bond and financial markets. *Economic Modelling, 88*, 25–38.
Sadorsky, P. (2012). Correlations and volatility spillovers between oil prices and the stock prices of clean energy and technology companies. *Energy Economics, 34*(1), 248–255.
Tiwari, A. K., Abakah, E. J. A., Gabauer, D., & Dwumfour, R. A. (2022). Dynamic spillover effects among green bond, renewable energy stocks and carbon markets during COVID-19 pandemic: Implications for hedging and investments strategies. *Global Finance Journal, 51*, 100692.
Umar, M., Farid, S., & Naeem, M. A. (2022). Time-frequency connectedness among clean-energy stocks and fossil fuel markets: Comparison between financial, oil and pandemic crisis. *Energy, 240*, 122702.
Van Hoang, T. H., Shahzad, S. J. H., Czudaj, R. L., & Bhat, J. A. (2019). How do oil shocks impact energy consumption? A disaggregated analysis for the US. *The Energy Journal, 40* (The New Era of Energy Transition).
Wu, Y. (2022). Are green bonds priced lower than their conventional peers? *Emerging Markets Review*, 100909.
Xiang, S., & Cao, Y. (2023). Green finance and natural resources commodities prices: Evidence from COVID-19 period. *Resources Policy, 80*, 103200.
Zerbib, O. D. (2019). The effect of pro-environmental preferences on bond prices: Evidence from green bonds. *Journal of Banking and Finance, 98*, 39–60.

Do Green Bonds Improve the Stock and Environmental Performance of Energy Firms? International Evidence

Burak Pirgaip, Mehmet Baha Karan, and Seçil Sayın Kutluca

Abstract Given that the global decarbonization of the energy sector entails huge amount of investment, green bonds have become an important tool and source of long-term capital for energy firms. This chapter examines the impact of green bond issuance on their stock and environmental performance. We analyze a sample of 239 green bonds issued by 80 unique energy firms in the period 2013–2021. We first follow the event study methodology and find that market reaction to green bond issuance announcements is largely positive. Using the difference-in-differences approach, we then show that energy firms generally perform better in their environmental practices. However, our results also imply that green bond issuance has a lagged and temporary effect on stock prices and environmental achievements are not that obvious, particularly in the short term. We draw attention to partly inconclusive nature of these findings emerging from our analyses and offer relevant policy implications for green bond market development on the basis of tackling with greenwashing and scaling up the market share.

Keywords Green bonds · Energy firms · Environmental performance · Greenwashing · Sustainability

JEL Classification G12 · G14 · O13 · Q56

1 Introduction

The combat against the negative impact of environmental degradation and the climate change on energy economics has become a worldwide priority. Recent international initiatives such as the Paris Agreement of 2015 and the European Green Deal of 2019

B. Pirgaip (✉) · M. B. Karan
Department of Business Administration, Hacettepe University, Ankara, Turkey
e-mail: burakpirgaip@hacettepe.edu.tr

S. S. Kutluca
Department of Strategy Development, Capital Markets Board of Turkey, Ankara, Turkey

J. Thewissen et al. (eds.), *The ESG Framework and the Energy Industry*,
https://doi.org/10.1007/978-3-031-48457-5_9

demonstrate that the agenda for "clean" energy transition has reached the highest political level. On top of that, the COVID-19 pandemic has accelerated the process of adjusting to change through global stimulus packages amounted to USD 17 trillion by October 2021 (IEA, 2021).[1] In this context, long-term funds to finance the investments required for the transition to a low-carbon economy as well as the projects that contribute to environmental sustainability have increased the significance of innovative financial instruments.

Among these instruments, green bonds are the most widely used and, accordingly, have the greatest appeal in the environmental, social, and governance (ESG) investing segment of the financial markets. Today, the market for "green bonds" has been expanding quickly for almost a decade as part of these developments. The Institute of International Finance announced that the volume of sustainable debt issued surpassed USD 4 trillion as of June 2022, of which the green bond market accounted for more than one-third at USD 1.7 trillion (IIF, 2022).

From a sustainable development perspective, as called for in the Addis Ababa Action Agenda, green bonds provide important contributions to bridging the Sustainable Development Goals (SDG) Financing Gap. They are distinguished from regular bonds by their green label, which signals a commitment to "exclusively" "use of proceeds" to "finance or refinance" new and/or existing eligible "green" projects, assets, or economic activities. Green projects are classified by taxonomies or other regulatory frameworks as projects that promote progress in environmentally sustainable activities. Thereby, green bonds support projects that fit into eligible categories of investments. These projects must have a significant, positive net benefit to the environment. Green bonds are considered innovative because they offer the opportunity to mobilize capital for green investments. They also offer investors the opportunity to make informed decisions to invest in green projects through more ambitious transparency requirements set by international standard setters such as International Capital Market Association (ICMA), Green Bond Principles. Standardized transparency frameworks through international standards or national regulatory frameworks require pre- and post-disclosure requirements related to clear environmental benefits, the targeted impacts of which should be assessed, quantified, and reported by the issuer using recognized metrics (e.g. tons of carbon (CO_2) equivalent). Measuring and reporting the impact of the green project is critical for the credibility of the green bond issuer to avoid accusations of greenwash and reputational risk.

This chapter centers on the question of whether green bonds are beneficial to both the investment community and the environment. We specifically ask how the market reacts when a firm announces to issue green bonds and the extent to which the environmental objectives are met after the issuance. We aim at providing a deeper understanding of the various aspects of green bonds and their potential impact on investor behavior and sustainability through the lens of energy firms. Green bonds are (very) relevant for firms in high energy-intensive sectors as to the growing need for them to incorporate ESG considerations into their business strategies. Recent

[1] Note that, the amount of approved government spending on clean energy has already hit USD 480 billion (IEA, 2021).

data show that energy firms, e.g. Chinese Three Gorges Group, Iberdrola, Engie SA, EDP, and State Grid Corporation of China, are among the group of top ten green bond issuers as of 2021, with a cumulative total value of USD 47.3 billion, representing 76.9% of the entire value of that group. Furthermore, energy is the largest category of use of proceeds in the global green bond market, contributing more than 40% to the 2021 total (Harrison & MacGeoch, 2022).

Despite its increasing popularity, however, the role of green bonds in the energy sector has attracted limited attention in the literature. Tang and Zhang (2020) argue that it would be timely to analyze the cross-industry effect in the green bond market starting with energy firms. This study fills the gap by focusing on the impact of green bond issuances on both stock and environmental performance of energy firms. For the impact on the stock performance, we test for the signaling hypothesis to explain how stock prices react to announcements of green bond issuance. This is important because investors do not have reliable, comparable, and relevant information on the environment criteria that helps them to distinguish firms with high or low commitment to the environment due to information asymmetry between managers and shareholders. Moreover, signaling constitutes a key channel of the stakeholder value maximization theory by evoking the investor awareness of ESG activities of firms (Servaes & Tamayo, 2013). We mitigate information asymmetry and assume that energy firms issue green bonds to send credible signals to the market regarding their environmental stewardship. We use the standard event methodology approach to cater to this research objective. Our results suggest that investors in the stock market react positively to the announcements of green bond issuances in general. For the impact on the environmental performance, we pursue an analytical approach to identify whether firms show the typical behavior of greenwashing. This term deserves special attention at this point. Greenwashing implies that firms pretend to care for the environment while doing little to actually do so. More specifically, it describes the practice of firms making false or misleading claims about the environmental benefits of their products or services. This can take many forms, such as exaggerating the recycled content of a product, claiming a product is "green" based on some small aspect of its manufacture or composition, or using vague or undefined terms such as "natural" or "environmentally friendly" without providing evidence to support the claim. From this point of view, green bonds can well be used for greenwashing purposes by simply not using the proceeds for the intended purpose or by exaggerating the environmental impact of the project that is being funded. Thus, we observe the evolution of the environmental performance of energy firms that issue green bonds in comparison with a matched group of non-issuer energy firms. In doing so, we utilize their environmental pillar scores disclosed alongside the ESG scores as well as the firm-level CO_2 emissions data. We employ the difference-in-differences approach for this purpose. We provide significant evidence of long-term improvement in the environmental performance of energy firms, which refutes the argument that green bond issuances are undertaken for reasons of greenwashing.

We contribute to the extant literature in two ways. First, we shed light on the valuation and environmental impact of green bonds in the energy sector, which is a major constituent of CO_2 emissions and environmental degradation. Second, we pave the way for a broader discussion of the role of green bonds as a contemporary means of changes in the energy sector for the transition to a clean economy.

Against this backdrop, Sect. 2 reviews the literature and presents our research hypotheses. Sections 3 and 4 explain the data and methodology, respectively. Section 5 provides the results along with a detailed discussion. Section 6 concludes.

2 Literature Review and Hypothesis Development

Green bond-related literature has exploded in recent years.[2] Among many strands of research, we confine ourselves to studies that examine the impact of green bonds on the stock and/or environmental performances of issuer firms. Both studies find their roots in the stakeholder value maximization theory, which posits that corporate social responsibility (CSR) that considers the consequences of firms' activities on various stakeholders positive impacts the firm value (Bae et al., 2011; Bénabou & Tirole, 2010; Deng et al., 2013; Lins et al., 2017). We elaborate on these studies as follows.

2.1 Studies Regarding the Impact of Green Bonds on the Stock Performance

Baulkaran (2019) provides the first evidence on the impact of green bond issuance on stock performance. The author utilizes the event study methodology for a sample of 54 firms across the Europe, Canada, the USA, China, and Australia and concludes that the cumulative abnormal returns are positive and statistically significant. Tang and Zhang (2020) conduct an event study of 132 public firms in 28 countries during 2007–2017 and find that market shows significantly positive reaction to announcements of green bond issuance, indicating that green bonds can improve the value of the issuer firms in the short term. Wang et al. (2020) examine stock market reactions following the issuance of green bonds in China. Based on an event study of 48 announcements of green bond issuances during the period from January 2016 to June 2019, the authors show that investors welcome these announcements with significantly positive price reactions. Flammer (2021) analyzes the market reaction to issuance announcements using firm-level data on 384 green bonds all over the world in the period 2013–2017 and confirms positive announcement returns on green bond issuances. While these studies document that market considers green bond issuance a value enhancement phenomenon for shareholders, there are also others that suggest the opposite mostly relying on the agency theory of Jensen and Meckling (1976). Lebelle et al. (2020), for 475 international green bonds issued by 145 firms from 2009 to 2018, indicate that green bond issuance decreases cumulative abnormal returns. The authors articulate

[2] The interested reader may refer to Bhutta et al. (2022) and the references therein.

that investors react in the same way for green bonds as they do for conventional or convertible bonds and that green bond issuances convey unfavorable information about the issuer firms.

Common to each of the abovementioned works is the concept of signaling in the background. It is well known in the literature that the information asymmetry between firms and their investors is costly (Healy & Palepu, 1993; Verrecchia, 1983) and can be reduced by sending credible signals that convey the firms' unobservable qualities (Connelly et al., 2011). Considering that green bond issuance may reduce information asymmetry (Zhang et al., 2021), signaling channel can be tested for explaining whether green bond issuers credibly signal their willingness and accountability to commit to environmental sustainability. The credibility of such a signal can generally manifest itself at least in two different ways. First, a green bond issuer should clearly lay out the use of proceeds and the environmental strategy behind the issuance in the prospectus. Second, an external review is required to verify the compliance with certain principles such as Climate Bonds Standards of Climate Bond Initiative. Therefore, we expect a positive market reaction to the issuance of green bonds by energy firms, as investors would view the "green" signal as valid due to its inherent credibility and we hypothesize the following:

H_1: Stock price reaction to the announcements of green bond issuances is positive for energy firms.

2.2 Studies Regarding the Impact of Green Bonds on the Environmental Performance

The credibility notion of "green" signaling also suggests that the environmental performance of the issuer should improve subsequent to the green bond issuance. This is plausible because the proceeds from the issuance should be directly invested in green projects that have positive externalities for the environment. However, the risk of "greenwashing" casts a shadow on this expectation. Greenwashing is one of the major problems frequently encountered in the green bond market (Berrone et al., 2017; Lyon & Montgomery, 2015; Marquis et al., 2016). Given the regulatory uncertainty surrounding the market and the lack of globally accepted enforceable criteria for evaluating the qualifications of the green bond, greenwashing has become a common concern among investors.

On the other hand, a growing number of studies pinpoint the positive impact of green bond issuance on firms' environmental performance. Upon a sample of 144 green bonds issued by 70 listed Chinese companies from 2016 to 2019, Zhou and Cui (2019) argue that green bond issuance increases CSR including responsibilities relating to environmental protection. Flammer (2021), in addition to her findings on the market reaction to green bond issuance, shows that environment ratings increase and CO_2 emissions decrease after green bond issuance, suggesting that green bonds are powerful tools in improving environmental performance. Yeow and Ng (2021) analyze the green bond issuances between 2015 and 2019 from various countries in North America, Asia, and Europe and corroborate these findings in terms of greenhouse gas emissions provided that green bonds are certified by third parties. Using a dataset of 1105 corporate green bonds issued worldwide by 92 issuers over the period 2007–2019, Fatica and Panzica (2021) demonstrate that green bond issuance is associated with a significant reduction in the intensity of both total and direct (Scope 1) emissions up to 2 years after the issuance. A recent paper by Wang et al. (2022) interestingly argues that firms pay more attention to climate risks following the green bond issuances. In this regard, we hypothesize the following for energy firms:

H_2. Environmental performance of energy firms improves following the issuance of green bonds.

3 Data

All the data come from Thomson Reuters Eikon in our study. The sample period is from 2013 to July 2022 since almost no corporate green bonds were issued before 2013. We initially determine 957 green bonds issued by energy firms in the sample period around the world. We drop 146 Islamic bonds, also known as Sukuk, due to their different issuance mechanisms. It is worth to expand on Sukuk and their "green" facet at this juncture. Sukuk are Islamic financial certificates, similar to bonds that represent ownership of a tangible asset, real estate, or a company, rather than the issuer's debt as in traditional bonds. They are structured to comply with the principles of Islamic finance, which prohibits the charging or payment of interest and also prohibits investment in certain types of businesses such as gambling, alcohol, and pornography. To comply with these principles, Sukuk are structured as profit-sharing contracts rather than debt obligations. Green Sukuk, in particular, are a type of Sukuk used to finance environmentally sustainable projects. Proceeds from the sale of green Sukuk are used to finance projects that have environmental benefits, such as renewable energy projects, sustainable agriculture, and water treatment plants. We do not include Sukuk issuers in the sample to ensure the homogeneity of the sample, especially for pricing reasons. The literature offers an increasing number of studies that intend to answer whether Sukuk are priced any different to their conventional counterparts. A majority of them indicate that Sukuk have a different pattern of yield spreads compared to conventional bonds (Ariff et al., 2017; Asmuni & Tan, 2021; Fathurahman & Fitriati, 2013; Haque et al., 2017; Saad et al., 2020; Saeed et al., 2021). These different pricing mechanisms preclude us from commingling (green) bonds with (green) Sukuk in the sample because both types of investors may have different attitudes toward risks and return, which would possibly distort our empirical analysis.

After excluding bonds with missing data, we reach 792 green bonds issued by public and private energy firms. Table 1 provides a brief overview of these green bonds issued by energy firms within the sample period.

As can be seen from Table 1, private energy firms issue more green bonds with larger sizes than publicly listed firms. Moreover, both the number of issuers and the total amount issued have increased dramatically over the years (Panel A). China and USA, the two largest CO_2 emitters, are the most prominent countries regarding the issuing activity of energy firms in the green bond market. It is worthy of note that, these two countries still maintain their position as the most prolific source of all types of green bonds with the highest volumes and number of issues (Harrison & MacGeoch, 2022). Cross-border issues of green bonds by energy firms also seem to be very attractive. We opt to leave these "Eurobonds," which are largely denominated in Euro and USD, as one of the countries of issue without converting them into the domicile country of the issuer (Panel B).

Since firm-level data such as the ones that belong to stock market, ESG scores, and accounting information are not available for private firms, we restrict our sample with green bonds issued by publicly listed energy firms. Thus, our final sample consists of 239 green bonds issued by 80 unique energy firms. Table 2 gives summary statistics, which we record in the fiscal year that ends prior to the date of green bond issuance.

In Table 2, total assets are the book value of total assets as reported. Market cap is calculated as the sum of market value for all relevant types of shares. Debt/Equity is the ratio of total debt to total equity as of the end of the fiscal period based on their book values. ROA measures operating efficiency and is calculated by dividing a net income prior to financing costs by total assets. Price-to-book ratio is the share price divided by its book value. ESG score is an overall grade based on the best management practices regarding environmental, social, and corporate governance pillars, which are key factors in determining the ability of a firm to generate long-term shareholder value. Environmental pillar score is an indicator of how well a firm avoids environmental risks and capitalizes on environmental opportunities. Social pillar score is a reflection of the firm reputation. Governance pillar score shows a firm's capacity to direct and control its rights and responsibilities. CO_2 emissions denote total CO_2 [direct (scope 1) + indirect (scope 2)] and CO_2 equivalents emission in tons. Accordingly, Table 2 suggests that issuers of green bonds in the energy sector have moderate size, are relatively leveraged, profitable, and trade at premium on average. The average scores imply that energy firms are mediocre performers of ESG and its pillars, while environmental score has the highest average value even beyond the overall ESG scores. We consider this a potential reference to the link between green bond issuance and environmental performance.

Table 1 An overview of green bonds issued by energy firms

	Public		Private		Total	
	# of issues	Total amount issued (bn USD)	# of issues	Total amount issued (bn USD)	# of issues	Total amount issued (bn USD)
Panel A: Year of issue						
2013	–	–	1	0.37	1	0.37
2014	3	2.43	–	–	3	2.43
2015	2	2.50	57	1.34	59	3.84
2016	2	1.94	16	4.51	18	6.45
2017	15	5.73	26	4.83	41	10.56
2018	9	4.18	25	8.58	34	12.76
2019	33	13.84	67	16.88	100	30.72
2020	42	20.58	91	24.37	133	44.95
2021	69	27.66	179	45.15	248	72.81
2022/7	64	15.83	91	22.52	155	38.35
Total	239	94.68	553	128.55	792	223.23
Panel B: Country of issue						
Argentina	1	0.03	9	0.34	10	0.37
Australia	–	–	1	0.21	1	0.21
Austria	1	0.11	4	0.01	5	0.12
Belgium	–	–	1	0.63	1	0.63
Brazil	6	0.73	27	1.33	33	2.06
Canada	–	–	6	2.04	6	2.04
Chile	2	0.13	–	–	2	0.13
China	56	10.17	114	22.35	170	32.52
Denmark	–	–	2	0.48	2	0.48
Eurobond	65	43.99	93	44.67	158	88.66
Finland	1	0.53	1	0.07	2	0.60
France	19	19.49	6	1.28	25	20.77
India	–	–	4	0.11	4	0.11
Italy	–	–	1	0.01	1	0.01
Japan	24	2.41	4	0.25	28	2.66
Latvia	–	–	3	0.26	3	0.26
Malaysia	–	–	2	0.03	2	0.03
New Zealand	6	0.58	–	–	6	0.58
Norway	3	0.41	42	3.03	45	3.44
Portugal	–	–	2	0.16	2	0.16
South Korea	1	0.05	56	3.20	57	3.25

(continued)

Table 1 (continued)

	Public		Private		Total	
	# of issues	Total amount issued (bn USD)	# of issues	Total amount issued (bn USD)	# of issues	Total amount issued (bn USD)
Spain	–	–	3	0.40	3	0.40
Sweden	2	0.12	11	1.19	13	1.31
Switzerland	3	0.42	2	0.24	5	0.66
Taiwan	–	–	18	2.59	18	2.59
Thailand	29	1.67	2	0.14	31	1.81
USA	20	13.85	139	43.54	159	57.39
Total	239	94.68	553	128.55	792	223.23

Note This table summarizes the data pertaining to green bonds issued by energy firms. Panel A demonstrates the data with respect to the year of issue, while the data in Panel B are based on the country of issue (not the issuer)
Source Thomson Reuters Eikon

Table 2 Summary statistics

	Mean	Median	St. dev.	Max	Min
Total assets (USD bn)	44.09	15.28	74.01	393.97	0.17
Market cap (USD bn)	14.70	6.74	23.66	134.55	0.13
Debt/equity	1.61	1.32	1.30	6.99	0.05
ROA	0.04	0.03	0.05	0.35	−0.04
Price-to-book	10.63	1.37	76.33	671.52	0.27
ESG score	52.85	56.93	19.69	90.16	16.27
Environmental pillar score	54.52	55.05	23.56	93.46	2.80
Social pillar score	49.30	51.56	24.21	91.84	3.31
Governance pillar score	54.30	55.44	21.20	96.81	11.05
CO_2 emissions (tons mn)	12.60	3.45	21.00	96.40	0.00

Note This table provides summary statistics of the data sample used in this study. Each item represents the firm-based average across the sample of 80 energy firms in the period 2013–2022
Source Thomson Reuters Eikon

4 Methodology

In this section, we describe our methodological approach, which is twofold. We start with examining the information content of the announcements of green bond issuances by applying the standard event study methodology. Afterward, we employ the difference-in-differences estimation method to investigate how the environmental performance of energy firms evolves following the issuance of green bonds. The reason behind the choice of this method is that it would not be possible to find an instrumental variable to deal with endogeneity due to the fact that green bonds are voluntarily (not randomly) issued (Flammer, 2021; Sisodia et al., 2022; Yeow & Ng, 2021). To this end, we match green bond issuers with their non-issuer counterparts and compare the evolution in environmental performance absent the green bond issue.

4.1 Event Study Approach

We obtain the USD-denominated stock returns of energy firms in the sample that announce the issuance of green bonds. Since the relevant information—credible signal—is transmitted to the market primarily at the time of the announcement, we use the "first announcement date" data provided by Thomson Reuters Eikon as the event date rather than the date of issuance. Next, we calculate the abnormal returns using the formula in Eq. (1):

$$\mathrm{AR}_{it} = R_{it} - \mathrm{ER}_{it}, \tag{1}$$

where AR_{it}, R_{it}, and ER_{it} denote the abnormal return, the actual return, and the expected return of firm i at time t, respectively. We regress actual return (R_{it}) on market portfolio return (R_{mt}) during an estimation window of 100 trading days [−11, +11] and a baseline event window of 21 trading days [−10, +10] as stated in the following market model (Brown & Warner, 1985):

$$R_{it} = a + \beta \times R_{mt} + \varepsilon_{it}. \tag{2}$$

The parameter estimates (α and β) that we obtain from these ordinary least squares (OLS) regressions are then used to calculate the expected return (ER_{it}) per day over the event window. Our market proxy is country-specific (e.g. FTSE Italian All Share for Italy, S&P CLX IGPA for Chile, etc.) (Flammer, 2021). The following formula is used to calculate cumulative abnormal returns (CAR):

$$\mathrm{CAR}_{it} = \sum_{t=1}^{n} \mathrm{AR}_{it}. \tag{3}$$

We derive the average abnormal returns (AAR) and cumulative abnormal returns (CAAR) by averaging the summed AR_{it} and CAR_{it} of the sample firms over the event window, and then we apply parametric t-test and nonparametric sign-test for the significance of the two returns. We also report the test results for various event windows to reveal the evolution of stock returns before and after the announcement date. In order to deal with the heterogeneity among the data, we disentangle subsequent issues made by the same firm from its first-ever issuance to capture any differences in the informational significance for each issuing type (Flammer, 2021;

Tang & Zhang, 2020). We do the same for certified and non-certified bond issuances with a similar perspective (Baulkaran, 2019; Flammer, 2021; Yeow & Ng, 2021).[3]

For robustness purposes, we proceed with taking into account the confounding events, which we define as a green bond issuance announcement made by the same energy firm within the event window as well as other relevant announcements. In addition to that, we consider excluding countries where green bonds are provided with fiscal (e.g. tax) incentives. USA, Chile, India, Brazil, China, Hong Kong, and Singapore are some of these countries that use subsidies for issuing green bonds. In this vein, we exclude green bond issuances made specifically in China since these issuances preponderate (around 41%) in the sample and China is one of the countries where green bond issuers are materially subsidized, both of which may affect the results (Azhgaliyeva & Kapsalyamova, 2021; Flammer, 2021). Currently, the Chinese government's strong support for green bonds can help issuers reduce issuance costs or obtain financial subsidies. Some provincial governments have already launched subsidy programs, and a single issuer can apply for a refund of up to USD 848,000 per year (CBI, 2020). We ultimately use the MSCI All Country World Equity Index instead of domestic market indices (Baulkaran, 2019; Flammer, 2021).

4.2 Difference-in-Differences Approach

We use all firm-year observations of the green bond issuing (treated) and matched non-issuing (control) energy firms in the sample period. Following Flammer (2021), we specify the following regression model:

$$y_{it} = \alpha_i + \alpha_c \times \alpha_t + \beta \times \text{Green Bond}_{it} + \varepsilon_{it} \tag{4}$$

where energy firms are indexed by i, years are indexed by t, and countries are indexed by c. y denotes for the environmental performance (in logarithmic form), α_i are firm fixed effects, $\alpha_c \times \alpha_t$ are country by year fixed effects, Green Bond is a dummy variable that takes the value of one if firm i is a green bond issuer by year t and zero otherwise, and ε_{it} is the error term. In this model, we measure the change in y following the green bond issuance announcement of issuer (treated) firms accounting for contemporaneous changes in y at otherwise corresponding non-issuer (control) firms by means of β. We extend Eq. (4) in order to differentiate the short-term evolution of the environmental performance from the long term by replacing Green Bond dummy with three dummies. These are Green Bond (pre-issue year) that is one in the year prior to the issuance of the green bond, Green Bond (short term, 1 year) that is one in the year following the issuance of the green bond, and Green Bond (long term, 2+ year) that is one in the succeeding years.

---

[3] Certification information is retrieved from the Certified Bonds Database of Climate Bond Initiative, which is available at https://www.climatebonds.net/certification/certified-bonds.

Our difference-in-differences approach requires two important steps: (1) proper determination of the control group and (2) proper measurement of the environmental performance. In order to match each of the 82 treated firms, we match a "control" firm that is equivalent to the treated firm in the year preceding the issuance of green bonds. We first identify pure bond issuers among the non-issuers of green bonds in the same country as its treated peer. Then, we select the most similar control firm based on the accounting and the ESG data previously reported in Table 2: total assets, market cap, debt/equity, ROA, price-to-book, the ESG and three pillar scores, and CO_2/total assets. By doing so, we ensure an ex-ante similarity between the treated and control firms so that non-issuers of green bonds operate under similar market conditions with similar financial capacity and environmental performance. We make use of the tests of differences in means and medians to illustrate this similarity.[4]

Besides, we mainly use the environmental pillar score as reported by Thomson Reuters Eikon. However, we also use the ratio of CO_2 emissions to total assets so as to avoid the ambiguity of linking green bond issuances with environmental scores and to provide a more concrete measure for environmental performance (Flammer, 2021).

5 Results and Discussion

5.1 Event Study Analysis and Stock Performance Results

Table 3 displays the event study analysis results for the whole sample. To start with, since some of the energy firms issue multiple green bonds even on the same day, the event study sample of announcements is 183, which is lower than the number of green bond issuances in the overall sample (i.e. 239). As the findings suggest, no information leakage occurs before the event date contrary to the previous literature (e.g. Baulkaran, 2019), while CAAR start to increase starting with the date of green bonds announcement [0, +0] and become significantly positive in the event window [+4, +5].

Figure 1 depicts the evolution of abnormal returns in the [−20, +20] event window. The CAAR in this period is around 0.45%.

When first and subsequent issues are considered separately, our findings dramatically change. We report this change in Panel A of Table 4. As is shown, the positive impact of announcements of green bond issuances is far more prominent for the first issues since it survives for 6 consecutive days following the 4th day after the event date. The CAAR range from 0.41 to 1.08% and are all statistically significant.

[4] Flammer (2021) determines the matched firms with regard to the nearest neighbor approach based on the Mahalanobis distances, whereas Yeow and Ng (2021), Zhang et al. (2021) and Sisodia et al. (2022) use the propensity score matching method for that purpose. We opt to follow Tang and Zhang (2020) in matching firms with each other.

Table 3 Cumulative average abnormal returns (whole sample)

Whole sample ($n = 183$)							
Event window	CAAR (%)	*t*(CAAR)	Sign-test	Event window	CAAR (%)	*t*(CAAR)	Sign-test
[−20, +20]	0.45	0.42	0.50	[+4, +4]	0.10	0.76	1.38
[−10, +10]	0.35	0.47	1.01	[+4, +5]	0.34	1.78*	2.40**
[−5, +5]	0.15	0.30	0.30	[+4, +6]	0.33	1.36	1.61
[−1, +1]	0.12	0.44	0.43	[+4, +7]	0.29	0.97	0.85
[0, +0]	0.01	0.10	0.50	[+4, +8]	0.24	0.70	0.73
[0, +1]	0.08	0.40	0.27	[+4, +9]	0.27	0.73	1.08
[0, +2]	0.13	0.53	0.56	[+4, +10]	0.30	0.75	0.96
[0, +3]	0.14	0.51	0.55	[+4, +20]	0.64	0.95	0.71
[0, +4]	0.24	0.76	1.08				

Note This table presents the results of our event study analysis for the whole sample. CAAR is average cumulative abnormal returns. *t*(CAAR) denotes the standard t-test and Wilcoxon sign-rank test is the nonparametric test. ** and * indicate 5% and 10% significance levels, respectively

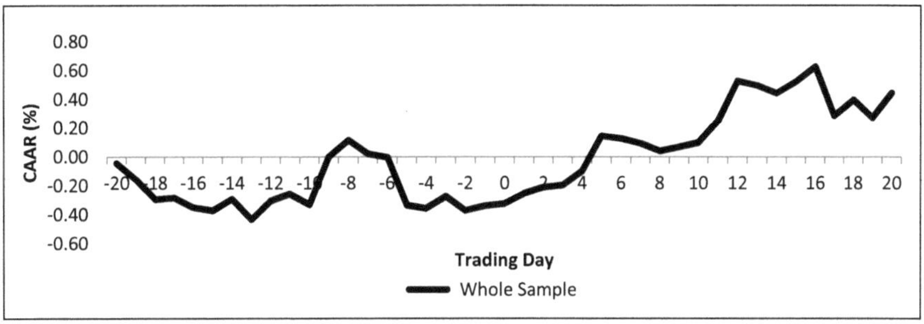

Fig. 1 Cumulative average abnormal returns for the whole sample in the event window [−20, + 20]

Furthermore, it seems possible to earn a 1.38% abnormal return in the [+4, +20] period, which is economically meaningful.

Abnormal returns are smaller and insignificant for subsequent issues. This concurs with the signaling argument in the sense that investors learn about the environmental commitment of the issuers by means of the announcement of the first-time issue. In contrast, investors' attention no longer exists after the first-time issuance. The trend in the abnormal returns around the date of announcements (i.e. [−20, +20]) of first and subsequent green bond issues is picturized in Fig. 2. The significant difference between the CAAR of the two types of issues (0.79% vs. 0.18%) in this period can be clearly noticed.

In Panel B of Table 4, we diagnose further heterogeneity in the sample this time considering the certification feature of green bond issuances. Our findings imply that third-party certification adds more value for the issuer. This manifests itself in the larger and more significant market response for certified green bonds, providing

Table 4 Cumulative average abnormal returns (first/subsequent and certified/non-certified issues)

Panel A	First issues ($n = 80$)			Subsequent issues ($n = 103$)		
Event window	CAAR (%)	t(CAAR)	Sign-test	CAAR (%)	*t*(CAAR)	Sign-test
[−20, +20]	0.79	0.46	1.04	0.18	0.13	−0.05
[−10, +10]	0.08	0.06	0.30	0.57	0.65	1.15
[−5, +5]	−0.07	0.08	0.00	0.32	0.57	0.39
[−1, +1]	−0.28	−0.61	−1.19	0.43	1.38	1.69*
[0, +0]	−0.19	−0.84	−1.03	0.18	1.03	1.68*
[0, +1]	−0.18	−0.47	−1.32	0.29	1.34	1.64
[0, +2]	−0.16	−0.37	−0.84	0.35	1.27	1.49
[0, +3]	−0.23	−0.49	−0.78	0.43	1.30	1.43
[0, +4]	0.18	0.36	0.24	0.28	0.71	1.21
[+4, +4]	0.41	2.10**	2.32**	−0.15	−0.90	−0.19
[+4, +5]	0.71	2.74***	2.64***	0.05	0.20	0.91
[+4, +6]	0.72	2.16**	1.81*	0.02	0.05	0.56
[+4, +7]	1.01	2.23**	1.65*	−0.27	−0.68	−0.33
[+4, +8]	1.08	2.02**	1.93*	−0.42	−0.97	−0.74
[+4, +9]	1.01	1.80*	2.09**	−0.31	−0.65	−0.39
[+4, +10]	0.76	1.23	1.34	−0.07	−0.13	0.13
[+4, +20]	1.38	1.27	1.27	0.07	0.09	0.02
Panel B	Certified issues ($n = 17$)			Non-certified issues ($n = 166$)		
Event window	CAAR (%)	*t*(CAAR)	Sign-test	CAAR (%)	*t*(CAAR)	Sign-test
[−20, +20]	2.04	0.74	0.78	0.46	0.40	0.52
[−10, +10]	0.63	0.34	0.40	0.33	0.40	0.91
[−5, +5]	0.97	0.90	0.92	0.03	0.06	−0.04
[−1, +1]	−0.25	−0.50	−0.31	0.12	0.42	0.34
[0, +0]	−0.15	−0.56	−0.78	0.03	0.19	0.67
[0, +1]	−0.27	−0.50	−0.45	0.08	0.37	0.21
[0, +2]	0.12	0.19	0.78	0.09	0.35	0.25
[0, +3]	−0.07	−0.11	0.50	0.12	0.38	0.28
[0, +4]	0.58	0.77	1.25	0.17	0.50	0.73
[+4, +4]	0.65	1.96**	1.97**	0.06	0.41	1.06
[+4, +5]	0.77	1.83*	1.78*	0.34	1.61	2.30**
[+4, +6]	0.26	0.37	−0.21	0.38	1.47	2.00**
[+4, +7]	0.56	0.97	0.12	0.33	1.10	1.02
[+4, +8]	0.16	0.25	0.07	0.30	0.81	0.92
[+4, +9]	0.65	0.94	0.54	0.29	0.71	1.20

(continued)

Table 4 (continued)

Panel B	Certified issues ($n = 17$)			Non-certified issues ($n = 166$)		
Event window	CAAR (%)	t(CAAR)	Sign-test	CAAR (%)	t(CAAR)	Sign-test
[+4, +10]	0.36	0.38	−0.02	0.36	0.83	1.23
[+4, +20]	2.45	1.64	1.35	0.67	0.91	0.64

Note This table presents the results of our event study analysis for the first and subsequent issues of green bonds. CAAR is average cumulative abnormal returns. t(CAAR) denotes the standard t-test, and Wilcoxon sign-rank test is the nonparametric test. ***, **, and * indicate 1%, 5%, and 10% significance levels, respectively

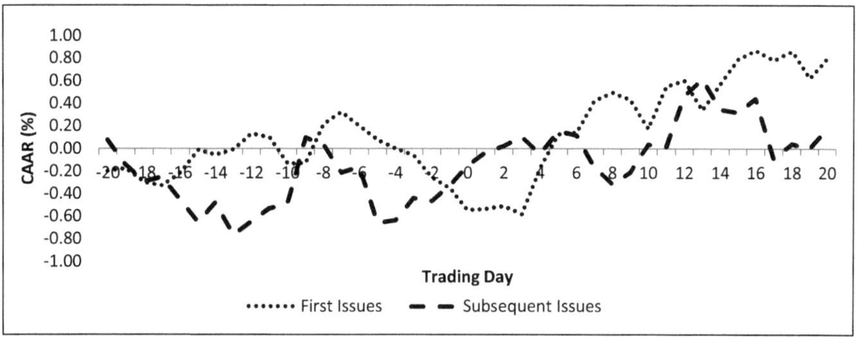

Fig. 2 Cumulative average abnormal returns for the first and subsequent issues in the event window [−20, +20]

additional evidence for the signaling argument. Investors possibly perceive the certification process as a valuable effort delivered by the firm to promote its environmental commitment even though it is a costly requirement. However, this value improvement is statistically significant only for a few days. This may be due to the low number of certified issues among the energy firms. Indeed, only 105 green bonds, which correspond to around 11% of total green bonds issued by energy firms, are certified according to the Climate Bonds Initiative database.[5] This implies that the certification process of the green bonds issued by energy firms is so costly that the worthiness of the certification is reflected in the stock value only on a limited scale. Therefore, the significance of green bond certification that is also evident in the literature (Flammer, 2021; Yeow & Ng, 2021) may not be fully recognized by the investors of energy firms. But note that the economic significance is the highest for certified issues with 2.04% and 2.45% of CAAR over the event windows [−20, +20] and [+4, +20], respectively.

In Fig. 3, it is possible to see how CAAR evolve around [−20, +20] with respect to the certification status of green bonds. It is apparent that certified green bonds have much stronger abnormal return effects on the stock market in economic terms.

[5] Note that the same database reveals that the number of certified green bonds (105) issued by energy firms corresponds to around 20% of total number of certified green bonds (527).

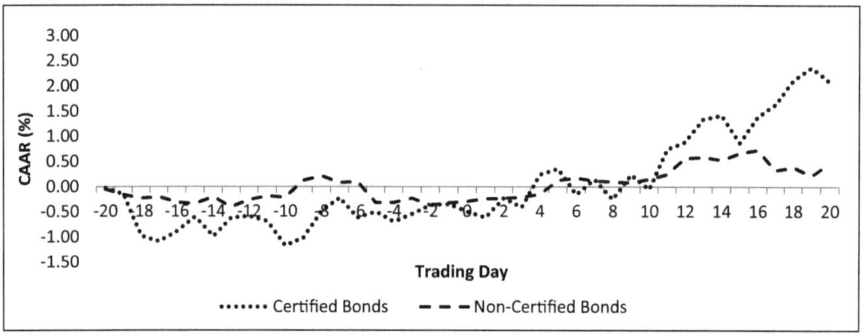

Fig. 3 Cumulative average abnormal returns for the certified and non-certified issues in the event window [−20, +20]

Taken together, our results indicate that green bond announcements, especially for the first-ever issuances, are taken as signals of environmental commitment and the consequent market reaction is largely positive pointing out a "green label" effect (Tang & Zhang, 2020). This is in line not only with the specific studies that find significantly positive response to the announcement of green bond issuances (Baulkaran, 2019; Flammer, 2021; Tang & Zhang, 2020; Wang et al., 2020) but also with a broader literature that shows the positive impact of announcement of eco-friendly actions on the stock market (Flammer, 2013; Klassen & McLaughlin, 1996; Krüger, 2015). That said, the overall staggered and somewhat transitory reaction of the market makes us think that investors may be facing several uncertainties that retard their response. For instance, they may speculate that green bond issues of energy firms are more costly than they are for firms in other sectors. Thus, a possible perception of future deterioration of profitability may be obscuring more significant and/or permanent valuation in the stock market (Lebelle et al., 2020). Another uncertainty may be associated with the relatively rare certification for green bonds issued by energy firms. Since certification is not always readily available for investors, the investment decision may be pending for some time.

We address robustness concerns in Table 5 by excluding confounding events (Panel A), excluding China (Panel B), and using a world market index (Panel C). Our results are, by and large, robust to these alternative treatments.

5.2 *Difference-in-Differences Analysis and Environmental Performance Results*

Before proceeding with the results of our difference-in-differences analysis, we illustrate the homogeneity between green bond issuer (treated) and matched non-issuer (control) firms in Table 6. Our findings indicate that non-issuer firms are highly

Table 5 Cumulative average abnormal returns (robustness check)

Event window	Panel A			Panel B			Panel C		
	Confounding Events ($n = 140$)			Excluding China ($n = 108$)			MSCI World Index ($n = 140$)		
	CAAR (%)	*t*(CAAR)	Sign-test	CAAR (%)	*t*(CAAR)	Sign-test	CAAR (%)	*t*(CAAR)	Sign-test
[−20, +20]	1.07	0.74	1.21	−0.31	−0.27	0.31	−1.41	−1.09	−1.18
[−10, +10]	0.45	0.43	0.86	−0.42	−0.49	0.25	−1.07	−1.11	−1.37
[−5, +5]	0.33	0.48	0.65	−0.55	−0.9	−0.38	−0.54	−0.87	−0.62
[−1, +1]	0.04	0.11	−0.14	−0.52	−1.95*	−1.25	−0.35	−1.05	−1.00
[0, +0]	−0.00	−0.02	0.24	−0.20	−1.23	−0.42	−0.06	−0.33	−0.17
[0, +1]	0.01	0.04	−0.33	−0.36	−1.71*	−1.06	−0.15	−0.57	−0.70
[0, +2]	0.05	0.15	0.28	−0.22	−0.83	−0.15	−0.17	−0.52	−0.55
[0, +3]	0.01	0.03	0.06	−0.41	−1.33	−0.61	−0.30	−0.83	−0.64
[0, +4]	0.30	0.73	0.91	−0.15	−0.44	0.12	−0.21	−0.53	−0.13
[+4, +5]	0.74	3.30***	3.85***	0.51	2.65***	2.82***	0.41	1.85*	1.93*
[+4, +6]	0.73	2.70***	2.85***	0.48	1.99**	1.91*	0.38	1.45	1.47
[+4, +7]	0.85	2.39**	2.47**	0.47	1.72*	1.70*	0.47	1.37	1.09
[+4, +8]	0.67	1.59	1.92*	0.21	0.63	1.03	0.16	0.40	0.16
[+4, +9]	0.59	1.26	2.01**	0.16	0.44	1.26	0.01	0.03	0.00
[+4, +10]	0.52	1.00	1.53	−0.01	−0.02	0.54	−0.21	−0.43	−0.55
[+4, +20]	1.28	1.42	1.49	0.64	0.90	0.86	0.05	0.07	−0.87

Note This table presents the results of our event study analysis for robustness purposes. CAAR is average cumulative abnormal returns. *t*(CAAR) denotes the standard *t*-test, and Wilcoxon sign-rank test is the nonparametric test. ***, **, and * indicate 1%, 5%, and 10% significance levels, respectively

Table 6 Comparison of treated and control firms

	Obs	Firm	Mean	Median	St. Dev	p-value	p-value
Log (total assets)	59	Treated	23.82	23.73	0.11	0.67	0.63
		Control	23.76	23.88	0.10		
Log (market cap)	59	Treated	22.91	22.87	0.08	0.71	0.12
		Control	22.86	22.64	0.09		
Debt/equity	59	Treated	1.54	1.22	0.12	0.73	0.10
		Control	1.62	0.98	0.20		
ROA	59	Treated	0.03	0.03	0.00	0.45	1.00
		Control	0.03	0.03	0.01		
Price-to-book	59	Treated	1.87	1.44	1.57	0.57	0.63
		Control	1.77	1.34	1.41		
ESG score	59	Treated	62.84	66.87	15.69	0.61	0.88
		Control	64.01	67.10	16.28		
Environmental pillar score	59	Treated	65.13	70.63	20.38	0.68	0.32
		Control	64.01	67.10	16.28		
Social pillar score	59	Treated	61.78	65.88	21.36	0.45	0.48
		Control	63.95	60.80	18.81		
Governance pillar score	59	Treated	60.61	59.50	20.77	1.00	0.67
		Control	60.59	64.05	21.54		
CO_2/Total Assets	59	Treated	0.00	0.00	0.00	0.32	0.47
		Control	0.05	0.00	0.52		

Note This table presents the tests of differences in means and medians of green bond issuer (treated) firms and non-issuer (control) firms

similar to their issuer peers and our difference-in-differences analysis may enable us to identify how these firms would behave absent the green bond issuance.

Eventually, our analysis reveals that the long-run environmental performance considerably improves. As shown in Table 7, the environmental pillar grade increases by 14.82%.[6] As such, CO_2 emissions/assets are reduced by 0.01433%, a reduction by 49.86%.[7] These enhancements in the environmental performance indicate that the greenwashing argument is not valid among energy firms. Rather, they complement our previous findings based on the signaling argument, since green bonds appear to possess the required level of signaling power in conveying information about the future performance of firms regarding their environmental commitments. Nevertheless, the positive contemporaneous impact on CO_2 emissions is remarkable. This

[6] Since the dependent variable (environmental pillar score) is log-transformed, we convert the coefficient 0.14 with the following formula: $100 * [\exp(0.14 - ½ * 0.06^2)) - 1]$.

[7] This is calculated by using the mean ratio of CO_2 emissions/total assets from Table 2 (0.02858%). So, (0.02858% – 0.01433%)/0.02858% = 49.86%.

Table 7 Difference-in-differences analysis results

	Environment pillar score		CO_2/Total Assets (in %)	
	(1)	(2)	(1)	(2)
Green Bond	3.02***		0.05***	
	(0.08)		(0.00)	
Green Bond (pre-issue year)		−0.03		0.00
		(0.06)		(0.00)
Green Bond (short term, 1 year)		−0.04		−0.01
		(0.06)		(0.00)
Green Bond (long term, 2+ years)		0.14**		−0.01*
		(0.06)		(0.00)
Firm fixed effects	Yes	Yes	Yes	Yes
Country-year fixed effects	Yes	Yes	Yes	Yes
Obs	200	200	200	200
R-sq	0.99	0.99	0.98	0.98

Note This table shows the results of the difference-in-differences analysis. ***, **, and * indicate 1%, 5%, and 10% significance levels, respectively. Green Bond is a dummy variable that is one if firm is a green bond issuer, Green Bond (pre-issue year) is a dummy variable that is one in the year prior to the issuance of the green bond. Green Bond (short term, 1 year) is a dummy variable that is one in the year following the issuance of the green bond. Green Bond (long term, 2+ years) is a dummy variable that is one in the succeeding years

finding suggests that green bonds issued with short maturities may not allow firms to reap their environmental benefits (Yeow & Ng, 2021).

Despite these potential conflicts, we substantially conclude that green bonds can be used to increase the environmental concerns of energy firms and help them alleviating the risks of transition to a low-carbon economy (Fatica & Panzica, 2021; Flammer, 2021; Wang et al., 2022; Yeow & Ng, 2021; Zhou & Cui, 2019).

6 Conclusion

Green bonds have become an important financing tool to accomplish environmental goals since their debut in 2007 by the European Investment Bank.[8] As they have surged in popularity also in the corporate world as of 2013, they have gained traction as an alternative asset class and a part of the ESG investing and impact investing universe that appeals investors in the market as well. Energy firms appear to exploit the advantages of issuing green bonds as they take place near the top issuers. Assuming

[8] The European Investment Bank and the World Bank pioneered the first green bonds, with the former issuing the Climate Awareness Bond in 2007 and the latter issuing its first green bond in 2008.

that a green bond issue sends credible signal to the investment community that the energy firm will use the proceeds from green bonds for improvements in energy efficiency and prevention of environmental pollution, one can expect that the market welcomes green bond issuances by positively responding to their announcements. It is also reasonable to anticipate that the environmental performance of energy firms improves following the green bond issuance.

On the other hand, these expectations might be disconfirmed by the incidence of greenwashing, where firms issue green bonds for deceptive advertising or intend to use the bond proceeds to support brown projects in substance. Hence, the real effects of green bonds may become blurred. This study examines such effects by analyzing the impact of green bond issuances on stock market valuation and on environmental performance of energy firms around the world. We find that the market reaction to green bond issuance announcements is positive. We also observe that environmental performance of energy firms improves in the long-run. However, we have some reservations about lagged and temporary investor response as well as conflicting results in the short-term environmental effects.

Scaling up green bond issuance with sound market practices depends on various key determinants such as existence and quality of sustainable finance policies and frameworks particularly on securing transparency by pre- and post-issuance disclosure requirements, credible external certification mechanisms, capacity to produce green project pipeline, the stage of capital market development, and sufficiently strong governance and political stability. Policymakers should exert collaborative effort in order to attain sustainable goals internationally. Valuation effect and environmental performance improvement appear to be attractive features of green bonds and can be used to elucidate investors on how green bonds may provide significant benefits not only for the individual firm but also for the environment as a whole. Hence, green bonds should be utilized for the decarbonization of energy firms provided that legislative frameworks that protect investors in the market from misconduct (e.g. greenwashing) are duly established.

It is noteworthy to highlight two limitations of the study. One is that we focus on the green bonds issued solely by energy firms and ignore "energy" green bonds issued by others such as banks or non-bank financial institutions including investment companies and insurance companies. Even though both types of green bonds mainly aim to fund environment-friendly projects, they may differ in many aspects that should be taken into consideration. The other one is the fact that we do not delve into the sub-sector of energy, e.g. renewables, oil, bioenergy, etc., which the issuer firm operates in. This is because our sample is not large enough to take such diversity into account. That being the case, this could even become a requirement for additional analysis as the number of issuer energy firms goes up in time. We leave these for future work.

References

Adamkaite, J., Streimikiene, D., & Rudzioniene, K. (2022). The impact of social responsibility on corporate financial performance in the energy sector: Evidence from Lithuania. *Corporate Social Responsibility and Environmental Management*, 1–14.

Aggarwal, P. (2013). Relationship between environmental responsibility and financial performance of firm: A literature review. *IOSR Journal of Business and Management, 13*(1), 13–22.

Alam, M. S., Atif, M., Chien-Chi, C., & Soytaş, U. (2019). Does corporate R&D investment affect firm environmental performance? Evidence from G-6 countries. *Energy Economics, 78*, 401–411.

Al-Tuwaijri, S. A., Christensen, T. E., & Hughes II, K. E. (2004). The relations among environmental disclosure, environmental performance, and economic performance: A simultaneous equations approach. *Accounting, Organizations and Society, 29*(5–6), 447–471.

Arellano, M. (1987). Computing robust standard errors for within-groups estimators. *Oxford Bulletin of Economics and Statistics, 49*(4), 431–434.

Ariff, M., Chazi, A., Safari, M., & Zarei, A. (2017). Significant difference in the yields of Sukuk bonds versus conventional bonds. *Journal of Emerging Market Finance, 16*(2), 115–135.

Asmuni, N. H., & Tan, K. S. (2021). Exploring the yield spread between Sukuk and conventional bonds in Malaysia. *Journal of Emerging Market Finance, 20*(2), 165–191.

Azhgaliyeva, D., & Kapsalyamova, Z. (2021). *Policy support in promoting green bonds in Asia.* Asian Development Bank Institute.

Bae, K. H., Kang, J. K., & Wang, J. (2011). Employee treatment and firm leverage: A test of the stakeholder theory of capital structure. *Journal of Financial Economics, 100*, 130–153.

Baltagi, B. H., Song, S. H., & Jung, B. C. (2001). The unbalanced nested error component regression model. *Journal of Econometrics, 101*(2), 357–381.

Baran, M., Kuźniarska, A., Makieła, Z. J., Sławik, A., & Stuss, M. M. (2022). Does ESG reporting relate to corporate financial performance in the context of the energy sector transformation? Evidence from Poland. *Energies, 15(2)*(477), 1–22.

Baulkaran, V. (2019). Stock market reaction to green bond issuance. *Journal of Asset Management, 20*(5), 331–340.

Bénabou, R., & Tirole, J. (2010). Individual and corporate social responsibility. *Economica, 77*(305), 1–19.

Berrone, P., Fosfuri, A., & Gelabert, L. (2017). Does greenwashing pay off? Understanding the relationship between environmental actions and environmental legitimacy. *Journal of Business Ethics, 144*(2), 363–379.

Bhutta, U. S., Tariq, A., Farrukh, M., Raza, A., & Iqbal, M. K. (2022). Green bonds for sustainable development: Review of literature on development and impact of green bonds. *Technological Forecasting and Social Change, 175*, 121378.

Brammer, S., Brooks, C., & Pavelin, S. (2006). Corporate social performance and stock returns: UK evidence from disaggregate measures. *Financial Management, 35*(3), 97–116.

Breusch, T. S., & Pagan , A. R. (1979). A simple test for heteroscedasticity and random coefficient variation. *Econometrica: Journal of the Econometric Society, 47*(5), 1287–1294.

Brown, S., & Warner, J. (1985). Using daily stock returns: The case of event studies. *Journal of Financial Economics, 14*, 3–31.

Castelo Branco, M., & Lima Rodriques, L. (2007). Positioning stakeholder theory within the debate on corporate social responsibility. *EJBO—Electronic Journal of Business Ethics and Organization Studies, 12*(1), 5–15.

CBI. (2020). *China's Green Bond Issuance and Investment Opportunity Report.* Climate Bonds Initiative and SynTao Green Finance.

Connelly, B., Certo, S., Ireland, R., & Reutzel, C. (2011). Signaling theory: A review and assessment. *Journal of Management, 37*(1), 39–67.

Cook, R. D., & Weisberg, S. (1983). Diagnostics for heteroscedasticity in regression. *Biometrika, 70*(1), 1–10.

Deng, X., Kang, J. K., & Low, B. S. (2013). Corporate social responsibility and stakeholder value maximization: Evidence from mergers. *Journal of Financial Economics, 110*(1), 87–109.
Donaldson, T., & Preston, L. E. (1995). The stakeholder theory of the corporation: Concepts, evidence, and implications. *Academy of Management Review, 20*(1), 65–91.
Ekatah, I., Samy, M., Bampton, R., & Halabi, A. (2011). The relationship between corporate social responsibility and profitability: The case of Royal Dutch Shell Plc. *Corporate Reputation Review, 14*(4), 249–261.
EU Climate Law. (2020).
European Commission. (2019). The European Green Deal. COM(2019) 640 final.
Fathurahman, H., & Fitriati, R. (2013). Comparative analysis of return on sukuk and conventional bonds. *American Journal of Economics*, 159–163.
Fatica, S., & Panzica, R. (2021). Green bonds as a tool against climate change? *Business Strategy and the Environment, 30*(5), 2688–2701.
Flammer, C. (2013). Corporate social responsibility and shareholder reaction: The environmental awareness of investors. *Academy of Management Journal, 56*(3), 758–781.
Flammer, C. (2021). Corporate green bonds. *Journal of Financial Economics, 142*(2), 499–516.
Freeman, R. E. (2010). *Strategic management: A stakeholder approach.* Cambridge University Press.
Friedman, M. (1970). The social responsibility of business ıs to ıncrease ıts profits. *New York Times Magazine.*
Froot, K. A. (1989). Consistent covariance matrix estimation with cross-sectional dependence and heteroskedasticity in financial data. *Journal of Financial and Quantitative Analysis, 24*(3), 333–355.
Frynas, J. G., & Yamahaki, C. (2016). Corporate social responsibility: Review and roadmap of theoretical perspectives. *Business Ethics: A European Review, 25*(3), 258–285.
Gonenc, H., & Scholtens, B. (2017). Environmental and financial performance of fossil fuel firms: A closer inspection of their interaction. *Ecological Economics, 132*, 307–328.
González-Benito, J., & González-Benito, Ó. (2005). Environmental proactivity and business performance: An empirical analysis. *Omega, 33*(1), 1–15.
Goodland, R. (1995). The concept of environmental sustainability. *Annual Review of Ecology and Systematics*, 1–24.
Gray, R., Owen, D., & Adams, C. (1996). *Accounting & accountability: Changes and challenges in corporate social and environmental reporting.* Prentice Hall.
Guenster, N., Bauer, R., Derwall, J., & Koedijk, K. (2011). The economic value of corporate eco-efficiency. *European Financial Management, 17*(4), 679–704.
Haque, M. M., Chowdhury, M. A., Buriev, A. A., Bacha, O. I., & Masih, M. (2017). Who drives whom-sukuk or bond? A new evidence from granger causality and wavelet approach. *Review of Financial Economics*, In Press.
Harrison, C., & MacGeoch, M. (2022). Sustainable debt, global state of the market 2021. *Climate Bonds Initiative.*
Hassel, L., Nilsson, H., & Nyquist, S. (2005). The value relevance of environmental performance. *European Accounting Review, 14*(1), 41–61.
Healy, P., & Palepu, K. (1993). The effect of firms' financial disclosure strategies on stock prices. *Accounting horizons, 7*(1–11).
IEA. (2021, January 12). *How much will renewable energy benefit from global stimulus packages?* Retrieved from IEA web site: https://www.iea.org/articles/how-much-will-renewable-energy-benefit-from-global-stimulus-packages
IEA. (2022, March). *Global energy review: CO_2 emissions in 2021.* Retrieved April 2022, from https://iea.blob.core.windows.net/assets/c3086240-732b-4f6a-89d7-db01be018f5e/GlobalEnergyReviewCO2Emissionsin2021.pdf
IIF. (2022). *ESG flows and markets: Q2 2022 chartbook.* Institute of International Finance.
Iwata, H., & Okada, K. (2011). How does environmental performance affect financial performance? Evidence from Japanese manufacturing firms. *Ecological Economics, 70*(9), 1691–1700.

Jensen, M. C. (2002). Value maximization, stakeholder theory, and the corporate objective function. *Business Ethics Quarterly, 12*(2), 235–256.

Jensen, M. C., & Meckling, W. (1976a). Theory of firm: Managerial behavior, agency costs, and ownership structure. *Journal of Financial Economics, 3*(4), 305–360.

King, A. A., & Lenox, M. J. (2001). Does it really pay to be green? An empirical study of firm environmental and financial performance: An empirical study of firm environmental and financial performance. *Journal of Industrial Ecology, 5*(1), 105–116.

Klassen, R. D., & McLaughlin, C. P. (1996). The impact of environmental management on firm performance. *Management Science, 42*(8), 1199–1214.

Kludacz-Alessandri, M., & Cygańska, M. (2021). Corporate social responsibility and financial performance among energy sector companies. *Energies, 14*(19, 6068), 1–16.

Konar, S., & Cohen, M. A. (2001). Does the market value environmental performance? *Review of Economics and Statistics, 83*(2), 281–289.

Krüger, P. (2015). Corporate goodness and shareholder wealth. *Journal of Financial Economics, 115*(2), 304–329.

Lebelle, M., Lajili Jarjir, S., & Sassi, S. (2020). Corporate green bond issuances: An international evidence. *Journal of Risk and Financial Management, 13*(2), 25.

Lech, A. (2013). Corporate social responsibility and financial performance. Theoretical and empirical aspects. *Comparative Economic Research. Central and Eastern Europe, 16*(3), 49–62.

Lee, S. (2021). Environmental responsibility, CEO power and financial performance in the energy sector. *Review of Managerial Science, 15*(8), 2407–2426.

Lins, K. V., Servaes, H., & Tamayo, A. (2017). Social capital, trust, and firm performance: The value of corporate social responsibility during the financial crisis. *The Journal of Finance, 72*(4), 1785–1824.

Lu, L. W., & Taylor, M. E. (2018). A study of the relationships among environmental performance, environmental disclosure, and financial performance. *Asian Review of Accounting.*

Lyon, T. P., & Montgomery, A. W. (2015). The means and end of greenwash. *Organization & Environment, 28*(2), 223–249.

Manrique, S., & Martí-Ballester, C. P. (2017). Analyzing the effect of corporate environmental performance on corporate financial performance in developed and developing countries. *Sustainability, 9, 1957*(11), 1–30.

Marquis, C., Toffel, M. W., & Zhou, Y. (2016). Scrutiny, norms, and selective disclosure: A global study of greenwashing. *Organization Science, 27*(2), 483–504.

Moneva, J. M., & Cuellar, B. (2009). The value relevance of financial and non-financial environmental reporting. *Environmental and Resource Economics, 44*(3), 441–456.

Montanarella, L., & Panagos, P. (2021). The relevance of sustainable soil management within the European Green Deal. *Land Use Policy, 100*(104950), 1–6.

Morelli, J. (2011). Environmental sustainability: A definition for environmental professionals. *Journal of environmental sustainability, 1(1)*(2), 1–9.

Nakao, Y., Amano, A., Matsumura, K., Genba, K., & Nakano, M. (2007a). Relationship between environmental performance and financial performance: An empirical analysis of Japanese corporations. *Business Strategy and the Environment, 16*(2), 106–118.

Nakao, Y., Nakano, M., Amano, A., Kokubu, K., Matsumura, K., & Gemba, K. (2007b). Corporate environmental and financial performances and the effects of information-based instruments of environmental policy in Japan. *International Journal of Environment and Sustainable Development, 6*(1), 1–22.

Orlitzky, M., Schmidt, F. L., & Rynes, S. L. (2003). Corporate social and financial performance: A meta-analysis. *Organization Studies, 24*(3), 403–441.

Pätäri, S., Arminen, H., Tuppura, A., & Jantunen, A. (2014). Competitive and responsible? The relationship between corporate social and financial performance in the energy sector. *Renewable and Sustainable Energy Reviews, 37*, 142–154.

Pekovic, S., Grolleau, G., & Mzoughi, N. (2018). Environmental investments: Too much of a good thing? *International Journal of Production Economics, 197*, 297–302.

Phillips, R. A., & Reichart, J. (2000). The environment as a stakeholder? A fairness-based approach. *Journal of Business Ethics, 23*(2), 185–197.
Refinitiv. (2022, May). *Environmental, social and governance scores from refinitiv.* Retrieved September 17, 2022, from https://www.refinitiv.com/content/dam/marketing/en_us/documents/methodology/refinitiv-esg-scores-methodology.pdf
Roberts, R. W. (1992). Determinants of corporate social responsibility disclosure: An application of stakeholder theory. *Accounting, Organizations and Society, 17*(6), 595–612. Retrieved from Accounting, Organizations and Society.
Rogers, W. (1993). Regression standard errors in clustered samples. *Stata Technical Bulletin, 3*(13), 19–23.
Rokhmawati, A., Gunardi, A., & Rossi, M. (2017). How powerful is your customers' reaction to carbon performance? Linking carbon and firm financial performance. *International Journal of Energy Economics and Policy, 7*(6), 85–95.
Rokhmawati, A., Sathye, M., & Sathye, S. (2015). The effect of GHG emission, environmental performance, and social performance on financial performance of listed manufacturing firms in Indonesia. *Procedia-Social and Behavioral Sciences, 211*, 461–470.
Ruf, B. M., Muralidhar, K., Brown, R. M., Janney, J. J., & Paul, K. (2001). An empirical investigation of the relationship between change in corporate social performance and financial performance: A stakeholder theory perspective. *Journal of Business Ethics, 32*(2), 143–156.
Russo, M. V., & Fouts, P. A. (1997). A resource-based perspective on corporate environmental performance and profitability. *Academy of Management Journal, 40*(3), 534–559.
Saad, N. M., Haniff, M. N., & Ali, N. (2020). Corporate governance mechanisms with conventional bonds and Sukuk'yield spreads. *Pacific-Basin Finance Journal, 62*, 101116.
Saeed, M., Elnahass, M., Izzeldin, M., & Tsionas, M. (2021). Yield spread determinants of sukuk and conventional bonds. *Economic Modelling, 105*, 105664.
Salvatore, R., & Heikki, L. (2017). Renewable energy growth and the financial performance of electric utilities: A panel data study. *Journal of Cleaner Production, 142*, 3676–3688.
Sarumpaet, S. (2005). The relationship between environmental performance and financial performance of Indonesian companies. *Jurnal Akuntansi Dan Keuangan, 7*(2), 89–98.
Saygili, E., Arslan, S., & Birkan, A. O. (2022). ESG practices and corporate financial performance: Evidence from Borsa Istanbul. *Borsa _Istanbul Review, 22*(3), 525–533.
Servaes, H., & Tamayo, A. (2013). The impact of corporate social responsibility on firm value: The role of customer awareness. *Management Science, 59*(5), 1045–1061.
Shahbaz, M., Karaman, A. S., Kilic, M., & Uyar, A. (2020). Board attributes, CSR engagement, and corporate performance: What is the nexus in the energy sector? *Energy Policy, 143*(111582), 1–14.
Sisodia, G., Joseph, A., & Dominic, J. (2022). Whether corporate green bonds act as armour during crises? Evidence from a natural experiment. *International Journal of Managerial Finance, 18*(4), 701–724.
Starik, M. (1995). Should trees have managerial standing? Toward stakeholder status for non-human nature. *Journal of Business Ethics, 14*(3), 207–217.
Stjepcevic, J., & Siksnelyte, I. (2017). Corporate social responsibility in energy sector. *Transformations in Business & Economics, 16*(1 (40)), 21–33.
Streimikiene, D., Simanaviciene, Z., & Kovaliov, R. (2009). Corporate social responsibility for implementation of sustainable energy development in Baltic States. *Renewable and Sustainable Energy Reviews, 13*(4), 813–824.
Suchman, M. C. (1995). Managing legitimacy: Strategic and institutional approaches. *Academy of Management Review, 20*(3), 571–610.
Talbot, D., & Boiral, O. (2018). GHG reporting and impression management: An assessment of sustainability reports from the energy sector. *Journal of Business Ethics, 147*(2), 367–383.
Tang, D. Y., & Zhang, Y. (2020). Do shareholders benefit from green bonds? *Journal of Corporate Finance, 61*, 101427.

Velte, P. (2017). Does ESG performance have an impact on financial performance? Evidence from Germany. *Journal of Global Responsibility, 80*(2), 169–178.

Verrecchia, R. E. (1983). Discretionary disclosure. *Journal of Accounting and Economics, 5*, 179–194.

Wahba, H. (2008). Does the market value corporate environmental responsibility? An empirical examination. *Corporate Social Responsibility and Environmental Management, 15*(2), 89–99.

Wang, C. W., Wu, Y. C., Hsieh, H. Y., Huang, P. H., & Lin, M. C. (2022). Does green bond issuance have an impact on climate risk concerns? *Energy Economics, 111*, 106066.

Wang, J., Chen, X., Li, X., Yu, J., & Zhong, R. (2020). The market reaction to green bond issuance: Evidence from China. *Pacific-Basin Finance Journal, 60*, 101294.

White, H. (1980). Heteroscedasticity-consistent covariance matrix estimator and a direct test for heteroscedasticity. *Econometrics, 48*(4), 817–838.

Wooldridge, J. M. (2002). *Econometric analysis of cross section and panel data.* MIT Press.

Yeow, K. E., & Ng, S. H. (2021). The impact of green bonds on corporate environmental and financial performance. *Managerial Finance, 47*(10), 1486–1510.

Yerdelen Tatoğlu, F. (2016). Üç boyutlu sabit ve tesadüfi etkili panel veri modellerinin tahmini için çeşitli yaklaşımlar. *Eurasian Econometrics, Statistics and Emprical Economics Journal, 5*, 60–70.

Zhang, R., Li, Y., & Liu, Y. (2021). Green bond issuance and corporate cost of capital. *Pacific-Basin Finance Journal, 69*, 101626.

Zhao, C., Guo, Y., Yuan, J., Wu, M., Li, D., Zhou, Y., & Kang, J. (2018). ESG and corporate financial performance: Empirical evidence from China's listed power generation companies. *Sustainability, 10*(8, 2607), 1–18.

Zhou, X., & Cui, Y. (2019). Green bonds, corporate performance, and corporate social responsibility. *Sustainability, 11*(23), 6881.

Zumente, I., Lāce, N., & Bistrova, J. (2020, May 7–8). ESG disclosure patterns in the Baltics. *Business and Management 2020* (pp. 28–37). Vilnius, Lithuania: 11th International Scientific Conference.

Dealing with ESG Issues: Creating Corporate Value

Resilience in Power Generation: Two Case Studies from Turkey

Fatih Avcı and Volkan Ş. Ediger

Abstract There is a growing interest in improving resilience in power systems to extreme climate events because of societies' high dependence on electrical energy and its vital role in economies. Resilience, which is closely linked with sustainability and the environmental, social, and governance (ESG), is especially important during the power system planning and implementation, and enhancement can accelerate the country's energy transition. In this chapter, we examined the lignite-fired Çan and hydroelectric Eğlence power plants as two cases in Turkey that can reveal the effects of extreme weather/climate events on electricity generation. This study used hourly air temperature data for Çan thermal power plants and daily precipitation data for Eğlence hydropower plants. The results of the investigation confirm the findings of previous studies: extreme weather/climatic conditions that occur because of global climate change cause considerable losses in electricity generation. Efficiency losses in power generation systems severely undermine Turkey's energy supply security and economy, especially given the country's high level of energy-import dependency. It is impossible to design every power plant to resist all possible events at the same time, but the effect of extreme climatic events can be reduced. We strongly recommend that the concept of resilience be immediately taken into consideration in designing new power plant investments and in adapting already existing ones to make them more flexible to any abrupt changes in climate. Resilience should top the energy agenda to enhance supply security and decrease dependence on foreign sources.

Keywords Energy resilience · Climate change · Power generation · Thermal and hydropower plants · Turkey

JEL Classification Q40 · Q41 · L94 · Q54 · Q01 · Q48

F. Avcı · V. Ş. Ediger (✉)
Center for Energy and Sustainable Development, Kadir Has University, Istanbul, Turkey
e-mail: volkanediger@gmail.com

J. Thewissen et al. (eds.), *The ESG Framework and the Energy Industry*,
https://doi.org/10.1007/978-3-031-48457-5_10

1 Introduction

Today's power systems are usually ill-prepared for large-scale extreme events (Lin et al., 2018), and power system master plans are often developed without consideration of the risks of current weather conditions and global climate change (Chattopadhyay et al., 2016). Resilience is a fundamental prerequisite for sustainability (Chaigneau et al., 2021; Editorial, 2019; Marchese et al., 2018; Pisano, 2012), and they are both related to environmental, social, and governance (ESG) issues, which have become a critical part of business strategy, including climate change, social inequality, and corporate governance (Sriyani et al., 2017).

This paper examines how extreme climate events affect electricity generation and what should be done to improve the resilience of power plants to climate change in Turkey. For this, one type of coal-fired power plants, 18 Mart Çan Thermal Power Plants (Çan TPP), located in Çanakkale province, and one type of hydroelectric power plants, Eğlence-2 Hydro Power Plants (Eğlence HPP), located in Adana have analyzed as case studies. The outage notification data related to weather or climate such as floods for Eğlence HPP and extreme temperatures for Çan TPP, which are obtained from the TEİAŞ webpage (TEİAŞ, 2020), are used to investigate the effect of climate change on electricity generation. The temperature data of the Çanakkale region where Çan PPP are located and precipitation data of the Adana region where Eğlence HPP are located are obtained from the Turkish State Meteorological Service (TSMS). The temperature data include minimum and maximum hourly temperatures, and the precipitation data include the amount of daily precipitation.

We studied the resilience-based planning stage, which is one of the three main stages of resilience (Huang et al., 2017; Mahzarnia et al., 2020). According to the authors' knowledge, this is the first study on energy resilience in Turkey and one of a few studies on the resilience of power generation carried out in the world and will contribute to the literature to a great extent.

The investigation of power outages together with temperature and precipitation data showed that the extreme weather conditions that resulted mainly from global climate change caused considerable losses in electricity generation in both cases. In Çan TPP, the increase in temperature from the long-term averages caused a loss of 60 MWe (19% of the installed capacity) and in Eğlence HPP, the increase of precipitation from the long-term averages caused a loss of 17.7 MW (65% of the installed capacity) as an average in electricity generation. These losses cause energy supply security as well as burden the economy. Both effects are of vital importance for countries such as Turkey, which are extremely dependent on foreign countries for energy.

The chapter is organized as follows. Section 2 discusses the conceptual evolution of resilience by reviewing the literature. The power sector of Turkey is summarized in the third section. The fourth section is devoted to the case studies of Çan Thermal Power Plant and Eğlence-2 Hydro Power Plants. The effect of climate change on electricity generation and the relationship between power decreases or outages and climate change are investigated in two cases in this section. The last section concludes the paper.

2 Literature Review and Conceptual Framework

Although the studies on resilience began with MacArthur (1955), its real spread was with the inspiring papers of Holling (1973) and Holling and Robin (1973) on ecological dynamics. The first authors defined the ecological concept of resilience in different ways, such as "a measure of the persistence of systems and of their ability to absorb change and disturbance and still maintain the same relationships between populations or state variables" (Holling, 1973, p. 14), "a measure of the ability of these systems to absorb changes of state variables, driving variables, and parameters" (Holling & Robin, 1973, p. 252), and a measure showing "how fast the variable return toward their equilibrium following a perturbation" (Pimm, 1984, p. 2). Recently, resilience is defined as "the ability of a system to absorb disturbances and still retain its basic function and structure" (Walker & Salt, 2006, p. 1), "the capacity to change in order to maintain the same identity" (Folke et al., 2010, p. 20), "the ability of an entity to anticipate, resist, absorb, respond to, adapt to and recover from a disturbance" (Carlson et al., 2012, p. 21), and "one which after an event has occurred, employs actions to return to its normal state by reducing its current level of stress quickly" (Hughes, 2015, p. 447).

Resilience has long been considered an important component of ecological stability (e.g., Batabyal, 1998; Neubert & Caswell, 1997). However, this tradition was later broken, and resilience was shown to be applicable not only to ecosystems but also to socioeconomic systems, and these two systems must be viewed as one single system (Levin et al., 1998, p. 234). Today, resilience is considered a multi-faceted concept, which can be adapted to various uses and contexts such as socioecological, psychiatric, engineering, disaster, urban, organizational, enterprise, community, infrastructure resilience, and environmental sciences (e.g., Alexander, 2013; Gatto & Drago, 2020; Sagintayev & Collins, 2017; Shakoua et al., 2019). However, it is mostly focused on the ability to deal with disruptions (Carlson et al., 2012) since resilience application in the systems will decrease the negative effects of disturbances via the flexibility and adaptability capability of the systems (Ghisellini et al., 2016; Leandro et al., 2020).

Recently, there is a growing interest in improving the adaptive capacity of energy systems to make the systems more resilient because of their vital role in economies (Erker et al., 2017; Molyneaux et al., 2016). Resilience is also an important factor of energy security, which aims at providing available, affordable, reliable, efficient, and clean energy services (e.g., Sovacool, 2011; Vivoda, 2010). Energy resilience can therefore be defined as "the capacity to successfully deal with any disruptions while continuing to provide affordable energy services to society" (Erker et al., 2017, p. 429).

The growing interest in energy resilience all around the world encouraged R&D activities on the subject (Gatto & Drago, 2020). Although energy resilience research started in 1994 and grew exponentially after 2000, it increased more rapidly in the last decade, especially in organizations located in the USA and the UK (Mola et al., 2018). In academia, continuous scientific production started in 2008 with an average rate of one paper per year until 2011 and increased rapidly from 2012 to the present (Gatto & Drago, 2020). However, most of the existing studies on energy resilience are carried out on individual energy systems not on the resilience of the integrated energy system (IES) (Lina & Biea, 2016) and on interdisciplinary analysis of the resilience of electrical systems such as a cross-epistemic resilience (CER) (Hamborg et al., 2020).

The previous studies used different parameters for energy resilience such as "share of renewable energy in the total energy consumption" and "share of energy used in the GDP structure" to evaluate a socioeconomic system's resilience (Bruneckiene et al., 2019, p. 10). Several climatic threats/challenges facing energy systems such as high temperatures and heat waves, changing precipitation patterns at all levels, rain with strong wings or lightning, sea-level changes, changes in river flows, including flooding, changes in wind patterns and intensity, storms, and hurricanes, changes in insolation, cold waves, heavy ice, and snow are also used in energy resilience studies (e.g., Chattopadhyay et al., 2016; Panteli & Mancarella, 2015; Sharifi & Yamagata, 2016).

Since power systems are vital for modern societies because of their high dependence on electrical energy and costly procedures for system recovery, it is very important to improve their resilience to especially extreme weather conditions and climate change (e.g., Chattopadhyay et al., 2016; Mahzarnia et al., 2020; Panteli & Mancarella, 2015; Sharifi & Yamagata, 2016; Tobin et al., 2018). The concept of resilience in power systems can be broadly defined as "the ability of a power system to withstand initial shock" (Pantelli & Mancerella, 2015, p. 260).

The resilience of power systems to climate change is a relatively new research area (Panteli & Mancarella, 2015) and becoming more popular because of the increase in the frequency and severity of power outages caused by extreme weather events (Jufri et al., 2019). However, this research is mostly concentrated on transmission and distribution systems (power grid resilience) rather than generation systems (e.g., Bhusal et al., 2020; Blaabjerg et al., 2017; Gatto & Drago, 2020; Jufri et al., 2019; National Academies, 2014; Rathor & Saxena, 2020; Scala et al., 2013; Ton & Wang, 2015; Totschniga et al., 2017; Vugrin et al., 2017; Wang et al., 2018; Willis & Loa, 2015).

Power outages, which threaten basic physiological and psychological needs (Moreno & Shaw, 2019), are caused by natural disasters, technical problems, or human-made reasons (Smith & Katz, 2013). Power generation is sensitive to severe weather, earthquakes, explosions, fires, and chemical releases (EPRI, 2016). However, the effect of climate change on electricity generation in various types of power plants is rarely studied (e.g., Cai et al., 2012; Ecoplan/Sigmaplan, 2007; Gonseth & Vielle, 2012; EPRI, 2016; Moreno & Shaw, 2019; Totschniga et al., 2017; WBCSD, 2014). According to Totschniga et al. (2017, p. 238), there are numerous effects of climate change on the electricity generation sector, including the type and location of infrastructure, the number of thermal and nuclear power plants relying on cooling water availability, and the number of hydropower plants.

The number and severity of weather-related events increased worldwide because of climatic changes in recent decades (Chen et al., 2017; IPCC, 2014). The number of extreme weather events has grown exponentially in the last three decades, increasing the number of heat waves in the world and such extreme events will presumably continue in different types to different regions (WBCSD, 2014). Because of extreme natural disasters, large-scale power electricity outages became more frequent, causing huge losses to society and the economy (Ton & Wang, 2015).

Temperature and water availability are the two most important factors affecting thermal and hydropower plants. Changes in temperature and water volumes resulting from climate change will decrease output by reducing generation (Çengel & Boles, 2005; WBCSD, 2014). Modeling the impacts of climate change on the energy sector in Switzerland, Gonseth and Vielle (2012) estimated that thermal power plants will lose 4.4% of capacity by 2050 due to increased river temperatures, and hydroelectric power plants will lose 2.2% due to reduced runoffs. The increase in temperature has two detrimental effects on thermal electricity generation: (1) it reduces the plant's efficiency, and (2) it forces operators to run the plant at partial load or to shut it down (Ecoplan/Sigmaplan, 2007; Gonseth & Vielle, 2012; Linnerud et al., 2011). The reduced gap between internal and external temperatures will permanently hit generating efficiency in warmer regions, and high humidity will reduce the efficiency of thermal plants in some locations (WBCSD, 2014). A reduction in runoff negatively affects hydropower production (Gonseth & Vielle, 2012).

3 Overview of Turkey's Power Sector

Studies in energy resilience have grown all around the world for the last decade, and there has been a growing interest in improving the adaptive capacity of power systems to make them more resilient. Turkey is one of the countries where electricity has a growing importance. It is 15th in electricity generation with 305.4 TWh (1.1% share) in the world, and the demand for electricity grew around 4.5% from 2009 to 2019, one of the fastest in the world (BP, 2021), in line with economic developments driven by industrialization and urbanization.

Turkey has predominantly a typical Mediterranean climate in most of its coastal areas, whereas the climate in the interior parts is dry with typical steppe vegetation (Ediger & Kentel, 1999). There are significant differences in climate from one region to the other; while the coastal areas have milder climates, the inland Anatolian plateau has extremes of hot summers and cold winters with limited rainfall (Şensoy et al., 2008, 2016).

Extreme weather events (also called natural disasters) have been increasing rapidly for the last two decades, and the hot waves had a considerable share in the weather extreme events (TSMS, 2020), hardening the operational conditions of electricity generation. According to Eroğlu et al. (2020), they increased from less than 100 in the 1990s to 936 in 2019. In 2019, heavy rain and flood were the most common climate-oriented natural disasters (332 events), consisting of 36%, storms were the second with 257 events, consisting of 27%, and hailing was the third with 167 events, consisting of 18%. In the future, a large part of the subtropical climatic belt covers the Eastern Mediterranean basin, and Turkey is expected to have a decreased precipitation, especially in winters in addition to long-term summer dryness (Türkeş et al., 2000).

Extreme temperature events are also an increasing trend. TSMS defines "heat wave" when the daily maximum temperature occurs above 5 °C from the long-term average in five consecutive days and "cold wave" when the daily maximum occurs below 5 °C from the long-term average. The annual average temperature in Turkey has been increasing trend since the 1990s (Şen, 2020). According to the models developed by Demircan et al. (2017) for the 2016 and 2099 period, an increase in mean temperature from 1 to 6 °C and a decrease in precipitation except winter season are expected. This means that the number of severities of heat waves due to climate change will increase (Kum & Çelik, 2014). Therefore, research on the effect of weather/climate change on electricity generation will have vital importance for the Turkish economy.

Energy plays an important role in the rapid development of Turkey. The country consumed 6.29 Exajoules (EJ) of primary energy (PEC) with a share of 1.1% in the world in 2020 (BP, 2021). It ranks 12th in rate of increase from 2009 to 2019 with 4.3%. In its energy mix, oil has the biggest share with 29.0% and it is followed by natural gas (26.5%) and coal (26.4%) (Table 1). Similarly, it ranks 15th in electricity generation with a share of 1.1% and increased its generation capacity by 4.5% from 2009 to 2019. This rate is relatively high compared to 2.9% of the world's average. However, coal and hydropower plants have the biggest shares in electricity generation with 34.7% and 25.6%, respectively. Therefore, their resilience is very important for the country.

Table 1 Primary energy consumption and electricity generation by fuel in Turkey in 2020

	Primary energy consumption (%)	Electricity generation (%)
Oil	29.0	0.05
Natural gas	26.5	22.9
Coal	26.4	34.7
Hydroelectricity	11.0	25.6
Renewables	7.1	16.3
Others[a]	–	0.42
Total	100.0	100.0

[a] Includes sources not specified elsewhere such as pumped hydro, non-renewable waste, and statistical discrepancies. Data from BP (2021)

In 2020, Turkey's power plant installed capacity reached 95,890.6 MW of which 49.8% thermal, 32.3% hydroelectricity, and 17.8% renewable sources. The distribution of the installed capacity of power plants among the production companies is 68% of private companies, 22% state-owned EÜAŞ, 7% unlicensed producers, and 3% auto producers. The power plants generated 306,703.1 GWh of electricity of which 57.7% is from thermal, 25.5% from hydro, and 16.8% from renewable sources in 2020.

Whereas the capacity factors of thermal, hydro, and total are in decreasing trend, renewables are increasing (Fig. 1). The average capacity factor of all power plants from 2010 to 2020 is 42.2%, whereas 50.7% in thermal, 29.8% in hydro, and 31.8% in renewable power plants. The reason why the capacity factors of thermal power plants are higher than others is that they operated as base load plants. The capacity factor of these plants is like other countries; for instance, in the USA in 2019, the average capacity factor of coal power plants was around 48% and natural gas power plants around 57% (Statista, 2020). The decreasing trend in capacity factors of thermal power plants is related to several factors such as technical constraints (e.g., unavailability of the plant because of equipment failures or maintenance), availability of fuel sources, and economic reasons.

The main reason for the reduced capacity factor in hydroelectric power plants is generally related to the rate of precipitation. The hydroelectric power plant's electricity generation may also be affected by the necessity to keep the water level at certain levels for agricultural, ecological, and risk management reasons. The average capacity factor of hydroelectric power plants in Turkey is low compared to the worldwide average of 44% (IPCC, 2011). Extreme climate events also decrease capacity factors by reducing the working hours of power plants. Therefore, for efficient and effective power generation, energy resilience of power plants should be improved.

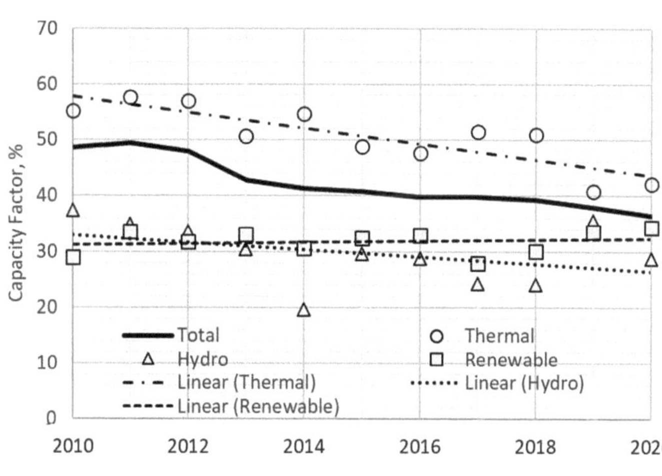

Fig. 1 Capacity factors of thermal, hydro, and renewable-based electricity generation in Turkey. Data from TEİAŞ

4 Case Studies on Thermal and Hydropower Plants

In this part, the effect of climate change on power generation in Çan TPP and Eğlence HPP is examined in detail by studying the maintenance and outage data together with temperature data for the thermal power plants and the precipitation data for the hydropower plants.

The Aegean and Mediterranean coasts where Çanakkale and Adana are located have cool, rainy winters, and hot, moderately dry summers (Şensoy et al., 2016). Şahin and Cigizoğlu (2012) separated Turkey into seven main precipitation regime regions and 16 sub-precipitation regime regions, including Çanakkale into the "Aegean" and Adana into the "Mediterranean" precipitation regimes, which has a monthly precipitation of 596.0 mm and 830.2 mm, respectively. Çanakkale is expected to have a warmer climate in the future, having an increase in mean annual temperature to 0.02977 °C per year by 2022 (Kale, 2017), and in Adana, the models projected an increase in temperature and a decrease in precipitation (Fujihara et al., 2008). Severe weather conditions are among the emergency situations that can occur in electric power plants (EPRI, 2016), and these extreme events affect all supply chains of power systems (WBCSD, 2014).

4.1 Çan TPP

The main characteristics of Çan TPP, which has been in operation since 2006, are given in Table 2. The power plants have two units; each has an installed capacity of 160 MWe, totaling 320 MWe. It uses a lignite-fired Circulating fluidized bed (CFB) combustion system, and the fuel is produced locally in the Çanakkale province.

The hourly generation capacity graph of Çan PPP in three years from January 1, 2016, to December 31, 2018, is given in Fig. 2. The plant generated 1,951,361 MWh of electricity in 2016, 1,864,369 MWh in 2017, and 2,449,067 MWh in 2018. In

Table 2 Main characteristics of the Çan TPP

Parameter	Characteristics
Installed capacity	320 MWe (2 units)
Designed generation capacity	2080 GWh/year
Realized generation—2018	2449 GWh
Fuel	Coal fired (Lignite)
Location	Çanakkale, Turkey
Operator company	EUAS
Boiler type	Circulating fluidized bed (CFB)
Cooling system	Dry-air (Heller type)
Installed capacity	320 MWe (2 units)

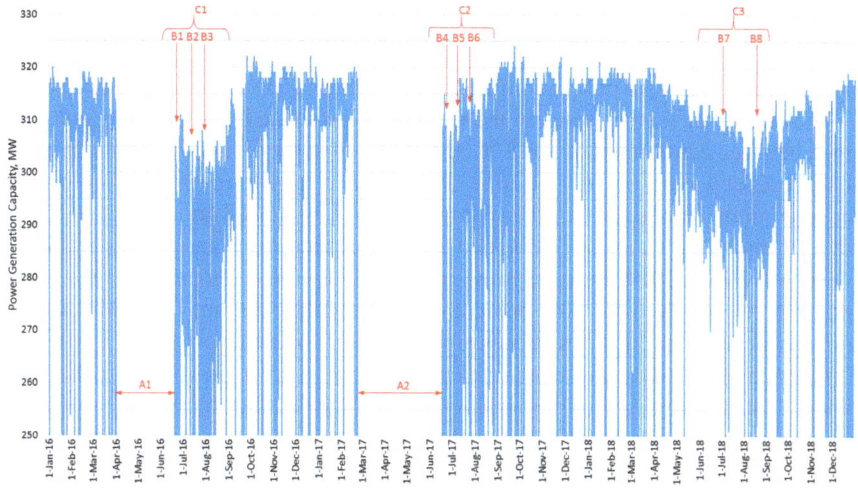

Fig. 2 Hourly generation capacity of Çan TPP between 1996 and 1998

other words, the capacity factors were 69.6%, 66.5%, and 87.3%, corresponding to working hours of 6098, 5826, and 7653, respectively.

During the studied period, the plant has never reached its full generation capacity of 320 MWe; its maximum electricity output has been 313 MWe. The power plant was taken in maintenance (shown with "A"), which are crucial operations carried out to provide reliable power generation to meet the demand, two times from April 2, 2016, to May 31, 2016, and from April 5, 2017, to May 22, 2017. Both units are stopped during these periods to carry out "corrective" that are performed after a breakdown occurred or "preventive" maintenance activities carried out to reduce the chance of failure of the system as suggested by Velayutham and Ismail (2018).

The power plant was broken down (shown with "B") because of unexpected reasons such as boiler valve problems, piping leakage, coal handling, ash handling system problems, fan problems, cardboard problems, and transformer-related problems (circuit breakers), etc. These mechanical problems can occur because of long-life operations and sudden thermal or physical forces. The problems in the coal handling system also decrease electricity generation due to the decrease in fuel supply for the boiler. Electricity generation decreases periodically during summer seasons because of the high temperature of intake air (shown with "C").

The capacity variations and losses of Çan TPP are summarized in Table 3. In the maintenance period, Çan TPP did not work for 2547 h in 106 days. The total duration of the breakdown period was 43 h in three years from 2016 to 2018. The power plants worked with a capacity ranging between 201 and 203 MWe with an average of 222 MWe during the breakdown period. During summer seasons between June and August, electricity generation capacity drops down to around 300 MWe. The average power generation capacities were 242 MWe in 2016, 243 MWe in 2017, and 292 MWe in 2018. The average electricity generation in the three summer seasons was 248 MW. The losses of electricity generation were 100% in maintenance, 31% in the breakdown, and 19% in regular summer operation periods, which correspond to total economic losses of $37.2 million, $207,035, and $18.5 million, respectively.[1]

The hourly air temperatures in the Çanakkale province between 2016 and 2018 range between a minimum of −8.5 °C at 4 a.m. on January 3, 2017, and a maximum of 40.6 °C at 1 p.m. on July 1, 2018 (Fig. 3). The long-term observed minimum and maximum temperatures of the years 2016, 2017, and 2018 are −8 °C and 37 °C, −8.5 °C and 40.6 °C, and −3.8 °C and 37.1 °C, respectively, and during 100 years between 1919 and 2019, the average minimum and maximum temperatures are 3.3 °C and 30.6 °C, respectively. The breakdown and regular summer operation periods correspond with the high-temperature periods. For instance, on July 13, 2017, at 12:43–19:59 h when the average air temperature was 36.5 °C in about 7 h, the plant generated 237 MWe (74% of the capacity) on average. In August 2018, the measured maximum temperature was 32.7 °C, and the plant generated an average of 252 MWe of electricity (80% of the capacity).

The details of maximum temperature events and the breakdown periods are given in Table 4. The minimum measured temperature during the breakdown events varies from 29.9 °C in B6 to 39.7 °C in B5, and the maximum from 32.3 °C in B8 and 38.4 °C in B5. These temperatures are much higher than the long-term average values. The difference between the averages varies from 6.5 °C in B8 and 16.2 °C in B5 whereas the maximums are from 2.4 °C in B8 and 12.5 °C in B5.

These extreme temperature events were much higher than the long-term average summer temperature of Çanakkale, which is 30 °C for the period from 1929 to 2019. The plant was designed in 2000 based on 30 °C but the temperature increased to 40 °C on July 1, 2017, at 1:00 p.m. As clearly shown in Fig. 3, the temperatures during the summer seasons of all three studied years are mostly above this temperature (shown with a thick line in the figure).

4.2 Eğlence HPP

The main characteristics of Eğlence HPP, which has been in operation since 2013 are given in Table 5. It is built on the Eğlence River, which is part of the Seyhan River system in Adana.

The hourly electricity generation capacity graph from 2016 to 2018 in Eğlence HPP is given in Fig. 4. The plant generated 39,729 MWh of electricity in 2016, 78,827 MWh in 2017, and 87,627 MWh in 2018. In other words, the capacity factors were 16.7%, 33.1%, and 36.8% corresponding to working hours of 1461, 2898, and 3222, respectively. The plant was not in operation (shown with "A") because of either maintenance (A3) or lack of available water for power generation (A1 and A2). For instance, the power plant stopped for 18 h or partially operated between March 29

[1] The electricity market prices in Turkey were 46.3 USD/MWh in 2016, 45.0 MW in 2017, and 47.4 MW in 2019.

Table 3 Summary of capacity variations and losses of Çan TPP between 2016 and 2018

Events		Timing			Power generation (MWe)			Loss of generation (%)	Average electricity price (USD/MWh)	Economical loss (USD)
		Start date	Stop date	Duration hours	Min	Max	Avr			
Maintenance	A1	2 Apr 2016 04:00	31 May 2016 02:00	1416	0	0	0	100	46.30	20,979,456
	A2	5 Apr 2017 02:00	22 May 2017 04:00	1131	0	0	0	100	45.00	16,286,400
	Overall			2547	0.0	0.0	0.0	100		37,265,856
Breakdown	B1	22 Jun 2016 12:00	22 Jun 2016 15:00	3	240	242	241	25	46.30	10,973
	B2	15 Jul 2016 13:00	15 Jul 2016 19:00	6	213	243	229	28	46.30	25,280
	B3	24 Jul 2016 13:00	24 Jul 2016 19:00	6	229	239	236	26	46.30	23,335
	B4	29 Jun 2017 13:00	29 Jun 2017 20:00	7	158	252	190	41	45.00	40,950
	B5	30 Jun 2017 11:00	30 Jun 2017 17:00	6	60	182	123	62	45.00	53,190
	B6	13 Jul 2017 12:00	13 Jul 2017 21:00	9	185	248	227	29	45.00	37,665
	B7	15 Jun 2018 15:00	15 Jun 2018 18:00	3	270	278	274	14	47.40	6541
	B8	19 Aug 2018 14:00	19 Aug 2018 17:00	3	252	259	256	20	47.40	9101
	Overall			43	201	243	222	31		207,035

(continued)

Table 3 (continued)

Events		Timing			Power generation (MWe)			Loss of generation (%)	Average electricity price (USD/MWh)	Economical loss (USD)
		Start date	Stop date	Duration hours	Min	Max	Avr			
Regular summer operation	C1	1 Jun 2016 00:00	31 Aug 2016 23:00	2208	127	311	242	24	46.30	7,973,971
	C2	1 Jun 2017 00:00	31 Aug 2017 23:00	2208	50	318	243	24	45.00	7,650,720
	C3	1 Jun 2018 00:00	31 Aug 2018 23:00	2208	140	313	292	9	47.40	2,930,458
	Overall			6624	8.4%	25.2%	105.7	314.0		18,555,149

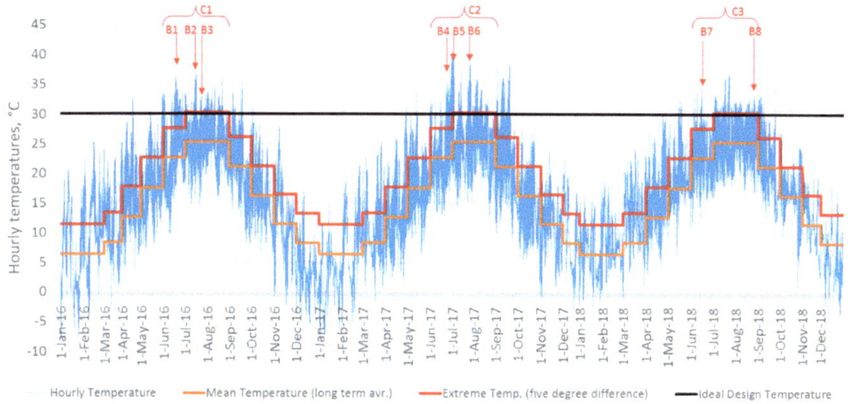

Fig. 3 Hourly air temperatures in the Çanakkale province between 2016 and 2018 and the breakdown and regular summer operations period

Table 4 Details of the maximum temperature events and breakdown events

Breakdown events	Measured hourly temperature (°C)			Long-term (1919–2019) temperatures (°C)	
	Minimum	Maximum	Average	Average	Maximum
B1	31.6	33.8	32.9	22.2	27.2
B2	30.6	35.9	33.6	25.0	30.0
B3	30.4	33.1	32.0	25.0	30.0
B4	30.8	39.6	36.4	22.2	27.2
B5	35.3	39.7	38.4	22.2	27.2
B6	29.9	37.2	34.6	25.0	30.0
B7	30.3	33.4	31.9	25.0	30.0
B8	30.3	32.3	31.4	24.9	29.9

Table 5 Main characteristics of the Eğlence HPP

Parameter	Characteristics
Installed capacity	27.2 MWe (3 unit)
Turbine types	Francis (5.2 MW + 11 MW × 2)
Designed head and flowrate	169 m and 17.4 m^3/s
Designed generation capacity	~52 GWh/year
Realized generation—2018	87.6 GWh
Location	Adana, Turkey
Operator company	Egenda Ege Enerji Üretim A.Ş

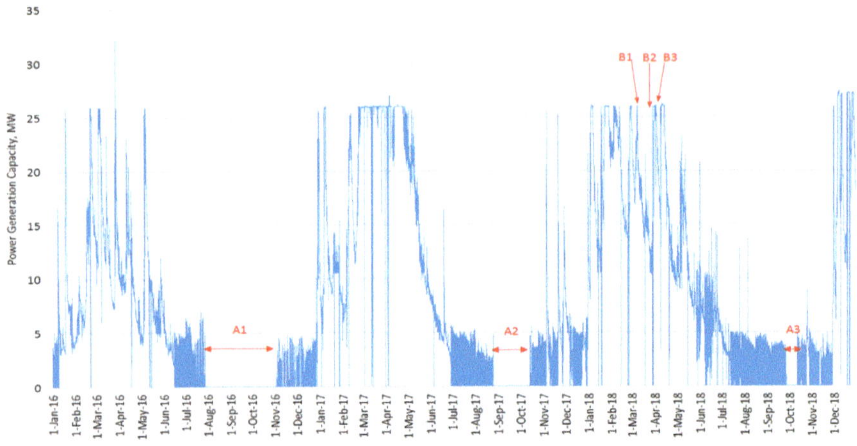

Fig. 4 Hourly generation capacity of Eğlence HPP between 2016 and 2018

and 31, 2018, because the flood clogged the filters and blocked the cooling system of the turbines. During the flood periods (shown with "B"), the electricity generation stopped or considerably decreased.

The capacity variations and losses are summarized in Table 6. The maintenance and no operation period last 3910 h of which 379 h are maintenance (A3). The breakdown period lasts 34 h. The losses of electricity generation were 100% in maintenance and 65% in breakdown periods, which correspond to total economic losses of 285,430 USD and 23,798 USD, respectively.[2]

Figure 5 shows the average monthly rainfall in the Adana province from January 2016 to December 2018. The maximum precipitation was in December 2018 with 400 mm, and the minimum precipitation was in August 2016 at 3 mm with an average of 6.34 mm on 395 rainy days. On the other hand, the daily precipitation varies between a minimum of 0.2 mm (several days) and a maximum of 119 mm (December 31, 2016) with an average of 10.5 mm. The outages seen during the last three days of March 2018 were caused by unexpected rains of up to 30 mm in one day compared to a long-term daily average of 8.95 mm. This extreme flooding the caused power plant to stop electricity generation.

The maximum daily precipitation occurred several times such as 88 mm on December 27, 2016, 119 mm on December 31, 2016, and 96.6 mm on Jan 23, 2018. During these days, plant operators stopped the plant in line with prior warnings about excessive rainfall. However, on March 29 and 30, 2018, unexpectedly high precipitation caused flooding (Fig. 6). There are a total of 12 rainy days with an average of 4.65 mm per rainy day in March.

The extreme precipitation seen in March is well above the long-term (90 years) average of the Adana region. As shown in Table 7, there are a total of 75 rainy days in a year with an average precipitation of 671 mm.

[2] The electricity feed-in tariffs for hydroelectricity were 73 USD/MWh for 2016, 2017, and 2018.

Table 6 Summary of capacity variations and losses of Eğlence HPP between 2016 and 2018

Events		Timing			Power generation (MWe)			Loss of generation (%)	Aver. electricity price (USD/MWh)	Economical loss (USD)
		Start date	Stop date	Duration hours	Min	Max	Aver			
Maintenance and no operation	A1	27 Jul 2016 17:00	3 Nov 2016 13:00	2360	0.0	0.0	0.0	100	73.0	172,280
	A2	26 Aug 2017 00:00	14 Oct 2017 03:00	1180	0.0	0.0	0.0	100	73.0	86,140
	A3	27 Sep 2018 06:00	12 Oct 2018 15:00	370	0.0	0.0	0.0	100	73.0	27,010
	Total			3910	0.0	0.0	0.0	100		285,430
Breakdown	B1	29 Mar 2018 16:00	30 Mar 2018 00:00	8	0.0	14.0	5.0	81	73.0	2920
	B2	30 Mar 2018 08:00	30 Mar 2018 23:00	15	0.0	19.0	11.0	58	73.0	12,045
	B3	31 Mar 2018 00:00	31 Mar 2018 11:00	11	0.0	24.6	11.0	58	73.0	8833
	Total			34	0.0	19.2	9.0	65		23,798

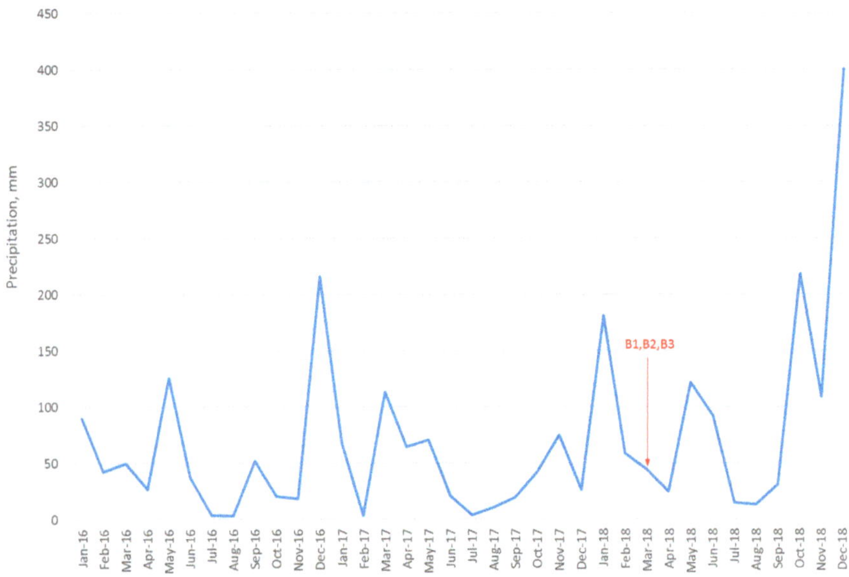

Fig. 5 Average monthly rainfall amount (mm) in Adana province between 2016 and 2018

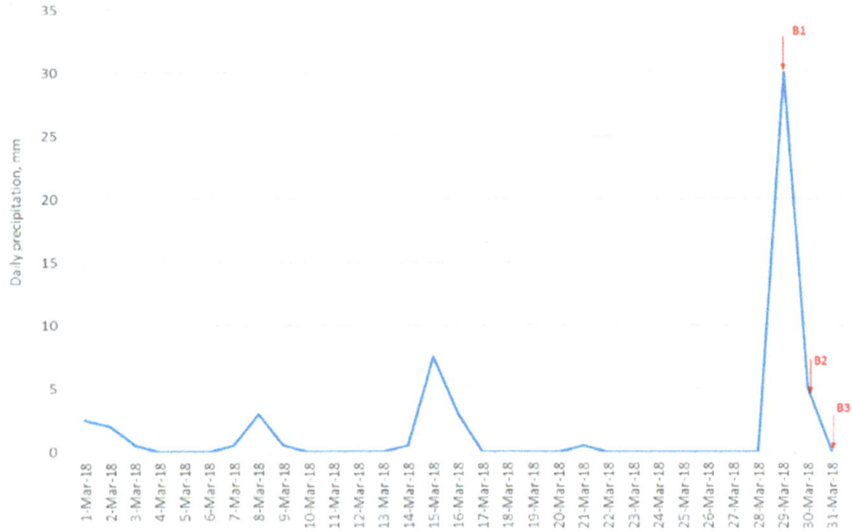

Fig. 6 Average daily precipitation in Adana region in March 2018

Table 7 Adana region's long-term monthly precipitation amounts between 1929 and 2019

1929–2019	Jan	Feb	Mar	Apr	May	June	July	Aug	Sept	Oct	Nov	Dec	Total
Average rainy days (number of days)	10.6	10.1	9.6	8.6	6.3	3.0	0.9	0.7	2.6	5.4	6.9	10.3	75.0
Average total precipitation amount (mm)	111.6	89.7	65.4	51.9	48.8	22.0	10.2	9.8	19.6	43.6	71.4	127.3	671.3

As a result of this unexpected flooding event, there was a power outage at Eğlence HPP on March 29–30, 2018. The operation capacity is reduced to two turbines and the plant stopped for 18 full hours. The plant was able to generate a maximum of 8.68 MW electricity on these days, much less than the March average of 16.92 MW.

As can be clearly seen in this section, climate change-induced changes in temperature and precipitation cause serious losses in electricity generation. This situation damages the economies of countries such as Turkey, which are developing rapidly and are extremely dependent on foreign countries for energy.

5 Conclusions

The climate is changing in Turkey at an increasing pace. Therefore, the concept of resilience should immediately be taken into consideration in designing new power plants as well as in adapting the already existing ones to make them more flexible to any changes in climate. Energy reliance should be urgently placed at the top of the agenda. In this study, we examined the power plants Çan TPP and Eğlence HPP as two cases from Turkey to investigate the effect of extreme weather/climate events on electricity generation. For this, the hourly air temperature data are used for Çan TPP and the daily precipitation data for Eğlence HPP together with their generation capacity graphs to compare extreme climate events with the electricity generation of power plants.

The main conclusion we draw from the study is that the extreme weather/climatic conditions that are resulted mainly from global climate change cause considerable losses in electricity generation. In Çan TPP, the increase of temperature from the long-term average of 25–40 °C especially in summer seasons caused a loss of 60 MWe on average (19% of the installed capacity) in electricity generation. In Eğlence HPP, the increase of precipitation from the long-term average of 8.95 mm per rainy day to 30 mm on March 29, 2018, caused a loss of 17.7 MW (65% of the installed capacity) as an average in electricity generation. The result of this study supports earlier studies. For instance, Tobin et al. (2018) showed that climate change has negative impacts on electricity production in most of the EU countries, and for most technologies; such impacts remain limited for a 1.5 °C warming and roughly double for a 3 °C warming.

The efficiency losses in power generation cause serious losses, which deeply affect the energy supply security and economy of countries that are highly dependent on foreign energy sources like Turkey. Turkey imports around 75% of its primary energy demand by paying $41 billion (in 2019) to support its rapidly growing economy. If we consider an average of 500 h of outage per year and an average market price of electricity of 47 USD/MWh, the loss at Çan TPP reaches $1.4 million in a year. On the other hand, the unexpected floods stopped turbines for 18 h in Eğlence HPP, causing a loss of $35,000 in the studied period.

Resilience should be studied in three stages such as planning, response, and restoration (Huang et al., 2017; Mahzarnia et al., 2020). In this paper, we studied only the planning stage. The most important policy recommendation we can make in this study is that climate change should be considered in designing power plants to maintain energy resilience. At present in Turkey, as in many other countries, the concept of resilience is not commonly applied in designing electricity power generation (EPRI, 2016; Lin et al., 2018). Of course, it is not possible to design every power plant to always resist all possible events, and most of the blackouts are caused by low-probability events (Panteli et al., 2017), but new strategies are needed for keeping electricity generation in three stages before, during, and after the external extreme event (Lin et al., 2018).

The historical data are not reliable for risk assessments on energy resilience applications. WBCSD (2014) demonstrated that relying only on historical data when planning for resilience can result in misunderstanding risk levels, particularly when the frequency and intensity of events are changing. Instead, weather forecasts are needed for consideration of all possibilities for global and regional climate change. Between 1980 and 2012, more than 21,000 natural catastrophes (disasters) occurred, of which 87% were weather-related in the world (WBCSD, 2014) and these figures are expected to increase in the future. Natural disasters bring unprecedented challenges to the power system if the power systems are ill-prepared for extreme events of different scales.

Acknowledgements The authors would like to thank Dr. John V. Bowlus, visiting scientist at the Center for Energy and Sustainable Development, Kadir Has University, for critically reviewing the manuscript and offering valuable suggestions.

References

Alexander, D. E. (2013). Resilience and disaster risk reduction: An etymological journey. *Natural Hazards and Earth System Sciences, 13*(11), 2707–2716.

Batabyal, A. A. (1998). The concept of resilience: retrospect and prospect. *Environment and Development Economics, 3*(2), 235–239.

Bhusal, N., Abdelmalak, M., Kamruzzaman, M., & Benidris, M. (2020). Power system resilience: Current practices, challenges, and future directions. *IEEE Access*. https://doi.org/10.1109/ACCESS.2020.2968586

Blaabjerg, F., Yang, Y., Yang, D., & Wang, X. (2017). Distributed power-generation systems and protection. *Proceedings of the IEEE, 105*(7), 1311–1331.

BP. (2021). Statistical review of world energy. BP plc. https://www.bp.com/en/global/corporate/energy-economics/statistical-review-of-worldenergy.html

Bruneckiene, J., Pekarskiene, I., Palekiene, O., & Simanaviciene, Z. (2019). An assessment of socio-economic systems' resilience to economic shocks: The case of Lithuanian regions. *Sustainability, 11*(566), 1–24.

Cai, Y. P., Huang, G. H., Yeh, S. C., Liu, L., & Li, G. C. (2012). A modeling approach for investigating climate change impacts on renewable energy utilization. *International Journal of Energy Research, 36*(6), 764–777.

Carlson, J. L., Haffenden, R. A., Bassett, G. W., et al. (2012). *Resilience: Theory and application*. Argonne, IL, United States.

Çengel, Y. A., & Boles, M. A. (2005). *Thermodynamics: An engineering approach*. McGraw-Hill Higher Education.

Chaigneau, T., Coulthard, S., Daw, T. M., et al. (2021). Reconciling well-being and resilience for sustainable development. *Nature Sustainability*. https://doi.org/10.1038/s41893-021-00790-8

Chattopadhyay, D., Spyrou, E., Mukhi, N., Bazilian, M., & Vogt-Schilb, A. (2016). Building climate resilience into power systems plans: Reflections on potential ways forward for Bangladesh. *The Electricity Journal, 29*, 32–41.

Chen, C., Wang, J., & Ton, D. (2017). Modernizing distribution system restoration to achieve grid resiliency against extreme weather events: An integrated solution. *Proceedings of the IEEE, 105*(7), 1267–1288.

Demircan, M., Gürkan, H., Eskioğlu, O., Arabacı, H., & Coşkun, M. (2017). Climate change projections for Turkey: Three models and two scenarios. *Turkish Journal of Water Science & Management, 1*(1), 22–43.

Ecoplan/Sigmaplan. (2007). *Auswirkungen der Klimaänderung auf die schweizer Volkswirtschaft (nationale Einflüsse)*. Technical report, Swiss Federal Office for the Environment and Swiss Federal Office of Energy, Bern.

Ediger, V. Ş, & Kentel, E. (1999). Renewable energy potential as an alternative to fossil fuels in Turkey. *Energy Conversion and Management, 40*, 743–755.

Editorial. (2019). Resilience and sustainability. *Nature Sustainability, 2*(249), 240.

EPRI (Electric Power Research Institute). (2016). *Electric power system resiliency: Challenges and opportunities*. Electric Power Research Institute.

Erker, S., Stangl, R., & Stoeglehner, G. (2017). Resilience in the light of energy crises, Part I: A framework to conceptualize regional energy resilience. *Journal of Cleaner Production, 164*, 420–433.

Eroğlu, H., Çetin, S., Erkan, M. A., Çamalan, G., Güseri, Y., Odabaşı, E., Soydam, M., & Arabacı, H. (2020). 2019 Yılı Meteorolojik Afetler Değerlendirmesi, Meteoroloji Genel Müdürlüğü, Araştırma Dairesi Başkanlığı, Meteorolojik Afetler Şube Müdürlüğü. file:///C:/Users/volkan.ediger/Desktop/2019MeteorolojikAfetlerDegerlendirmesi.pdf

Folke, C., Carpe, S. R., Walker, B., Scheffer, M., Chapin, T., & Rockström, J. (2010). Resilience thinking: Integrating resilience, adaptability and transformability. *Ecology and Society, 15*(4), 20. http://www.ecologyandsociety.org/vol15/iss4/art20/

Fujihara, Y., Tanaka, K., Watanabe, T., Nagano, T., & Kojiri, T. (2008). Assessing the impacts of climate change on the water resources of the Seyhan River Basin in Turkey: Use of dynamically downscaled data for hydrologic simulations. *Journal of Hydrology, 353*, 33–48.

Gatto, A., & Drago, C. (2020). A taxonomy of energy resilience. *Energy Policy, 136*, 111007. https://doi.org/10.1016/j.enpol.2019.111007

Ghisellini, P., Cialani, C., & Ulgiati, S. (2016). A review on circular economy: The expected transition to a balanced interplay of environmental and economic systems. *Journal of Cleaner Production, 114*, 11–32.
Gonseth, C., & Vielle, M. (2012). *Modeling the impacts of climate change on the energy sector: A Swiss perspective.* EPFL and Swiss Climate Research Working Paper.
Hamborg, S., Meya, J. N., Eisenack, K., & Raabe, T. (2020). Rethinking resilience: A cross-epistemic resilience framework for interdisciplinary energy research. *Energy Research & Social Science, 59*, 101285.
Holling, C. S., & Robin, L. (1973). Resilience and stability of ecological systems. In: L. Robin, S. Sörlin, & P. Warde (Eds.), *The future of nature: Documents of global change.* Yale University Press.
Holling, C. S. (1973). Resilience and stability of ecological systems. *Annual Review of Ecology and Systematics, 4*, 1–23.
Huang, G., Wang, J., Chen, C., Qi, J., & Guo, C. (2017). Integration of preventive and emergency. Responses for power grid resilience enhancement. *IEEE Transactions on Power Systems, 32*(6), 4451–4463.
Hughes, L. (2015). The effects of event occurrence and duration on resilience and adaptation in energy systems. *Energy, 84*, 443–454.
IPCC (Intergovernmental Panel on Climate Change). (2011). Hydropower. In: O. Edenhofer, R. Pichs Madruga, Y. Sokona, K. Seyboth, P. Matschoss, S. Kadner, T. Zwickel, P. Eickemeier, G. Hansen, S. Schlömer, & C. von Stechow (Eds.), *IPCC Special report on renewable energy sources and climate change mitigation.* Cambridge University Press.
IPCC (Intergovernmental Panel on Climate Change). (2014). Climate change 2014: Synthesis report. In Core Writing Team, R. K. Pachauri, & L. A. Meyer (Eds.), *Contribution of Working Groups I, II and III to the Fifth Assessment Report of the Intergovernmental Panel on Climate Change.* IPCC. https://ar5.syr.ipcc.ch/ipcc/ipcc/resources/pdf/IPCC_SynthesisReport.pdf
Jufri, F. H., Widiputra, V., & Jung, J. (2019). State-of-the-art review on power grid resilience to extreme weather events: Definitions, frameworks, quantitative assessment methodologies, and enhancement strategies. *Applied Energy, 239*, 1049–1065.
Kale, S. (2017). Climatic trends in the temperature of Çanakkale city, Turkey. *NE Sciences, 2*(3), 14–27.
Kum, G., & Çelik, M. A. (2014). Impact of global climate change on the Mediterranean Region; Adanaas a case study. *Procedia—Social and Behavioral Sciences, 120*, 600–608.
Leandro, J., Chen, K. F., Wood, R. R., & Ludwig, R. (2020). A scalable flood-resilience-index for measuring climate change adaptation: Munich city. *Water Research, 173*, 115502. https://doi.org/10.1016/j.watres.2020.115502
Levin, S. A., Barrett, S., Aniyar, S., Baumol, W., Bliss, C., Bolin, B., Dasgupta, P., Ehrlich, P., Folke, C., Gren, I. M., Holling, C. S., Jansson, A., Jansson, B. O., Mäler, K., Martin, D., Perrings, C., & Sheshinski, E. (1998). Resilience in natural and socioeconomic systems. *Environment and Development Economics, 3*(2), 222–235.
Lin, Y., Bie, Z., & Qiu, A. (2018). A review of key strategies in realizing power system resilience. *Global Energy Interconnection, 1*(1), 70–78.
Lina, Y., & Biea, Z. (2016). Study on the resilience of the integrated energy system. *Energy Procedia, 103*, 171–176.
Linnerud, K., Mideksa, T. K., & Eskeland, G. S. (2011). The impact of climate change on nuclear power supply. *Energy Journal, 32*(1), 149–170.
MacArthur, R. (1955). Fluctuations of animal populations and a measure of community stability. *Ecology, 36*(3), 533–536.
Mahzarnia, M., Moghaddam, M. P., Baboli, P. T., & Siano, P. (2020). A review of the measures to enhance power systems resilience. *IEEE Systems Journal, 14*(3), 4059–4070. https://ieeexplore.ieee.org/document/8974395

Marchese, D., Reynolds, E., Bates, M. E., Morgan, H., Clark, S. S., & Linkov, I. (2018). Resilience and sustainability: Similarities and differences in environmental management applications. *Science of the Total Environment, 613–614*, 1275–1283.

Mola, M., Feofilovs, M., & Romagnoli, F. (2018). Energy resilience: Research trends at urban, municipal, and country level. *Energy Procedia, 147*, 104–113.

Molyneaux, L., Brown, C., Wagner, L., & Foster, J. (2016). Measuring resilience in energy systems: Insights from a range of discipline. *Renewable and Sustainable Energy Reviews, 59*, 1068–1079.

Moreno, J., & Shaw, D. (2019). Community resilience to power outages after disaster: A case study of the 2010 Chile earthquake and tsunami. *International Journal of Disaster Risk Reduction, 34*, 448–458.

National Academies. (2014). *Improving power system resilience, Resilient America Roundtable 2* (pp. 1–12). National Academy of Sciences.

Neubert, M. G., & Caswell, H. (1997). Alternatives to resilience for measuring the responses of ecological systems to perturbations. *Ecology, 78*(3), 653–665.

Panteli, M., & Mancarella, P. (2015). Influence of extreme weather and climate change on the resilience of power systems: Impacts and possible mitigation strategies. *Electric Power Systems Research, 127*, 259–270.

Panteli, M., Pickering, C., Wilkinson, S., Dawson, R., & Mancarella, P. (2017). Power system resilience to extreme weather: Fragility modeling, probabilistic impact assessment, and adaptation measures. *IEEE Transactions on Power Systems, 32*(5), 3747–3757.

Pimm, S. L. (1984). The complexity and stability of ecosystems. *Nature, 307*, 321–326.

Pisano, U. (2012). *Resilience and sustainable development: Theory of resilience, systems thinking and adaptive governance.* European Sustainable Development Network (ESDN) Quarterly Report N°26.

Rathor, S. K., & Saxena, D. (2020). Energy management system for smart grid: An overview and key issues. *International Journal of Energy Research, 44*(6), 4067–4109.

Sagintayev, Z., & Collins, N. (2017). Power to the people: Disaster resilience support with advance energy storage systems. *Materials Today: Proceedings, 4*, 4555–4560.

Şahin, S., & Cigizoglu, H. K. (2012). The sub-climate regions and the sub-precipitation regime regions in Turkey. *Journal of Hydrology, 450*, 180–189.

Scala, A., Mureddu, M., Chessa, A., Caldarelli, G., & Damiano, A. (2013). Distributed generation and resilience in power grids. In: B.M. Hämmerli, N. Kalstad Svendsen, & J. Lopez (Eds.), *Critical information infrastructures security*. Lecture Notes in Computer Science (vol. 7722). Springer. https://doi.org/10.1007/978-3-642-41485-5_7

Şen, Ö. L. (2020). How does the global climate change affect the climate of Turkey? http://climatechangeinturkey.com/climate-change-basics-how-does-the-climate-of-turkey-change.html

Şensoy, S., Demircan, M., Ulupınar, U., & Balta, İ. (2008). Türkiye iklimi. MGM. http://www.mgm.gov.tr/FILES/iklim/turkiye_iklimi.pdf

Şensoy, S., Demircan, M., & Ulupınar, Y. (2016). Climate of Turkey. https://www.researchgate.net/publication/296597022_Climate_of_Turkey

Shakoua, L. M., Wybob, J. L., Reniers, G., & Boustras, G. (2019). Developing an innovative framework for enhancing the resilience of critical infrastructure to climate change. *Safety Science, 118*, 364–378.

Sharifi, A., & Yamagata, Y. (2016). Principles and criteria for assessing urban energy resilience: A literature review. *Renewable and Sustainable Energy Reviews, 60*, 1654–1677.

Smith, A. B., & Katz, R. W. (2013). US billion-dollar weather and climate disasters: Data sources, trends, accuracy and biases. *Natural Hazards, 67*(2), 387–410.

Sovacool, B. K. (2011). Evaluating energy security in the Asia pacific: Towards a more comprehensive approach. *Energy Policy, 39*, 7472–7479.

Sriyani, C., Lokuwaduge, D. S., & Heenetigala, K. (2017). Integrating environmental, social and governance (ESG) disclosure for a sustainable development: An Australian study. *Business Strategy and the Environment, 26*(4), 438–450. https://doi.org/10.1002/bse.1927

Statista. (2020). Capacity factor of coal power plants in the United States from 2010 to 2020. https://www.statista.com/statistics/744947/capacity-factor-of-coal-power-plants-in-the-us-by-unit-type/#:~:text=In%202019%2C%20the%20average%20capacity,produced%20at%20full 20rated%20power
TEİAŞ (Turkish Electricity Transmission Corporation). (2020). Outage/maintenance notification system database. https://seffaflik.epias.com.tr/transparency/piyasa-mesaj-sistemi.xhtml
Tobin, I., Greuell, W., Jerez, S., Ludwig, F., Vautard, R., van Vliet, M. T. H., & Breon, F.-M. (2018). Vulnerabilities and resilience of European power generation to 1.5 °C, 2 °C and 3 °C warming. *Environmental Research Letters, 13*, 1–8, 044024. https://doi.org/10.1088/1748-9326/aab211
Ton, D. T., & Wang, W. T. P. (2015). A more resilient grid: The US department of energy joins with stakeholders in an R&D Plan. *IEEE Power & Energy Magazine, 13*(3), 26–34.
Totschniga, G., Hirner, R., Müller, A., Kranzl, L., Hummel, M., Nachtnebel, H. P., Schicker, S. I., & Formayer, H. (2017). Climate change impact and resilience in the electricity sector: The example of Austria and Germany. *Energy Policy, 103*, 238–248.
TSMS (Turkish State Meteorological Service). (2020). Turkish meteorology database. https://www.mgm.gov.tr/veridegerlendirme/il-ve-ilceleristatistik.aspx?k=A&m=ADANA; https://www.mgm.gov.tr/veridegerlendirme/il-ve-ilceleristik.aspx?k=A&m=CANAKKALE
Türkeş, M., Sümer, U. M., & Çetiner, G. (2000). Küresel iklim değişikliği ve olası etkileri. Çevre Bakanlığı, Birleşmiş Milletler İklim Değişikliği Çerçeve Sözleşmesi Seminer Notları, 724, ÇKÖK Gn. Md., Ankara.
Velayutham, P., & Ismail, F. B. (2018). A review on power plant maintenance and operational performance. *MATEC Web of Conference, 225*, 05003. https://doi.org/10.1051/matecconf/201 8225050003
Vivoda, V. (2010). Evaluating energy security in the Asia-Pacific region: A novel methodological approach. *Energy Policy, 38*, 5258–5263.
Vugrin, E., Castillo, A., & Silva-Monroy, C. (2017). *Resilience metrics for the electric power system: A performance-based approach*, Sandia Report, SAND2017-1493.
Walker, H., & Salt, D. (2006). *Resilience thinking: Sustaining ecosystems and people in a changing world*. Island Press.
Wang, J., Xie, N., Wu, W., Han, D., Wang, C., & Zhu, B. (2018). Resilience enhancement strategy using microgrids in distribution network. *Global Energy Interconnection, 1*(5), 537–543.
WBCSD (World Business Council of Sustainable Development). (2014). Building a resilient power sector. https://docs.wbcsd.org/2014/03/Building_A_Resilient_Power_Sector.pdf.
Willis, H. H., & Loa, K. (2015). *Measuring the resilience of energy distribution systems*. Rand Corporation.

The Effect of Environmental Scores on Financial Performance of Energy Companies in the European Region

Gizem Arı and Z. Göknur Büyükkara

Abstract Increasing awareness and expectations for a sustainable environment increases the pressure on the energy industry to reduce its pollution. Despite the importance of the subject, the number of studies examining the effect of environmental responsibility activities on financial performance of companies operating in the energy sector is limited. Also, the findings obtained from previous studies are mixed about the direction of the relevant relationship. This study examines the impact of environmental responsibility on financial performance within the framework of companies operating in the energy sector in the European Region. In doing so, it probes the validity of the stakeholder theory and agency theory in explaining the relationship between corporate social-environmental responsibility and financial performance. We consider 58 European energy companies that have detailed and classified environmental responsibility scores between 2011 and 2020. According to the applied three-dimensional panel data regression results, we find that the aggregate environmental score of the European energy companies has not a significant effect on their financial performance. However, the resource use score, which is one of the environmental sub-scores, is negatively related to both the return on assets and return on equity of the companies. Moreover, the emission reduction and environmental innovation scores, which are the other environmental sub-scores, do not have a significant effect on the environmental-financial performance relationship. Although we have obtained findings showing that activities aimed at reducing the use of environmentally harmful resources, energy and water have a reducing effect on financial performance by shedding light on the validity of the agency theory, we see that a neutral effect is dominant between the environmental responsibility activities and financial performance carried out in European energy companies in general.

G. Arı · Z. G. Büyükkara (✉)
Department of Business Administration, Hacettepe University, Beytepe, Ankara 06800, Turkey
e-mail: goknur@hacettepe.edu.tr

G. Arı
e-mail: gizemari@hacettepe.edu.tr

J. Thewissen et al. (eds.), *The ESG Framework and the Energy Industry*,
https://doi.org/10.1007/978-3-031-48457-5_11

Keywords Emissions score · Resource use score · Environmental innovation score · Return on asset (ROA) · Return on equity (ROE) · Energy industry · European Region

1 Introduction

This study investigates the interaction between corporate environmental responsibility and corporate financial performance of companies operating in the European energy sector. The concept of environmental sustainability, which was first discussed in detail by Goodland (1995), is generally defined as the preservation of the continuity of natural capital such as soil, atmosphere, forests, water, and wetlands. Moreover, it has been stated that all these concepts are interrelated so that environmental sustainability cannot be considered independently of social and economic capital. The energy sector is recognized as an important source of environmental pollution (Bose, 2010). It has a higher level of influence compared to other sectors within the scope of environmental sustainability and climate change issues, and for this reason, it attracts increasing pressure and incentives for sustainability activities. Also, the European Region is taking important initiatives to support and promote environmental responsibility activities. For example, the European Green Deal, which aims to make the European Region a carbon-neutral continent until 2050, and RePowerEU, which aims to expand the use of energy conservation and clean energy, are on the agenda. Therefore, in our research, we focus on companies operating in the European energy sector. By proceeding in this way, we think that we have eliminated some problems that may arise from geographical region differences in the findings we will obtain. Moreover, we proceed in a way that supports the view that the environmental/social-financial performance relationship should be examined on an industry-specific basis (Gonenc & Scholtens, 2019), based on the idea that the economic benefits to be gained from the investments made in this field will differ according to the industry structure (Orsato, 2006).

We are not conducting the first study to examine the relationship between environmental responsibility and financial performance. The ever-increasing awareness of the need to consider social and environmental issues in commercial activities (Baran et al., 2022) and the increase in concerns about environmental protection and climate change have motivated many researchers to examine the impact of firms' environmental responsibility performance on firm performance (Rokhmawati et al., 2017). There are many studies in the literature that provide evidence that corporate social-environmental responsibility activities have a positive effect on firm performance (Orlitzky et al., 2003). However, the literature is still mixed due to the subjectivity or sample size of the selected environmental performance variables (Aggarwal, 2013). For example, Rokhmawati et al. (2015) examine the impact of greenhouse gas emissions (GHG), environmental performance, and social performance on financial performance of Indonesian companies. As a result, it is argued that CO_2 intensity and social reporting score have a significant positive impact on financial performance. However, the results are not significant for the relationship between environmental performance and financial performance. In addition, the economic development levels of the countries in which the companies operate play a decisive role in the impact of environmentally responsible activities on financial performance. Manrique and Martí-Ballester (2017) investigate the environmental-financial performance relationship of a firm depending on the level of economic development of the country in which it operates during the global financial crisis. They provide evidence that the adoption of environmental practices significantly and positively impacts corporate financial performance in developed and developing countries. However, this effect is stronger for companies located in developing countries than for developed countries. Similarly, Naeem et al. (2022) discuss the relationship between environmental, social, and governance (ESG) performance and financial performance of environmentally sensitive sectors with a recent study. When investigating this relationship, they refer to the stakeholder theory and the shareholder theory. The findings show that ESG performance has a significant positive impact on financial performance in environmentally sensitive sectors. Contrary to claims by Manrique and Martí-Ballester (2017), this effect is more evident in developed countries. Ultimately, the authors argue for the validity of the stakeholder theory. Velte (2017), investigating the validity of stakeholder theory within the scope of corporate social responsibility, argues that ESG and its sub-scores have a positive effect on return on asset (ROA), but not had a significant effect on Tobin's Q. The main inference obtained from these findings generally shows that stakeholders appreciate the socially responsible investments of companies. However, there is also the view that firm-level investments in social-environmental activities may cause agency costs and negatively affect financial performance (Gonenc & Scholtens, 2017; Vural-Yavas, 2021). Zumente et al. (2020) claim that an increase in the ESG performance of companies traded on the Baltic stock exchange reduces return on equity (ROE). Ruggiero and Lehkonen (2017) explore the supportability of the natural-resource-based view and find that the increase in the firm-level use of renewable energy negatively affects the financial performance. Based on this, we are decisively considering and testing the findings obtained on the relationship between environmental responsibility activities and financial performance.

Our main motivation for this study is to provide evidence of whether investments in environmental responsibility have a significant impact on corporate financial performance. Moreover, if this effect is significant, it is to contribute to the existing discussion by determining its direction. For this, we refer to stakeholder theory, which argues that the interests of all stakeholder groups should be considered, and agency theory, employing the view that corporate social responsibility activities can cause agency costs. In our study, we rely on the observation data of 58 energy companies with environmental scores from 19 different European countries for the period 2011–2020. Accordingly, we comprehensively answer the following research question:

RQ: *"Do companies with higher environmental performance operating in the European energy sector show better financial performance than others?"*

As a corporate environmental performance proxy, we examine the general environmental performance score and sub-scores within the scope of ESG separately and associate them with ROA and ROE, which are accounting-based performance measures, as corporate financial performance proxies. We consider the emission score, resource use score, and environmental innovation score as environmental sub-scores. We think that it is important to examine the sub-scores separately from the aggregate environmental score, because sub-scores may have a higher level of information than the aggregated score (Gonenc & Scholtens, 2019). We use three-dimensional nested panel regression for models to examine the relationship between financial performance and environmental performance. Our aim here is to consider possible firm, country, and year fixed effects. We think that it is especially important whether there are country effects in econometric models because the fact that countries are different from each other will ensure the differentiation of regulations and government incentives related to social and environmental responsibility.

Our main finding is that we do not support the view that environmental responsibility improvement activities of European energy companies will have a positive impact on their financial performance. Our regression results show that there is no statistically significant interaction between the aggregate environmental score and financial performance. However, the resource use sub-score has a significant negative impact on both the ROA and ROE. Further, we observe firm, year, and country fixed effects in models. This indicates that the results may differ at the firm level, at the country level, and over the years. In short, although most of the current findings in the literature reveal that the environmental-financial performance relationship is positive, our findings reveal that having a higher environmental resource use performance will decrease financial performance, at least for the 58 companies examined in the European energy sector. This indicates that improvements in environmental performance do not offer a reward in terms of profitability. When the primary goal of the investors is wealth maximization, the high cost of environmental investments cannot prevent them from being perceived as greenwashing.

The following sections of the study are structured as follows. Section 2 focuses on the importance of the concept of environmental responsibility in the European energy sector. Section 3 highlights the theoretical background, presents the literature, and develops the hypotheses. We present the research methodology and information on the dataset in Sect. 4. In Sect. 5, we show the findings and implications of our econometric analysis, while concluding the study in Sect. 6 with a conclusion, limitations of our study, and recommendations for future research.

2 Environmental Responsibility in European Energy Sector

In this study, we mentioned earlier that we focus on companies operating in the energy industry in the European Region. We can list the industry groups that are within the scope of the energy sector and that we have included in the scope of our review as follows:

- Coal (TRBC Industry Code: 50101010)
- Oil and Gas (TRBC Industry Code: 50102030)
- Oil and Gas-Related Equipment and Services (TRBC Industry Code: 50103020)
- Renewable Energy (TRBC Industry Code: 50201010).

The coal industry covers the fields of activity related to coal mining and coal sales. The oil and gas industry includes onshore and offshore oil, natural gas, unconventional oil and gas exploration and production, and oil and gas refining and marketing activities. The oil and gas-related equipment and service industry refers to oil or gas drilling operations, transportation, storage operations and other related activities. The renewable energy industry, on the other hand, covers fuel groups such as biodiesel, ethanol fuels, biomass and biogas fuels, hydrogen fuels and services related to these fuel groups such as geothermal equipment, hydropower equipment, wind system, and equipment.

The energy sector is being encouraged to take on more and more responsibility in terms of environmental sustainability compared to other sectors, as it is the business line that most affects environmental instability (Stjepcevic & Siksnelyte, 2017). Therefore, the gradual increase in global energy demand brings up the importance of climate change and sustainability issues. Climate change is closely related to minimizing waste in energy use, environmental innovation activities, and sensitivity to carbon emissions.

Minimizing greenhouse gas emissions and turning to renewable energy sources by reducing the use of resources that harm the environment can be said to be important actions in supporting environmental sustainability. The energy sector is recognized as an important source of environmental pollution. It is one of the leading sectors that cause greenhouse gas emissions, which is one of the leading factors in climate change. In particular, all stages from the production of electricity to its use pose a threat to the ecosystem. Figure 1 shows the sectoral distribution of carbon dioxide emissions in the European Region in 2020. It is seen that the energy supply constitutes the main source of carbon dioxide emissions with a share of 30.1% of the total. Respectively, domestic transportation ranks second with a share of 27.1%, and industry ranks third with a share of 23.5% as sectors that cause carbon dioxide emissions. It is visible that the emission caused by only these three sectors corresponds to 80.7% of the total emissions.

According to a report published by the International Energy Agency (IEA) in March 2022, while the global economy has successfully eliminated the effects of the Covid-19 pandemic in 2021, renewable energy production has grown significantly annually, but an increase in coal use has not been prevented. The 6% increase in CO_2 emissions in 2021 reaching its highest-ever level of 36.3 gigatons (Gt) is in line with the 5.9% increase in global economic output. It is also underlined that since 2010, CO_2 emissions point to a strong combination with gross domestic product (GDP) growth (IEA, 2022).

When viewed based on selected developed countries, as can be seen in Fig. 2, CO_2 emissions, which have been decreasing for the last ten years for the European Union, have started to increase as of 2020. It can be said that there is a similar

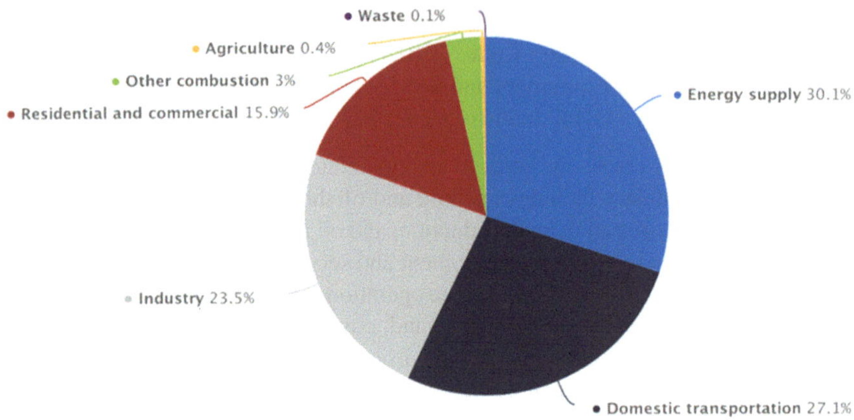

Fig. 1 Distribution of carbon dioxide emissions in the European Union in 2020, by sector. *Source* Statista (2022)

situation in the USA. However, there is no doubt that the European Union has made significant progress in sustainable environmental regulations in recent years. The European Green Deal (Montanarella & Panagos, 2021), which aims to make the European Union the first climate-neutral continent by 2050, emerges as a growth strategy that aims to transform it into a society with a competitive economy that adopts efficient resource use and has no net greenhouse gas emissions (European Commission, 2019). In line with this goal, the 2050 Energy Roadmap explores the transition of the energy system in line to reduce greenhouse gases, while increasing competitiveness and security of supply. The national energy and climate action plans (NECPs) introduced in 2019 are based on the Regulation on the Governance of the Energy Union and Climate Action (EU 2018/1999) for all Europeans. On the other hand, the European Climate Law is the enactment of the goal set in the European Green Deal for the European economy and society to become climate neutral by 2050 (EU Climate Law, 2020). In addition, the current energy crisis poses a threat to the energy security of the European Union. The main reason for the crisis is the ever-increasing global demand for natural gas and the Chinese government's large amount of LNG imports. This situation has become more severe with the military attack of Russia against the Ukraine. To cope with the effects of the crisis, Europe implements activities to diversify its gas supply and intensify renewable energy sources. In this direction, the European Union Commission has proposed the REPowerEU plan (Calanter & Zisu, 2022). The aim of REPowerEU plan is to increase energy savings, diversify energy sources, and support the transition to clean energy production financially and legally (European Commission, 2022).

Following the increasing awareness of environmental and social issues in the last two decades, it is not unfair to blame the energy industry for the increase in greenhouse gas emissions that cause global warming. Therefore, concerns about the environmental impacts of the industry have increased significantly in recent years, encouraging companies to engage in responsible practices. In this context, it is

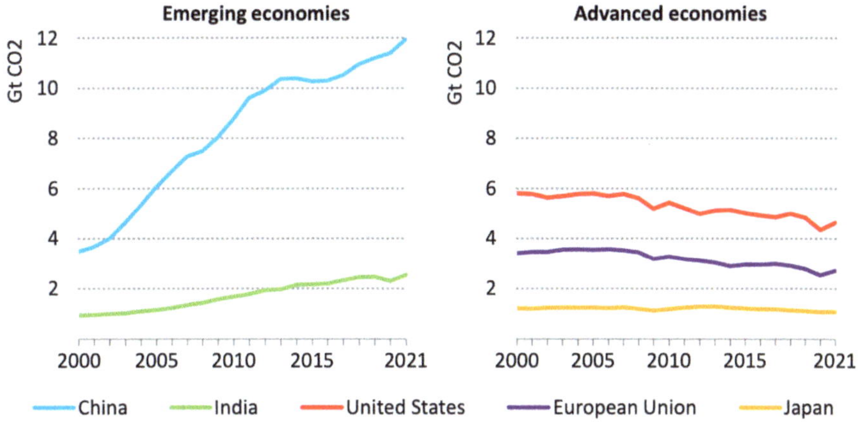

Fig. 2 CO_2 emissions for selected emerging and advanced economies, 2000–2021. *Source* IEA (2022)

essential to emphasize the importance of corporate social responsibility and corporate environmental responsibility activities for companies operating in the energy sector, as well as companies operating in all other sectors, to reduce the risk of climate change. Considering the increase in energy demand, energy production, and energy use that account for most of the greenhouse gas emissions of the European Union, it has become an inevitable necessity, and not a choice anymore, for companies operating in the energy sector to try to minimize the environmental impact of their outputs from resource inputs to waste products throughout the entire activity cycle.

As the global energy demand continues to increase, the concern for environmental damage caused by the energy sector will also increase (Talbot & Boiral, 2018). Minimizing the use of energy resources that cause environmental destruction and providing efficient, clean, affordable, and socially reliable energy services have an important role in the sustainable development of the energy sector (Pätäri et al., 2014). Therefore, what is expected from energy companies is to adopt a corporate social responsibility approach at the company level, which includes decisions such as on reducing carbon emissions and investing in renewable energy resources within the scope of combating climate change. In this context, energy companies do not only have the option to create value for their shareholders now and in the future, but they must also undertake business that is both profitable for shareholders and socially environmentally responsible (Streimikiene et al., 2009).

3 Theoretical Background and Literature Review

3.1 Theoretical Background

The basis of studies examining the relationship between corporate social-environmental performance and corporate financial performance in the literature points to two theories: stakeholder theory and agency theory. One of the two perspectives on the responsibility of business to society and based on neoclassical economic theory, the "classical view," suggests that the aim of businesses is to generate profit by focusing on shareholder wealth growth (Friedman, 1970). In contrast, stakeholder theory claims that companies should consider the interests of all stakeholder groups affected by their decisions and activities, and they have a social responsibility toward it (Castelo Branco & Lima Rodriques, 2007). Stakeholder theory meets the demand of stakeholders, which creates trust and cooperation that leads to competitive advantage and better financial performance (Freeman, 1984; Freeman & Phillips, 2002; Harrison et al., 2010; Jones, 1995). According to the stakeholder theory, corporate social responsibility activities are positively related to corporate financial performance. At this point, the aim of firms acts as a tool to coordinate the expectations of various stakeholders (Donaldson & Preston, 1995). That is, the main purpose of the firms is to balance the conflicting expectations of various stakeholders (Roberts, 1992). In addition, the theory points out how to balance the various demands of the stakeholders by gathering the expectations of all stakeholders, from customers to employees, from capital suppliers to the benefits to be provided to society in general, around a common decision criterion, value maximization (Jensen, 2002). From this point of view, stakeholder theory offers a perspective to measure the relationship between corporate social performance and corporate financial performance through financial accounting indicators (Ruf et al., 2001).

On the other hand, from the perspective of agency theory (Jensen & Meckling, 1976), which examines the relationship between social responsibility efforts, agents, and owners at the point where the decision mechanism is delegated, Friedman (1970) stated that the benefit that companies will gain from social-environmental responsibility activities will be less than the expected cost. The reason behind this view is that companies are responsible for increasing profitability and social-environmental responsibility activities can be explained as an agency problem between managers and shareholders. In other words, managers can use responsible behavior for their own interests and while doing this, they can ignore the interests of all other stakeholder groups (Vural-Yavas, 2021). Moreover, according to Gonenc and Scholtens (2017), managers may exhibit socially environmentally responsible behaviors with an opportunistic perspective, and this approach may conflict with the expectations of stakeholders and cause agency costs. In addition, while companies claim to be socially responsible, they may engage in greenwashing behavior by not making any improvements in this direction. In terms of companies, the reasons attributed to social-environmental responsibility behavior may also represent the difference in the results obtained.

3.2 Literature Review and Hypothesis Development

The previous literature offers mixed results on the relationship between corporate environmental responsibility and corporate financial performance. Some studies reveal a positive relationship between environmental performance and financial performance. Others argue that this relationship is negative or that there is no relationship. There are even studies showing an inverted U-shaped relationship. There are many reasons why previous studies have offered mixed results. For example, the use of different research methodologies can be shown as a reason, but it can be said that the most important reason is that environmental responsibility activities are generally judged subjectively, and proxies used are different from each other (Moneva & Cuellar, 2009). The different responsibility proxies used include (i) environmental responsibility indicators derived from various environmental reports prepared by companies, (ii) environmental responsibility indices prepared using the content analysis method, (iii) environmental performance rating data obtained from international databases such as Thomson Reuters, Bloomberg, and MSCI. In addition, data on the intensity of use of renewable and clean energy sources, which are considered the representative of environmental performance, decrease in carbon emissions, and environmental and water pollution is also used (Al-Tuwaijri et al., 2004; Guenster et al., 2011; Kalash, 2021; Lech, 2013; Lu & Taylor, 2018; Ruggiero & Lehkonen, 2017; Shahbaz et al., 2020).

As discussed in Sect. 3.1, stakeholder theory and resource-based views argue that the relationship between environmental performance and financial performance is positive. This positive relationship has been proven by numerous studies in the literature. For example, King and Lenox (2001) examine the relationship between corporate environmental performance and profitability on 652 publicly traded US manufacturing companies between 1987 and 1996. Tobin's Q, return on assets and return on equity and return on investment are used as profitability representations. As an environmental performance indicator, capital expenditures on pollution control technology, emission data, compliance with environmental management standards, environmental performance ratings, and more are used. The findings show that the relationship between reducing environmental pollution and financial performance is positive, and firms operating in clean industries have higher Tobin's Q. Similarly, Al-Tuwaijri et al. (2004) show a significant positive relationship between environmental performance and economic performance. The primary task of the managers is to make decisions that support the long-term goals of the companies, and the managers who adopt this behavior accept the necessity of the company to exhibit socially responsible behavior and to adopt strategies that will minimize environmental pollution. 198 US companies traded in the Standard and Poor's 500 (S&P500) Index are included in the sample. In addition, in the study, market-based performance measure is used as a financial performance proxy and the ratio of toxic waste recycled to total toxic waste generated as an environmental performance proxy. Finally, the study documents a positive relationship between the past and present values of the environmental performance indicators. It seems that investors support environmentally responsible behaviors. Nakao et al. (2007a, 2007b) provide evidence that corporate environmental activities have a positive impact on financial performance in Japanese firms. Guenster et al. (2011) consider the concept of eco-efficiency and examine the relationship between eco-efficiency and financial performance for the period 1997–2004. Results show that eco-efficiency is positively related to firm performance and market value in the US market. Another study supporting the stakeholder theory is held by Pätäri et al. (2014). The results of the study using KLD rating data for the corporate social responsibility proxy show that corporate social responsibility leads to better financial performance for 14 energy sector companies in the period covering 1991 and 2009, but better financial performance does not lead to better corporate social responsibility. Gonenc and Scholtens (2017) state that environmental responsibility activities are positively related to Tobin's Q, a market-based performance indicator, and negatively related to stock returns. Pekovic et al. (2018) examined over 6000 French firms for five years. Based on environmental responsibility data from survey data, the authors argue that this relationship follows an inverted U-curve. The sample consists of 29,719 observations covering the period 2003–2007. The companies in the dataset belong to manufacturing sectors such as agriculture-food, energy, consumer goods etcetera. The findings reveal that environmental responsibility investments improve firm performance, but these investments should be at an optimal level. Investing too little or too much in the environment can be economically detrimental. Lee (2021), using a sample of 75 companies traded in the MSCI World Energy index for a five-year period starting from 2013, states that there is a positive relationship between firm performance and environmental responsibility practices. When the sub-dimensions are examined in addition to the general environmental dimension, it is documented that the improvements in environmental innovation and resource use have a positive effect on financial performance. However, it is seen that emission reduction does not affect financial performance. The findings show that corporate social responsibility is something that increases value, in line with stakeholder theory. Kludacz-Alessandri and Cygańska (2021) studied an international sample of 32 countries and 219 companies for 2020 and observed that there is a statistically significant relationship between the financial performance of energy sector firms and the implementation of the corporate social responsibility strategy. Return on assets (ROA) and earnings before interest and taxes (EBIT) are found to be significantly higher in companies that implement a corporate social responsibility strategy. However, the authors find no evidence that return on equity (ROE), beta coefficient, and EBITDA per share are associated with corporate social responsibility adoption. Kalash (2021) examines the impact of environmental performance on capital structure and financial performance by using the data of 49 companies traded on the Istanbul Stock Exchange (ISE) between 2014 and 2019. Findings document a positive relationship between environmental performance and firm leverage. In addition, a positive relationship is detected between profitability indicators and environmental performance, but the results for stock returns are the opposite.

Contrary to the stakeholder theory, there are also studies in the literature that support the idea that the benefits to be gained from environmental responsibility activities will be less than the costs to be incurred within the scope of agency theory. Wagner et al. (2002) state that environmental performance negatively affects the economic performance of companies operating in the European paper manufacturing industry, making the traditional view to be valid to this relationship. Hassel et al. (2005), using measurements from Caring Company (CC) Research AB as an environmental performance proxy, provide evidence in their study of Swedish firms that environmental performance has a negative impact on the market value of firms. Similarly, Brammer et al. (2006) show a negative relationship between environmental indicators and stock returns, according to the cross-sectional regression results obtained using the EIRIS social responsibility data for 2003 in the UK. Fisher-Vanden and Thorburn (2011) examine the relationship between membership in Climate Leaders, one of the voluntary environmental programs (VEPs) that aims to reduce greenhouse gas emissions, with stock returns. After the announcement of participation in the related program, a decrease was observed in share prices. Overall, the findings seem to conflict with firm value maximization of corporate commitments to reduce greenhouse gas emissions. Iwata and Okada (2011) examine the relationship between waste emissions and gas emission reduction performance and financial performance for Japanese manufacturing firms over the period 2004–2008. Results differ for each environmental indicator. While waste emissions do not have a significant effect on financial performance, a meaningless relationship is also seen in polluted industries in terms of greenhouse gas emissions. However, in cleaner industries, greenhouse gas emissions reduction appears to have a positive impact on financial performance. Ruggiero and Lehkonen (2017) present evidence of a negative relationship between firm-level renewable energy growth and short-term and long-term financial performance in a study of 66 energy firms for the period 2005–2014. Lu and Taylor (2018) examine the relationship between environmental performance, environmental disclosures, and financial performance for large-scale companies in the USA, using Newsweek's green rankings. The estimation results provide evidence of a negative relationship between environmental performance and financial performance while providing evidence of a positive relationship for environmental disclosures.

On the other hand, according to González-Benito and González-Benito (2005), Sarumpaet (2005), Lech (2013), Shahbaz et al. (2020), Adamkaite et al. (2022), there is mixed or no relationship between corporate environmental performance and financial performance. González-Benito and González-Benito (2005) find no evidence to support that environmental responsibility results in higher profitability, at least in the short run. The results obtained are generally mixed. Therefore, the authors state that there is no single correct answer to the environmental responsibility-financial performance relationship. Sarumpaet (2005) examines the relationship between environmental performance and financial performance in a sample of Indonesian firms. According to the results, there is no significant relationship between the environmental performance proxy and ROA. Lech (2013) considers participation in the Respect Index, which aims to determine the companies operating in the most appropriate way with environmental, social, and corporate governance criteria, as a corporate social responsibility proxy. The results show that participation in the Respect

Index is not statistically significant in determining the financial performance of Polish firms. Shahbaz et al. (2020) use Tobin's Q and ROA as a proxy of financial performance indicators in their study where they examined the relationship between ESG and sub-scores and financial performance for the energy sector. As a result, higher social responsibility performance does not necessarily result in higher financial performance for both ROA and Tobin's Q. The results of the study by Adamkaite et al. (2022), examining nine Lithuanian energy companies, show that there is a neutral relationship between corporate social responsibility and financial performance in the period 2017–2020.

Considering that previous literature has offered arguments supporting corporate environmental performance has positive and negative, neutral, and mixed effects on financial performance, we propose the following hypotheses:

If the stakeholder theory is valid:

H_1: There is a positive relationship between aggregate environmental performance and financial performance.

H_2: There is a positive relationship between individual dimensions of environmental performance and financial performance.

If the agency theory is valid:

H_3: There is a negative relationship between aggregate environmental performance and financial performance.

H_4: There is a negative relationship between individual dimensions of environmental performance and financial performance.

4 Data and Research Methodology

4.1 *Measurement of Variables*

This study aims to determine the relationship between the environmental responsibility performance and financial performance indicators of publicly traded companies operating in the energy sector in the European Region between 2011 and 2020. In this study, we contribute to the ongoing debate about whether companies' environmental performance is important to their corporate financial performance by starting with the following research question: "Do companies with higher environmental responsibility scores operating in the European energy sector perform better financially?"

We consider financial performance as the dependent variable. Financial performance proxies are return on assets (ROA) and return on equity (ROE), which are accounting-based performance measures. According to Keats and Hitt (1988), accounting-based performance measures reflect past or current short-term operating performance, while market-based performance measures offer a long-term and future-oriented approach. Gentry and Shen (2010) state in their study that there is a positive correlation between accounting-based performance and market-based performance measures, but that the covariance is less than 10%, and that the two financial performance indicators represent different dimensions. For this reason, we only use accounting-based performance measures in our study. ROA is calculated by dividing total net income after taxes by total assets. It shows how profitably the assets are used in the company. ROE is calculated by dividing net income after tax by total equity. It shows how efficiently management is using equity capital to generate profits. The annual financial data of the firms are taken from the Thomson Reuters Eikon database, previously called Asset4.

The independent variables considered as proxy for environmental responsibility are the environmental pillar scores (EPS and sub-scores) obtained from the Thomson Reuters Eikon database. The database formulates the final environmental, social, and governance (ESG) score by grouping three sub-scores and ten separate categories, which reflect the ESG performance of companies considered as corporate social responsibility proxy, their effectiveness based on company commitments, and publicly disclosed information. ESG sub-components are named environmental, social, and governance, respectively. The environment sub-component consists of three categories in total, corresponding to emission reduction scores, resource utilization scores, and environmental innovation scores, respectively. The emission reduction score measures the rate of implementation, in other words, the effectiveness of the decisions taken by companies to reduce environmental emissions in both production and operational processes. The resource use score measures the performance of a company in reducing the use of environmentally harmful materials, energy, or water in all operational processes and producing more eco-efficient solutions for this. The innovation score reflects the ability of companies to reduce environmental costs for all their stakeholders while creating new market opportunities through new eco-designed environmental technologies, products, or processes. Each sub-score and the final ESG performance can take a value between 0 and 100. The Eikon database maintains ESG data and calculates ESG scores for a total of more than 2,100 companies in the European Region for all sectors (Refinitiv, 2022). However, the number of companies operating in the energy sector and having an environmental pillar score during the analysis period is limited to 58. The distribution information of the companies included in the analysis regarding the countries in which they operate is given in Table 1.

Firm characteristics are included in the model as control variables, following previous studies (Chen & Xie, 2022; Lee, 2021; Okafor et al., 2021; Saygili et al., 2022; Velte, 2017; Zhao et al., 2018; Wahba, 2008; Zhou et al., 2022). These characteristics are firm size (SIZE), financial leverage (LEV), the market-to-book ratio (MTB), and firm age (AGE). Table 2 shows calculation methods and explanations for dependent, independent, and control variables.

Table 1 Number of firms included in the analysis by country

Country	*n*	Fraction
Austria	1	0.02
Belgium	1	0.02
Denmark	1	0.02
Finland	1	0.02
France	4	0.07
Germany	1	0.02
Greece	2	0.03
Hungary	1	0.02
Italy	4	0.07
Jersey	1	0.02
Luxembourg	1	0.02
Netherlands	4	0.07
Norway	6	0.10
Poland	3	0.05
Portugal	1	0.02
Russia	9	0.16
Spain	4	0.07
Switzerland	1	0.02
United Kingdom	12	0.21
Total	58	100

Table 2 Variables of the study

Dependent variables	**Explanation**
ROA	Return on asset: net income after taxes to total assets, percent
ROE	Return on equity: net income after taxes to total equity, percent
Independent variables	**Explanation**
EPS	Environmental pillar score
ES	Emission score
RUS	Resource use score
EIS	Environmental innovation score
Control variables	**Explanation**
SIZE	Natural logarithm of total asset (firm size)
LEV	Total debt to total equity (leverage), percent
MTB	Market-to-book ratio
AGE	Current year – company founding year

4.2 Model Specification and Estimation Method

In the study, an unbalanced three-dimensional nested fixed effects panel regression model, which considers the data structure in which firms are nested within countries, is used as an econometric analysis method. The estimated three-dimensional panel data model consists of two-unit dimensions and a time dimension, in which one unit, which is a firm, is nested in the other unit, which is a country.

In panel data models with nested dimensions, Baltagi et al. (2001) first studied the model in which two-unit effects are nested within each other, but the time dimension is not included. Later, in 2012, Matyas and Balazsi proposed a three-dimensional panel data model that includes two-unit dimensions interactively and a time dimension (Yerdelen Tatoglu, 2016).

From this point of view, the models established to analyze the effect of environmental responsibility performance on financial performance, which considers two units and a time dimension, are as follows:

Model 1

$$\begin{aligned}\mathrm{CFP(ROA)_{fct}} &= \beta_0 + \beta_1\mathrm{EPS_{fct}} + \beta_2\mathrm{SIZE_{fct}} + \beta_3\mathrm{LEV_{fct}} + \beta_4\mathrm{MTB_{fct}} \\ &\quad + \beta_5\mathrm{AGE_{fct}} + \mu_\mathrm{f} + \gamma_\mathrm{c} + \lambda_\mathrm{t} + \varepsilon_\mathrm{fct}.\end{aligned}$$

Model 2

$$\begin{aligned}\mathrm{CFP(ROA)_{fct}} &= \beta_0 + \beta_1\mathrm{ES_{fct}} + \beta_2\mathrm{RUS_{fct}} + \beta_3\mathrm{EIS_{fct}} + \beta_4\mathrm{SIZE_{fct}} \\ &\quad + \beta_5\mathrm{LEV_{fct}} + \beta_6\mathrm{MTB_{fct}} + \beta_7\mathrm{AGE_{fct}} + \mu_\mathrm{f} \\ &\quad + \gamma_\mathrm{c} + \lambda_\mathrm{t} + \varepsilon_\mathrm{fct}.\end{aligned}$$

Model 3

$$\begin{aligned}\mathrm{CFP(ROE)}_{fct} &= \beta_0 + \beta_1\mathrm{EPS}_{fct} + \beta_2\mathrm{SIZE}_{fct} + \beta_3\mathrm{LEV}_{fct} + \beta_4\mathrm{MTB}_{fct} \\ &\quad + \beta_5\mathrm{AGE}_{fct} + \mu_f + \gamma_c + \lambda_t + \varepsilon_{fct}.\end{aligned}$$

Model 4

$$\begin{aligned}\mathrm{CFP(ROE)_{fct}} &= \beta_0 + \beta_1\mathrm{ES_{fct}} + \beta_2\mathrm{RUS_{fct}} + \beta_3\mathrm{EIS_{fct}} + \beta_4\mathrm{SIZE_{fct}} \\ &\quad + \beta_5\mathrm{LEV_{fct}} + \beta_6\mathrm{MTB_{fct}} + \beta_7\mathrm{AGE_{fct}} \\ &\quad + \mu_\mathrm{f} + \gamma_\mathrm{c} + \lambda_\mathrm{t} + \varepsilon_\mathrm{fct}.\end{aligned}$$

In the established models, μ_f represents the energy companies, γ_c represents the countries in which the companies operate, and λ_t represents the time dimension. In addition, the number of companies that make up the sample of the research is 58. The companies operate in 19 different European countries. The period of the sample is

2011–2020. The data are unbalanced in the sense that the number of firms operating in each country is different from each other.

The established models are based on stakeholder theory and agency theory. Models 1 and 3 are estimated to test hypotheses 1 and 3; models 2 and 4 are estimated to test hypotheses 2 and 4.

5 Results and Analysis

Panel A in Table 3 presents descriptive statistics for financial performance indicators (ROA and ROE), Panel B for environmental responsibility performance (environmental pillar score and its sub-scores), and Panel C for control variables (SIZE, LEV, MTB, and AGE). Among the financial performance indicators presented in Panel A, the mean value of ROA for the relevant period and 580 observations is 2.03 and the mean value of ROE is 2.65. Environmental performance scores range from 0 to 100 as stated above. While the mean value for the overall environmental score is 56.95, the mean values of the emission and resource use scores, excluding the environmental innovation score, are higher than the overall environmental score, with 67.82 and 66.57, respectively in Panel B. The reason for this is that the low mean value in the environmental innovation score reduces the overall environmental score. In Panel C, which includes descriptive statistics on control variables, mean values are 22.85 for firm size, 77.20 for leverage, 1.77 for market-to-book ratio, and 29.37 for firm age. The calculated skewness and kurtosis values show that the variables are not normally distributed.

Table 3 Descriptive statistics of variables

Variables	Obs	Mean	Std. dev.	Skewness	Kurtosis
ROA	580	2.035	9.481	−0.686	5.801
ROE	580	2.658	31.997	−1.503	11.342
EPS	580	56.952	22.267	−0.377	2.406
ES	580	67.820	26.496	−0.876	2.999
RUS	580	66.579	26.239	−0.872	3.028
EIS	580	22.768	30.169	0.985	2.472
SIZE	580	22.855	1.665	0.370	2.551
LEV	570	77.204	76.632	1.731	6.180
MTB	575	1.776	3.062	6.939	56.846
AGE	576	29.371	22.344	1.268	4.116

Note All financial variables are winsorized at the 1 and 99% levels to mitigate the potential influence of outliers. Variable definitions are in Table 2

Table 4 presents the pair-wise correlation matrix for variables. It is not surprising that ES, RUS, and EIS as components of EPS are positively and significantly correlated with each other. As expected, size and market-to-book ratio are positively and significantly correlated with ROA and ROE. In contrast, the correlation coefficient between leverage and financial performance is negative. This also applies to the age variable. In addition, variance inflation factors (VIF) are calculated to test for multicollinearity. However, no VIF value exceeds threshold 10 in our data. Our results are not affected by multicollinearity.

Since the established model is a three-dimensional panel data model, we test the unit and time dimensions together and separately via the likelihood-ratio (LR) test. The basic hypothesis in the combined LR test is that the standard error of at least one of the firms, country, and time effects is different from 0. For the LR tests, which are set up individually or in pairs, the hypotheses are that the standard errors of the firm (or country, time) effects are 0. LR test results are presented in Appendix Table 9. According to the results, each model is suitable for the three-dimensional panel data model.

After this stage, random effects are estimated using the maximum likelihood estimator and fixed effects are estimated using the within-group estimator. It is clear that the two-unit (firm and country) effects are not independent of each other in our models which two units and a time dimension are important. In order to overcome the biased estimation results arising from the multicollinearity problem for fixed effects estimation, we construct models in which two-unit effects are interactive as suggested by Matyas and Balazsi (2012) and apply the following within-group transformations. η_{fc} represents the interaction of firm and country unit effects.

Model 1a

$$\begin{aligned}\mathrm{CFP(ROA)}_{\mathrm{fct}} = {} & \beta_0 + \beta_1\mathrm{EPS}_{\mathrm{fct}} + \beta_2\mathrm{SIZE}_{\mathrm{fct}} + \beta_3\mathrm{LEV}_{\mathrm{fct}} + \beta_4\mathrm{MTB}_{\mathrm{fct}} \\ & + \beta_5\mathrm{AGE}_{\mathrm{fct}} + \eta_{\mathrm{fc}} + \lambda_{\mathrm{t}} + \varepsilon_{\mathrm{fct}}.\end{aligned}$$

Model 2a

$$\begin{aligned}\mathrm{CFP(ROA)}_{\mathrm{fct}} = {} & \beta_0 + \beta_1\mathrm{ES}_{\mathrm{fct}} + \beta_2\mathrm{RUS}_{\mathrm{fct}} + \beta_3\mathrm{EIS}_{\mathrm{fct}} + \beta_4\mathrm{SIZE}_{\mathrm{fct}} \\ & + \beta_5\mathrm{LEV}_{\mathrm{fct}} + \beta_6\mathrm{MTB}_{\mathrm{fct}} + \beta_7\mathrm{AGE}_{\mathrm{fct}} \\ & + \eta_{\mathrm{fc}} + \lambda_{\mathrm{t}} + \varepsilon_{\mathrm{fct}}.\end{aligned}$$

Model 3a

$$\begin{aligned}\mathrm{CFP(ROE)}_{\mathrm{fct}} = {} & \beta_0 + \beta_1\mathrm{EPS}_{\mathrm{fct}} + \beta_2\mathrm{SIZE}_{\mathrm{fct}} + \beta_3\mathrm{LEV}_{\mathrm{fct}} + \beta_4\mathrm{MTB}_{\mathrm{fct}} \\ & + \beta_5\mathrm{AGE}_{\mathrm{fct}} + \eta_{\mathrm{fc}} + \lambda_{\mathrm{t}} + \varepsilon_{\mathrm{fct}}.\end{aligned}$$

Model 4a

Table 4 Correlation results

Variables	ROA	ROE	EPS	ES	RUS	EIS	SIZE	LEV	MTB	AGE
ROA	1									
ROE	0.689***	1								
EPS	−0.068	0.003	1							
ES	−0.004	0.019	0.893***	1						
RUS	−0.058	−0.006	0.861***	0.722***	1					
EIS	−0.060	0.029	0.616***	0.375***	0.356***	1				
SIZE	0.177***	0.116***	0.522***	0.544***	0.492***	0.336***	1			
LEV	−0.261***	−0.317***	0.138***	0.155***	0.072*	−0.006	−0.149***	1		
MTB	0.297***	0.372***	−0.094**	−0.102**	−0.115***	−0.044	−0.251***	0.175***	1	
AGE	−0.137***	−0.015	0.386***	0.323***	0.320***	0.300***	0.198***	0.160***	−0.028	1

Note This table represents the pair-wise correlation coefficients between the environmental performance, financial performance and control variables for the sample. Variable definitions are in Table 2. ***, **, * significance at $p < 0.01$; $p < 0.05$ and $p < 0.10$, respectively

$$\begin{aligned}\text{CFP(ROE)}_{\text{fct}} = {} & \beta_0 + \beta_1\text{ES}_{\text{fct}} + \beta_2\text{RUS}_{\text{fct}} + \beta_3\text{EIS}_{\text{fct}} + \beta_4\text{SIZE}_{\text{fct}} \\ & + \beta_5\text{LEV}_{\text{fct}} + \beta_6\text{MTB}_{\text{fct}} + \beta_7\text{AGE}_{\text{fct}} \\ & + \eta_{\text{fc}} + \lambda_{\text{t}} + \varepsilon_{\text{fct}}\end{aligned}$$

$$(Y_{\text{fct}} - Y_{\text{fc}} - Y_{\text{t}} + Y) = \beta'(X_{\text{fct}} - X_{\text{fc}} - X_{\text{t}} + X) + (\varepsilon_{\text{fct}} - \varepsilon_{\text{fc}} - \varepsilon_{\text{t}} + \varepsilon).$$

We compare the fixed effects regression estimation results in Table 6 with the random effects estimation results in Table 5. Accordingly, we observe that the externality assumption cannot be met, in other words, the variables are internal, and we find that the fixed effects model is valid.

Table 7 presents the diagnostic test results. The results of the Breusch–Pagan (1979)/Cook–Weisberg (1983) and White (1980) tests applied for detecting heteroscedasticity, which is suitable for our panel data model, confirm heteroscedasticity. In addition, to clarify the autocorrelation problem in the model, the Wooldridge

Table 5 Random effects estimators

Maximum likelihood method	Model1	Model2	Model3	Model4
EPS	−0.0441* *(0.0229)*		−0.0469 *(0.0685)*	
ES		0.0173 *(0.0212)*		0.0890 *(0.0636)*
RUS		−0.0487** *(0.0203)*		−0.1312** *(0.0610)*
EIS		−0.0123 *(0.0143)*		−0.0057 *(0.0429)*
SIZE	1.5113*** *(0.3593)*	1.4697*** *(0.3629)*	3.4626*** *(1.0672)*	3.3119*** *(1.0686)*
LEV	−0.0360*** *(0.0049)*	−0.0364*** *(0.0048)*	−0.1725*** *(0.0147)*	−0.1720*** *(0.0146)*
MTB	1.2606*** *(0.1474)*	1.2443*** *(0.1452)*	4.6554*** *(0.4416)*	4.5897*** *(0.4324)*
AGE	−0.0321 *(0.0254)*	−0.0317 *(0.0249)*	0.0235 *(0.0751)*	0.0237 *(0.0728)*
Firm fixed effect	Yes	Yes	Yes	Yes
Country fixed effect	Yes	Yes	Yes	Yes
Year fixed effect	Yes	Yes	Yes	Yes
Wald Test	141.27***	145.62***	248.45***	254.01***
Number of Obs	568	568	568	568

Note This table presents maximum likelihood estimator results of random effects regressions of EPS scores on financial performance (ROA and ROE) for each model and the values of the control variables over the period 2011–2020 for the sample. Variable definitions are in Table 2. Standard errors are provided in parentheses below the coefficient values. ***, **, * significance at $p < 0.01$; $p < 0.05$ and $p < 0.10$, respectively

Table 6 Fixed effects estimator

Fixed effects estimator (Within-group estimator)	Model1**a**	Model2**a**	Model3**a**	Model4**a**
EPS	−0.0412 *(0.0258)*		−0.1170 *(0.0787)*	
ES		0.0123 *(0.0228)*		0.0258 *(0.0695)*
RUS		−0.0489** *(0.0218)*		−0.1526** *(0.0665)*
EIS		−0.0090 *(0.0162)*		−0.0088 *(0.0495)*
SIZE	1.4124*** *(0.4446)*	1.4387*** *(0.4567)*	4.5581*** *(1.3537)*	4.6495*** *(1.3902)*
LEV	−0.0368*** *(0.0051)*	−0.0372*** *(0.0051)*	−0.1864*** *(0.0157)*	−0.1872*** *(0.0157)*
MTB	1.2078*** *(0.1683)*	1.1958*** *(0.1682)*	4.8795*** *(0.5125)*	4.8425*** *(0.5121)*
AGE	−0.0299 *(0.0384)*	−0.0369 *(0.0387)*	−0.1462 *(0.1171)*	−0.1719 *(0.1180)*
Firm fixed effect	Yes	Yes	Yes	Yes
Country fixed effect	Yes	Yes	Yes	Yes
Year fixed effect	Yes	Yes	Yes	Yes
R^2	16.95%	17.43%	30.74%	31.19%
Adj. R^2	16.21%	16.40%	30.12%	30.33%
F test	22.98***	16.92***	49.96***	36.32***
Number of Obs	568	568	568	568

Note This table presents the within-group estimator results of fixed effects regressions of EPS scores on financial performance (ROA and ROE) for each model and the values of the control variables over the period 2011–2020 for the sample. Variable definitions are in Table 2. Standard errors are provided in parentheses below the coefficient values. ***, **, * significance at $p < 0.01$; $p < 0.05$ and $p < 0.10$, respectively

(2002) test, which was shown to be strong in small samples as well, is applied, and there is an autocorrelation problem in the model according to the test results.

We base our tests on standard errors of the Prais–Winsten Regression type, which is robust for both heteroscedasticity and serial correlation. Table 8 shows the robustness estimator results. Wald tests show the overall significance of the tested models. The estimation results show that EPS has no significant effect on ROA and ROE. It seems that being sensitive to the environment does not result in favor of the financial performance of enterprises. We support the findings of Shahbaz et al. (2020) that environmental responsibility performance is not explicitly related to accounting-based financial performance and the neutral relationship between corporate social responsibility and financial performance achieved by Adamkaite et al. (2022). As Sarumpaet (2005), mentioned, when the favors done on behalf of the environment result in high

Table 7 Diagnostic tests

	Model1**a**	Model2**a**	Model3a	Model4**a**
White's test H_0: Homoskedasticity	87.06*** *(0.0000)*	115.69*** *(0.0000)*	203.31*** *(0.0000)*	261.38*** *(0.0000)*
Breusch–Pagan/Cook–Weisberg test H_0: Constant variance	12.09*** *(0.0005)*	10.12*** *(0.0015)*	233.48*** *(0.0000)*	243.55*** *(0.0000)*
Wooldridge test H_0: no first-order autocorrelation	9.267*** *(0.0035)*	9.905*** *(0.0026)*	11.256*** *(0.0014)*	14.019*** *(0.0004)*

Note This table presents the diagnostic tests for each model. *p*-values are provided in parentheses below the coefficient values. ***, **, * significance at $p < 0.01$; $p < 0.05$ and $p < 0.10$, respectively

prices for products and services, people may prefer the price instead of the environment. On the other hand, there is evidence that RUS ($p < 0.05$) has a negative significant effect on ROA and ROE when individual dimensions of the environment are tested. When RUS increases by one unit, ROA and ROE decrease by 0.05% and 0.18%, respectively. Allocating resources to environmental responsibility activities will result in a reduction in resources directed to production activities, resulting in a decrease in profits (Zhao & Murrell, 2016). Although we do not support the findings that the environmental-financial performance relationship is positive (Al-Tuwaijri et al., 2004; Lee, 2021; Nakao et al., 2007a, 2007b; Pätäri et al., 2014), we consider the opinion of Arslan-Ayaydin and Thewissen (2015) that companies can improve their economic performance if they reduce their environmental concerns instead of increasing their environmental performance. In competitive market conditions, we think that it would be more rational for companies that focus on their profits to lessen their concerns on this issue rather than increase their environmental performance. Results are similar for ROE and ROA. Although we have obtained results that some environmental proxies have a negative effect on financial performance, we cannot obtain evidence that any theory is valid. However, the results shed some light on the agency theory. In addition, the significant effect of SIZE ($p < 0.05$ and $p < 0.10$), LEV ($p < 0.01$) and MTB ($p < 0.01$) on financial performance in all models is as expected. As the total assets of the companies increase, their profitability also increases. A higher market-to-book ratio results in higher profitability. On the contrary, an increase in leverage level negatively affects profitability. For firms, the AGE is not associated with financial performance in any model.

In all models, there are visible effects of each company, the countries in which the companies operate, and the years. The effect of advantages and disadvantages arising from differences between countries on environmental performance may result from the differences in perceptions of investors as well as the regulations and incentives offered by countries on sustainability. From this point of view, we can say that there is a divergence or convergence effect between countries in terms of environmental performance, even if we cannot obtain results specific to countries in the analysis.

Table 8 Robustness estimator results

Prais–Winsten regression	Model1a	Model2**a**	Model3a	Model4**a**
EPS	−0.0349 *(0.0364)*		−0.1114 *(0.1184)*	
ES		0.0221 *(0.0344)*		0.0511 *(0.1137)*
RUS		−0.0591** *(0.0297)*		−0.1891** *(0.0847)*
EIS		−0.0006 *(0.0152)*		0.0151 *(0.0445)*
SIZE	1.7217** *(0.8720)*	1.7127* *(0.8844)*	5.0376* *(2.8254)*	5.0419* *(2.9178)*
LEV	−0.0416*** *(0.0112)*	−0.0420*** *(0.0115)*	−0.2221*** *(0.0610)*	−0.2258*** *(0.0632)*
MTB	1.0816*** *(0.2440)*	1.0648*** *(0.2540)*	4.4737*** *(0.9624)*	4.3953*** *(0.9732)*
AGE	−0.0422 *(0.0439)*	−0.0523 *(0.0422)*	−0.1611 *(0.1531)*	−0.1983 *(0.1569)*
Firm fixed effect	Yes	Yes	Yes	Yes
Country fixed effect	Yes	Yes	Yes	Yes
Year fixed effect	Yes	Yes	Yes	Yes
R^2	13.08%	13.69%	28.32%	28.82%
Wald X^2	53.66***	71.75***	94.19***	187.62***
Number of Obs.	568	568	568	568

Note This table presents the Prais–Winsten Regression robust estimator results of fixed effects regressions of EPS scores on financial performance (ROA and ROE) for the four established models and the values of the control variables over the period 2011–2020 for the sample. Variable definitions are in Table 2. Robust standard errors are provided in parentheses below the coefficient values. ***, **, * significance at $p < 0.01$; $p < 0.05$ and $p < 0.10$, respectively

6 Conclusion, Limitations, and Future Scope

In general, the concept of corporate social-environmental responsibility has a wide scope and theoretical perspectives sometimes seem to compete (Frynas & Yamahaki, 2016). Within the scope of corporate environmental responsibility, we are interested in the energy sector, as it is one of the leading sectors that pose a threat to the environment and is of undeniable importance for the global economy.

The main purpose of this study is to contribute to the literature by examining the relationship between environmental responsibility performance and financial performance of companies operating in the energy sector. For this purpose, the sample consists of data from 58 European energy companies for the period 2011–2020. We use environmental scores calculated by Thomson Reuters Eikon as a proxy of environmental responsibility, and ROA and ROE data as indicators of financial performance. Previous studies have provided mixed results on environmental-financial performance, and most studies sampled more than one sector. First, we examine a specific sector in the environmental-financial performance relationship and focus on the energy sector, which has the highest share as a source of environmental damage. In addition, to eliminate geographical differences, we take into account the European Region, which has made important studies in environmental sustainability practices in recent years. Our study provides specific evidence for the European energy sector using firm-level comparable environmental sub-scores. We believe that by using environmental sub-scores, we can provide more detailed information compared to the general environmental score. In addition, we test the country fixed effects in the econometric model, considering that each country may have different environmental sustainability approaches and practices, as well as firm and year fixed effects.

Findings from the three-dimensional panel regression results show that the aggregate environmental score has not a significant effect on ROA and ROE. When the individual dimensions of environmental performance are examined, a negative relationship is detected between resource reduction and financial performance. However, emission reduction and environmental innovation scores do not have a significant impact on financial performance in all models. Based on the results, we support the view that the stakeholder theory is not valid for the environmental performance-financial performance relationship of energy companies. In general, the findings indicate that the relationship between environmental and financial performance is negative, but insufficient because the effects of environmental performance are mostly insignificant. Findings on a negative relationship are consistent with studies such as done by Fisher-Vanden and Thorburn (2011), Ruggiero and Lehkonen (2017), Lu and Taylor (2018). On the other hand, the lack of a significant relationship between environmental performance and financial performance is in line with the findings obtained by Sarumpaet (2005), Lech (2013), Shahbaz et al. (2020), Adamkaite et al. (2022). In summary, the results shed some light on agency theory, from which we can denote that better environmental performance does not necessarily lead to higher financial performance. Considering the findings of Walker and Wan (2012), which states that realistic actions toward environmental responsibility behavior have a neutral effect on the financial performance of firms, but that deception behaviors harm financial performance, another question that comes to mind is whether company investments directed to environmental responsibility are perceived as greenwashing by stakeholders. In our opinion, this subject becomes even more interesting, and we leave the answer to this question to future studies. From this point of view, whether environmental/social responsibility activities are an agency cost or not is an important topic of discussion (Cheung, 2016; Liang & Renneboog, 2018). In addition, agency costs such as monitoring or bonding costs arising from the principal-agent relationship, which are not examined in detail in this study, may be addressed in future studies.

The findings of the study include the following results. First, environmental responsibility activities have large costs, and the fact that the energy sector is one of the sectors that cause environmental problems brings with it a necessity of allocating more budget to these costs. Therefore, investments in environmental responsibility may reduce the profitability of the company. In addition, while investors generally prefer short-term investments, environmental sustainability efforts include long-term goals and investments. On the other hand, actions toward environmental responsibility at the company level may be perceived as greenwashing or window dressing by investors and other stakeholders. Companies operating in sectors where compliance costs are higher in terms of environmental benefits may face a disadvantage in terms of financial performance, as the related costs outweigh the added value created for the company. Although the energy sector is under pressure to focus on socially responsible activities for a sustainable environment, our evidence shows that positive activities in this field result in neutral or even negative results in terms of profitability. Ceteris paribus seems unnecessary or inconvenient for companies that only want to increase their profitability to focus on activities that will increase their environmental performance score. From this point of view, another research question comes to mind: could there be a U-shaped or an inverted U-shaped relationship between environmental and financial performance for energy companies?

The generalizability of the findings to other regions and sectors is limited, as the sample of the study includes only energy companies operating in the European Region. Another limitation is the use of only accounting-based profitability indicators as a representative of financial performance. Future studies can provide more robustness to the social responsibility literature with a comparative analysis of other sectors and regions by examining different environmental representatives, market-based profitability indicators or stock price performance. Additionally, future studies may examine the moderating effect of government-led green regulations and incentives on the corporate environmental-financial performance relationship.

Appendix

See Table 9.

Table 9 LR test results

Maximum likelihood method	EPS	ES	RUS	EIS	SIZE	LEV	MTB	AGE	Hypothesis	LR Test Statistics (χ^2)
Model1	−0.0441* *(0.0229)*				1.5113*** *(0.3593)*	−0.0360*** *(0.0049)*	1.2606*** *(0.1474)*	−0.0321 *(0.0254)*	$H_0 = \sigma_\mu = \sigma_\gamma = \sigma_\lambda = 0$	99.22***
	−0.0459** *(0.0226)*				1.7224*** *(0.3540)*	−0.0367*** *(0.0049)*	1.3035*** *(0.1501)*	−0.0403 *(0.0251)*	$H_0 = \sigma_\mu = \sigma_\lambda = 0$	97.59***
	−0.0457* *(0.0238)*				1.6029*** *(0.3715)*	−0.0421*** *(0.0051)*	1.3328*** *(0.1543)*	−0.0469* *(0.0258)*	$H_0 = \sigma_\mu = \sigma_\gamma = 0$	47.61***
	−0.0322 *(0.0201)*				1.1161*** *(0.2717)*	−0.0267*** *(0.0043)*	1.1245*** *(0.1089)*	−0.0184 *(0.0178)*	$H_0 = \sigma_\gamma = \sigma_\lambda = 0$	67.17***
	−0.0458* *(0.0236)*				1.7337*** *(0.3666)*	−0.0426*** *(0.0051)*	1.3650*** *(0.1559)*	−0.0514** *(0.0256)*	$H_0 = \sigma_\mu = 0$	46.91***
	−0.0361* *(0.0209)*				1.1903*** *(0.2829)*	−0.0309*** *(0.0045)*	1.1768*** *(0.1148)*	−0.0270 *(0.0184)*	$H_0 = \sigma_\gamma = 0$	19.08***
	−0.0469*** *(0.0175)*				1.6217*** *(0.2299)*	−0.0260*** *(0.0043)*	1.1898*** *(0.1048)*	−0.0408*** *(0.0149)*	$H_0 = \sigma_\lambda = 0$	40.58***
Model2		0.0173 *(0.0212)*	−0.0487** *(0.0203)*	−0.0123 *(0.0143)*	1.4697*** *(0.3629)*	−0.0364*** *(0.0048)*	1.2443*** *(0.1452)*	−0.0317 *(0.0249)*	$H_0 = \sigma_\mu = \sigma_\gamma = \sigma_\lambda = 0$	92.74***
		0.0160 *(0.0213)*	−0.0502** *(0.0206)*	−0.0114 *(0.0145)*	1.6984*** *(0.3576)*	−0.0372*** *(0.0049)*	1.2886*** *(0.1484)*	−0.0399 *(0.0247)*	$H_0 = \sigma_\mu = \sigma_\lambda = 0$	90.94***
		0.0194 *(0.0223)*	−0.0521** *(0.0214)*	−0.0143 *(0.0151)*	1.5631*** *(0.3740)*	− 0.0424*** *(0.0051)*	1.3128*** *(0.1515)*	−0.0451* *(0.0252)*	$H_0 = \sigma_\mu = \sigma_\gamma = 0$	41.49***

(continued)

Table 9 (continued)

Maximum likelihood method	EPS	ES	RUS	EIS	SIZE	LEV	MTB	AGE	Hypothesis	LR Test Statistics (χ^2)
		0.0292 *(0.0189)*	−0.0406** *(0.0174)*	−0.0262** *(0.0121)*	1.1266*** *(0.2805)*	−0.0293*** *(0.0043)*	1.1206*** *(0.1082)*	−0.0179 *(0.0178)*	$H_0 = \sigma_\gamma = \sigma_\lambda = 0$	65.14***
		0.0118 *(0.0224)*	−0.0526** *(0.0216)*	−0.0133 *(0.0152)*	1.7113*** *(0.3689)*	−0.0430*** *(0.0051)*	1.3478*** *(0.1536)*	−0.0497** *(0.0250)*	$H_0 = \sigma_\mu = 0$	40.66***
		0.0312 *(0.0199)*	−0.0449** *(0.0183)*	−0.0284** *(0.0127)*	1.1978*** *(0.2917)*	−0.0336*** *(0.0045)*	1.1731*** *(0.1139)*	−0.0260 *(0.0183)*	$H_0 = \sigma_\gamma = 0$	17.57***
		0.0310* *(0.0182)*	−0.0470*** *(0.0171)*	−0.0317*** *(0.0112)*	1.5467*** *(0.2379)*	−0.0290*** *(0.0043)*	1.1960*** *(0.1040)*	−0.0371** *(0.0149)*	$H_0 = \sigma_\lambda = 0$	40.38***
Model3	−0.0469 *(0.0685)*				3.4626*** *(1.0672)*	−0.1725*** *(0.0147)*	4.6554*** *(0.4416)*	0.0235 *(0.0751)*	$H_0 = \sigma_\mu = \sigma_\gamma = \sigma_\lambda = 0$	71.65***
	−0.0386 *(0.0676)*				3.5870*** *(1.0450)*	−0.1740*** *(0.0148)*	4.7842*** *(0.4452)*	0.0232 *(0.0738)*	$H_0 = \sigma_\mu = \sigma_\lambda = 0$	71.07***
	−0.0593 *(0.0713)*				3.7165*** *(1.1265)*	−0.1904*** *(0.0153)*	4.9004*** *(0.4661)*	−0.0169 *(0.0783)*	$H_0 = \sigma_\mu = \sigma_\gamma = 0$	33.18***
	−0.0082 *(0.0595)*				2.5475*** *(0.8012)*	−0.1308*** *(0.0128)*	4.0078*** *(0.3242)*	0.0227 *(0.0522)*	$H_0 = \sigma_\gamma = \sigma_\lambda = 0$	49.56***
	−0.0496 *(0.0705)*				3.7429*** *(1.1005)*	−0.1912*** *(0.0154)*	4.9987*** *(0.4672)*	−0.0133 *(0.0770)*	$H_0 = \sigma_\mu = 0$	32.91***
	−0.0209 *(0.0615)*				2.7277*** *(0.8316)*	−0.1416** *(0.0133)*	4.1648*** *(0.3389)*	0.0013 *(0.0540)*	$H_0 = \sigma_\gamma = 0$	10.94***

(continued)

Table 9 (continued)

Maximum likelihood method	EPS	ES	RUS	EIS	SIZE	LEV	MTB	AGE	Hypothesis	LR Test Statistics (χ^2)
	0.0152 *(0.0518)*				2.8592*** *(0.6794)*	−0.1229*** *(0.0127)*	4.2460*** *(0.3096)*	−0.0021 *(0.0442)*	$H_0 = \sigma_\lambda = 0$	35.07***
Model4		0.0890 *(0.0636)*	−0.1312** *(0.0610)*	−0.0057 *(0.0429)*	3.3119*** *(1.0686)*	−0.1720*** *(0.0146)*	4.5897*** *(0.4324)*	0.0237 *(0.0728)*	$H_0 = \sigma_\mu = \sigma_\gamma = \sigma_\lambda = 0$	65.36***
		0.0905 *(0.0637)*	−0.1314** *(0.0616)*	0.0020 *(0.0431)*	3.4513*** *(1.0490)*	−0.1737*** *(0.0147)*	4.7187*** *(0.4373)*	0.0243 *(0.0719)*	$H_0 = \sigma_\mu = \sigma_\lambda = 0$	64.81***
		0.0891 *(0.0666)*	−0.1455** *(0.0641)*	−0.0067 *(0.0452)*	3.5773*** *(1.1229)*	−0.1895*** *(0.0152)*	4.8215*** *(0.4564)*	−0.0128 *(0.0760)*	$H_0 = \sigma_\mu = \sigma_\gamma = 0$	27.13***
		0.1334** *(0.0563)*	−0.1119** *(0.0519)*	−0.0569 *(0.0357)*	2.5834*** *(0.8259)*	−0.1377*** *(0.0129)*	3.9969*** *(0.3215)*	0.0256 *(0.0520)*	$H_0 = \sigma_\gamma = \sigma_\lambda = 0$	47.96***
		0.0916 *(0.0666)*	−0.1442** *(0.0645)*	0.0000 *(0.0453)*	3.6185*** *(1.1025)*	−0.1904*** *(0.0153)*	4.9226*** *(0.4587)*	−0.0085 *(0.0750)*	$H_0 = \sigma_\mu = 0$	26.86***
		0.1376** *(0.0588)*	−0.1258** *(0.0542)*	−0.0626* *(0.0374)*	2.7743*** *(0.8584)*	−0.1490*** *(0.0134)*	4.1493*** *(0.3361)*	0.0048 *(0.0538)*	$H_0 = \sigma_\gamma = 0$	9.90***
		0.1630*** *(0.0539)*	−0.1153** *(0.0505)*	−0.0440 *(0.0332)*	2.6187*** *(0.7024)*	−0.1299*** *(0.0127)*	4.2574*** *(0.3070)*	0.0103 *(0.0440)*	$H_0 = \sigma_\lambda = 0$	35.07***

Note This table presents the LR test results from the maximum likelihood estimator for all models. Variable definitions are in Table 2. Standard errors are provided in parentheses below the coefficient values. ***, **, * significance at $p < 0.01$; $p < 0.05$ and $p < 0.10$, respectively

References

Adamkaite, J., Streimikiene, D., & Rudzioniene, K. (2022). The impact of social responsibility on corporate financial performance in the energy sector: Evidence from Lithuania. *Corporate Social Responsibility and Environmental Management*, 1–14.

Aggarwal, P. (2013). Relationship between environmental responsibility and financial performance of firm: A literature review. *IOSR Journal of Business and Management, 13*(1), 13–22.

Al-Tuwaijri, S. A., Christensen, T. E., & Hughes II, K. E. (2004). The relations among environmental disclosure, environmental performance, and economic performance: A simultaneous equations approach. *Accounting, Organizations and Society, 29*(5–6), 447–471.

Arslan-Ayaydin, Ö., & Thewissen, J. (2015). *The impact of environmental strengths and concerns on the accounting performance of firms in the energy sector.* Springer International Publishing, 83–107.

Baltagi, B. H., Song, S. H., & Jung, B. C. (2001). The unbalanced nested error component regression model. *Journal of Econometrics, 101*(2), 357–381.

Baran, M., Kuźniarska, A., Makieła, Z. J., Sławik, A., & Stuss, M. M. (2022). Does ESG reporting relate to corporate financial performance in the context of the energy sector transformation? Evidence from Poland. *Energies, 15(2)*(477), 1–22.

Bose, B. K. (2010). Global warming: Energy, environmental pollution, and the impact of power electronics. *IEEE Industrial Electronics Magazine, 4*(1), 6–17.

Brammer, S., Brooks, C., & Pavelin, S. (2006). Corporate social performance and stock returns: UK evidence from disaggregate measures. *Financial Management, 35*(3), 97–116.

Breusch, T. S., & Pagan , A. R. (1979). A simple test for heteroscedasticity and random coefficient variation. *Econometrica: Journal of the Econometric Society, 47*(5), 1287–1294.

Calanter, P., & Zisu, D. (2022). EU policies to combat the energy crisis. *Global Economic Observer, 10*(1), 26–33.

Castelo Branco, M., & Lima Rodriques, L. (2007). Positioning stakeholder theory within the debate on corporate social responsibility. *EJBO—Electronic Journal of Business Ethics and Organization Studies, 12*(1), 5–15.

Chen, Z., & Xie, G. (2022). ESG disclosure and financial performance: Moderating role of ESG investors. *International Review of Financial Analysis, 83,* 102291.

Cheung, A. (2016). Corporate social responsibility and corporate cash holdings. *Journal of Corporate Finance, 37,* 412–430.

Cook, R. D., & Weisberg, S. (1983). Diagnostics for heteroscedasticity in regression. *Biometrika, 70*(1), 1–10.

Donaldson, T., & Preston, L. E. (1995). The stakeholder theory of the corporation: Concepts, evidence, and implications. *Academy of Management Review, 20*(1), 65–91.

EU Climate Law. (2020).

European Commission. (2019). The European Green Deal. COM(2019) 640 final.

European Commission. (2022). *REPowerEU: Affordable, secure and sustainable energy for Europe.* Retrieved September 19, 2022 from https://ec.europa.eu/info/strategy/priorities-2019-2024/european-green-deal/repowereu-affordable-secure-and-sustainable-energy-europe_en.

Fisher-Vanden, K., & Thorburn, K. S. (2011). Voluntary corporate environmental initiatives and shareholder wealth. *Journal of Environmental Economics and Management, 62*(3), 430–445.

Freeman, R. E. (1984). *Strategic management: A stakeholder approach.* Cambridge University Press.

Freeman, R. E., & Phillips, R. A. (2002). Stakeholder theory: A libertarian defense. *Business Ethics Quarterly, 12*(3), 331–349.

Friedman, M. (1970). The social responsibility of business ıs to ıncrease ıts profits. *New York Times Magazine.*

Frynas, J. G., & Yamahaki, C. (2016). Corporate social responsibility: Review and roadmap of theoretical perspectives. *Business Ethics: A European Review, 25*(3), 258–285.

Gentry, R. J., & Shen, W. (2010). The relationship between accounting and market measures of firm financial performance: How strong is it? *Journal of Managerial Issues, 22*(4), 514–530.
Gonenc, H., & Scholtens, B. (2017). Environmental and financial performance of fossil fuel firms: A closer inspection of their interaction. *Ecological Economics, 132*, 307–328.
Gonenc, H., & Scholtens, B. (2019). Responsibility and performance relationship in the banking industry. *Sustainability, 11*(12), 3329.
González-Benito, J., & González-Benito, Ó. (2005). Environmental proactivity and business performance: An empirical analysis. *Omega, 33*(1), 1–15.
Goodland, R. (1995). The concept of environmental sustainability. *Annual Review of Ecology and Systematics*, 1–24.
Guenster, N., Bauer, R., Derwall, J., & Koedijk, K. (2011). The economic value of corporate eco-efficiency. *European Financial Management, 17*(4), 679–704.
Harrison, J. S., Bosse, D. A., & Phillips, R. A. (2010). Managing for stakeholders, stakeholder utility functions, and competitive advantage. *Strategic Management Journal, 31*(1), 58–74.
Hassel, L., Nilsson, H., & Nyquist, S. (2005). The value relevance of environmental performance. *European Accounting Review, 14*(1), 41–61.
IEA. (2022, March). *Global energy review: CO_2 emissions in 2021*. Retrieved April 2022, from https://iea.blob.core.windows.net/assets/c3086240-732b-4f6a-89d7-db01be018f5e/GlobalEnergyReviewCO2Emissionsin2021.pdf
Iwata, H., & Okada, K. (2011). How does environmental performance affect financial performance? Evidence from Japanese manufacturing firms. *Ecological Economics, 70*(9), 1691–1700.
Jensen, M. C. (2002). Value maximization, stakeholder theory, and the corporate objective function. *Business Ethics Quarterly, 12*(2), 235–256.
Jensen, M. C., & Meckling, W. (1976). Theory of firm: Managerial behavior, agency costs, and ownership structure. *Journal of Financial Economics, 3*(4), 305–360.
Jones, T. M. (1995). Instrumental stakeholder theory: A synthesis of ethics and economics. *Academy of Management Review, 20*(2), 404–437.
Kalash, I. (2021). The impact of environmental performance on capital structure and firm performance: The case of Turkey. *Society and Business Review, 16*(2), 255–277.
Keats, B. W., & Hitt, M. A. (1988). A causal model of linkages among environmental dimensions, macro organizational characteristics, and performance. *Academy of Management Journal, 31*(3), 570–598.
King, A. A., & Lenox, M. J. (2001). Does it really pay to be green? An empirical study of firm environmental and financial performance: An empirical study of firm environmental and financial performance. *Journal of Industrial Ecology, 5*(1), 105–116.
Kludacz-Alessandri, M., & Cygańska, M. (2021). Corporate social responsibility and financial performance among energy sector companies. *Energies, 14*(19, 6068), 1–16.
Lech, A. (2013). Corporate social responsibility and financial performance. Theoretical and empirical aspects. *Comparative Economic Research. Central and Eastern Europe, 16*(3), 49–62.
Lee, S. (2021). Environmental responsibility, CEO power and financial performance in the energy sector. *Review of Managerial Science, 15*(8), 2407–2426.
Liang., H, & Renneboog., L. (2018). *Is corporate social responsibility an agency problem?* In Research Handbook of Finance and Sustainability, Edward Elgar Publishing, 54–71.
Lu, L. W., & Taylor, M. E. (2018). A study of the relationships among environmental performance, environmental disclosure, and financial performance. *Asian Review of Accounting*.
Manrique, S., & Martí-Ballester, C. P. (2017). Analyzing the effect of corporate environmental performance on corporate financial performance in developed and developing countries. *Sustainability, 9, 1957*(11), 1–30.
Matyas, L., & Balazsi, L. (2012). *The estimation of multidimensional fixed effects panel data models*. CEU, Department of Economics Working Papers.
Moneva, J. M., & Cuellar, B. (2009). The value relevance of financial and non-financial environmental reporting. *Environmental and Resource Economics, 44*(3), 441–456.

Montanarella, L., & Panagos, P. (2021). The relevance of sustainable soil management within the European Green Deal. *Land Use Policy, 100*(104950), 1–6.

Naeem, N., Cankaya, S., & Bildik, R. (2022). Does ESG performance affect the financial performance of environmentally sensitive industries? A comparison between emerging and developed markets. *Borsa Istanbul Review, 22*(2), 128–140.

Nakao, Y., Amano, A., Matsumura, K., Genba, K., & Nakano, M. (2007a). Relationship between environmental performance and financial performance: An empirical analysis of Japanese corporations. *Business Strategy and the Environment, 16*(2), 106–118.

Nakao, Y., Nakano, M., Amano, A., Kokubu, K., Matsumura, K., & Gemba, K. (2007b). Corporate environmental and financial performances and the effects of information-based instruments of environmental policy in Japan. *International Journal of Environment and Sustainable Development, 6*(1), 1–22.

Okafor, A., Adeleye, B. N., & Adusei, M. (2021). Corporate social responsibility and financial performance: Evidence from US tech firms. *Journal of Cleaner Production, 292,* 126078.

Orlitzky, M., Schmidt, F. L., & Rynes, S. L. (2003). Corporate social and financial performance: A meta-analysis. *Organization Studies, 24*(3), 403–441.

Orsato, R. J. (2006). Competitive environmental strategies: when does it pay to be green? *California Management Review, 48*(2), 127–143.

Pätäri, S., Arminen, H., Tuppura, A., & Jantunen, A. (2014). Competitive and responsible? The relationship between corporate social and financial performance in the energy sector. *Renewable and Sustainable Energy Reviews, 37*, 142–154.

Pekovic, S., Grolleau, G., & Mzoughi, N. (2018). Environmental investments: Too much of a good thing? *International Journal of Production Economics, 197*, 297–302.

Refinitiv. (2022, May). *Environmental, social and governance scores from refinitiv.* Retrieved September 17, 2022, from https://www.refinitiv.com/content/dam/marketing/en_us/documents/methodology/refinitiv-esg-scores-methodology.pdf

Roberts, R. W. (1992). Determinants of corporate social responsibility disclosure: An application of stakeholder theory. *Accounting, Organizations and Society, 17*(6), 595–612. Retrieved from Accounting, Organizations and Society.

Rokhmawati, A., Gunardi, A., & Rossi, M. (2017). How powerful is your customers' reaction to carbon performance? Linking carbon and firm financial performance. *International Journal of Energy Economics and Policy, 7*(6), 85–95.

Rokhmawati, A., Sathye, M., & Sathye, S. (2015). The effect of GHG emission, environmental performance, and social performance on financial performance of listed manufacturing firms in Indonesia. *Procedia-Social and Behavioral Sciences, 211*, 461–470.

Ruf, B. M., Muralidhar, K., Brown, R. M., Janney, J. J., & Paul, K. (2001). An empirical investigation of the relationship between change in corporate social performance and financial performance: A stakeholder theory perspective. *Journal of Business Ethics, 32*(2), 143–156.

Ruggiero, S., & Lehkonen, H. (2017). Renewable energy growth and the financial performance of electric utilities: A panel data study. *Journal of Cleaner Production, 142,* 3676–3688.

Sarumpaet, S. (2005). The relationship between environmental performance and financial performance of Indonesian companies. *Jurnal Akuntansi Dan Keuangan, 7*(2), 89–98.

Saygili, E., Arslan, S., & Birkan, A. O. (2022). ESG practices and corporate financial performance: Evidence from Borsa Istanbul. *Borsa _Istanbul Review, 22*(3), 525–533.

Shahbaz, M., Karaman, A. S., Kilic, M., & Uyar, A. (2020). Board attributes, CSR engagement, and corporate performance: What is the nexus in the energy sector? *Energy Policy, 143*(111582), 1–14.

Statista. (2022).*Distribution of Carbon Dioxide Emissions in the European Union in 2020.* Retrieved March 15, 2022 from https://www.statista.com/statistics/999398/carbon-dioxide-emissions-sources-european-union-eu/.

Stjepcevic, J., & Siksnelyte, I. (2017). Corporate social responsibility in energy sector. *Transformations in Business & Economics, 16*(1 (40)), 21–33.

Streimikiene, D., Simanaviciene, Z., & Kovaliov, R. (2009). Corporate social responsibility for implementation of sustainable energy development in Baltic States. *Renewable and Sustainable Energy Reviews, 13*(4), 813–824.
Talbot, D., & Boiral, O. (2018). GHG reporting and impression management: An assessment of sustainability reports from the energy sector. *Journal of Business Ethics, 147*(2), 367–383.
Velte, P. (2017). Does ESG performance have an impact on financial performance? Evidence from Germany. *Journal of Global Responsibility, 80*(2), 169–178.
Vural-Yavaş, Ç. (2021). Economic policy uncertainty, stakeholder engagement, and environmental, social, and governance practices: The moderating effect of competition. *Corporate Social Responsibility and Environmental Management, 28*(1), 82–102.
Wagner, M., Van Phu, N., Azomahou, T., & Wehrmeyer, W. (2002). The relationship between the environmental and economic performance of firms: An empirical analysis of the European paper industry. *Corporate Social Responsibility and Environmental Management, 9*(3), 133–146.
Wahba, H. (2008). Does the market value corporate environmental responsibility? An empirical examination. *Corporate Social Responsibility and Environmental Management, 15*(2), 89–99.
Walker, K., & Wan, F. (2012). The harm of symbolic actions and green-washing: Corporate actions and communications on environmental performance and their financial implications. *Journal of Business Ethics, 109,* 227–242.
White, H. (1980). Heteroscedasticity-consistent covariance matrix estimator and a direct test for heteroscedasticity. *Econometrics, 48*(4), 817–838.
Wooldridge, J. M. (2002). *Econometric analysis of cross section and panel data.* MIT Press.
Yerdelen Tatoğlu, F. (2016). Üç boyutlu sabit ve tesadüfi etkili panel veri modellerinin tahmini için çeşitli yaklaşımlar. *Eurasian Econometrics, Statistics and Empirical Economics Journal, 5*, 60–70.
Zhao, C., Guo, Y., Yuan, J., Wu, M., Li, D., Zhou, Y., & Kang, J. (2018). ESG and corporate financial performance: Empirical evidence from China's Listed power generation companies. *Sustainability, 10*(8, 2607), 1–18.
Zhou, G., Liu, L., & Luo, S. (2022). Sustainable development, ESG performance and company market value: Mediating effect of financial performance. *Business Strategy and the Environment, 31*(7), 3371–3387.
Zhao, X., & Murrell, A. J. (2016). Revisiting the corporate social performance-financial performance link: A replication of W addock and G raves. *Strategic Management Journal, 37*(11), 2378–2388.
Zumente, I., Lāce, N., & Bistrova, J. (2020, May 7–8). ESG disclosure patterns in the Baltics. *Business and Management 2020* (pp. 28–37). Vilnius, Lithuania: 11th International Scientific Conference.

The Impact of Executive Pay Gap on Environmental and Social Performance in the Energy Sector: Worldwide Evidence

Halit Gonenc and Deniz Kartal

Abstract This study examines the impact of the executive pay gap on corporate social performance (CSP), which is the average of social and environmental performance scores for firms in the energy sector worldwide. Following agency theory, we find that firms that pay their executives more than the industry average (pay gap) have lower CSP. We also examine the role of corporate governance at the firm level and market-supporting institutions at the country level to explain the relationship between the pay gap and CSP. The negative effect of the pay gap on CSP is less pronounced for firms located in countries with weaker market-supporting institutions. This evidence is consistent with the idea that firms use CSP to reach a broad investor base in weak market conditions. However, our results show that firm-level corporate governance is not as effective as country-level market institutions. This evidence supports the notion that development of country-level institutions drives CSP in the energy sector.

Keywords Executive pay gap · Energy sector · Corporate social performance · Environmental performance · Corporate governance · Institutional settings

1 Introduction

Modern society consumes large amounts of fuel, and the energy industry is a crucial part of the infrastructure and maintenance of society in almost all countries. Nevertheless, global warming has created growing interest in social and environmental issues in societies worldwide. Companies that are especially involved in production, including fossil fuel extraction, manufacturing, and refining, which operate in the energy industry are affected by actions that take responsibility to protect the environment. These actions put more pressure on companies to meet stakeholder expectations, rather than serving shareholder interests only. The main goal of this study

---

H. Gonenc (✉) · D. Kartal
University of Groningen, Groningen, The Netherlands
e-mail: h.gonenc@rug.nl

J. Thewissen et al. (eds.), *The ESG Framework and the Energy Industry*,
https://doi.org/10.1007/978-3-031-48457-5_12

is to examine how one such pressure, namely, pay gap in executives' compensation, is associated with corporate social performance (CSP), in terms of a combination of social and environmental concerns, of energy companies across countries. Executive pay gap is calculated as the difference in the highest remuneration package in the US dollars between the firm and the two-digit industry average. The international nature of our sample also allows us to capture the county-level factors that contribute to such efforts.

Related literature has documented that CSP enhances the financial performance and reputation of companies. This evidence implies that managers are more motivated to increase CSP. Ferrel et al. (2016) demonstrate that firm-level proxies for strong governance lead to better CSP. Positive pay-for-performance, which is one of the proxies used by the authors to measure strong firm-level governance, drives higher levels of CSP. This finding implies that if compensation policies are used to extract benefits by increasing social reputation rather than being linked with firm performance, additional payments that are not considered to motivate managers for higher financial performance would lead to some agency concerns. Then, it can be argued that executives being paid more would lead to lower CSP. Companies in the energy sector have a high value of assets, which would likely lead to high compensation for their managers. However, additional spending, especially over an industry average, could be at the expense of shareholders.

When the institutional market characteristics of a country are strong, there may be less need for companies to make considerable individual efforts to contribute to higher levels of CSP (El Ghoul et al., 2016). However, with weak institutional settings, there may be more room for companies to determine their own environmental strategies. There could also be more pressure from stakeholders. In such an environment, a company can differentiate itself from other similar companies. This finding implies that the strategic value of CSP is greater in countries with weak market-supporting institutions.

Using a sample of 2502 firm/year observations of companies in the energy sector from 19 countries over the period 2002–2016, we find a significant and negative relationship between executive pay gap and CSP, indicating that companies paying their executives on the board of directors more than the industry average have lower CSP. Moreover, we examine the effect of the executive pay gap on CSP in relation to corporate governance as well as the strength of market-supporting institutions. We find that firm-level governance in general increases CSP, but it does not help energy firms to reduce the negative effect of pay gap on CSP. For market-supporting institutions, we use proxies including stock market efficiency, credit market efficiency, business freedom, and legal system and property rights. Our results show that that there are no significant differences on the effect of the pay gap on CSP between countries with strong and weak market institutions, but the negative relationship between pay gap and CSP is less relevant in countries with weak market institutions, except for the legal system and property rights.

This study contributes to the literature by investigating the relationship between the executive pay gap and CSP in the energy sector, which plays a key role in reducing global warming. More importantly, we consider country-level market-supporting institutions to create awareness of the country-level factors driving the overall firm-level CSP. When market-supporting institutions are weak, CSP could be recognized by companies to create reputation, which in turn the role of pay gap is negligible in such countries. It is important for today's managers to understand the institutional factors that affect CSP but cannot be controlled directly (Ioannou & Serafeim, 2012). The increased pressure from stakeholders to conduct business in a socially responsible manner underlines this need. Policymakers should be aware of the significance of national institutions for CSP. To improve CSP, managers and policymakers must be able to adopt different policies and be prepared to take different actions in different circumstances if needed (Hartmann & Uhlenbruch, 2015).

The remainder of this paper is organized as follows. Section 2 reviews the literature and develops a discussion as a base for the hypotheses to be tested. Section 3 describes the sample and methodology used in this analysis. Section 4 presents the main results of the study. Section 5 presents the conclusions, limitations, and possible subjects for future research.

2 Literature Review and Hypothesis Development

Corporate social responsibility (CSR) is an effort by companies to meet stakeholder demands. Socially responsible companies should integrate social and environmental concerns into their business. CSP measures corporate performance by showing how companies perform with responsible actions.

2.1 Executive Compensation and CSP

Top managers play an important role in coordinating their activities as firms become larger and more difficult to manage (Chandler, 1962). As CSR can be considered a strategic decision, the industry labor market incentive could influence a CEO's decision to invest in more CSR rather than investing in more firm-specific projects. The key idea of CSR is to satisfy a wider stakeholder group, which includes employees, suppliers, customers, investors, communities, and the government (Freeman et al., 2007; Jiao, 2010; Yuen et al., 2016). The reasons for a company to engage in CSR involve multiple actors, with a different set of motives ranging from reactions to pressure from stakeholders to proactive strategies (Aguilera et al., 2007). This is in line with stakeholders' theory, in which the main goal is to satisfy stakeholders. Stakeholder theory has frequently been used to explain a firm's motivation to practice sustainability (Meixell & Luoma, 2015). For example, this orientation leads to a lower cost of equity for firms (El Ghoul et al., 2011), a lower cost of debt (Goss & Roberts, 2011), lower risk exposure, and a lower probability of financial distress (Albuquerque et al., 2018; Cheung, 2016; Jo & Na, 2012). CSR is positively related to customer loyalty (Du et al., 2007), willingness to pay premium prices (Creyer &

Ross, 1996), and a positive attitude toward the brand (Perez et al., 2009). All of these contribute to better performance of the company and ultimately to a better review of the CEO. This implies that in this case, CSR is used as a tool by CEOs to enhance positive reviews and secure their positions.

Few studies examine the relationship between executive compensation and CSP. According to Indjejikian (1999), the CEO compensation structure is a crucial factor in letting executives pursue long-term profits in alignment with the interests of shareholders. Deckop et al. (2006) identify a significant positive relationship between a long-term focus and CSP. Karim et al. (2021) find that the proportion of cash-based compensation decreases, while the proportion of equity-based compensation increases with it. This implies that executive compensation aligned with better corporate governance leads to a higher CSP. On the other hand, this would also indicate that agency problems existing with the compensation structure could affect CSP negatively (Bhandari & Javakhadze, 2017; Cespa & Cestone, 2007; Masulis & Reza, 2015). Wade et al. (2006) highlight that CSP is more likely to recognize the demotivating effect of large gaps between workers and executive pay. This could be used to argue that executives who are paid more would be less involved in CSR, which leads to a lower CSP. Since the money not spent on executives can be saved and transferred to spending more on the broader society, it may also lead to more corporate philanthropy. This discussion leads to the following hypotheses:

H1: *There is a significant and negative relationship between the executive pay gap and CSP.*

2.1.1 Moderating Role of Corporate Governance

Khan (2010) defines corporate governance as a broad term describing the processes, customs, policies, laws, and institutions that direct organizations and corporations in the way the act. Executive compensation can be seen as a part of corporate governance, as it can be seen as a part of policies. The related literature has reported mixed results, finding negative (David et al., 2007), positive (Ferrel et al., 2016; Jo & Harjoto, 2011; Rupley et al., 2012), and insignificant (Schnatterly, 2003) relationships between corporate governance and CSP.

If we consider CSR value-creating activities, firms with better corporate governance should be less likely to compensate their managers very high because additional spending would all be at the expense of shareholders. The other point of view is stakeholder theory, which indicates that corporations conduct CSR not only because they want to make profits and follow laws, but also because they are required to be ethical and socially supportive (Carroll, 1979). This argument implies that the effect of the gap in executive compensation from industry peers for firms with strong governance is weaker than that for firms with weak governance.

H2: *Firm-level level corporate governance weakens the negative relationship between executive pay gap and CSP.*

2.2 *Moderating Role of Country-Level Market-Supporting Institutions*

Ringov and Zollo (2007) point out that there is no solid empirical base linking national specificity with CSP. This could lead to the critical question of why firms in some countries are more socially responsible than those in other countries. In addition, the focus of this study has been extended to investor protection and, more specifically, on how this variable affects the aforementioned effect of executive compensation on CSR. Jackson and Apostolakou (2010) show that companies located in countries with the Anglo-Saxon model are more likely to engage in voluntary CSR policies and practices. This is compared to coordinated market economies, which are embedded and shaped by legal regulations and other institutions.

El Ghoul et al. (2016) argue similarly but distinguish between weaker and stronger market institutions. Proxies for this are stock market efficiency, credit market efficiency, business freedom, legal system, and property rights. They state that "where market-supporting institutions are absent or weak, firms must develop solutions to overcome market failures" (El Ghoul et al., 2016, p. 3). This implies that with weak-supporting institutions, firms have the freedom to decide what to do instead of taking on the solutions given by the government. Under these circumstances, the Anglo-Saxon model can be linked with weaker market institutions and coordinated market economies can be linked with stronger market institutions. These governance systems, in which firms are embedded, are also likely to influence the degree and strength of the internal and external pressures the firm will face to engage in social responsibility initiatives (Matten & Crane, 2005). According to Aguilera and Jackson (2003), differences in corporate governance systems influence corporate social responsibility systems. Campbell (2007) argues that companies that belong to trade or employee associations and companies that are engaged in dialogue with unions, employees, and other stakeholders are more likely to behave socially responsibly. These characteristics are most common in countries with stronger market institutions.

There are companies that ensure that the outside world knows about their CSR initiatives, communicating it properly to their stakeholders, for example, in their reports. On the other hand, some companies operate in countries with certain laws and regulations. These companies do not describe the CSR activities that extend because they simply follow rules/laws. Thus, the stricter the regulations of a country related to CSR, the less room there is for companies to develop their own CSR policies. When there are fewer regulations, there is more room for companies to determine their own strategy but also more pressure from stakeholders. In this environment, a company can differentiate itself from other similar companies. El Ghoul et al. (2016) suggest that the strategic value of CSR is greater when a lack of institutions leads to higher transaction costs. This implies that the strategic value of CSR is higher in countries with weaker institutions. This discussion leads to the following hypothesis:

H3: *The negative relationship between executive pay gap and CSP is weaker in countries with weak institutional settings.*

3 Data and Methodology

3.1 Sample

The data for the empirical analysis consist of firm-level financial and CSP information and country-level institutional variables for the period 2003–2016. Thomson Reuters ASSET4 data is used to collect executive payments and corporate government, social, and environmental scores for companies in energy-related industries.[1] Firms from the utilities, which would include the majority of energy service industries, are excluded because their regulatory settings are different from those of other firms. We obtain firm/year observations with both variables available from 28 countries, but we drop countries with less than ten observations. Thus, our final sample contains energy firms from 19 countries. The data on the GDPs are extracted from the World Bank (www.data.worldbank.org). CSP is considered as the dependent variable and is equal to the average of environmental and social performance. The executive pay gap is the independent variable calculated as the difference in the remuneration package between the highest compensation and industry average. The distinction between countries with strong and weak market institutions makes use of the framework created by El Ghoul et al. (2016). Based on this process, we retained 2502 firm/year observations belonging to 398 unique firms from 19 countries.[2]

3.2 Variables

We identify several variables to capture possible effects on CSP based on the previous literature. First, we calculate the natural logarithm of total assets in millions of $US to control firm size. Return on assets (Roa), measured as the ratio of net income before extraordinary items to total assets, is included to control for the effect of the accounting-based performance. Leverage, measured as the ratio of total debt to total assets, is included to account for the debt resources available to invest in CSP. In addition, we include short-term total assets, capital expenditures, corporate governance score, whether a company pays dividends, and Tobin's Q, measured as the ratio of the market value of assets to the book value of assets to control market-based performance. Country-level variable gross domestic product (GDP) is measured by the natural logarithm of the GDP of a country. Definitions of all variables are presented in the appendix.

---

[1] The following four-digit sic codes are included in the energy-related industries in our sample: 1221, 1222, 1241, 1311, 1321, 1381, 1382, 1389, 2813, 2816, 2819, 2821, 2822, 2823, 2824, 2851, 2865, 2869, 2873, 2874, 2875, 2879, 2891, 2892, 2893, 2895, 2899, 2911, 2992, 3433, 3511, 3511, 3542, 3699, 3568. A name list of these industries is given in Panel C of Table 2.

[2] The potential number of firm/year observations for all industries, excluding financial and utilities, is 19,967 for the same sample period. Thus, our sample size for the energy industry is 12.5% of a possible full sample.

We use four indices for country-level market-supporting institutions as these measurements are performed by El Ghoul et al. (2016).[3] The focus is on stock and credit market efficiency, regulatory systems, legal systems, and property rights. The indices range from 0 to 10. Higher values indicate more efficient stock markets, easier access to external financing, fewer regulatory hurdles to firm entry and operations, and better contract and property rights enforcement.

3.3 Methodology

We perform ordinary least squares (OLS) regressions to test our hypotheses. We calculate standard errors that are heteroskedasticity-robust and clustered at the firm level. We take all the explanatory variables lagged by one year. The following regression equation captures all relationships we include into our analyses.

$$\begin{aligned}\text{CSP}_{it} = {} & \alpha_0 + \beta_1 \text{PayGap}_{it} - 1 + \beta_2 \text{CGVSCORE}_{it-1} + \beta_3 \text{PayGap}_{it-1} \\ & \times \text{CGVSCORE}_{it-1} + \beta_4 \text{Dividend}_{it-1} + \beta_5 \text{Leverage}_{it-1} \\ & + \beta_6 \text{Size}_{it-1} + \beta_7 \text{Roa}_{it-1} + \beta_8 \text{TobinQ}_{it-1} + \beta_9 \text{Cash}_{it-1} \\ & + \beta_{10} \text{Capex}_{it-1} + \beta_{11} \text{GDP}_{it-1} + \beta_{12} \text{Market} \\ & - \text{Supporting Institution Proxy}_{it-1} + \beta_{13} \text{PayGap}_{it-1} \\ & \times \text{Market - Supporting Institution Proxy}_{it-1} \\ & + \text{Industry Fixed Effects} + \text{Year Fixed Effects} + \varepsilon_{it}.\end{aligned}$$

The estimated coefficient of the variable PayGap tests Hypothesis 1, which states whether the pay gap has a significant and negative influence on CSP. Hypothesis 2 examines how corporate governance affects the relationship between executive pay gap and CSP. The estimated coefficient of interaction variable $\text{PayGap}_{it-1} \times \text{CGVSCORE}_{it-1}$ tests this hypothesis. To examine how the strength of a country's market-supporting institution affects the relation between executives' pay gap and CSP, four separate interaction variables between variable PayGap and proxies of market-supporting intuitions are included in our equations separately.

[3] Detailed definitions of these variables are given by El Ghoul et al. (2016) as follows: (1) Stock market efficiency shows whether stock markets provide adequate financing. (2) Credit market efficiency captures whether credit is available to business. (3) Business freedom assesses freedom from regulations as reflected by administrative requirements, ease of entry, bribes/other extra payments required, licensing restrictions, bureaucratic costs, and the cost of tax compliance. (4) Legal system and property rights evaluate the quality of the legal system based on judicial independence, impartial courts, military interference in the rule of law and politics, integrity of the legal system, protection of property rights, legal enforcement of contracts, regulatory restrictions on the sale of real property, reliability of police, and business cost of crime.

3.4 Sample Statistics

Table 1 provides the summary statistics of the dependent, CSP, and the main independent variable, PayGap, as well corporate governance scores and mean values of Tobin's Q and all our country-level variables by sample countries. The distribution of sample countries shows that there is wide variation in countries with different scores for the proxies of market-supporting institutions, with the USA as the largest number of observations. There are sufficient variations among the values of CSP and PayGap across sample countries.

Table 2 shows sample descriptive statistics for the full sample, by year, and by sub-sector in the energy industry in Panels A, B, and C, respectively. Panel A reports sample descriptive statistics based on the number of observations, mean, median, standard deviation, minimum, and maximum—for all the variables we use in our empirical analysis. Over the sample period, the mean of CSP is 0.5119, ranging between 0.069 and 0.9756. The mean of PayGap equals −0.0027, which indicates that, on average, the executives of energy firms are paid $2700, which corresponds to 6.3% of the total gap, less than their industry peers are. Corporate governance score is on average high for our sample energy firms with a mean of 0.6709. Firms paid dividends about 70% of the time in the sample period. Thirty-two % of capital structure of the sample firms refers to debt financing. Sample firms have 8% profits over assets, the average market value is 1.6 times higher than the book value of assets, and the firms hold 9.86% of their assets in cash and short-term investments.

Panel B of Table 2 reports that the number of observations increased steadily over the sample period, from 40 in 2003 to 245 in 2016. The mean values of CSP stayed stable, but the pay gap, on average, increased with our sample of energy firms. Panel C presents the descriptive statistics by sub-sector of sample firms in the energy industry. Fossil fuel firms capture the majority of observations. CSP on average varies across sectors and the mean of PayGap is negative in all sectors.

Table 3 reports the Pearson correlations between pairs of all firm-level and country-level variables. It provides concerns if there are any with the strength of the linear relationship between the two variables. One important point is very high correlations among our country-level variables. This is the main reason that we do not include them in one equation model all together in our regression analysis.

4 Regression Results

Table 4 reports the results from OLS regression estimation for testing Hypothesis 1. We find that the effect of PayGap on CSP is negative and statistically significant at the 1% level in all models. This shows that a higher pay gap leads to a decrease in CSP. This means that paying executives more than the average leads to a decrease in CSP. The effect is also economically significant. From the results with model 1, one standard deviation change in the pay gap changes the mean CSP by [(the

Table 1 Sample countries and descriptive statistics

Country	N	CSP	PayGap in millions of US$	CGVSCORE	TobinQ	Stock market efficiency	Credit market efficiency	Business freedom	Legal systems and property rights	GDP
Australia	293	0.4095	−0.0136	0.6195	1.6648	7.5400	7.3100	7.0600	8.4200	7.1478
Austria	11	0.9234	−0.0004	0.4979	1.0172	5.8700	6.6400	6.9100	8.5400	5.9184
Belgium	18	0.4517	−0.0001	0.4678	0.9459	6.1200	6.2300	6.7400	7.2600	6.1799
Canada	464	0.3623	−0.0034	0.7604	1.5580	7.2000	7.1600	7.3900	8.2900	7.3809
China	63	0.5618	−0.0005	0.3209	1.4583	4.8700	4.0700	5.4500	6.3500	8.8533
Denmark	10	0.9106	−0.0014	0.5760	3.7748	6.5700	7.2400	7.6800	8.9600	5.8024
France	98	0.7640	−0.0006	0.6340	1.3485	5.9500	5.6300	6.8400	7.4700	7.8500
Germany	65	0.8932	−0.0002	0.4646	1.4115	6.3900	5.3800	6.9100	8.5100	8.1576
Hong Kong	52	0.3185	−0.0015	0.3992	1.4135	8.1100	7.7900	7.9000	8.0700	5.5290
India	54	0.7024	−0.0009	0.2750	2.1547	6.6400	5.9400	5.1300	5.8000	7.4877
Italy	18	0.8704	−0.0005	0.4678	1.2793	4.1500	4.3500	5.8600	5.8900	7.6060
Netherlands	58	0.7486	−0.0006	0.6090	1.2934	6.7900	6.7600	6.7600	8.4100	6.6764
Norway	59	0.6360	−0.0021	0.5467	2.2574	6.8400	7.1800	7.1700	8.8400	6.0425
Poland	17	0.4749	−0.0019	0.2451	1.2761	5.0200	4.8000	5.6700	6.1300	6.2354
South Africa	30	0.7797	−0.0036	0.6278	1.4716	6.8500	5.0600	6.4000	5.5500	5.8902
Sweden	33	0.6576	−0.0020	0.5564	1.8116	7.1000	7.0600	7.5100	8.4400	6.1527
Switzerland	57	0.7044	−0.0006	0.5128	1.8041	7.1700	6.7300	7.4800	8.6200	6.3416
UK	226	0.5730	−0.0029	0.7465	1.8099	6.3200	5.8500	7.1800	8.2200	7.8859
USA	876	0.4830	0.0001	0.7547	1.6751	7.3800	7.2200	7.0400	7.4600	9.6236
Total	2502	0.5119	−0.0027	0.6709	1.6460	7.0244	6.7930	7.0325	7.8316	8.0907

This table presents the sample distribution. The sample period is from 2003 to 2016. The definitions of the variables are given in Appendix

Table 2 Sample descriptive statistics

Panel A: Descriptive statistics of all variables

Variables	*N*	Mean	Median	Std. dev.	Minimum	Maximum
CSP	2502	0.5119	0.4941	0.2957	0.0690	0.9756
PayGap in Mil. of US$	2502	−0.0027	−0.0003	0.0083	−0.0606	0.0031
CGVSCORE	2502	0.6709	0.7316	0.2276	0.0252	0.9756
Dividend	2502	0.7030	1.0000	0.4570	0.0000	1.0000
Leverage	2502	0.3207	0.3172	0.1962	0.0000	1.0000
Size	2502	15.3818	15.3299	1.6839	9.4917	19.7696
Roa	2502	0.0803	0.0840	0.0941	−0.3690	0.3870
TobinQ	2502	1.6460	1.4042	1.0384	0.5913	9.1242
Cash	2502	0.0977	0.0653	0.1109	0.0003	0.8289
Casg	2502	0.0986	0.0916	0.0579	0.0005	0.1804
Stock market efficiency	2502	7.0244	7.2000	0.6547	4.1500	8.1100
Credit market efficiency	2502	6.7930	7.1800	0.8014	4.0700	7.7900
Business freedom	2502	7.0325	7.0400	0.4732	5.1300	7.9000
Legal sys. & property rights	2502	7.8316	8.2200	0.6884	5.5500	8.9600
GDP	2502	8.0907	7.8002	1.2753	5.2016	9.8048

Panel B: Descriptive statistics by year

year	*N*	CSP		PayGap in millions of US$	
		Mean	Median	Mean	Median
2003	40	0.5050	0.5200	−0.0003	−0.0001
2004	41	0.6251	0.6629	−0.0006	−0.0003
2005	69	0.4687	0.3565	−0.0016	−0.0004
2006	106	0.5457	0.5599	−0.0012	−0.0002
2007	115	0.5295	0.5690	−0.0011	−0.0003
2008	146	0.5645	0.5789	−0.0012	−0.0003
2009	206	0.5014	0.4790	−0.0015	−0.0004
2010	229	0.4968	0.4212	−0.0021	−0.0002
2011	250	0.4915	0.4931	−0.0022	−0.0003
2012	273	0.4838	0.4595	−0.0020	−0.0002
2013	279	0.4795	0.4336	−0.0028	−0.0002
2014	266	0.4928	0.4563	−0.0042	−0.0003
2015	237	0.5421	0.5268	−0.0068	−0.0011
2016	245	0.5557	0.5444	−0.0033	−0.0003

(continued)

Table 2 (continued)

Panel B: Descriptive statistics by year

year	*N*	CSP		PayGap in millions of US$	
		Mean	Median	Mean	Median
Total	2502	0.5119	0.4941	−0.0027	−0.0003

Panel C: Descriptive statistics by sub-sectors of energy industry

Sub-sectors	*N*	CSP		PayGap in millions of US$	
		Mean	Median	Mean	Median
Bituminous coal and lignite-surface	90	0.3365	0.3329	−0.0027	−0.0003
Bituminous coal-underground mining	58	0.4247	0.3157	−0.0047	−0.0003
Coal mining services	10	0.3545	0.3456	−0.0110	−0.0034
Crude petroleum and natural gas	908	0.3918	0.3029	−0.0048	−0.0005
Natural gas liquids	33	0.2589	0.2453	−0.0084	−0.0024
Drilling oil and gas wells	160	0.2978	0.2637	−0.0010	−0.0003
Oil and gas exploration services	20	0.2992	0.1937	−0.0011	−0.0007
Oil and gas field services	226	0.4667	0.4335	−0.0027	−0.0012
Industrial gases	40	0.8066	0.9145	−0.0006	0.0000
Industrial inorganic chemicals	62	0.7334	0.8526	−0.0011	−0.0006
Plastics materials and resins	144	0.6245	0.6845	−0.0010	−0.0001
Synthetic rubber	6	0.2315	0.1622	−0.0036	−0.0035
Paints and allied products	80	0.6923	0.7561	−0.0004	0.0000
Cyclic crudes and intermediates	18	0.4239	0.1368	−0.0002	−0.0002
Industrial organic chemicals	73	0.8061	0.8711	−0.0002	−0.0002
Nitrogenous fertilizers	46	0.6759	0.7286	−0.0004	−0.0002
Phosphatic fertilizers	11	0.6959	0.8520	0.0002	0.0002
Agricultural chemicals	48	0.7595	0.8373	−0.0002	0.0001
Adhesives and sealants	30	0.8615	0.9020	−0.0005	−0.0004
Explosives	25	0.8287	0.8371	−0.0009	−0.0005
Carbon black	14	0.7103	0.8089	0.0000	0.0000
Chemical preparations	45	0.4839	0.4647	−0.0026	−0.0004
Petroleum refining	274	0.7177	0.8302	−0.0004	0.0000
Lubricating oils and greases	2	0.4668	0.4668	−0.0058	−0.0058
Heating equipment, except electric	2	0.7629	0.7629	0.0000	0.0000
Turbines and turbine generator sets	47	0.7429	0.8679	−0.0002	−0.0001
Power transmission equipment	14	0.8105	0.8178	0.0002	0.0002
Electrical equipment and supplies	16	0.5753	0.6369	−0.0080	−0.0004
Total	2502	0.5119	0.4941	−0.0027	−0.0003

This table reports number of observations (*N*), mean, median, standard deviation, minimum, and maximum values of all variables by the full sample (Panel A), the mean and median values of CSP and PayGap by year (Panel B), and sub-sectors of the energy industry (Panel C). The sample period is from 2003 to 2016. The definitions of the variables are given in Appendix

Table 3 Pearson correlations

		[1]	[2]	[3]	[4]	[5]	[6]	[7]	[8]
CSP	[1]	1							
PayGap	[2]	0.2994*	1						
CGVSCORE	[3]	0.1888*	0.1999*	1					
Dividend	[4]	0.4264*	0.3490*	0.0661*	1				
Leverage	[5]	0.1294*	0.2523*	0.0837*	0.0795*	1			
Size	[6]	0.5951*	0.5981*	0.1599*	0.5057*	0.2754*	1		
Roa	[7]	0.1811*	0.2741*	0.0902*	0.3856*	0.0243	0.3609*	1	
TobinQ	[8]	−0.0961*	−0.0844*	−0.0631*	−0.0774*	−0.1795*	−0.2986*	0.0004	1
Cash	[9]	−0.1078*	−0.3393*	−0.2346*	−0.2254*	−0.3512*	−0.3774*	−0.2817*	0.2793*
Capex	[10]	−0.3276*	−0.1184*	0.1011*	−0.2104*	−0.1184*	−0.1549*	0.0354	0.0751*
Stock market efficiency	[11]	−0.3109*	−0.1230*	0.3539*	−0.1954*	−0.0508*	−0.2972*	−0.1162*	0.1201*
Credit market efficiency	[12]	−0.3211*	−0.1009*	0.3705*	−0.2059*	−0.0275	−0.2693*	−0.1208*	0.1133*
Business freedom	[13]	−0.1965*	−0.0629*	0.3286*	−0.1527*	0.0127	−0.2169*	−0.0840*	0.0235
Legal rights and property rights	[14]	−0.1219*	−0.2210*	0.1862*	−0.1834*	−0.1019*	−0.3049*	−0.1763*	0.0947*
GDP	[15]	−0.0663*	0.2248*	0.3378*	0.0181	0.1919*	0.2904*	0.1468*	−0.0904*

		[9]	[10]	[11]	[12]	[13]	[14]	[15]
CSP	[1]							
PayGap	[2]							
CGVSCORE	[3]							
Dividend	[4]							
Leverage	[5]							
Size	[6]							

(continued)

Table 3 (continued)

		[9]	[10]	[11]	[12]	[13]	[14]	[15]
Roa	[7]							
TobinQ	[8]							
Cash	[9]	1						
Capex	[10]	−0.1104*	1					
Stock market efficiency	[11]	0.0323	0.1713*	1				
Credit market efficiency	[12]	0.006	0.1840*	0.9379*	1			
Business freedom	[13]	−0.0585*	0.1357*	0.5965*	0.6636*	1		
Legal rights and property rights	[14]	0.0877*	0.1211*	0.4880*	0.5470*	0.7800*	1	
GDP	[15]	−0.1984*	0.0551*	0.1868*	0.1737*	−0.0358*	−0.1883*	1

This table reports Pearson correlations among CSP, corporate governance, market institution-specific variables, and all control variables. The sample period is from 2003 to 2016. The definitions of the variables are given in Appendix. Correlations with '*' represent significance at 1% level coefficient of PayGap × standard deviation of PayGap)/mean CSP] = (−2.127 × 0.0083)/0.5119 = −0.0345. Therefore, a one standard deviation change in the pay gap ($8300 in Panel A of Table 2) causes a 3.45% decrease in the mean CSP. These results provide supporting evidence to the first hypothesis.

The positive and statistically significant estimated coefficient of CGVSCORE indicates that firms with stronger governance have a higher CSP. All our control variables with exceptions of Leverage, Roa, and Cash are significant determinants of CSP. Finally, it can be determined that there are significant effects of market-supporting institutions, except legal system and property rights, on CSP.

Table 5 reports the results of Hypotheses 2 and 3 for the moderating roles of firm-level corporate governance and market-supporting intuitions on the main relationship we examine. The results with the coefficients of stand-alone variable PayGap show that the effect of pay gap on CSP is significant and negative for firms with weak corporate governance. The estimated coefficient of CGVSCORE is positive and significant, indicating that CSP increases with strong governance. The interaction variable for PayGap with CGVSCORE is negative and significant, suggesting that firms with strong governance have more decrease in CSP when PayGap increases. There are two implications with the results. First, we can say that high level of PayGap decreases CSP of strong governance firms. Second, for the role of corporate governance in explaining the effect of pay gap on CSP, we can say that firm-level governance is not effective to adjust overall executive payments in energy companies. Therefore, our sample does not provide evidence to support our hypothesis 2.

In models 2 to 5 in Table 5, the coefficients of the interactions between the proxies for market institutions and PayGap in testing hypothesis 3 are all statistically insignificant. Thus, we cannot show that the effect of the pay gap on CSP differs between countries with strong and weak institutions. These findings do not support our hypothesis 3 that implies that the negative impact of PayGap on CSP is more pronounced in countries with weak market-supporting intuitions. We find that decreasing in CSP with increase in PayGap is similar between weak and strong market-supporting institutions. However, stand-alone effects of the proxies of market intuitions, except legal system and property rights, have still significant effects on CSP.

The findings combining the effects of stand-alone and interaction variables of the proxies of market-supporting institutions reserve further investigation. In Table 6, we perform regressions with PayGap and control variables including CGVSCORE against CSP for subsamples created by the level of proxies of market-supporting institutions. We use median of country-level proxies of market-supporting institutions to classify sample countries into weak and strong markets. We find that, in countries with strong market-supporting institutions, again with the exemption of legal and property rights where the effects are similar in those countries, the effect of the pay gap on CSP is negative and significant, but the effect is insignificant in countries with weak market-supporting intuitions. This finding implies that the effect of the pay gap on CSP is relevant in countries with strong stock and credit market efficiencies and high business freedom. Thus, in those markets, a higher pay gap leads to a decrease

Table 4 Regression of PayGap with CSP

	Model 1	Model 2	Model 3	Model 4	Model 5
PayGap	−2.127***	−3.802***	−3.637***	−3.287***	−3.876***
	[0.806]	[0.833]	[0.827]	[0.820]	[0.860]
CGVSCORE	0.373***	0.351***	0.365***	0.388***	0.312***
	[0.035]	[0.043]	[0.043]	[0.047]	[0.042]
Dividend	0.053***	0.042**	0.041**	0.035*	0.040**
	[0.017]	[0.019]	[0.018]	[0.018]	[0.019]
Leverage	0.03	0.033	0.045	0.04	0.037
	[0.037]	[0.050]	[0.049]	[0.049]	[0.051]
Size	0.093***	0.094***	0.093***	0.095***	0.102***
	[0.008]	[0.008]	[0.008]	[0.008]	[0.007]
Roa	−0.002	0.051	0.045	0.064	0.07
	[0.074]	[0.085]	[0.082]	[0.083]	[0.088]
TobinQ	0.017***	0.021***	0.022***	0.020***	0.020***
	[0.006]	[0.006]	[0.006]	[0.006]	[0.006]
Cash	0.005	0.086	0.077	0.069	0.104
	[0.063]	[0.064]	[0.061]	[0.065]	[0.066]
Capex	−0.307**	−0.359**	−0.377**	−0.400**	−0.418**
	[0.147]	[0.172]	[0.172]	[0.171]	[0.180]
GDP	−0.070**	−0.046***	−0.048***	−0.061***	−0.057***
	[0.034]	[0.009]	[0.009]	[0.008]	[0.011]
Stock market efficiency		−0.072***			
		[0.017]			
Credit market efficiency			−0.068***		
			[0.014]		
Business freedom				−0.110***	
				[0.024]	
Legal systems and property rights					−0.024
					[0.018]
Constant	−0.744***	−0.475***	−0.501***	−0.126	−0.801***
	[0.252]	[0.165]	[0.145]	[0.208]	[0.215]
Adj R−squared	0.689	0.615	0.621	0.617	0.597
Observations	2502	2502	2502	2502	2502
Industry	Yes	Yes	Yes	Yes	Yes
Year	Yes	Yes	Yes	Yes	Yes

This table reports results from regressing pay gap with CSP. Appendix provides definitions for all variables. Standard errors are reported in brackets below the estimated coefficients, and '***', '**', and '*' represent significance at 1%, 5%, and 10% levels, respectively

Table 5 Regression of PayGap with CSP and the interactions

	Model 1	Model 2	Model 3	Model 4	Model 5
PayGap	−7.587***	−7.961	−15.158	−17.485	−24.033*
	[1.834]	[20.281]	[10.844]	[24.820]	[13.451]
CGVSCORE	0.308***	0.380***	0.396***	0.419***	0.332***
	[0.045]	[0.047]	[0.047]	[0.051]	[0.045]
Dividend	7.730**	10.919***	11.980***	11.058***	8.772***
	[3.114]	[3.179]	[3.167]	[3.088]	[3.187]
Leverage	0.039**	0.040**	0.038**	0.032*	0.038**
	[0.019]	[0.019]	[0.018]	[0.018]	[0.019]
Size	0.035	0.03	0.044	0.038	0.036
	[0.050]	[0.050]	[0.049]	[0.049]	[0.051]
Roa	0.102***	0.092***	0.090***	0.092***	0.100***
	[0.008]	[0.008]	[0.008]	[0.008]	[0.008]
TobinQ	0.101	0.081	0.074	0.095	0.095
	[0.090]	[0.086]	[0.084]	[0.085]	[0.090]
Cash	0.018***	0.018***	0.019***	0.017***	0.018***
	[0.006]	[0.006]	[0.006]	[0.006]	[0.006]
Capex	0.1	0.079	0.07	0.06	0.104
	[0.066]	[0.062]	[0.060]	[0.063]	[0.066]
GDP	−0.405**	−0.344**	−0.363**	−0.387**	−0.409**
	[0.178]	[0.171]	[0.172]	[0.171]	[0.180]
PayGap * CGVSCORE	−0.052***	−0.048***	−0.049***	−0.063***	−0.058***
	[0.009]	[0.009]	[0.009]	[0.008]	[0.011]
Stock market efficiency		−0.075***			
		[0.018]			
PayGap * stock market efficiency		−0.162			
		[2.667]			
Credit market efficiency			−0.070***		
			[0.015]		
PayGap * Credit market efficiency			0.774		
			[1.470]		
Business freedom				−0.114***	
				[0.025]	
PayGap * Business freedom				1.236	
				[3.486]	

(continued)

Table 5 (continued)

	Model 1	Model 2	Model 3	Model 4	Model 5
Legal systems & property rights					−0.023
					[0.019]
PayGap * Legal sys. & property rgt					1.892
					[1.564]
Constant	−1.020***	−0.413**	−0.455***	−0.061	−0.800***
	[0.117]	[0.172]	[0.151]	[0.217]	[0.237]
R-squared	0.597	0.618	0.625	0.62	0.599
Observations	2502	2502	2502	2502	2502
Industry	Yes	Yes	Yes	Yes	Yes
Year	Yes	Yes	Yes	Yes	Yes

This table reports results from regressing pay gap with CSP. Appendix provides definitions for all variables. Standard errors are reported in brackets below the estimated coefficients, and '***', '**', and '*' represent significance at 1%, 5%, and 10% levels, respectively

in CSP because CSP is more important for firms in countries with weak market-supporting institutions to create reputations among their stakeholders. This evidence supports our theoretical discussion for hypothesis 3.

The reason for the absence of a negative relationship for firms located in countries with weak market-supporting institutions could be limited variability in CSP activity.[4] This would mean that CSP activities in these countries are generally low, regardless of the executives' pay gap. To rule out this possibility, we compared the mean and median CSP levels between countries with weak and strong market institutions. Panel B in Table 6 presents the results. We find that CSP levels in weak market institutions are higher than those in strong market institutions based on all four proxies. Therefore, we can conclude that the non-negative and insignificant explanatory power of PayGap among weak institutional countries is not because of the already low CSP levels in these countries.

5 Conclusion

This study aims to investigate the effect of the executive pay gap on the CSP for a sample of firms operating energy industries across countries. We develop a framework to investigate the effect of the pay gap on CSP in countries with weak and strong market-supporting institutions. First, we show that there is a negative and significant relationship between the executives' pay gap and CSP, indicating that paying executives more than the industry average leads to less CSP. Second, when firm-level corporate governance is high, the decreasing effect of the pay gap on CSP is

[4] We are grateful to one anonymous reviewer for this suggestion.

Table 6 Relationship between PayGap and CSP and proxies of market-supporting institutions

Panel A: Regression results

	Stock market efficiency		Credit market efficiency		Business freedom		Legal system and property rights	
	Weak	Strong	Weak	Strong	Weak	Strong	Weak	Strong
PayGap	2.937	−5.480***	1.767	−5.201***	−3.444	−3.725***	−9.163***	−4.052***
	[3.591]	[0.945]	[3.378]	[0.929]	[4.616]	[0.896]	[3.378]	[0.906]
CGVSCORE	0.255***	0.494***	0.245***	0.452***	0.308***	0.323***	0.414***	0.167***
	[0.059]	[0.060]	[0.061]	[0.057]	[0.053]	[0.049]	[0.055]	[0.050]
Dividend	0.066*	0.038*	0.052	0.041**	0.056**	0.018	0.037	0.079***
	[0.036]	[0.021]	[0.037]	[0.020]	[0.025]	[0.029]	[0.024]	[0.029]
Leverage	0.082	−0.01	0.087	0.018	0.066	0.044	0.045	−0.004
	[0.108]	[0.051]	[0.114]	[0.051]	[0.079]	[0.068]	[0.068]	[0.071]
Size	0.062***	0.105***	0.067***	0.106***	0.094***	0.105***	0.096***	0.107***
	[0.013]	[0.010]	[0.013]	[0.009]	[0.011]	[0.010]	[0.012]	[0.010]
Roa	−0.002	−0.019	−0.08	0.023	−0.004	0.128	−0.079	0.045
	[0.243]	[0.077]	[0.270]	[0.078]	[0.174]	[0.101]	[0.159]	[0.091]
TobinQ	0.007	0.027***	0.02	0.025***	0.030***	0.019**	0.039***	0
	[0.013]	[0.006]	[0.013]	[0.007]	[0.011]	[0.009]	[0.012]	[0.007]
Cash	−0.152	0.08	−0.122	0.097	−0.025	0.150**	0.021	0.107
	[0.126]	[0.069]	[0.141]	[0.067]	[0.143]	[0.072]	[0.123]	[0.081]
Capex	0.037	−0.386**	0.144	−0.434**	−0.632*	−0.287	−0.650**	0.001
	[0.357]	[0.186]	[0.383]	[0.187]	[0.346]	[0.199]	[0.266]	[0.216]
GDP	−0.017	−0.035***	−0.016	−0.045***	−0.080***	−0.006	−0.056***	−0.082***
	[0.021]	[0.013]	[0.023]	[0.011]	[0.016]	[0.029]	[0.017]	[0.028]

(continued)

Table 6 (continued)

Panel A: Regression results

	Stock market efficiency		Credit market efficiency		Business freedom		Legal system and property rights	
	Weak	Strong	Weak	Strong	Weak	Strong	Weak	Strong
Constant	−0.538**	−1.331***	−0.636**	−1.257***	−0.680***	−1.283***	−0.993***	−0.820***
	[0.229]	[0.130]	[0.247]	[0.129]	[0.223]	[0.262]	[0.225]	[0.239]
Adj R-squared	0.52	0.616	0.508	0.614	0.589	0.615	0.528	0.728
Observations	817	1685	748	1754	1308	1194	1452	1050
Industry	Yes	Yes	Yes	Yes	Yes	Yes	Yes	Yes
Year	Yes	Yes	Yes	Yes	Yes	Yes	Yes	Yes

Panel B: Univariate comparisons of CSP

	Stock market efficiency		Credit market efficiency		Business freedom		Legal system and property rights	
CSP	Weak	Strong	Weak	Strong	Weak	Strong	Weak	Strong
Mean	0.6769	0.4319***	0.6770	0.4415***	0.5644	0.4545***	0.5321	0.4840***
Median	0.7744	0.3452***	0.7670	0.3552***	0.5988	0.3813***	0.5222	0.4251***

This table reports results from regressing pay gap with CSP for those groups (Panel A) and from univariate comparisons of mean and median of CSP between groups of pairs (Panel B). Sample countries are classified in weak and strong market-supporting institutions based on the median of each proxy which is conducted to determine whether the means differ significantly. Statistical tests for the differences in mean and median are based on a two-tailed t-test and Wilcoxon rank-sum test, respectively. Appendix provides definitions for all variables. Standard errors are reported in brackets below the estimated coefficients, and '***', '**', and '*' represent significance at 1%, 5%, and 10% levels, respectively small, indicating that firm-level governance doesn't play an important role to modify the effect of pay gap on CSP. Third, the executive pay gap has a stronger negative effect on CSP with strong stock and credit efficient markets that have easier access to external financing and fewer regulatory hurdles. This finding shows that CSP is used to reduce the negative effects of market-supporting intuitions and the pay gap cannot affect the level of CSP in such environments.

This study has some limitations to keep in mind. First, the pay gap is only calculated based on total compensation provided to all executives on the board. Focusing on CEO or CFO compensation structure could have reduced the sample size for the energy industry dramatically. Future studies with more data availability can eliminate this limitation. Second, there are differences in the availability of data across countries. For example, there is much more data from the USA than from any other country. The final sample size consisted of almost 40% of the data from the USA. Third, this study focuses on how market-supporting institutions influence the relationship between the executive pay gap and CSP. Other types of institutions or other factors, such as national culture, might affect this relationship. Future research could examine the effects of other factors on CSP.

The evidence provided by this study makes managers of energy firms be more aware of the drivers of CSP. Today's investors are not only looking for a good return on their investment but also for sustainable investments, giving attention to climate change and other benefits to society. If the pay gap is an important driver of the overall CSP score, it might affect the attitude of stakeholders toward the firm. This is valuable information for managers, because it gives them possible insight as to why some firms might attract more investors than others. This can help them to adopt different policies or take action in countries with different market-supporting institutions.

Appendix

Variable	Definition	Source
CSP	The CSP score is equal to the average of environmental performance and social performance. The environmental performance measures the impact on living and non-living natural systems, including the air, land, and water, as well as complete ecosystems. The social performance measures the capacity to generate trust and loyalty with its workforce, customers, and society, through its use of best management practices	ASSET4

(continued)

(continued)

Variable	Definition	Source
PayGap	The pay gap is calculated by the difference in highest remuneration package in the US dollars between the firm and the four-digit industry average	Authors' calculation based on data in ASSET4
CGVSCORE	The overall corporate governance score	ASSET4
Dividend	Whether a company paid dividend or not	Datastream
Leverage	Measured as the ratio of total debt to total assets	Datastream
Size	Measured as the natural logarithm of total assets in millions of $US	Datastream
Roa	Return on assets measured as the ratio of net income before extraordinary items to total assets	Datastream
TobinQ	Measured as the ratio of the market value of assets to the book value of assets, where the market value of assets is total assets plus market capitalization minus book equity	Datastream
Cash	Cash and short-term assets divided by the total assets	Datastream
Capex	Capital expenditures divided by the total assets	Datastream
Stock market efficiency	Shows whether stock markets provide adequate financing. Based on an index from 0 to 10	El Ghoul et al. (2016)
Credit market efficiency	Captures if credit is available to business. Based on an index from 0 to 10	El Ghoul et al. (2016)
Business freedom	Assesses freedom from regulations as reflected by administrative requirements, ease of entry, bribes/other extra payments required, licensing restrictions, bureaucratic cost, and the cost of tax compliance. Based on an index from 0 to 10	El Ghoul et al. (2016)
Legal systems and property rights	Evaluates the quality of the legal system based on judicial independence, impartial courts, military interference in the rule of law and politics, integrity of the legal system, protection of property rights, legal enforcement of contracts, regulatory restrictions on the sale of real property, reliability of police, and business cost of crime. Based on an index from 0 to 10	El Ghoul et al. (2016)
GDP	Measures as the natural logarithm of the country's GDP in Billions of $US	World Bank

References

Aguilera, R. V., & Jackson, G. (2003). The cross-national diversity of corporate governance: Dimensions and determinants. *Academy of Management Review, 28*, 447–465.

Aguilera, R. V., Rupp, D. E., Williams, C. A., & Ganapathi, J. (2007). Putting the S back in corporate social responsibility: A multilevel theory of social change in organizations. *Academy of Management Review, 32*, 836–863.

Albuquerque, R., Durnev, A., & Koskinen, Y. (2018). Corporate social responsibility and firm risk: Theory and empirical Evidence. *Management Science, 65*, 4451–4469.

Bhandari, A., & Javakhadze, D. (2017). Corporate social responsibility and capital allocation efficiency. *Journal of Corporate Finance, 43*, 354–377.

Campbell, J. L. (2007). Why would corporations behave in socially responsible ways? An institutional theory of corporate social responsibility. *Academy of Management Review, 32*, 946–967.

Carroll, A. (1979). A three-dimensional conceptual model of corporate social performance. *Academy of Management Review, 4*, 497–505.

Cespa, G., & Cestone, G. (2007). Corporate social responsibility and managerial entrenchment. *Journal of Economics and Management Strategy, 16*, 741–771.

Chandler, A. D. (1962). Strategy and structure. In *The history of the American-industrial enterprise*. MIT Press.

Cheung, A. W. K. (2016). Corporate social responsibility and corporate cash holdings. *Journal of Corporate Finance, 37*, 412–430.

Creyer, E. H., & Ross, W. T., Jr. (1996). The impact of corporate behavior on perceived product value. *Marketing Letters, 7*, 173–185.

David, P., Bloom, M., & Hillman, A. J. (2007). Investor activism, managerial responsiveness, and corporate social performance. *Strategic Management Journal, 28*, 91–100.

Deckop, J. R., Merriman, K. K., & Gupta, S. (2006). The effects of CEO pay structure on corporate social performance. *Journal of Management, 32*, 329–342.

Du, S., Bhattacharya, C. B., & Sen, S. (2007). Reaping relational rewards from corporate social responsibility: The role of competitive positioning. *International Journal of Research in Marketing, 24*, 224–241.

El Ghoul, S., Guedhami, O., Kwok, C. C., & Mishra, D. R. (2011). Does corporate social responsibility affect the cost of capital? *Journal of Banking & Finance, 35*, 2388–2406.

El Ghoul, S., Guedhami, O., & Yongtae, K. (2016). Country-level institutions, firm value, and the role of corporate social responsibility initiatives. *Journal of International Business Studies*, 1–26.

Ferrel, A., Liang, H., & Renneboog, L. (2016). Socially responsible firms. *Journal of Financial Economics, 122*, 585–606.

Freeman, R. E., Harrison, J. S., & Wicks, A. C. (2007). *Managing for stakeholders: Survival, reputation, and success*. Yale University Press.

Hartmann, J., & Uhlenbruck, K. (2015). National institutional antecedents to corporate environmental performance. *Journal of World Business, 50*, 729–741.

Indjejikian, R. J. (1999). Performance evaluation and compensation research: An agency perspective. *Accounting Horizons, 13*, 147–157.

Jackson, G., & Apostolakou, A. (2010). Corporate social responsibility in Western Europe: An institutional mirror or substitute. *Journal of Business. Ethics, 94*, 371–394.

Jiao, Y. (2010). Stakeholder welfare and firm value. *Journal of Banking and Finance, 34*, 2549–2561.

Jo, H., & Na, H. (2012). Does CSR reduce firm risk? Evidence from controversial industry sectors. *Journal of Business Ethics, 110*, 441–456.

Jo, H., & Harjoto, M. A. (2011). Corporate governance and firm value: The impact of corporate social responsibility. *Journal of Business Ethics, 103*, 351–383.

Karim, A. E., Albitar, K., & Elmarzouky, M. (2021). A novel measure of corporate carbon emission disclosure, the effect of capital expenditures and corporate governance. *Journal of Environmental Management, 290*, 112581.

Khan, M. H. U. Z. (2010). The effect of corporate governance elements on corporate social responsibility (CSR) reporting: Empirical evidence from private commercial banks of Bangladesh. *International Journal of Law and Management, 52*, 82–109.

Ioannou, I., & Serafeim, G. (2012). What drives corporate social performance? The role of nation-level institutions. *Journal of International Business Studies, 43*, 834–864.

Masulis, R. W., & Reza, S. W. (2015). Agency problems of corporate philanthropy. *Review of Financial Studies, 28*, 592–636.

Matten, D. A., & Crane, A. (2005). Corporate citizenship: Towards an extended theoretical conceptualization. *Academy of Management Review, 30*, 166–180.

Meixell, M. J., & Luoma, P. (2015). Stakeholder pressure in sustainable supply chain management. *International Journal of Physical Distribution & Logistics Management, 45*, 69–89.

Perez, R. C., Alcanniz, E. B., & Herrera, A. A. (2009). The role of self-definitional principles in consumer identification with a socially responsible company. *Journal of Business Ethics, 89*, 547–564.

Ringov, D., & Zollo, M. (2007). The impact of national culture on corporate social performance. *Corporate Governance: The International Journal of Business in Society, 7*, 476–485.

Rupley, K. H., Brown, D., & Marshall, R. S. (2012). Governance, media and the quality of environmental disclosure. *Journal of Accounting and Public Policy, 31*, 610–640.

Schnatterly, K. (2003). Increasing firm value through detection and prevention of white-collar crime. *Strategic Management Journal, 24*, 587–614.

Wade, J., O'Reilly, C., & Pollock, T. (2006). Overpaid CEOs and underpaid managers: Fairness and executive compensation. *Organization Science, 17*, 527–544.

Yuen, K. F., Thai, V. V., & Wong, Y. D. (2016). The effect of continuous improvement capacity on the relationship between of corporate social performance and business performance in maritime transport in Singapore. *Transportation Research Part E: Logistics and Transportation Review, 95*, 62–75.

Sector and Country Effects of Carbon Reduction and Firm Performance

Robin van Emous, R. Krušinskas, and W. Westerman

Abstract Previous studies have indicated a positive association between carbon reduction and firm performance. Using a dataset covering firms across 10 sectors and 53 countries over the period 2004–2019, we add to the literature by showing the differences between sectors and various groupings of countries on carbon reduction and firm performance in terms of the return on assets, the return on equity and the return on sales, as well as the Tobin's Q and the current ratio. The services sector shows a positive result in relation to most of the corporate financial performance variables. The results also provide evidence for a negative relationship for agricultural and mining firms. The findings indicate that differences in carbon reduction are limited when allowing for various ways of grouping countries.

1 Introduction

The presence of carbon legislation and the level of overall country emissions have an impact on carbon reduction and financial performance, as shown by the literature. However, the effects on sector and country levels, as well as various groupings thereof, have not yet been studied. This paper aims to identify differences in this respect. It therefore covers the suggestion of Gallego-Alvarez (2015) to research the impact of country characteristics and in particular the differences between sectors. In doing so, we provide insight on the differences between countries in carbon reduction, financial performance, and additional measurements. Our dataset covers observations from 10 sectors and 53 countries over the period 2004–2019.

In pursuing so-called 3P goals, firms have lately been expressing that next to traditional 'Profit' goals, also social ('People') and environmental ('Planet') goals

R. van Emous (✉) · R. Krušinskas
School of Economics and Business, Kaunas University of Technology, Kaunas, Lithuania
e-mail: robin.van@ktu.edu

W. Westerman
Faculty of Economics and Business, University of Groningen, Groningen, The Netherlands

J. Thewissen et al. (eds.), *The ESG Framework and the Energy Industry*,
https://doi.org/10.1007/978-3-031-48457-5_13

matter. An example of such a view can be drawn from the 2018 Annual Report of the Dutch multinational firm DSM, where CEO Feike Sijbesma writes:

> Ten years ago, many people believed that contributing to a better and a more sustainable world could not go hand in hand with financial returns and profit. Today, we are proving that doing well financially can go together with doing good for the world. We are convinced this will only become more important in the future. Within the next ten years, good financial results will have to go hand in hand with purpose, providing companies with their continued license to operate in a broad sense. We currently see a growing belief among our shareholders confirming this view. (DSM, 2019, p. 10)

Whereas doing good for the world may go together with doing well financially, it may not be that it also goes with doing *better* financially. Indeed, DSM may have purposely given up some of its possible shareholder value while transforming itself from a bulk chemical firm into a nutrition and materials firm. However, Other firms such as the Dutch/British oil and gas major Shell, may have been less transformational toward serving environmental goals to the detriment of their financial goals. Firms must make cost benefit trade-offs, at least in terms of timing of their measures, but maybe also in terms of making money versus being green.

Companies are also facing a changing policy environment pressure and variety of regulations on corporate financial management activities. The United Nation Global Compact (2013) initiative issued the Ten Principles to support companies in the transition to sustainable development and to leverage corporate finance and investments toward the realization of the Sustainable Development Goals (SDGs). The European Union is increasingly putting efforts on supporting the European Green Deal strategy, directing private investments toward the transition to a climate-neutral economy. The European Commission (2019) published new climate-related reporting guidelines to assist companies, but not to create new legal obligations. However, the aim to spread more widely sustainable finance targets was implemented.

Meanwhile, prior research still debates on whether it does pay to be green or not. Whereas a recent study by Busch et al. (2020) claims that more polluting firms have a better financial performance, Galama and Scholtens (2021) has recently shown the opposite in a survey article. Van Emous et al. (2021) find that carbon reduction increases the return on assets, the return on equity and the return on sales, whereas it has no effect on Tobin's Q and the current ratio. Additional measurements, such as responsibility scores of firms, overall emissions of CO_2 in a country, presence of carbon legislation in a country and GDP growth per country, have a limited positive effect or no effect at all. While dealing with a large global sample, Van Emous et al. (2021) do not include sector and country effects.

Our present study provides an initial insight to identify the differences among sectors and country groupings by providing in-depth descriptive statistics. To strengthen the analysis, we conducted a variety of statistical tests to determine the significance of the sector and country groupings differences. We grouped the companies in ten sectors to find differences amongst them. We created multiple country groupings. We looked into differences among continents, sectors and continents combined, between countries with or without carbon legislation and between countries with either the highest or lowest overall carbon emissions.

The study indicates that firms in every continent are reducing their carbon emissions. Firms that reduce their carbon emissions in general show a higher financial performance in terms of return on assets, return on equity, and return on sales, whereas we find no relationship with Tobin's Q and the current ratio. Finally, while we do find some sector level and country level effects related to financial performance variables, they are often insignificant or contradict each other. Therefore, we cannot show that greening the company pays off more in specific sectors or continents than other ones. However, we also do not find the opposite result, namely that greening initiatives cannot simply be rejected for financial performance reasons.

In Sect. 2, we briefly discuss the core literature. The selected data, variables and methodology follow in Sect. 3. In Sect. 4, the findings on sectors, countries, and various groupings of these are presented. Section 5 shows the country level findings on carbon legislation and carbon emission. Finally, we conclude with a brief overview and an outlook.

2 Literature Review

Relations between carbon emission policies and financial performance of firms have been well-studied (Brouwers et al., 2016, 2018; Jong et al., 2014; Luo & Tang, 2013; Marin et al., 2018; Sariannidis et al., 2013). Field studies on carbon emissions of firms and their financial performance have been done by Gallego-Alvarez et al. (2015), Delmas et al. (2015), Lewandowski (2017), Busch et al. (2020) and Van Emous et al. (2021). As to the two most recent studies just mentioned, it is striking that Busch et al. (2020) find that more polluting firms have a better financial performance, whereas Van Emous et al. (2021) show that carbon reduction increases the return on assets, the return on equity and the return on sales, while having no effect on Tobin's Q and the current ratio.

Table 1 provides an overview of financial performance indicators used in the field studies discussed above.

The field study researchers mainly focus on accounting-based profitability measures by using returns on assets, equity, and sales, which all deal with the short-term performance of firms. In addition, most of their studies implement Tobin's Q as a stock market performance indicator, which includes the long-term perspective

Table 1 Overview of financial performance measures in studies on carbon reduction

Research	Financial performance measures
Gallego-Alvarez (2015)	ROA, ROE
Delmas et al. (2015)	ROA, Tobin's Q
Lewandowski (2017)	ROA, ROE, ROS, ROIC, and Tobin's Q
Busch et al. (2020)	ROE, Revenue
Van Emous et al. (2021)	ROA, ROE, ROS, Tobin's Q, and CR

of investors. Van Emous et al. (2021) started including liquidity, measured by the current ratio into this research field.

3 Data and Methodology

3.1 Data

Our research uses a large global sample referring to the years 2004–2019. The sample covers 1785 firms from 10 sectors and 53 countries, making the total number of observations equal to 9265. Financial data are drawn from the Thomson Reuters Eikon Database. The carbon emission data are drawn from the same database and are part of the ASSET4 Database, as are the responsibility scores of the firms. We follow the methodology of Lewandowski (2017) by including only scope one emissions that cover all the direct emissions on-site from production process and scope two emissions that refer to the indirect emissions from purchased energy. Scope three emissions, which cover the all the other emissions sources, are excluded. Lewandowski (2017) argues that the scope three emissions lack reliable data and are not impacted by regulatory pressures. Observations with negative assets and sales are excluded from the study. The sectors are grouped by Standard Industrial Classification (SIC) codes. The country level data are all drawn from the World Bank Database. In line with previous research (Delmas, 2015; Lewandowski, 2017; Van Emous et al., 2021), financial firms are included in our study.

The data are merged into one general database and winsorized at the 1 and 99% level to counter outlier effects. We specifically look at differences across sectors and for effects accounting for country differences. Moreover, we cluster the countries on a continent level and next combine sectors and continents to analyze the differences. Where applicable, we test for differences on carbon reduction on the firm level financial performance as measured with five different indicators: as well as selected other additional measurements on country characteristics and firm-level responsibility scores. We perform ordinary least squares (OLS) regressions and cluster the standard errors on the firm level. To reduce the impact of endogeneity, the financial performance indicators and additional measurements are lagged with $t - 1$, in line with the approach of Van Emous et al. (2021).

3.2 Variables

We use multiple variables that measure the financial performance of firms. Based on the literature, we selected the return on assets (*ROA*), the return on sales (*ROS*), the return on equity (*ROE*), and the Tobin's Q (*TOBIN*). As an addition to the recent field studies and following Van Emous et al. (2021), we also include the current ratio (*CR*) that measures the ability to repay short-term liabilities. The main variable employed in the present study is the difference in carbon reduction (divided by sales to account for the corporate level of growth) on the firm level (*DELTACO2*). Next to the above-mentioned variables, we study the responsibility scores per firm (*ESG*), GDP growth per country (*GDPGROWTH*), CO2 emissions per country (*CO2EMISSION*), and the presence of CO2 legislation (*LEGAL*). Moreover, we specifically search for sector level and country level effects in our sample and add variables that indicate these. To reduce the impact of omitted variable bias we include a wide variety of control variables. First, we control for *SIZE* measured by the logarithm of the total market capitalization of a firm. The second control variable is *LEVERAGE,* which is calculated by dividing the long-term debts of a firm by the total assets. The third variable is *CAPINT,* which represents the capital intensity and is calculated by dividing the total assets by the total sales. The fourth variable we control for is *DELTASALES* which measures the change in sales compared to year $t - 1$. The fifth control variable is *CASHFLOW,* which represents the firm's free cashflow at the end of year t. The sixth control variable is GDPGROWTH, which represents the economic development of the country. We also included the following three moderating variables: *CO2EMISSION,* which measures the overall carbon emissions of a country divided by its GDP, *LEGAL* that indicates the presence of carbon legislation within a country and *ESG,* which measures the responsibility shown by a firm.

3.3 Methodology

The paper contains four different statistical tests. First, to analyze differences between two groups we included a two-sides T-Test to test for differences in mean values and the Mann–Whitney Test for differences in median values. We also performed an ANOVA test to test for differences in values between multiple groups. Finally, we performed an OLS regression to add statistical robustness to our results. We included year, country, and sector fixed effect to account for differences caused by time-invariant characteristics that are unobserved. All the standard errors are clustered at firm level. To reduce the impact of endogeneity, we lagged the main independent variable DELTACO2 with $t - 1$. For each of the financial performance indicators, we have included three models. The first model tests for the relation between carbon emissions reduction and Corporate Financial Performance, CFP. The regression function used is the following:

$$\begin{aligned} \text{CFP}_{i,t} &= \beta_0 + \beta_1 \text{DELTACO2}_{i,t-1} + \beta_2 \text{DELTACO2}^2_{i,t-1} \\ &\quad + \beta_3 \text{CONTROLVARIABLES} + \text{Fixed Effects}_{i,c,t,u} + \varepsilon_t \end{aligned} \tag{1}$$

Model 2 introduces the three moderating variables. The first variable *CO2EMISSION* measures the impact the countries emissions where firm i is registered, the variable *LEGAL* indicates the presence of carbon legislation in the country of firm *i* and *ESG* represents the ESG score of firm *i*. Model 2 also introduces the sector or country level control variables that indicate the firm's presence in a specific country or in a sector grouping, these variables are added as control variables. We employ the following regression equation:

$$\begin{aligned}\mathrm{CFP}_{i,t} = \beta_0 + \beta_1\mathrm{DELTACO2}_{i,t-1} + \beta_2\mathrm{DELTACO2}^2_{i,t-1} \\ + \beta_3\mathrm{CONTROLVARIABLES} + \beta_4\mathrm{CO2EMISSION}_{i,t} \\ + \beta_5\mathrm{LEGAL}_{i,t} + \beta_6\mathrm{ESG}_{i,t} + \text{Fixed Effects}_{i,c,t,u} + \varepsilon_t \end{aligned} \quad (2)$$

Model 3 tests include the three interaction variables to measure the moderating effect of a certain variable on the relation between carbon emissions reduction and CFP. The variable *DELTACO2* × *CO2EMISSION* measures the impact of the carbon emissions in the country where firm i is registered, while *DELTACO2* × *LEGAL* measures the impact of the presence of carbon legislation in the country where firm *i* is registered, the third variable *DELTACO2* × *ESG* finally measures the effect of the ESG score of firm i.

$$\begin{aligned}\mathrm{CFP}_{i,t} = \beta_0 + \beta_1\mathrm{DELTACO2}_{i,t-1} + \beta_2\mathrm{DELTACO2}^2_{i,t-1} \\ + \beta_3\mathrm{CONTROLVARIABLES} + \beta_4\mathrm{DELTACO2} \times \mathrm{CO2EMISSION}_{i,t} \\ + \beta_5\mathrm{DELTACO2} \times \mathrm{LEGAL}_{i,t} + \beta_6\mathrm{DELTACO2} \times \mathrm{ESG}_{i,t} \\ + \text{Fixed Effects}_{i,c,t,u} + \varepsilon_t \end{aligned} \quad (3)$$

To implement the influence of country and sector differences, we create three different sets of regression analysis for each of the financial performance indicators. The first set of regression analysis focuses on sector differences, in this analysis the financial services firms are first excluded, to avoid the so-called dummy variable trap. For the remaining sectors, dummy variables are created, indicating the sector in which a firm is operating. For the analysis on the continent level differences, we excluded the Oceanian firms and firms in the remaining sector due to the low number of observations. For the remaining continents, dummy variables are created indicating the location of a firm in a continent. Regarding the analysis on the country's emissions, we created a dummy variable indicating whether a firm is operating in a country that is either in top five or bottom five countries based on countries emissions scaled by the GDP.

4 Analysis by Sector and Country Groupings

4.1 Analysis by Sector

Table 2 provides the descriptive statistics of mean values for the main variables by sector. The results in Table 2 show that the manufacturing sector has the highest representation within the sample ($n = 4864$). The mean values for the variable *DELTACO2* show that among every sector, on average, firms are reducing their emissions. The mean values also show that the firms in the mining industry have on average the highest emission reduction, followed by firms operating in the agriculture, forestry, and fishing industry. On the other hand, firms in the wholesale trade, retail, services, and the firms that cannot be classified have on average the lowest emission reduction among the sample (mean = – 0.000002). The regression results for the sector analysis can be found in Tables 12, 13, 14, 15 and 16 in Appendix 1.

Looking at the results for the variables *ROA* and *ROE*, the results show that the agricultural, forestry, and fishing industry outperforms the other industries. These findings are not supported by the regression results in the Tables 12 and 13 in Appendix

Table 2 Descriptive statistics by sector

Sector	*N*	DELTACO2	ROA	ROE	ROS	TOBIN	CR
(1) Agriculture, forestry, and fishing	23	– 0.000015	0.115	0.182	0.1114	1.926	1.752
(2) Mining	794	– 0.000022	0.046	0.007	0.041	1.345	2.073
(3) Construction	268	– 0.000005	0.049	0.081	0.045	0.472	1.604
(4) Manufacturing	4864	– 0.000007	0.070	0.112	0.116	1.299	1.678
(5) Transportation, communication, electricity, gas, and sanitary services	1470	– 0.000009	0.067	0.141	0.118	1.347	1.084
(6) Wholesale trade	212	– 0.000002	0.070	0.138	0.038	1.030	1.679
(7) Retail	557	– 0.000002	0.084	0.125	0.041	1.323	1.324
(8) Finance, insurance, and real estate	20	– 0.000003	0.065	0.107	0.323	1.378	1.284
(9) Services	902	– 0.000002	0.070	0.110	0.089	1.690	1.312
(10) Other	155	– 0.000002	0.050	0.106	0.090	0.851	1.447

Descriptive statistics by sector of the full sample with 9265 observations covering 53 countries over the period 2004–2019. The industries are classified according to the SIC standards. The presented variables are *DELTACO2* to measure the change in carbon emissions compared to year $t - 1$ and *ROA, ROS, ROE, TOBIN,* and *CR* to measure the firm's financial performance. The variable *DELTACO2* is lagged with $t - 1$

Table 3 Descriptive statistics by country

Country	*N*	GDPGROWTH	CO2EMISSION	LEGAL	ESG
Argentina	9	− 0.023	0.277	1	53.208
Australia	522	0.027	0.474	0.761	52.228
Austria	54	0.014	0.207	1	56.032
Belgium	80	0.014	0.272	1	57.582
Bermuda	56	− 0.001	0.131	0	52.274
Brazil	35	0.015	0.167	0	54.709
Canada	382	0.021	0.436	0.113	56.565
Cayman Islands	35	0.034	0.146	0	48.708
Chile	16	0.022	0.266	0.625	59.631
China	96	0.065	0.751	0	52.200
Colombia	18	0.035	0.165	0.333	70.413
Cyprus	1	0.031	0.324	1	60.220
Denmark	126	0.014	0.221	1	55.689
Finland	129	0.011	0.303	1	62.084
France	536	0.012	0.175	0.979	62.655
Germany	347	0.014	0.265	0.988	61.438
Greece	39	− 0.013	0.306	1	67.491
Hong Kong SAR. China	111	0.022	0.147	0	55.050
Hungary	11	0.029	0.279	1	59.830
India	113	0.065	0.361	0	62.934
Indonesia	27	0.051	0.226	0	68.312
Ireland	29	0.069	0.223	1	45.706
Israel	38	0.034	0.313	0	50.908
Italy	142	0.001	0.228	1	61.209
Japan	1775	0.007	0.285	0.682	54.056
Kazakhstan	3	0.042	0.783	1	29.245
Kenya	2	0.056	0.127	0	47.891
Korea. Rep	113	0.029	0.380	0.619	57.758
Liberia	1	− 0.023	0.192	0	72.343
Luxembourg	27	0.031	0.272	1	62.559
Malaysia	29	0.050	0.381	0	54.440
Mexico	93	0.022	0.296	0.667	64.358
Morocco	1	0.030	0.282	0	50.419
Netherlands	189	0.015	0.261	0.974	61.748
New Zealand	57	0.029	0.278	0.982	48.311
Norway	48	0.015	0.184	1	50.597
Panama	2	0.033	0.172	0	64.584

(continued)

Table 3 (continued)

Country	*N*	GDPGROWTH	CO2EMISSION	LEGAL	ESG
Papua New Guinea	15	0.064	0.252	0	48.889
Philippines	55	0.065	0.184	0	52.784
Poland	23	0.038	0.475	1	51.462
Portugal	46	0.000	0.220	1	63.934
Russian Federation	28	0.017	0.809	0	37.793
Saudi Arabia	5	0.024	0.356	0	47.388
Singapore	56	0.034	0.147	0.196	52.497
South Africa	350	0.013	0.849	0.140	53.638
Spain	196	0.009	0.231	1	64.436
Sweden	222	0.020	0.139	1	62.004
Switzerland	256	0.019	0.109	0.875	60.238
Thailand	22	0.031	0.310	0	61.159
Turkey	3	0.062	0.259	0	60.843
United Arab Emirates	3	0.017	0.300	0	52.712
United Kingdom	1570	0.015	0.235	0.989	51.122
United States	1123	0.020	0.396	0.922	54.054
Total	9265				
Mean		0.025	0.299	0.525	55.619

Descriptive statistics of mean values by country of the full sample with 9265 observations covering 53 countries

1. In fact, the results provide statistical evidence that the profitability of agricultural firms is lower. The sectors with the lowest mean value for *ROA* are the mining and construction industry, which can be caused by the large amount of assets that are necessary for operations within these industries. The mining industry also has on average the lowest value for *ROE,* which can indicate either low net incomes or high amounts of equity compared to other sectors. The low performance of mining firms on profitability is partially confirmed on a five (*ROA)* or ten (*ROS* and *ROE*) percent confidence level in the regression results in Tables 12, 13 and 14 in Appendix 1. Looking at the *ROS,* the results in Table 2 show that the financial, insurance, and real estate firms on average outperform the other industries (mean = 0.323), whereas the industry with the second highest value is the manufacturing industry (mean = 0.118). The large gap between the financial firms and firms in other industries can be explained by differences in profitability and regulations. For the variable *TOBIN,* the mean results show that the firms that operate in the agriculture, forestry, and fishing industry have the highest stock market performance. However, these results

Table 4 Descriptive statistics by continent

Continent	N	Value	DELTACO2	ROA	ROE	ROS	TOBIN	CR
Europe	4098	Mean	– 0.0000075	0.073	0.133	0.073	1.363	1.402
	4098	Median	– 0.0000008	0.069	0.133	0.062	0.982	1.236
Asia	2450	Mean	– 0.0000013	0.054	0.076	0.151	0.853	1.653
	2450	Median	– 0.0000063	0.049	0.086	0.044	0.532	1.408
Northern America	1691	Mean	– 0.0000109	0.075	0.113	0.107	1.706	1.762
	1691	Median	– 0.0000010	0.079	0.128	0.078	1.205	1.492
Oceania	594	Mean	– 0.0000189	0.060	0.058	0.047	1.335	1.574
	594	Median	– 0.0000013	0.071	0.079	0.056	1.075	1.337
Other	432	Mean	– 0.0000187	0.074	0.094	0.084	1.902	1.603
	432	Median	– 0.0000009	0.077	0.103	0.055	0.878	1.449
Total	9265							
Mean			– 0.0000077	0.068	0.108	0.108	1.314	1.554
Median			– 0.0000062	0.065	0.109	0.109	0.897	1.344

Continent	N	Value	GDPGROWTH	CO2EMISSION	LEGAL	ESG
Europe	4098	Mean	0.014	0.225	0.976	57.080
	4098	Median	0.017	0.235	1.000	57.161
Asia	2450	Mean	0.018	0.301	0.529	54.686
	2450	Median	0.015	0.285	1.000	55.450
Northern America	1691	Mean	0.020	0.385	0.674	55.031
	1691	Median	0.023	0.396	1.000	55.213
Oceania	594	Mean	0.028	0.450	0.763	51.678
	594	Median	0.253	0.474	1.000	51.425
Other	432	Mean	0.014	0.726	0.171	54.646
	432	Median	0.012	0.849	0.000	54.126
Total	9265					
Mean			0.017	0.312	0.752	55.619
Median			0.019	0.285	1.000	55.847

Descriptive statistics of mean and median values of the full sample with 9265 observations, by continent. The presented variables are *DELTACO2* to measure the change in carbon emissions compared to year $t - 1$ and *ROA, ROS, ROE, TOBIN,* and *CR* to measure the firm's financial performance, *GDPGROWTH* to measure the financial development of a country, *CO2EMISSION* to measure the overall carbon emissions of a country scaled by its GDP, *LEGAL* which is a dummy indicating the presence of carbon legislation and *ESG* to represent the average responsibility score of the firms within a country

Table 5 ANOVA test for equality in means among continents

	Chi-square value	*P*-value
DELTACO2	2600	< 0.001
ROA	728,037	< 0.001
ROE	1200	< 0.001
ROS	3300	< 0.001
TOBIN	950.943	< 0.001
CR	275.844	< 0.001
GDPGROWTH	1200	< 0.001
CO2EMISSION	3000	< 0.001
LEGAL	4700	< 0.001
ESG	37.499	< 0.001

Results for the performed ANOVA test for equality in means across multiple continents. The Chi-square value represents the difference between the expected and observed frequencies of the outcomes, and the *P*-value represents the probability that the data represents the same population. The presented variables are *DELTACO2* to measure the change in carbon emissions compared to year $t - 1$ and *ROA, ROS, ROE, TOBIN,* and *CR* to measure the firm's financial performance, *GDPGROWTH* to measure the financial development of a country, *CO2EMISSION* to measure the overall carbon emissions of a country scaled by its GDP, *LEGAL,* which is a dummy indicating the presence of carbon legislation, and *ESG* to represent the average responsibility score of the firms within a country

can be biased by the low number of observations within this sector, which is further supported by the negative coefficient found in the regression results in Table 15 in Appendix 1. The mean values of *TOBIN* show that also firms that operate in the mining, manufacturing, transportation, wholesale trade, retail, financial, and services sector have on average a Tobin's Q above one, meaning that investors value the firm higher than the book value of the assets of the firm. The firms that operate in the construction sector have on average the lowest Tobin's Q (mean = 0.472), meaning that the market value of these firms is on average 47.2% of the total book value of the assets. When looking at the liquidity of the different industries, which is measured with the variable *CR*, the results show that firms among all industries on average can repay their short-term liabilities. The mining industry has the highest value (mean = 2.073), which indicates that its current assets are sufficient to repay their short-term liabilities twice. The regression results provided in Table 16 in Appendix 1 provide no statistical evidence that the liquidity of mining firms outperforms other sectors.

4.2 Analysis by Country

Table 3 provides the descriptive statistics by country for the following country level variables: *GDPGROWTH, CO2EMISSION,* and *LEGAL,* as well as the responsibility scores of firms, *ESG*. The sample contains observations covering 53 countries

Table 6 Descriptive statistics by continent by sector (performance variables)

Continent/industry	*N*	DELTACO2	ROA	ROE	ROS	TOBI	CR
Europe							
(2) Mining	211	– 0.0000072	0.060	0.048	0.039	1.131	1.804
(3) Construction	143	– 0.0000091	0.058	0.090	0.054	0.522	1.882
(4) Manufacturing	1995	– 0.0000092	0.081	0.148	0.077	1.470	1.545
(5) Transportation	755	– 0.0000097	0.065	0.158	0.093	1.261	0.986
(6) Wholesale trade	119	– 0.0000025	0.088	0.181	0.046	1.386	1.741
(7) Retail	314	– 0.0000019	0.067	0.099	0.034	1.133	1.263
(8) Financial services	1	– 0.0000006	0.074	0.341	0.083	1.643	1.288
(9) Services	492	– 0.0000027	0.071	0.102	0.086	1.644	1.157
(10) Other	68	– 0.0000001	0.048	0.083	0.047	0.796	1.376
Asia							
(1) Agriculture	2	– 0.0000001	0.024	0.071	0.131	0.817	1.937
(2) Mining	58	0.0000000	0.088	0.075	0.314	2.215	2.502
(3) Construction	92	– 0.0000001	0.039	0.077	0.032	0.416	1.302
(4) Manufacturing	1705	– 0.0000008	0.051	0.063	0.157	0.765	1.750
(5) Transportation	350	– 0.0000037	0.068	0.126	0.173	1.167	1.276
(6) Wholesale trade	37	0.0000000	0.027	0.094	0.046	0.337	1.465
(7) Retail	34	– 0.0000007	0.057	0.108	0.037	1.059	1.050
(9) Services	115	– 0.0000012	0.052	0.094	0.094	0.989	1.582
(10) Other	57	– 0.0000040	0.048	0.094	0.117	0.831	1.378
Northern America							
(1) Agriculture	15	– 0.0000217	0.136	0.224	0.138	2.537	1.845
(2) Mining	299	– 0.0000125	0.024	– 0.049	– 0.019	0.990	2.182
(3) Construction	7	0.0000021	0.060	0.159	0.127	0.808	1.177
(4) Manufacturing	843	– 0.0000125	0.085	0.140	0.154	1.896	1.826
(5) Transportation	159	– 0.0000196	0.074	0.148	0.130	1.619	1.080
(6) Wholesale trade	44	– 0.0000011	0.067	0.103	0.021	0.786	1.746
(7) Retail	126	– 0.0000053	0.121	0.181	0.048	1.812	1.435
(8) Financial services	19	– 0.0000030	0.064	0.095	0.336	1.364	1.284
(9) Services	173	0.0000005	0.082	0.165	0.116	2.302	1.659
(10) Other	6	– 0.0000012	0.039	0.220	– 0.073	0.474	1.734
Oceania							
(2) Mining	136	– 0.0000634	0.064	0.022	0.050	1.442	2.276
(3) Construction	2	0.0000056	0.057	0.080	0.033	0.485	1.148
(4) Manufacturing	192	– 0.0000141	0.055	0.041	0.028	1.442	1.782
(5) Transportation	133	0.0000042	0.057	0.093	0.070	1.118	1.025
(6) Wholesale trade	9	– 0.0000095	0.069	0.024	– 0.000	0.617	1.448

(continued)

Table 6 (continued)

Continent/industry	*N*	DELTACO2	ROA	ROE	ROS	TOBI	CR
(7) Retail	38	– 0.0000012	0.097	0.117	0.054	1.384	1.032
(9) Services	79	– 0.0000034	0.054	0.078	0.054	1.334	1.128
(10) Other	5	– 0.0000134	0.050	0.065	0.071	1.377	0.682
Other							
(1) Agriculture	6	– 0.0000032	0.095	0.114	0.051	0.768	1.460
(2) Mining	90	– 0.0000421	0.029	0.026	0.055	2.318	1.758
(3) Construction	24	– 0.0000014	0.034	0.022	0.012	0.292	1.274
(4) Manufacturing	129	– 0.0000156	0.088	0.104	0.067	1.581	1.679
(5) Transportation	73	– 0.0000236	0.087	0.120	0.169	2.915	1.295
(6) Wholesale trade	3	0.0000016	– 0.054	– 0.220	– 0.043	0.298	1.535
(7) Retail	45	– 0.0000005	0.108	0.172	0.062	1.430	1.885
(9) Services	43	– 0.0000103	0.100	0.094	0.067	2.290	1.307
(10) Other	19	– 0.0000026	0.065	0.200	0.221	1.092	2.016

Descriptive statistics of mean values of the full sample with 9265 observations, by continent and by sector. The presented variables are *DELTACO2* to measure the change in carbon emissions compared to year $t-1$ and *ROA, ROS, ROE, TOBIN,* and *CR* to measure the firm's financial performance

of which 19 countries cover over 100 observations. The countries with the largest representation are Japan ($n = 1775$), the United Kingdom ($n = 1570$), and the United States ($n = 1123$). The results for the variable *GDPGROWTH* show that 50 countries had an increase in GDP over the sample period. Of these countries Ireland has the highest economic growth (mean = 0.069) followed by China, India, and the Philippines (mean = 0.065 for these countries). Within the sample, there are four countries with a decrease in GDP. The countries with the largest economic decline are Argentina (mean = – 0.023), Liberia (mean = – 0.023), and Greece (mean = – 0.013). Looking at the average GDP growth (mean = 0.025), the results show that 24 countries experience more economic growth and 29 countries less economic growth. The results for the variable *CO2EMISSION* represent the total CO2 emissions of a country scaled by its GDP. The mean values in Table 3 show that South Africa (mean = 0.849), the Russian Federation (mean = 0.809), and Kazakhstan (mean = 0.783) are the most polluting countries. Switzerland (mean = 0.109), Kenya (mean = 0.127), and Bermuda (mean = 0.131), on the other hand, have the lowest overall carbon emissions in terms of GDP. The overall mean value for the overall emissions is 0.299 kg emission per unit of GDP. The results indicate that 35 countries emit less than this average and 18 countries emit more. The results for the variable *LEGAL* show that 17 countries had participated in carbon legislation throughout the entire sample period (mean = 1.000). On the other hand, 20 countries did not enforce any carbon regulations. The remaining 17 countries only enforced carbon legislation over a part of the sample period. Except for two outliers, namely Kazakhstan (mean = 29.245) and the Russian Federation (mean = 37.793),

Table 7 Descriptive statistics on firms that operate in countries without or with carbon legislation

Variables	*N*	Mean	Median	STD
DELTACO2	2301	– 0.000011	– 0.000003	0.000114
ROA	2301	0.066	0.622	0.077
ROE	2301	0.093	0.101	0.252
ROS	2301	0.176	0.060	0.555
TOBIN	2301	1.368	0.779	1.861
CR	2301	1.592	1.352	0.894
GDPGROWTH	2301	0.022	0.022	0.028
CO2EMISSION	2301	0.404	0.361	0.222
ESG	2301	54.314	54.606	13.700
(1) Firms that are registered in countries without carbon legislation				
DELTACO2	6964	– 0.000648	– 0.000008	0.000108
ROA	6964	0.068	0.066	0.074
ROE	6964	0.108	0.109	0.322
ROS	6964	0.099	0.057	0.347
TOBIN	6964	1.314	0.897	1.485
CR	6964	1.554	1.344	0.863
GDPGROWTH	6694	0.015	0.018	0.016
CO2EMISSION	6694	0.282	0.265	0.101
ESG	6964	56.050	56.301	15.827
(2) Firms that are registered in countries with carbon legislation				

Full sample descriptive statistics of mean, median, and standard deviation values with 9265 observations, divided in firms that are registered in countries with and without carbon legislation. The presented variables are *DELTACO2* to measure the change in carbon emissions compared to year $t-1$ and *ROA, ROS, ROE, TOBIN,* and *CR* to measure the firm's financial performance, *GDPGROWTH* to measure the financial development of a country, *CO2EMISSION* to measure the overall carbon emissions of a country scaled by its GDP and *ESG* to represent the average responsibility score of the firms within a country

values for the responsibility score *ESG* do not vary much country by country from the sample mean of 55.619.

4.3 Analysis by Continent

In this part, we will look at similarities and differences across different continents. The following continents are represented in the sample: Europe ($n = 4098$), Asia ($n = 2450$), Northern America ($n = 1691$), Oceania ($n = 594$), Africa ($n = 354$), and South America ($n = 78$). To reduce the impact of single observations on the overall results, Africa and South America are grouped together as Other, since both continents

Table 8 Descriptive statistics by sector on countries without or with carbon legislation—performance

Without legislation	Value	*N*	DELTACO2	ROA	ROE	ROS	TOBIN	CR
(1) Agriculture, forestry, and fishing	Mean	11	– 0.00002640	0.086	0.111	0.087	1.482	1.742
	Median	11	– 0.00000251	0.079	0.103	0.062	0.817	1.625
(2) Mining	Mean	324	– 0.00003590	0.051	0.053	0.089	1.746	2.253
	Median	324	– 0.00000477	0.055	0.052	0.099	0.908	1.889
(3) Construction	Mean	61	– 0.00000049	0.033	0.064	0.031	0.376	1.228
	Median	61	– 0.00000035	0.035	0.096	0.026	0.307	1.100
(4) Manufacturing	Mean	1149	– 0.00001020	0.067	0.079	0.231	1.261	1.604
	Median	1149	– 0.00000002	0.064	0.099	0.050	0.658	1.415
(5) Transportation	Mean	444	– 0.00000393	0.073	0.143	0.173	1.624	1.182
	Median	444	– 0.00000002	0.066	0.119	0.109	1.046	1.047
(6) Wholesale trade	Mean	24	– 0.00000299	0.049	0.041	0.019	0.499	1.901
	Median	24	– 0.00000001	0.053	0.095	0.020	0.413	1.698
(7) Retail	Mean	80	– 0.00000181	0.097	0.172	0.049	1.377	1.629
	Median	80	– 0.00000065	0.085	0.180	0.039	1.054	1.308
(8) Financial services	Mean	7	– 0.00000831	0.056	0.106	0.593	1.005	0.579
	Median	7	– 0.00000640	0.052	0.091	0.566	0.993	0.529
(9) Services	Mean	134	– 0.00000046	0.065	0.093	0.099	1.414	1.342
	Median	134	– 0.00000009	0.059	0.108	0.057	1.020	1.208
(10) Other	Mean	67	– 0.00000789	0.053	0.138	0.137	0.833	1.679
	Median	67	– 0.00000013	0.049	0.105	0.090	0.860	1.414
With legislation	Value	*N*	DELTACO2	ROA	ROE	ROS	TOBIN	CR
(1) Agriculture, forestry, and fishing	Mean	12	– 0.00000451	0.143	0.246	0.139	2.333	1.762
	Median	12	0.00000051	0.151	0.252	0.154	2.506	1.878

(continued)

Table 8 (continued)

With legislation	Value	*N*	DELTACO2	ROA	ROE	ROS	TOBIN	CR
(2) Mining	Mean	470	− 0.00001290	0.042	− 0.025	0.007	1.068	1.949
	Median	470	− 0.00000026	0.061	0.064	0.071	0.760	1.576
(3) Construction	Mean	207	− 0.00000624	0.054	0.086	0.049	0.500	1.715
	Median	207	− 0.00000002	0.053	0.110	0.041	0.449	1.248
(4) Manufacturing	Mean	3715	− 0.00000624	0.071	0.122	0.081	1.310	1.701
	Median	3715	− 0.00000004	0.069	0.111	0.060	0.929	1.514
(5) Transportation	Mean	1026	− 0.00001080	0.064	0.141	0.094	1.227	1.042
	Median	1026	− 0.00000027	0.061	0.117	0.068	0.964	0.929
(6) Wholesale trade	Mean	188	− 0.00000190	0.073	0.150	0.040	1.098	1.650
	Median	188	− 0.00000007	0.073	0.127	0.035	0.896	1.512
(7) Retail	Mean	477	− 0.00000251	0.082	0.117	0.040	1.314	1.272
	Median	477	− 0.00000114	0.073	0.119	0.036	0.942	0.999
(8) Financial services	Mean	13	− 0.00000001	0.069	0.108	0.177	1.579	1.664
	Median	13	− 0.00000022	0.056	0.085	0.130	1.053	1.288
(9) Services	Mean	768	− 0.00000266	0.071	0.113	0.087	1.739	1.307
	Median	768	− 0.00000016	0.068	0.122	0.062	1.275	1.158
(10) Other	Mean	88	0.00000191	0.047	0.082	0.054	0.866	1.270
	Median	88	− 0.00000074	0.046	0.108	0.054	0.839	1.257
Total		9265						
	Mean		− 0.00000770	0.068	0.108	0.099	1.314	1.554
	Median		− 0.00000006	0.065	0.109	0.057	0.897	1.344

Full sample descriptive statistics of mean and median values with 9265 observations, divided in firms that are registered in countries with and without carbon legislation by sector. The presented variables are *DELTACO2* to measure the change in carbon emissions compared to year $t-1$ and *ROA, ROS, ROE, TOBIN*, and *CR* to measure the firm's financial performance

Table 9 *T*-test for equality of means and Mann–Whitney test for equality of medians on countries without and with carbon legislation

	T-test		Mann–Whitney	
	T-value	*P*-value	*Z*-value	*P*-value
DELTACO2	– 1.875	0.061	0.945	0.345
ROA	– 1.389	0.165	– 3.311	< 0.001
ROE	– 2.531	0.011	– 6.313	< 0.001
ROS	12.401	< 0.001	3.176	0.002
TOBIN	2.031	0.042	– 7.355	< 0.001
CR	2.460	0.014	2.153	0.031
GDPGROWTH	13.989	< 0.001	14.192	< 0.001
CO2EMISSION	36.103	< 0.001	26.487	< 0.001
ESG	– 4.711	< 0.001	– 5.058	< 0.001

Results of the two-sided *T*-test for equality and means and the Mann–Whitney test for equality in medians. The presented variables are *DELTACO2* to measure the change in carbon emissions compared to year $t - 1$ and *ROA, ROS, ROE, TOBIN,* and *CR* to measure the firm's financial performance, *GDPGROWTH* to measure the financial development of a country, *CO2EMISSION* to measure the overall carbon emissions of a country scaled by its GDP and *ESG* to represent the average responsibility score of the firms within a country

represent less than 500 observations. Table 4 provides the descriptive statistics of mean values by continent for the performance measures *DELTACO2, ROA, ROE, ROS, TOBIN,* and *CR,* as well as for the additional measurements *GDPGROWTH, CO2EMISSION, LEGAL,* and *ESG.* Table 4 presents the mean and median value for all the stated variables. The regression results for this analysis can be found in the Tables 17, 18, 19, 20 and 21 in Appendix 2.

For the variable *DELTACO2,* the results show that across all continent firms are on average cutting their emissions. For all these continents, the median value is lower than the mean value, which implies that the overall carbon reduction of 50% of the firms within a continent is less than the average. On average, Oceanian, Other, and Northern American firms have the overall highest carbon reduction Asian firms have the lowest overall carbon reduction.

The first financial performance indicator is *ROA*. The results show that Northern American firms (mean = 0.075), Other firms (mean = 0.074), and European firms (mean = 0.073) have the highest values for ROA, whereas Asian firms (mean = 0.054) have on average the lowest ROA. For the variable *ROE* Europe (mean = 0.133) and Northern America (mean = 0.113) are the only continents with an ROE above 0.100. Oceania (mean = 0.058) and Asia (mean = 0.076) have the lowest ROE. The third profitability indicator is *ROS*. Asia (mean = 0.151) and Northern America (mean = 0.107) have the highest value for ROS and are the only continents with a value above 0.100. Oceania (mean = 0.047) and Europe (mean = 0.073) have the lowest ROS. Looking at the overall profitability by continents, the results show that Northern America has one of the highest values for all the performance indicators,

Table 10 Descriptive statistics for countries with highest and lowest carbon emissions

Country	*N*	DELTACO2	ROA	ROS	ROE	TOBIN	CR
South Africa	350	– 0.000007700	0.068	0.099	0.108	1.314	1.554
Australia	522	– 0.000017300	0.055	0.044	0.051	1.298	1.546
Canada	382	– 0.000024400	0.047	0.076	0.035	1.079	1.720
United States	1123	– 0.000006400	0.088	0.125	0.148	1.678	1.793
Korean Republic	113	– 0.000000001	0.054	0.112	0.075	0.733	1.327
Total	2490						
Mean		– 0.000012400	0.071	0.095	0.101	1.489	1.687

Country	*N*	GDPGROWTH	CO2EMISSION	LEGAL	ESG
South Africa	350	0.013	0.849	0.140	53.638
Australia	522	0.027	0.474	0.761	52.228
Canada	382	0.021	0.436	0.113	56.565
United States	1123	0.020	0.397	0.922	54.054
Korean Republic	113	0.029	0.380	0.619	57.758
Total	2490				
Mean		0.021	0.482	0.640	54.166

Countries with the highest carbon emission scaled by GDP

Country	*N*	DELTACO2	ROA	ROS	ROE	TOBIN	CR
Switzerland	256	– 0.000004030	0.096	0.098	0.157	1.893	1.796
Sweden	222	– 0.000000312	0.085	0.066	0.152	1.197	1.483
Hong Kong SAR	111	– 0.000004600	0.080	0.246	0.132	1.257	1.612
France	536	– 0.000012200	0.066	0.071	0.099	1.245	1.233
Denmark	126	– 0.000001850	0.109	0.096	0.164	3.031	1.480
Total	1251						
Mean		– 0.000006690	0.081	0.094	0.130	1.550	1.451

Country	*N*	GDPGROWTH	CO2EMISSION	LEGAL	ESG
Switzerland	256	0.019	0.109	0.875	60.238
Sweden	222	0.012	0.139	1.000	62.004
Hong Kong SAR	111	0.022	0.147	0.000	55.050
France	536	0.012	0.175	0.979	65.655
Denmark	126	0.014	0.221	1.000	55.689
Total	1251				
Mean		0.016	0.157	0.877	60.669

Countries with the lowest carbon emission scaled by GDP

Descriptive statistics of mean values of a sample divided in the five countries with the highest and lowest overall carbon emissions. The presented variables are *DELTACO2* to measure the change in carbon emissions compared to year $t - 1$ and *ROA, ROS, ROE, TOBIN,* and *CR* to measure the firm's financial performance, *GDPGROWTH* to measure the financial development of a country, *CO2EMISSION* to measure the overall carbon emissions of a country scaled its GDP, *LEGAL,* which is a dummy indicating the presence of carbon legislation, and *ESG* to represent the average responsibility score of the firms within a country

Table 11 *T*-test for equality of means and Mann–Whitney test for equality of medians for countries with highest and lowest carbon emissions

	T-test		Mann–Whitney	
	T-value	*P*-value	*Z*-value	*P*-value
DELTACO2	− 1.397	0.163	− 3.996	< 0.001
ROA	− 3.338	< 0.001	− 0.835	0.404
ROE	− 2.525	0.011	− 3.591	< 0.001
ROS	0.112	0.911	− 3.706	< 0.001
TOBIN	− 1.148	0.251	− 0.816	0.415
CR	7.9198	< 0.001	6.691	< 0.001
GDPGROWTH	11.130	< 0.001	13.647	< 0.001
CO2EMISSION	74.555	< 0.001	50.877	< 0.001
LEGAL	− 15.692	< 0.001	− 15.201	< 0.001
ESG	− 12.531	< 0.001	− 11.845	< 0.001

The results of the two-sided *T*-test for equality and means and Mann–Whitney test for equality in medians. The presented variables are *DELTA_CO2* to measure the change in carbon emissions compared to year $t - 1$ and *ROA, ROS, ROE, TOBIN,* and *CR* to measure the firm's financial performance

indicating that on average Northern American firms are the most profitable. European firms outperform Other firms on the ROA and ROE but underperform on the ROS indicating that these firms require more sales to make profit. Asia on the other hand underperforms for the variables *ROA* and *ROE* but outperforms for the variable *ROS,* which can indicate that Asian firms require more assets or equity compared to Other firms. Overall, Oceanian firms have the lowest profitability for all the indicators.

For the variable *TOBIN,* the results show that the other continents (mean = 1.902) and Northern America (mean = 1.706) have the highest stock market performance. Asia (mean = 0.853) has the lowest value, and it is the only continent with an average value below 1.000. This indicates that the market value of Asian firms is lower than their book value of the total assets. The variable *CR* measures the liquidity of firms. Northern American (mean = 1.762) and Asian (mean = 1.653) firms have on average the overall highest current ratio. European firms (mean = 1.402) have the lowest value, indicating that European firms on average have a lower liquidity than Oceanian and Other firms. The regression results that can be found in Table 21 in Appendix 2 do not show statistical evidence for a relation between operating in a certain continent and liquidity.

The economic growth of countries is measured with the variable *GDPGROWTH,* which represents the annual growth in GDP, compared to year $t - 1$. The results for this variable show that European and Other countries (mean = 0.014) have the lowest economic growth, whereas Oceanian countries have the highest economic growth (mean = 0.028). The variable *CO2EMISSION* represents the average of the overall carbon emissions of a country scaled by the country's GDP over the sample period. The results show that Other countries firms have the highest overall carbon emissions; on average, the emissions of these continents are three times higher than the continent with the lowest emissions, Europe. A higher median value compared to the mean value implies that over 50% of the observations represent a country with higher emissions than the continent average. The variable *LEGAL* indicates the presence of a trading emissions scheme or carbon taxation within a country. The results show that European firms have the highest mean value, which is likely to be caused by the EU ETS program that covers 31 European countries (European Union, 2015). The Other group has the lowest value, which indicates the little presence of carbon legislation, and this lack of carbon legislation may be a reason for the high mean value for their overall emissions. A median value of 1.000 for the variable *LEGAL* indicates that over 50% of the observations within the sample are registered in a country with carbon legislation. The mean value of the ESG variable is on every continent higher than 50. It differs between 51.425 for Oceania and 57.080 for Europe.

Table 5 provides the results of the ANOVA test to see whether the differences in means as provided in the descriptive statistics above are significant. The results in Table 5 imply that for the variables *DELTACO2, ROA, ROE, ROS, TOBIN, CR, GDPGROWTH, CO2EMISSION, LEGAL,* and *ESG* there are significant differences across the different continents. A higher Chi-square value implies that the probability that there are significant differences between the different groups is higher compared to variables with a lower Chi-square value. The results for all these variables suggest that the earlier explained differences as provided in Table 4 are statistically supported.

The results of the continent analysis show significant differences across continents in emission reduction, financial performance, and additional measurements. In every continent, firms are cutting their emissions. Oceanian, South American, African, and Northern American firms have the highest overall carbon reduction and Asian firms have the lowest overall carbon reduction. The results show that Northern American firms have the best overall financial performance when considering all the performance indicators, *ROA, ROE,* and *ROS*. European firms have high values for *ROA, ROE,* and *TOBIN*, but the lowest value for Tobin's Q and Asian firms have the highest values for the ROS, but the lowest value for the ROA, the ROE, and Tobin's Q. Overall the Oceanian firms have the worst financial performance.

4.4 Analysis by Sector and Continent

Table 6 provides the descriptive statistics by continent and by sector to analyze differences in carbon emission and financial performance among different sectors in different continents. The results of the sector analysis presented in Sect. 4.1 in Table 2 show that the firms operating in the mining, agricultural, and transportation industry have the overall highest carbon reduction. The results in Table 6 show that the mining industry firms in Oceania, Northern America, and Other have the highest overall carbon reduction; firms in the mining industry in Asia on the other hand have on average no carbon reduction. As to the agricultural sector, Asian firms have the worst carbon performance and Northern American firms have the best carbon performance, however this sector has a low representation within the sample ($n = 23$), which indicates that single observations may bias the results for this sector. For the transportation sector, the results show that among all continents, firms are reducing their emissions, except for Oceanian firms within this sector. For this sector firms in Southern America and Africa have the highest carbon reduction and European and Northern American firms have a better carbon performance compared to the overall sector average (mean = – 0.000009). Looking at the results for the sector with the highest representation within the sample, the results show that manufacturing firms in South America and Africa, Oceania and Northern America have the highest overall carbon reduction. Looking at the overall average carbon reduction of the manufacturing firms the results show that all firms on all continents except Asia reduce their emissions more than the overall sector average (mean = – 0.00007).

Within the sample, there are seven sectors within continents that are not reducing their overall emissions. In Europe throughout all the different sectors, firms are cutting their emissions and the construction firms within Europe have on average the overall highest emission reduction compared to the construction firms in different continents. For Asia, the results show that no single sector has the overall highest carbon reduction, whereas for the agriculture, mining, and manufacturing sector Asian firms even have the lowest carbon performance, compared to similar industries in different continents. Comparing the emission reduction from Asian firms to the overall averages per sector as presented in Sect. 4.1 the results show that for almost all the sectors' firms in Asia are underperforming, only firms placed in the remaining sectors are performing better than the overall average. Firms in Northern America are in almost all sectors reducing their emissions, only firms within the services sector had on average an increase in emissions. Oceania has the two sectors with the worst overall carbon performance, the construction and transportation firms and the sector with highest overall carbon reduction, representing the firms in the mining industry. Northern American firms within the agriculture, retail, and financial services sectors outperform similar companies in the other continents. The results for Other firms show that among almost all sectors' firms are cutting their emissions, except for the wholesale trade firms. However, this group of firms represents just three firm year observations, so individual observations may bias the results.

Table 6 provides insights in the financial performance per sector for all the different continents. The financial performance is measured with the variables *ROA, ROE, ROS, TOBIN,* and *CR*. For the variable *ROA,* the results as presented in Sect. 4.1 show that firms in most European sectors outperform the overall average value for *ROA*. The analysis by sector in Sect. 4.1 showed that the agricultural and retail firms have the highest value for the variable *ROA*, whereas for both sectors Northern American firms have the highest profitability. Table 6 shows that Asian firms in the agriculture, manufacturing, retail, and services sectors have the overall lowest return on assets compared to similar firms in different continents, whereas also most of the sectors have a lower ROA than the overall sector average value presented in Sect. 4.1. Other firms in the manufacturing, transportation, services, and remaining sectors have the highest ROA of the firms within the sample. The results for the variable *ROE* show similar trends for European and Asian firms, since in Europe most sectors perform above average, with firms in the manufacturing, transportation, wholesale trade, and financial services having the overall highest ROE compared to similar firms in different continents. Looking at the Asian firms, the results show that firms in most sectors are performing worse than the sector average. Northern American firms on the other hand are outperforming the sector average for most sectors and Oceanian firms are underperforming. The results for the variable *ROS* are contradicting the earlier trends found for *ROA* and *ROE*, since for this variable European firms are underperforming and firms in Asia are outperforming the sector averages. Firms in Europe and Asia that have the same profitability may show differences in assets, equity, and sales. For Northern American and Oceanian firms, the results show similar trends to the results on the ROA and the ROE. Looking at the profitability of the sector with the highest representation within the sample, the manufacturing sector, the results show that Other firms have the highest ROA, European firms have the highest ROE and Asian firms have the highest ROS. The results also show that only Northern American firms outperform the sector average for all these profitability indicators. Oceanian manufacturing firms on the other hand underperform in comparison to the overall sector average for these financial performance indicators. The stock market performance indicator in this research is *TOBIN*. The results show that Asian firms among almost all sectors are underperforming on Tobin's Q ratio compared to the sector average provided in Sect. 4.1. Asian manufacturing, retail and services firms even have the overall lowest value per sector. The Northern American agriculture, construction, manufacturing, retail, and services sector firms have the overall highest Tobin's Q compared to similar companies elsewhere. Looking at the results for *CR*, the results show that European and Oceanian firms underperform for most of the sectors, compared to the overall sector average. Asian and Northern American firms tend to outperform the sector average for most of the sectors. Table 22 in Appendix 3 provides insight on the additional measurements *GDPGROWTH, CO2EMISSION, LEGAL,* and *ESG*. Among others, interesting differences in terms of legislation can be noticed and this is where the next section will focus upon.

5 Country Level Analysis

5.1 Country Level Analysis on Carbon Legislation

Many countries installed carbon legislation to enforce firms to reduce their emissions. We analyze whether there are differences in carbon reduction and financial performance for firms that are registered in countries with carbon legislation. To indicate that a firm is registered in a country with carbon legislation, we created the dummy variable *LEGAL*, which has a value of zero for countries without carbon legislation and of one for countries with carbon legislation. Basically, there are two forms of carbon legislation: emission trading schemes and carbon taxation. Table 7 provides the descriptive statistics for both groups for the following variables: *DELTACO2, ROA, ROE, ROS, TOBIN, CR, GDPGROWTH, CO2EMISSION,* and *ESG.* The results for the variable *DELTACO2* imply that firms being registered in a country with carbon legislation have a higher carbon reduction (mean = – 0.000648) compared to firms that are not registered in a country with carbon legislation (mean = – 0.000011). The results for the median value of firms that are registered in a country with carbon legislation (median = – 0.000008) is higher, suggesting that these firms reduce more of their emissions compared to firms that are registered in a country that has no carbon legislation (median = – 0.000003). The findings suggest that the enforcement of governments plays an important role in the reduction of corporate emissions. For both groups, the median values are lower than the mean value, suggesting that less than 50% of the observations are performing better than the average. The statistics for the variables *ROA* and *ROE* show that firms that are registered in a country with carbon legislation perform slightly better. Firms registered in a country without carbon legislation outperform firms being from a country with carbon legislation in terms of *ROS, TOBIN,* and *CR*, suggesting that the firms within the sample that must pay for their carbon emissions are not able to pass these costs along to their customers (Brouwers et al., 2018).

Countries with carbon legislation have on average a low *GDPGROWTH*, indicating that they experience lower economic growth than others. As to the overall emissions of countries scaled by the countries' GDP, we find that on average countries with carbon legislation (mean = 0.282) outperform countries without carbon legislation (mean = 0.404). These findings suggest that the presence of carbon legislation in a country leads to an overall lowering of emissions, possibly caused by the higher carbon reduction of firms being registered here, such as presented by the mean values for the variable *DELTACO2.* The results for the variable *ESG* suggest that firms being registered in a country with carbon legislation (mean = 56.050) are more responsible compared to firms in countries without carbon legislation (mean = 54.314), indicating that firms that are forced to reduce their emissions have a higher ESG score.

Table 8 presents the descriptive statistics for countries with and without carbon legislation by sector. The results for the variable *DELTACO2* show that companies that are registered in countries without carbon legislation and that are operating in the agricultural, mining, manufacturing, wholesale trade, financial services, and other sectors have on average a higher carbon reduction compared to similar companies that are registered in a country with carbon legislation, which suggests that companies within those sectors are not impacted by carbon legislation. The companies within the construction, transportation, and communication, retail and services firms that are registered in countries with carbon legislation achieved a higher reduction in overall carbon emissions. Looking at one of the largest carbon legislation systems worldwide (the EU ETS), carbon legislation systems mainly influence companies that operate in the manufacturing, transportation, and utilities sectors (European Union, 2015). The provided results in Table 8 show that on average for the manufacturing companies the presence of carbon legislation leads to a lower carbon reduction, indicating that the carbon reduction for these companies is not driven by governmental enforcement but by other incentives. As to the transportation and utilities companies, the results show that the presence of carbon legislation improves the carbon reduction.

Looking at the profitability of firms, as measured with the variable *ROA* and *ROE,* the results show that on average for most sectors firms that are registered in countries with carbon legislation perform better. As to the profitability indicator *ROS*, the profitability of firms that are registered in countries with or without carbon legislation differs per sector. Looking at the sector with the highest representation within the sample, the manufacturing sector, the results show that countries with carbon legislation have on average higher values for *ROA* and *ROE.* Countries with carbon legislation have a lower ROS on average, but also a higher median value. The variable *TOBIN* represents the stock market performance of firms. The results show that agricultural, construction, manufacturing, wholesale trade, financial services, services, and remaining firms in countries with carbon legislation have higher values for *TOBIN* implying that carbon legislation does not affect the market value of firms in these sectors. As to the liquidity ratio *CR* the results show that for the mining, transportation, wholesale trade, retail, services, and remaining sector firms that are registered in countries without carbon legislation perform better, which may suggest that the firms that are registered in a country with carbon legislation dip into their liquidity to repay the government for their emissions. Table 23 in Appendix 3 shows the descriptive statistics for the additional measurements *GDPGROWTH, CO2EMISSION,* and *ESG.*

To test whether there are significant differences between firms that are registered in countries with or without carbon legislation, we conduct two statistical analyses. The first test is the two-sided T-test for means to find out whether the mean of both groups is equal. The second test is the two-sided Mann–Whitney test for medians to see whether the median of both groups is equal. Both tests are conducted for the following variables: *DELTACO2, ROA, ROE, ROS, TOBIN, CR, GDPGROWTH, CO2EMISSION,* and *ESG.* The results are provided in Table 9. Firms that are registered in countries with carbon legislation have on average a higher lowering in emissions and the mean value is higher for those firms, as shown with the variable *DELTACO2* in Table 9. The T-test thus indicates that the firms that are registered in countries with carbon legislation have significantly higher carbon reduction on a 10% confidence interval (p-value $= 0.068$). The results for the Mann–Whitney test provide no evidence for a significant difference between both groups for the variable *DELTACO2* (p-value $= 0.345$). As to the financial performance indicators, the results of a two-sided T-test only show a significant difference in *ROS* between both groups, indicating that firms that are registered in countries with carbon legislation have on average a lower return on sales. The results for the Mann–Whitney test show that the median value for the financial performance measures *ROA, ROE,* and *TOBIN* shows significant differences between both groups. The results for the country level variables *GDPGROWTH* and *CO2EMISSION* show that countries with carbon legislation on average experience less economic growth measured as growth of GDP. The average emissions scaled by the country's GDP are relatively lower for countries with carbon legislation, implying that the implementation of carbon legislation reduces a country's overall emissions. The significant results for the variable *ESG* indicate that there are significant differences in mean and median values of both groups.

The overall results of this analysis show that firms that are registered in countries with carbon legislation have a higher level of carbon reduction, at a 10% confidence interval. In addition, the results of the performed *T*-test show that firms that are registered in countries without carbon legislation have a significantly better financial performance. The results of the Mann–Whitney test also show that the median value for the financial performance variables is higher for firms in countries with carbon legislation. Regarding the financial performance indicators ROA, ROE, ROS, Tobin's Q, and CR, firms in countries without carbon legislation perform better, when looking at the median values. The results finally show that countries with carbon legislation have lower overall emissions, but experience less economic growth. Also, in countries with carbon legislation firms tend to be more responsible.

5.2 Country Level Analysis on Overall Emissions

The results in Table 10 show that the average value for the variable *DELTACO2* is higher in more polluting countries, but among all countries, firms are reducing their overall emissions. The regression results supporting this analysis can be found in the Tables 24, 25, 26, 27 and 28 in Appendix 4. In this analysis, we created dummy variables for both country groups indicating the location of a firm in a country in either the top five or bottom five countries based on their overall emissions. The results also indicate that on average firms in Canada have the overall highest carbon reduction and firms in the Korean Republic have the lowest carbon reduction, followed by Australia. Looking at the corporate profitability, the results show that the firms in the countries with the lowest emissions tend to be more profitable on average, based on return on assets and return on equity, whereas firms in more polluting countries have on average a better return on sales. For the variable *ROA,* on average Danish companies have the highest mean values and Canadian firms have the lowest mean values. As to the variable *ROS*, firms in Hong Kong SAR have the highest values and Australian firms the lowest values. Looking at the results for *ROE*, we find that Danish companies have the highest values and Canadian firms the lowest values. The regression results in Table 26 in Appendix 4 provide no evidence for differences in profitability between both groups and the Other firms in the sample. Also, as to the stock market performance indicator *TOBIN* companies in less polluting countries tend to score better: companies in Denmark have the highest mean value and Korean firms have the lowest mean value. The regression results in Table 27 in Appendix 4 statistically support this claim. These regression results show that both groups have a positive coefficient for the variable *TOBIN* indicating that both country groups outperform the countries in the middle. The regression results further provide no evidence for a relation between inclusion in one of the country groups and liquidity. Looking at the liquidity of the firms, the results for the variable *CR* show that firms in more polluting countries tend to outperform firms in less polluting countries. Firms in Switzerland have the highest liquidity and firms in France have the lowest current ratio on average.

As to the country level variables, the results show that Sweden and South Africa have the lowest economic growth and the Korean Republic and Australia have the highest economic growth. Looking at the overall emissions within a country, measured with *CO2EMISSION*, the result show that countries with carbon legislation have lower overall emissions. The results for the variable *LEGAL* show that countries with lower emissions have on average more carbon legislation, indicating that carbon legislation does lead to an overall reduction in greenhouse gasses. The results of the variable *ESG* suggest that on average countries with lower emissions household firms with higher ESG scores.

Table 11 presents the results of a two-sided *T*-test for equality in means and Mann–Whitney test for equality in medians for both groups of countries. The results show that there are significant differences in means for the variables *ROA, ROE,* and *CR* on a 95% confidence level. These findings show that firms in less polluting countries have on average a better return on assets and return on equity and firms in more polluting countries have a better liquidity, measured with the current ratio. For the variables *DELTACO2, ROS,* and *TOBIN,* no significant differences are found, suggesting that there are no statistical differences between both country groups. The results of the Mann–Whitney test in Table 11 show that there is a significant difference in median for the variables *DELTACO2, ROE, ROS,* and *CR.* The results for *GDPGROWTH* indicate that countries with lower overall emissions experience less economic growth. The results for *CO2EMISSION* show that the difference in emissions for both groups is statistically significant. The significant values for *LEGAL* suggest that the presence of carbon legislation lowers a country's overall emissions. The results for *ESG* show that firms in countries with lower emissions are more responsible.

6 Conclusions

We confirm the general findings of earlier research in that carbon emissions reduction is either unrelated or positively related to corporate financial performance indicators and moreover, we show the differences between sectors and various groupings of countries on carbon reduction and firm performance. The sector level results indicate that the services sector shows a positive result in relation to the return on assets, the return on equity, the return on sales, and the current ratio, but a negative result in relation to Tobin's Q. Specifically, the agriculture, forestry, and fishing sector show either a negative or insignificant relationship with the performance variables. With the other sectors, the relationships are either contradictory or insignificant. These findings are confirmed by our regression results, which are only providing some statistical evidence for a negative relation with corporate financial performance for agricultural and mining firms.

The results from the country level analysis show that, on average, firms among every continent are reducing their carbon emissions. Firms registered in countries with carbon legislation have a slightly higher average level of carbon reduction. The results provide evidence for significant differences in financial performance between both country groups. For firms in the countries with the overall highest and lowest carbon emissions the results show limited statistical evidence for differences in carbon reduction between the groups. We find insignificant or conflicting effects of continent groupings on the financial performance indicators. In general, the effects found are insignificant.

Overall, our findings contribute to the existing literature on the relation between carbon reduction and financial performance, looking at sector and country differences. The results provide some further support for a positive relationship between carbon reduction and profitability and provide more insight in differences in carbon reduction and financial performance among sectors and countries. Our study can be extended by performing more in-depth sector-specific and country-specific analyses. Moreover, several other financial performance measures, such as Revenues, EBITDA, and EBIT, can be applied by researchers as well. We do control for endogeneity to some extent by performing an OLS regression. Follow-up studies might further the statistical analysis on the provided insight in countries and sectors differences. Finally, future research might focus on both new and non-financial performance indicators since existing studies mainly focus on traditional corporate financial performance indicators. It can be noted that corporate reporting of those non-financial indicators is also strongly promoted by the United Nations and the European Commission, but data availability is still remaining an issue. Besides implementing new variables, future research could also consider implementing carbon emission data from independent sources that are not related to regular financial databases.

Appendix 1: Regression Analysis with Inclusion of Sectors

See Tables 12, 13, 14, 15 and 16.

Appendix 2: Regression Analysis with Inclusion of Continents

See Tables 17, 18, 19, 20 and 21.

Appendix 3: Descriptive Statistics by Sector and Country (Groups), Additional Measurements

See Tables 22 and 23.

Table 12 Regression analysis on ROA

Dependent variable	ROA	ROA	ROA
Variable	Model 1	Model 2	Model 3
DELTACO2	– 31.7559***	– 31.8168***	– 66.2760*
	[7.3145]	[7.3349]	[34.4802]
DELTACO2^2	– 9020	– 8880	– 9580
	[6243.3670]	[6245.1541]	[6263.9008]
SIZE	0.0106***	0.0102***	0.0101***
	[0.0010]	[0.0010]	[0.0010]
LEVERAGE	– 0.0217**	– 0.0225**	– 0.0225**
	[0.0110]	[0.0110]	[0.0110]
DELTASALES	0.0640***	0.0645***	0.0645***
	[0.0060]	[0.0060]	[0.0060]
INTENSITY	– 0.0113***	– 0.0112***	– 0.0113***
	[0.0019]	[0.0019]	[0.0019]
GDPGROWTH	0.0063	0.0036	– 0.0032
	[0.0513]	[0.0511]	[0.0509]
CASHFLOW	0.1320***	0.1318***	0.1320***
	[0.0201]	[0.0200]	[0.0199]
CO2EMISSION		0.0190	0.0196
		[0.0252]	[0.0253]
ESG		0.0002***	0.0002***
		[0.0001]	[0.0001]
LEGAL		0.0011	0.0012
		[0.0030]	[0.0029]
(1) AGRICULTURE		– 0.0405***	– 0.0407***
		[0.0112]	[0.0111]
(2) MINING		– 0.0244*	– 0.0248*
		[0.0148]	[0.0148]
(3) CONSTRUCTION		– 0.0185*	– 0.0180*
		[0.0098]	[0.0096]
(4) MANUFACTURING		– 0.0087	– 0.0087
		[0.0076]	[0.0076]
(5) TRANSPORTATION		– 0.0068	– 0.0066
		[0.0125]	[0.0125]
(6) WHOLESALE TRADE		– 0.0099	– 0.0094
		[0.0091]	[0.0091]
(7) RETAIL		0.0078	0.0077
		[0.0168]	[0.0168]

(continued)

Table 12 (continued)

Dependent variable	ROA	ROA	ROA
(9) SERVICES		0.0112	0.0110
		[0.0153]	[0.0153]
(11) OTHER		– 0.0439**	– 0.0438**
		[0.0213]	[0.0211]
DELTAC02_X_ESG			0.8079*
			[0.4263]
DELTAC02_X_LEGAL			10.4208
			[18.6720]
DELTAC02_X_CO2			– 56.6007
			[46.3057]
CONSTANT	– 0.1729***	– 0.1735***	– 0.1741***
	[0.0267]	[0.0315]	[0.0316]
FIXED EFFECTS	Yes	Yes	Yes
Adjusted *R*-squared	0.4737	0.4749	0.4753
Observations	9265	9265	9265

Estimates of the OLS regressions for *ROA*. The included variables are as defined in the main text. The models use industry, year, and country fixed effects. Robust firm-level clustered standard errors are presented in square brackets. The symbols ***, **, * denote statistical significance at the 1%, 5%, and 10% levels

Appendix 4: Regression Analysis with Inclusion of Countries Emissions

See Tables 24, 25, 26, 27 and 28.

Table 13 Regression analysis on ROS

Dependent variable	ROS	ROS	ROS
Variable	Model 1	Model 2	Model 3
DELTACO2	– 78.2878**	– 78.0989**	– 420.4692*
	[36.5323]	[36.4607]	[248.6165]
DELTACO2^2	– 50,300	– 50,600	– 49,900
	[49,700]	[49,900]	[48,100]
SIZE	0.0099***	0.0099***	0.0099***
	[0.0018]	[0.0017]	[0.0017]
LEVERAGE	– 0.0901***	– 0.0896***	– 0.0904***
	[0.0251]	[0.0248]	[0.0246]
DELTASALES	0.0763***	0.0759***	0.0762***
	[0.0239]	[0.0239]	[0.0239]
INTENSITY	– 0.0214***	– 0.0214***	– 0.0214***
	[0.0032]	[0.0032]	[0.0032]
GDPGROWTH	– 0.1122	– 0.1139	– 0.1143
	[0.1641]	[0.1636]	[0.1640]
CASHFLOW	0.6838***	0.6839***	0.6846***
	[0.0506]	[0.0507]	[0.0500]
CO2EMISSION		0.1816	0.1880
		[0.1264]	[0.1276]
ESG		– 0.0000	– 0.0000
		[0.0002]	[0.0002]
LEGAL		0.0075	0.0069
		[0.0083]	[0.0078]
(1) AGRICULTURE		– 0.0631***	– 0.0637***
		[0.0221]	[0.0217]
(2) MINING		– 0.0611**	– 0.0617**
		[0.0248]	[0.0245]
(3) CONSTRUCTION		– 0.0290*	– 0.0295*
		[0.0170]	[0.0172]
(4) MANUFACTURING		– 0.0285**	– 0.0279**
		[0.0111]	[0.0112]
(5) TRANSPORTATION		– 0.0158	– 0.0159
		[0.0204]	[0.0203]
(6) WHOLESALE TRADE		– 0.0184	– 0.0186
		[0.0122]	[0.0124]
(7) RETAIL		– 0.0152	– 0.0151
		[0.0196]	[0.0200]

(continued)

Table 13 (continued)

Dependent variable	ROS	ROS	ROS
(9) SERVICES		– 0.0000	0.0001
		[0.0208]	[0.0209]
(11) OTHER		0.1595**	0.1586**
		[0.0631]	[0.0634]
DELTAC02_X_ESG			53.308
			[3.3611]
DELTAC02_X_LEGAL			– 60.941
			[62.3319]
DELTAC02_X_CO2			173.6231
			[168.6131]
CONSTANT	– 0.2803***	– 0.3293***	– 0.3367***
	[0.0792]	[0.1143]	[0.1154]
FIXED EFFECTS	Yes	Yes	Yes
Adjusted R-squared	0.8242	0.8242	0.8249
Observations	9265	9265	9265

Estimates of the OLS regressions for *ROS*. The included variables are as defined in the main text. The models use industry, year, and country fixed effects. Robust firm-level clustered standard errors are presented in square brackets. The symbols ***, **, * denote statistical significance at the 1%, 5%, and 10% levels

Table 14 Regression analysis on ROE

Dependent variable	ROE	ROE	ROE
Variable	Model 1	Model 2	Model 3
DELTACO2	– 67.2307**	– 67.1948**	– 116.4070
	[32.0351]	[32.1056]	[125.0350]
DELTACO2^2	– 59,500**	– 59,500**	– 59,100**
	[28,500]	[28,400]	[27,900]
SIZE	0.0340***	0.0326***	0.0326***
	[0.0048]	[0.0048]	[0.0048]
LEVERAGE	0.0916	0.0896	0.0897
	[0.0585]	[0.0585]	[0.0585]
DELTASALES	0.1269***	0.1277***	0.1274***
	[0.0227]	[0.0228]	[0.0229]
INTENSITY	– 0.0279***	– 0.0278***	– 0.0278***

(continued)

Table 14 (continued)

Dependent variable	ROE	ROE	ROE
	[0.0059]	[0.0059]	[0.0059]
GDPGROWTH	– 0.1490	– 0.1596	– 0.1616
	[0.2117]	[0.2124]	[0.2118]
CASHFLOW	0.3362***	0.3356***	0.3359***
	[0.0634]	[0.0633]	[0.0634]
CO2EMISSION		0.1755**	0.1762**
		[0.0802]	[0.0800]
ESG		0.0006*	0.0006*
		[0.0003]	[0.0003]
LEGAL		0.0122	0.0126
		[0.0126]	[0.0125]
(1) AGRICULTURE		– 0.0694**	– 0.0693**
		[0.0353]	[0.0353]
(2) MINING		– 0.1319**	– 0.1320**
		[0.0552]	[0.0553]
(3) CONSTRUCTION		– 0.0279	– 0.0280
		[0.0332]	[0.0331]
(4) MANUFACTURING		– 0.0196	– 0.0201
		[0.0256]	[0.0256]
(5) TRANSPORTATION		– 0.0212	– 0.0214
		[0.0307]	[0.0307]
(6) WHOLESALE TRADE		– 0.0029	– 0.0032
		[0.0254]	[0.0254]
(7) RETAIL		– 0.0132	– 0.0137
		[0.0616]	[0.0616]
(9) SERVICES		0.0047	0.0041
		[0.0767]	[0.0767]
(11) OTHER		– 0.0306	– 0.0309
		[0.0318]	[0.0317]
DELTAC02_X_ESG			0.0477
			[1.9778]
DELTAC02_X_LEGAL			469.072
			[77.3637]
DELTAC02_X_CO2			396.869
			[180.2594]

(continued)

Table 14 (continued)

Dependent variable	ROE	ROE	ROE
CONSTANT	– 0.7536***	– 0.7841***	– 0.7832***
	[0.1208]	[0.1339]	[0.1340]
FIXED EFFECTS	Yes	Yes	Yes
Adjusted R-squared	0.2035	0.2040	0.2038
Observations	9265	9265	9265

Estimates of the OLS regressions for *ROE*. The included variables are as defined in the main text. The models use industry, year, and country fixed effects. Robust firm-level clustered standard errors are presented in square brackets. The symbols ***, **, * denote statistical significance at the 1%, 5%, and 10% levels

Table 15 Regression analysis on TOBIN

Dependent variable	TOBIN	TOBIN	TOBIN
Variable	Model 1	Model 2	Model 3
DELTACO2	– 174.3528	– 176.8120	– 462.5821
	[130.1209]	[129.9563]	[826.8382]
DELTACO2^2	291,000**	295,000**	279,000*
	[147,000]	[147,000]	[148,000]
SIZE	0.3044***	0.3101***	0.3092***
	[0.0256]	[0.0262]	[0.0261]
LEVERAGE	0.6971**	0.7004***	0.7038***
	[0.2705]	[0.2700]	[0.2705]
DELTASALES	0.1957	0.1972*	0.1956*
	[0.1194]	[0.1190]	[0.1188]
INTENSITY	– 0.0646***	– 0.0650***	– 0.0654***
	[0.0137]	[0.0137]	[0.0135]
GDPGROWTH	2.2703**	2.3406**	2.1651**
	[0.9520]	[0.9552]	[0.9401]
CASHFLOW	0.7730***	0.7749***	0.7787***
	[0.1500]	[0.1500]	[0.1487]
CO2EMISSION		2.6519***	2.6535***
		[0.8503]	[0.8397]
ESG		– 0.0024	– 0.0023
		[0.0017]	[0.0017]
LEGAL		– 0.1473***	– 0.1405***
		[0.0534]	[0.0527]

(continued)

Table 15 (continued)

Dependent variable	TOBIN	TOBIN	TOBIN
(1) AGRICULTURE		– 2.6998***	– 2.7021***
		[0.8482]	[0.8480]
(2) MINING		0.4203	0.4126
		[0.5937]	[0.5932]
(3) CONSTRUCTION		– 0.6590***	– 0.6451***
		[0.1606]	[0.1605]
(4) MANUFACTURING		– 0.4159***	– 0.4198***
		[0.1367]	[0.1372]
(5) TRANSPORTATION		– 1.0202***	– 1.0162***
		[0.2660]	[0.2656]
(6) WHOLESALE TRADE		– 1.3629***	– 1.3524***
		[0.2906]	[0.2857]
(7) RETAIL		– 0.0474	– 0.0541
		[0.3764]	[0.3775]
(9) SERVICES		– 0.3932***	– 0.4020***
		[0.1930]	[0.1932]
(11) OTHER		– 1.2785***	– 1.2764***
		[0.3403]	[0.3329]
DELTAC02_X_ESG			65.853
			[8.4203]
DELTAC02_X_LEGAL			561.3319
			[375.6054]
DELTAC02_X_CO2			– 1570
			[1770.3055]
CONSTANT	– 6.3711***	– 7.3371***	– 7.3255***
	[0.7133]	[0.9026]	[0.8971]
FIXED EFFECTS	Yes	Yes	Yes
Adjusted R-squared	0.4384	0.4392	0.4399
Observations	9265	9265	9265

Estimates of the OLS regressions for *TOBIN*. The included variables are as defined in the main text. The models use industry, year, and country fixed effects. Robust firm-level clustered standard errors are presented in square brackets. The symbols ***, **, * denote statistical significance at the 1, 5, and 10% levels

Table 16 Regression analysis on CR

Dependent variable	CR	CR	CR
Variable	Model 1	Model 2	Model 3
DELTACO2	117.9604	119.8409	355.6842
	[80.4411]	[80.3802]	[443.6451]
DELTACO2^2	45,300	41,700	38,100
	[87,700]	[87,300]	[87,300]
SIZE	− 0.0216*	− 0.0176	− 0.0175
	[0.0116]	[0.0119]	[0.0119]
LEVERAGE	− 0.7259***	− 0.7159***	− 0.7165***
	[0.1580]	[0.1574]	[0.1574]
DELTASALES	− 0.0055	− 0.0121	− 0.0109
	[0.0669]	[0.0663]	[0.0664]
INTENSITY	− 0.0148**	− 0.0150**	− 0.0149**
	[0.0066]	[0.0066]	[0.0066]
GDPGROWTH	− 0.5644	− 0.5570	− 0.5607
	[0.7016]	[0.7020]	[0.7026]
CASHFLOW	0.1324**	0.1342**	0.1329**
	[0.0646]	[0.0647]	[0.0646]
CO2EMISSION		− 0.4147	− 0.4183
		[0.4715]	[0.4727]
ESG		− 0.0019*	− 0.0019*
		[0.0011]	[0.0011]
LEGAL		0.0483	0.0468
		[0.0336]	[0.0335]
(1) AGRICULTURE		0.2625	0.2620
		[0.3892]	[0.3883]
(2) MINING		1.9483***	1.9481***
		[0.2713]	[0.2724]
(3) CONSTRUCTION		0.9808***	0.9826***
		[0.2073]	[0.2070]
(4) MANUFACTURING		2.2900***	2.2921***
		[0.0997]	[0.0996]
(5) TRANSPORTATION		0.9693***	0.9708***
		[0.2332]	[0.2333]
(6) WHOLESALE TRADE		0.9849***	0.9869***
		[0.1021]	[0.1020]
(7) RETAIL		0.3390***	0.3409***
		[0.1294]	[0.1292]

(continued)

Table 16 (continued)

Dependent variable	CR	CR	CR
(9) SERVICES		0.3131***	0.3153***
		[0.0780]	[0.0777]
(11) OTHER		1.9609***	1.9628***
		[0.4011]	[0.4011]
DELTAC02_X_ESG			0.4445
			[5.7339]
DELTAC02_X_LEGAL			– 210.6681
			[201.9915]
DELTAC02_X_CO2			– 342.7303
			[512.5218]
CONSTANT	1.4722***	1.6007***	1.5963***
	[0.3688]	[0.4828]	[0.4833]
FIXED EFFECTS	Yes	Yes	Yes
Adjusted *R*-squared	0.4056	0.4065	0.4064
Observations	9265	9265	9265

Estimates of the OLS regressions for *CR*. The included variables are as defined in the main text. The models use industry, year, and country fixed effects. Robust firm-level clustered standard errors are presented in square brackets. The symbols ***, **, * denote statistical significance at the 1%, 5%, and 10% levels

Table 17 Regression analysis on ROA

Dependent variable	ROA	ROA	ROA
Variable	Model 1	Model 2	Model 3
DELTACO2	– 31.7559***	– 31.8168***	– 66.2760*
	[7.3145]	[7.3349]	[34.4802]
DELTACO2^2	– 9020	– 8880	– 9580
	[6243.3670]	[6245.1541]	[6263.9008]
SIZE	0.0106***	0.0102***	0.0101***
	[0.0010]	[0.0010]	[0.0010]
LEVERAGE	– 0.0217**	– 0.0225**	– 0.0225**
	[0.0110]	[0.0110]	[0.0110]
DELTASALES	0.0640***	0.0645***	0.0645***
	[0.0060]	[0.0060]	[0.0060]
CAPINT	– 0.0113***	– 0.0112***	– 0.0113***
	[0.0019]	[0.0019]	[0.0019]

(continued)

Table 17 (continued)

Dependent variable	ROA	ROA	ROA
CASHFLOW	0.1320***	0.1318***	0.1320***
	[0.0201]	[0.0200]	[0.0199]
GDPGROWTH	0.0063	0.0036	– 0.0032
	[0.0513]	[0.0511]	[0.0509]
CO2EMISSION		– 1.3915***	– 1.4147***
		[0.3572]	[0.3578]
ESG		0.0002***	0.0002***
		[0.0001]	[0.0001]
LEGAL		0.0011	0.0012
		[0.0030]	[0.0029]
EUROPE		– 0.9946***	– 1.0107***
		[0.2539]	[0.2543]
NORTH AMERICA		– 0.7742***	– 0.7873***
		[0.2060]	[0.2064]
ASIA		– 0.6249***	– 0.6349***
		[0.1618]	[0.1621]
DELTAC02_X_ESG			0.8079*
			[0.4263]
DELTAC02_X_LEGAL			104.208
			[18.6720]
DELTAC02_X_CO2			– 56.6007
			[46.3057]
CONSTANT	– 0.1729***	1.0243***	1.0440***
	[0.0267]	[0.3019]	[0.3023]
FIXED EFFECTS	Yes	Yes	Yes
Adjusted R-squared	0.4737	0.4749	0.4753
Observations	9265	9265	9265

Estimates of the OLS regressions for *ROA*. The included variables are as defined in the main text. The models use industry, year, and country fixed effects. Robust firm-level clustered standard errors are presented in square brackets. The symbols ***, **, * denote statistical significance at the 1%, 5%, and 10% levels

Table 18 Regression analysis on ROS

Dependent variable	ROS	ROS	ROS
Variable	Model 1	Model 2	Model 3
DELTACO2	– 78.2878**	– 78.0989**	– 420.4692*
	[36.5323]	[36.4607]	[248.6165]
DELTACO2^2	– 50,300	– 50,600	– 49,900
	[49,700]	[49,900]	[48,100]
SIZE	0.0099***	0.0099***	0.0099***
	[0.0018]	[0.0017]	[0.0017]
LEVERAGE	– 0.0901***	– 0.0896***	– 0.0904***
	[0.0251]	[0.0248]	[0.0246]
DELTASALES	0.0763***	0.0759***	0.0762***
	[0.0239]	[0.0239]	[0.0239]
CAPINT	– 0.0214***	– 0.0214***	– 0.0214***
	[0.0032]	[0.0032]	[0.0032]
CASHFLOW	0.6838***	0.6839***	0.6846***
	[0.0506]	[0.0507]	[0.0500]
GDPGROWTH	– 0.1122	– 0.1139	– 0.1143
	[0.1641]	[0.1636]	[0.1640]
CO2EMISSION		– 3.1160*	– 3.1591*
		[1.7273]	[1.7412]
ESG		– 0.0000	– 0.0000
		[0.0002]	[0.0002]
LEGAL		0.0075	0.0069
		[0.0083]	[0.0078]
EUROPE		– 2.2360*	– 2.2683*
		[1.2269]	[1.2368]
NORTH AAERICA		– 1.8101*	– 1.8373*
		[1.0144]	[1.0227]
ASIA		– 1.4163*	– 1.4366*
		[0.7825]	[0.7888]
DELTAC02_X_ESG			53,308,00
			[3.3611]
DELTAC02_X_LEGAL			– 6.0941
			[62.3319]
DELTAC02_X_CO2			173.6231
			[168.6131]
CONSTANT	– 0.2803***	2.4711*	2.5058*
	[0.0792]	[1.4665]	[1.4782]

(continued)

Table 18 (continued)

Dependent variable	ROS	ROS	ROS
FIXED EFFECTS	Yes	Yes	Yes
Adjusted R-square	0.8242	0.8242	0.8249
Observations	9265	9265	9265

Estimates of the OLS regressions for *ROS*. The included variables are as defined in the main text. The models use industry, year, and country fixed effects. Robust firm-level clustered standard errors are presented in square brackets. The symbols ***, **, * denote statistical significance at the 1%, 5%, and 10% levels

Table 19 Regression analysis on ROE

Dependent variable	ROE	ROE	ROE
Variable	Model 1	Model 2	Model 3
DELTACO2	– 67.2307**	– 67.1948**	– 116.4070
	[32.0351]	[32.1056]	[125.0350]
DELTACO2^2	– 59,500**	– 59,500**	– 59,100**
	[28,500]	[28,400]	[27,900]
SIZE	0.0340***	0.0326***	0.0326***
	[0.0048]	[0.0048]	[0.0048]
LEVERAGE	0.0916	0.0896	0.0897
	[0.0585]	[0.0585]	[0.0585]
DELTASALES	0.1269***	0.1277***	0.1274***
	[0.0227]	[0.0228]	[0.0229]
CAPINT	– 0.0279***	– 0.0278***	– 0.0278***
	[0.0059]	[0.0059]	[0.0059]
CASHFLOW	0.3362***	0.3356***	0.3359***
	[0.0634]	[0.0633]	[0.0634]
GDPGROWTH	– 0.1490	– 0.1596	– 0.1616
	[0.2117]	[0.2124]	[0.2118]
CO2EMISSION		– 5.0405***	– 5.0278***
		[1.0264]	[1.0245]
ESG		0.0006*	0.0006*
		[0.0003]	[0.0003]
LEGAL		0.0122	0.0126
		[0.0126]	[0.0125]
EUROPE		– 3.6043***	– 3.5955***
		[0.7302]	[0.7288]

(continued)

Table 19 (continued)

Dependent variable	ROE	ROE	ROE
NORTH AMERICA		− 2.8631***	− 2.8566***
		[0.5990]	[0.5977]
ASIA		− 2.2777***	− 2.2722***
		[0.4666]	[0.4658]
DELTAC02_X_ESG			0.0477
			[1.9778]
DELTAC02_X_LEGAL			46.9072
			[77.3637]
DELTAC02_X_CO2			39.6869
			[180.2594]
CONSTANT	− 0.7536***	3.6455***	3.6363***
	[0.1208]	[0.8619]	[0.8595]
FIXED EFFECTS	Yes	Yes	Yes
Adjusted R-squared	0.2035	0.2040	0.2038
Observations	9265	9265	9265

Table 20 Regression analysis on TOBIN

Dependent variable	TOBIN	TOBIN	TOBIN
Variable	Model 1	Model 2	Model 3
DELTACO2	− 174.3528	− 176.8120	− 462.5821
	[130.1209]	[129.9563]	[826.8382]
DELTACO2^2	291,000**	295,000**	279,000*
	[147,000]	[147,000]	[148,000]
SIZE	0.3044***	0.3101***	0.3092***
	[0.0256]	[0.0262]	[0.0261]
LEVERAGE	0.6971**	0.7004***	0.7038***
	[0.2705]	[0.2700]	[0.2705]
DELTASALES	0.1957	0.1972*	0.1956*
	[0.1194]	[0.1190]	[0.1188]
CAPINT	− 0.0646***	− 0.0650***	− 0.0654***
	[0.0137]	[0.0137]	[0.0135]
CASHFLOW	0.7730***	0.7749***	0.7787***
	[0.1500]	[0.1500]	[0.1487]
GDPGROWTH	2.2703**	2.3406**	2.1651**
	[0.9520]	[0.9552]	[0.9401]

(continued)

Table 20 (continued)

Dependent variable	TOBIN	TOBIN	TOBIN
CO2EMISSION		– 58.3481***	– 58.7270***
		[9.7317]	[9.6785]
ESG		– 0.0024	– 0.0023
		[0.0017]	[0.0017]
LEGAL		– 0.1473***	– 0.1405***
		[0.0534]	[0.0527]
EUROPE		– 42.0563***	– 42.3136***
		[6.9395]	[6.9052]
NORTH AMERICA		– 33.4838***	– 33.6928***
		[5.6833]	[5.6535]
ASIA		– 26.7722***	– 26.9317***
		[4.4347]	[4.4140]
DELTAC02_X_ESG			6.5853
			[8.4203]
DELTAC02_X_LEGAL			561.3319
			[375.6054]
DELTAC02_X_CO2			– 15700
			[1770.3055]
CONSTANT	– 6.3711***	44.4664***	44.8012***
	[0.7133]	[8.2443]	[8.1957]
FIXED EFFECTS	Yes	Yes	Yes
Adjusted R-squared	0.4384	0.4392	0.4399
Observations	9265	9265	9265

Estimates of the OLS regressions for *TOBIN*. The included variables are as defined in the main text. The models use industry, year, and country fixed effects. Robust firm-level clustered standard errors are presented in square brackets. The symbols ***, **, * denote statistical significance at the 1, 5, and 10% levels

Table 21 Regression analysis on CR

Dependent variable	CR	CR	CR
Variable	Model 1	Model 2	Model 3
DELTACO2	117.9604	119.8409	355.6842
	[80.4411]	[80.3802]	[443.6451]
DELTACO2^2	45,300	41,700	38,100
	[87,700]	[87,300]	[87,300]
SIZE	– 0.0216*	– 0.0176	– 0.0175

(continued)

Table 21 (continued)

Dependent variable	CR	CR	CR
	[0.0116]	[0.0119]	[0.0119]
LEVERAGE	– 0.7259***	– 0.7159***	– 0.7165***
	[0.1580]	[0.1574]	[0.1574]
DELTASALES	– 0.0055	– 0.0121	– 0.0109
	[0.0669]	[0.0663]	[0.0664]
CAPINT	– 0.0148**	– 0.0150**	– 0.0149**
	[0.0066]	[0.0066]	[0.0066]
CASHFLOW	0.1324**	0.1342**	0.1329**
	[0.0646]	[0.0647]	[0.0646]
GDPGROWTH	– 0.5644	– 0.5570	– 0.5607
	[0.7016]	[0.7020]	[0.7026]
CO2EMISSION		– 0.1238	– 0.2261
		[7.6934]	[7.7105]
ESG		– 0.0019*	– 0.0019*
		[0.0011]	[0.0011]
LEGAL		0.0483	0.0468
		[0.0336]	[0.0335]
EUROPE		– 0.1200	– 0.1906
		[5.4659]	[5.4780]
NORTH AMERICA		0.1597	0.1055
		[4.4122]	[4.4221]
ASIA		0.1878	0.1438
		[3.4850]	[3.4928]
DELTAC02_X_ESG			0.4445
			[5.7339]
DELTAC02_X_LEGAL			– 210.6681
			[201.9915]
DELTAC02_X_CO2			– 342.7303
			[512.5218]
CONSTANT	1.4722***	1.3536	1.4331
	[0.3688]	[6.5309]	[6.5455]
FIXED EFFECTS	Yes	Yes	Yes
Adjusted *R*-squared	0.4056	0.4065	0.4064
Observations	9265	9265	9265

Estimates of the OLS regressions for *CR*. The included variables are as defined in the main text. The models use industry, year, and country fixed effects. Robust firm-level clustered standard errors are presented in square brackets. The symbols ***, **, * denote statistical significance at the 1%, 5%, and 10% levels

Table 22 Descriptive statistics by continent by sector (additional measurements)

Continent/industry	*N*	GDPGROWTH	CO2EMISSION	LEGAL	ESG
Europe					
(2) Mining	211	0.018	0.249	0.976	48.757
(3) Construction	143	0.014	0.229	1.000	56.050
(4) Manufacturing	1995	0.014	0.218	0.964	58.531
(5) Transportation	755	0.013	0.231	0.977	59.373
(6) Wholesale trade	119	0.015	0.231	1.000	54.840
(7) Retail	314	0.014	0.227	1.000	56.483
(8) Financial services	1	0.013	0.235	1.000	33.662
(9) Services	492	0.015	0.225	0.998	52.642
(10) Other	68	0.021	0.252	0.971	56.195
Asia					
(1) Agriculture	2	0.037	0.346	0.000	40.927
(2) Mining	58	0.038	0.345	0.241	56.486
(3) Construction	92	0.016	0.359	0.641	54.325
(4) Manufacturing	1705	0.014	0.303	0.581	54.720
(5) Transportation	350	0.031	0.283	0.277	53.428
(6) Wholesale trade	37	0.013	0.310	0.892	57.204
(7) Retail	34	0.022	0.359	0.765	52.070
(9) Services	115	0.016	0.276	0.539	59.982
(10) Other	57	0.033	0.250	0.246	49.882
Northern America					
(1) Agriculture	15	0.019	0.396	0.733	41.320
(2) Mining	299	0.019	0.407	0.485	56.382
(3) Construction	7	0.027	0.141	0.000	41.266
(4) Manufacturing	843	0.020	0.376	0.752	55.076
(5) Transportation	159	0.020	0.380	0.453	53.452
(6) Wholesale trade	44	0.020	0.404	0.705	49.400
(7) Retail	126	0.021	0.393	0.778	59.088
(8) Financial services	19	0.019	0.415	0.632	46.641
(9) Services	173	0.021	0.396	0.786	54.935
(10) Other	6	0.025	0.381	0.167	58.812
Oceania					
(2) Mining	136	0.031	0.449	0.706	51.271
(3) Construction	2	0.032	0.474	0.500	48.601
(4) Manufacturing	192	0.027	0.459	0.734	49.015
(5) Transportation	133	0.027	0.431	0.782	51.227
(6) Wholesale trade	9	0.027	0.409	0.556	40.269

(continued)

Table 22 (continued)

Continent/industry	*N*	GDPGROWTH	CO2EMISSION	LEGAL	ESG
(7) Retail	38	0.028	0.443	0.816	69.900
(9) Services	79	0.027	0.464	0.886	54.253
(10) Other	5	0.028	0.474	1.000	30.294
Other					
(1) Agriculture	6	0.010	0.849	0.167	59.928
(2) Mining	90	0.014	0.781	0.100	59.506
(3) Construction	24	0.012	0.849	0.167	41.248
(4) Manufacturing	129	0.017	0.691	0.202	59.031
(5) Transportation	73	0.013	0.534	0.205	50.399
(6) Wholesale trade	3	0.012	0.849	0.000	37.928
(7) Retail	45	0.011	0.819	0.178	56.013
(9) Services	43	0.010	0.796	0.209	49.664
(10) Other	19	0.013	0.849	0.105	44.116

The descriptive statistics of mean values of the full sample with 9265 observations, by continent and by sector. The presented variables are *DELTACO2* to measure the change in carbon emissions compared to year $t - 1$ and *ROA, ROS, ROE, TOBIN,* and *CR* to measure the firm's financial performance

Table 23 Descriptive statistics by sector on countries without or with carbon legislation—moderators

Without legislation	Value	*N*	GDPGROWTH	CO2EMISSION	ESG
(1) Agriculture, forestry, and fishing	Mean	11	0.019	0.593	48.594
	Median	11	0.018	0.396	47.981
(2) Mining	Mean	324	0.024	0.494	57.745
	Median	324	0.022	0.436	55.728
(3) Construction	Mean	61	0.023	0.567	47.655
	Median	61	0.018	0.751	48.641
(4) Manufacturing	Mean	1149	0.019	0.366	53.941
	Median	1149	0.020	0.285	53.511
(5) Transportation	Mean	444	0.030	0.352	53.920
	Median	444	0.028	0.285	55.716
(6) Wholesale trade	Mean	24	0.021	0.501	41.894
	Median	24	0.020	0.436	38.728
(7) Retail	Mean	80	0.021	0.613	57.608
	Median	80	0.019	0.613	56.891

(continued)

Table 23 (continued)

Without legislation	Value	*N*	GDPGROWTH	CO2EMISSION	ESG
(8) Financial services	Mean	7	0.020	0.436	50.662
	Median	7	0.020	0.436	50.763
(9) Services	Mean	134	0.018	0.463	56.333
	Median	134	0.018	0.436	56.889
(10) Other	Mean	67	0.031	0.399	50.605
	Median	67	0.028	0.285	53.628
With legislation	Value	*N*	GDPGROWTH	CO2EMISSION	ESG
(1) Agriculture, forestry, and fishing	Mean	12	0.017	0.434	43.890
	Median	12	0.022	0.396	37.181
(2) Mining	Mean	470	0.020	0.352	51.152
	Median	470	0.022	0.396	50.517
(3) Construction	Mean	207	0.013	0.259	55.469
	Median	207	0.015	0.235	55.140
(4) Manufacturing	Mean	3715	0.015	0.276	56.943
	Median	3715	0.017	0.285	57.043
(5) Transportation	Mean	1026	0.014	0.267	57.093
	Median	1026	0.018	0.235	58.108
(6) Wholesale trade	Mean	188	0.015	0.271	54.718
	Median	188	0.018	0.235	56.512
(7) Retail	Mean	477	0.016	0.289	57.693
	Median	477	0.019	0.235	58.081
(8) Financial services	Mean	13	0.019	0.390	43.478
	Median	13	0.017	0.396	41.873
(9) Services	Mean	768	0.017	0.286	53.613
	Median	768	0.019	0.235	53.094
(10) Other	Mean	88	0.020	0.289	52.461
	Median	88	0.015	0.265	53.606
Total		9265			
	Mean		0.017	0.434	43.890
	Median		0.022	0.396	37.181

Full sample descriptive statistics of mean and median values with 9265 observations, divided in firms that are registered in countries with and without carbon legislation by sector. The presented variables are *GDPGROWTH* to measure the financial development of a country, *CO2EMISSION* to measure the overall carbon emissions of a country scaled by the country's GDP and *ESG* to represent the average responsibility score of the firms within a country

Table 24 Regression analysis on ROA

Dependent variable	ROA	ROA	ROA
Variable	Model 1	Model 2	Model 3
DELTACO2	– 31.7559***	– 31.8168***	– 66.2760*
	[7.3145]	[7.3349]	[34.4802]
DELTACO2^2	– 9020	– 8880	– 9580
	[6243.3670]	[6245.1541]	[6263.9008]
SIZE	0.0106***	0.0102***	0.0101***
	[0.0010]	[0.0010]	[0.0010]
LEVERAGE	– 0.0217**	– 0.0225**	– 0.0225**
	[0.0110]	[0.0110]	[0.0110]
DELTASALES	0.0640***	0.0645***	0.0645***
	[0.0060]	[0.0060]	[0.0060]
CAPINT	– 0.0113***	– 0.0112***	– 0.0113***
	[0.0019]	[0.0019]	[0.0019]
CASHFLOW	0.0063	0.0036	– 0.0032
	[0.0513]	[0.0511]	[0.0509]
GDPGROWTH	0.1320***	0.1318***	0.1320***
	[0.0201]	[0.0200]	[0.0199]
CO2EMISSION		– 0.0118	– 0.0129
		[0.0178]	[0.0178]
ESG		0.0002***	0.0002***
		[0.0001]	[0.0001]
LEGAL		0.0011	0.0012
		[0.0030]	[0.0029]
COUNTRYTOP5		0.0169	0.0178
		[0.0136]	[0.0136]
COUNTRYBOTTOM5		0.0021	0.0026
		[0.0143]	[0.0143]
DELTAC02_X_ESG			104.208
			[18.6720]
DELTAC02_X_LEGAL			-566.007
			[46.3057]
DELTAC02_X_CO2			-566.007
			[46.3057]
CONSTANT	-0.1729***	-0.1643***	-0.1643***
	[0.0267]	[0.0277]	[0.0277]

(continued)

Table 24 (continued)

Dependent variable	ROA	ROA	ROA
FIXED EFFECTS	Yes	Yes	Yes
Adjusted R-squared	0.4737	0.4749	0.4753
Observations	9265	9265	9265

Estimates of the OLS regressions for *ROA*. The included variables are as defined in the main text. The models use industry, year, and country fixed effects. Robust firm-level clustered standard errors are presented in square brackets. The symbols ***, **, * denote statistical significance at the 1, 5, and 10% levels

Table 25 Regression analysis on ROS

Dependent variable	ROS	ROS	ROS
Variable	Model 1	Model 2	Model 3
DELTACO2	– 78.2878**	– 78.0989**	– 420.4692*
	[36.5323]	[36.4607]	[248.6165]
DELTACO2^2	– 50,300	– 50,600	– 49,900
	[49,700]	[49,900]	[48,100]
SIZE	0.0099***	0.0099***	0.0099***
	[0.0018]	[0.0017]	[0.0017]
LEVERAGE	– 0.0901***	– 0.0896***	– 0.0904***
	[0.0251]	[0.0248]	[0.0246]
DELTASALES	0.0763***	0.0759***	0.0762***
	[0.0239]	[0.0239]	[0.0239]
CAPINT	– 0.0214***	– 0.0214***	– 0.0214***
	[0.0032]	[0.0032]	[0.0032]
CASHFLOW	– 0.1122	– 0.1139	– 0.1143
	[0.1641]	[0.1636]	[0.1640]
GDPGROWTH	0.6838***	0.6839***	0.6846***
	[0.0506]	[0.0507]	[0.0500]
CO2EMISSION		0.0111	0.0128
		[0.0325]	[0.0324]
ESG		– 0.0000	– 0.0000
		[0.0002]	[0.0002]
LEGAL		0.0075	0.0069
		[0.0083]	[0.0078]
COUNTRYTOP5		0.0781	0.0803
		[0.0696]	[0.0702]

(continued)

Table 25 (continued)

Dependent variable	ROS	ROS	ROS
COUNTRYBOTTOM5			53.308
			[3.3611]
DELTAC02_X_ESG			53.308
			[3.3611]
DELTAC02_X_LEGAL			– 60.941
			[62.3319]
DELTAC02_X_CO2			173.6231
			[168.6131]
CONSTANT	– 0.2803***	– 0.2781***	– 0.2840***
	[0.0792]	[0.0797]	[0.0804]
FIXED EFFECTS	Yes	Yes	Yes
Adjusted *R*-square	0.8242	0.8242	0.8249
Observations	9265	9265	9265

Estimates of the OLS regressions for *ROS*. The included variables are as defined in the main text. The models use industry, year, and country fixed effects. Robust firm-level clustered standard errors are presented in square brackets. The symbols ***, **, * denote statistical significance at the 1, 5, and 10% levels

Table 26 Regression analysis on ROE

Dependent variable	ROE	ROE	ROE
Variable	Model 1	Model 2	Model 3
DELTACO2	– 67.2307**	– 67.1948**	– 116.4070
	[32.0351]	[32.1056]	[125.0350]
DELTACO2^2	– 59,500**	– 59,500**	– 59,100**
	[28,500]	[28,400]	[27,900]
SIZE	0.0340***	0.0326***	0.0326***
	[0.0048]	[0.0048]	[0.0048]
LEVERAGE	0.0916	0.0896	0.0897
	[0.0585]	[0.0585]	[0.0585]
DELTASALES	0.1269***	0.1277***	0.1274***
	[0.0227]	[0.0228]	[0.0229]
CAPINT	– 0.0279***	– 0.0278***	– 0.0278***
	[0.0059]	[0.0059]	[0.0059]
CASHFLOW	– 0.1490	– 0.1596	– 0.1616
	[0.2117]	[0.2124]	[0.2118]
GDPGROWTH	0.3362***	0.3356***	0.3359***
	[0.0634]	[0.0633]	[0.0634]

(continued)

Table 26 (continued)

Dependent variable	ROE	ROE	ROE
CO2EMISSION		0.0111	0.0128
		[0.0325]	[0.0324]
ESG		– 0.0000	– 0.0000
		[0.0002]	[0.0002]
LEGAL		0.0075	0.0069
		[0.0083]	[0.0078]
COUNTRYTOP5		0.0936	0.0962
		[0.0698]	[0.0704]
COUNTRYBOTTOM5		0.0781	0.0803
		[0.0696]	[0.0702]
DELTAC02_X_ESG			53.308
			[3.3611]
DELTAC02_X_LEGAL			– 60.941
			[62.3319]
DELTAC02_X_CO2			396.869
			[180.2594]
CONSTANT	– 0.7536***	– 0.7279***	– 0.7269***
	[0.1208]	[0.1256]	[0.1258]
FIXED EFFECTS	Yes	Yes	Yes
Adjusted *R*-squared	0.2035	0.2040	0.2038
Observations	9265	9265	9265

Estimates of the OLS regressions for *ROE*. The included variables are as defined in the main text. The models use industry, year, and country fixed effects. Robust firm-level clustered standard errors are presented in square brackets. The symbols ***, **, * denote statistical significance at the 1, 5, and 10% levels

Table 27 Regression analysis on TOBIN

Dependent variable	TOBIN	TOBIN	TOBIN
Variable	Model 1	Model 2	Model 3
DELTACO2	– 174.3528	– 176.8120	– 462.5821
	[130.1209]	[129.9563]	[826.8382]
DELTACO2^2	291,000**	295,000**	279,0005*
	[147,000]	[147,000]	[148,000]
SIZE	0.3044***	0.3101***	0.3092***
	[0.0256]	[0.0262]	[0.0261]

(continued)

Table 27 (continued)

Dependent variable	TOBIN	TOBIN	TOBIN
LEVERAGE	0.6971**	0.7004***	0.7038***
	[0.2705]	[0.2700]	[0.2705]
DELTASALES	0.1957	0.1972*	0.1956*
	[0.1194]	[0.1190]	[0.1188]
CAPINT	– 0.0646***	– 0.0650***	– 0.0654***
	[0.0137]	[0.0137]	[0.0135]
CASHFLOW	2.2703**	2.3406**	2.1651**
	[0.9520]	[0.9552]	[0.9401]
GDPGROWTH	0.7730***	0.7749***	0.7787***
	[0.1500]	[0.1500]	[0.1487]
CO2EMISSION		0.7612	0.7344
		[0.7051]	[0.6915]
ESG		– 0.0024	– 0.0023
		[0.0017]	[0.0017]
LEGAL		– 0.1473***	– 0.1405***
		[0.0534]	[0.0527]
COUNTRYTOP5		1.0378***	1.0534***
		[0.3869]	[0.3832]
COUNTRYBOTTOM5		0.9552**	0.9636**
		[0.4060]	[0.4028]
DELTAC02_X_ESG			561.3319
			[375.6054]
DELTAC02_X_LEGAL			– 1570
			[1770.3055]
DELTAC02_X_CO2			– 15700
			[1770.3055]
CONSTANT	– 6.3711***	– 6.7693***	– 6.7492***
	[0.7133]	[0.8177]	[0.8122]
FIXED EFFECTS	Yes	Yes	Yes
Adjusted *R*-squared	0.4384	0.4392	0.4399
Observations	9265	9265	9265

Estimates of the OLS regressions for *TOBIN*. The included variables are as defined in the main text. The models use industry, year, and country fixed effects. Robust firm-level clustered standard errors are presented in square brackets. The symbols ***, **, * denote statistical significance at the 1, 5, and 10% levels

Table 28 Regression analysis on CR

Dependent variable	CR	CR	CR
Variable	Model 1	Model 2	Model 3
DELTACO2	117.9604	119.8409	355.6842
	[80.4411]	[80.3802]	[443.6451]
DELTACO2^2	45,300	41,700	38,100
	[87,700]	[87,300]	[87,300]
SIZE	– 0.0216*	– 0.0176	– 0.0175
	[0.0116]	[0.0119]	[0.0119]
LEVERAGE	– 0.7259***	– 0.7159***	– 0.7165***
	[0.1580]	[0.1574]	[0.1574]
DELTASALES	– 0.0055	– 0.0121	– 0.0109
	[0.0669]	[0.0663]	[0.0664]
CAPINT	– 0.0148**	– 0.0150**	– 0.0149**
	[0.0066]	[0.0066]	[0.0066]
CASHFLOW	– 0.5644	– 0.5570	– 0.5607
	[0.7016]	[0.7020]	[0.7026]
GDPGROWTH	0.1324**	0.1342**	0.1329**
	[0.0646]	[0.0647]	[0.0646]
CO2EMISSION		– 0.5385**	– 0.5435**
		[0.2326]	[0.2323]
ESG		– 0.0019*	– 0.0019*
		[0.0011]	[0.0011]
LEGAL		0.0483	0.0468
		[0.0336]	[0.0335]
COUNTRYTOP5		0.0679	0.0687
		[0.2612]	[0.2618]
COUNTRYBOTTOM5		– 0.3465	– 0.3473
		[0.2636]	[0.2643]
DELTAC02_X_ESG			– 210.6681
			[201.9915]
DELTAC02_X_LEGAL			– 342.7303
			[512.5218]
DELTAC02_X_CO2			– 342.7303
			[512.5218]
CONSTANT	1.4722***	1.6378***	1.6339***
	[0.3688]	[0.3782]	[0.3783]
FIXED EFFECTS	Yes	Yes	Yes
Adjusted *R*-squared	0.4056	0.4065	0.4064
Observations	9265	9265	9265

Estimates of the OLS regressions for *CR*. The included variables are as defined in the main text. The models use industry, year, and country fixed effects. Robust firm-level clustered standard errors are presented in square brackets. The symbols ***, **, * denote statistical significance at the 1%, 5%, and 10% levels

References

Brouwers, R., Schoubben, F., & Van Hulle, C. (2018). The influence of carbon cost on the link between carbon emission and corporate financial performance in the context of the European Union Emission Trading Scheme. *Business Strategy and the Environment, 27*, 1422–1436.

Brouwers, R., Schoubben, F., Van Hulle, C., & Van Uytbergen, S. (2016). The initial impact of EU ETS verification events on stock prices. *Energy Policy, 94*(1), 138–149.

Busch, T., Bassen, A., Lewandowski, S., & Sump, F. (2020). Corporate carbon and financial performance revisited. *Organization & Environment*, 5–18.

Delmas, M., Nairn-Birch, N., & Lim, J. (2015). Dynamics of environmental and financial performance: The case of greenhouse gas emissions. *Organization & Environment, 28*(4), 374–393.

DSM. (2019). *DSM integrated annual report*. Heerlen.

van Emous, R., Krušinskas, R., & Westerman, W. (2021). Carbon emissions and corporate financial performance: the influence of country characteristics, *Energies*, 14, 6029 1–20 (Special Issue "Energy Security and the Transition toward Green Energy Production").

EU Commission. (2019). Guidelines on non-financial reporting: Supplement on reporting climate-related information (C/2019/4490). Retrieved on January 12, 2022 from: https://eur-lex.europa.eu/legal-content/EN/TXT/?uri=CELEX:52019XC0620(01)

European Union. (2015). *EU ETS handbook*. Retrieved on November 19, 2021 from: https://ec.europa.eu/clima/sites/clima/files/docs/ets_handbook_en.pdf

Galama, J., & Scholtens, B. (2021). A meta-analysis of the relationship between companies' greenhouse gas emissions and financial performance. *Environmental Research Letters, 16*, 1–24.

Gallego-Alvarez, I., Segura, L., & Martinez-Ferrero, J. (2015). Carbon emissions reduction: The impact on the financial and operational performance of international companies. *Journal of Cleaner Production, 103*, 149–159.

Jong, T., Couwenberg, O., & Woerdman, E. (2014). Does EU emissions trading bite? An event study. *Energy Policy, 69*, 510–519.

Lewandowski, S. (2017). Corporate carbon and financial performance: The role of emission reduction. *Business Strategy and the Environment, 26*, 1196–1211.

Luo, L., & Tang, Q. (2013). Carbon tax, corporate carbon profile and financial return. *Pacific Accounting Review, 26*(3), 351–373.

Marin, G., Marino, M., & Pellegrin, C. (2018). The impact of the European Emission Trading Scheme on multiple measures of economic performance. *Environmental & Resource Economics, 71*, 551–582.

Sariannidis, N., Zafeiriou, E., Giannarakis, G., & Arabatzis, G. (2013). CO_2 emissions and financial performance of socially responsible firms: An empirical survey. *Business Strategy and the Environment, 22*(2), 109–120.

United Nations Global Compact. (2013). Retrieved on 13 January 2022 from: https://www.unglobalcompact.org/what-is-gc/mission/principles

FSC
www.fsc.org

MIX
Papier aus verantwortungsvollen Quellen
Paper from responsible sources
FSC® C105338

If you have any concerns about our products,
you can contact us on
ProductSafety@springernature.com

In case Publisher is established outside the EU,
the EU authorized representative is:
Springer Nature Customer Service Center GmbH
Europaplatz 3, 69115 Heidelberg, Germany

Printed by Libri Plureos GmbH
in Hamburg, Germany